THE USES OF MASS COMMUNICATIONS
Current Perspectives on
Gratifications Research

SAGE ANNUAL REVIEWS OF COMMUNICATION RESEARCH

SERIES EDITORS

F. Gerald Kline, *University of Michigan*
Peter Clarke, *University of Michigan*

Other Books in this Series:

Volume I — *Current Perspectives in Mass Communication Research*
F. Gerald Kline and Phillip J. Tichenor, Editors

Volume II — *New Models for Communication Research*
Peter Clarke, Editor

Volume III — *The Uses of Mass Communications:*
Current Perspectives on Gratifications Research
Jay G. Blumler and Elihu Katz, Editors

Volume IV — *Political Communication* (forthcoming)
Steven H. Chaffee, Editor

Volume III

SAGE ANNUAL REVIEWS OF COMMUNICATION RESEARCH

The Uses
of
Mass Communications

Current Perspectives
on Gratifications Research

JAY G. BLUMLER
and
ELIHU KATZ

Editors

SAGE PUBLICATIONS / Beverly Hills / London

For information address:

SAGE PUBLICATIONS, INC. 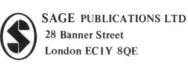 SAGE PUBLICATIONS LTD
275 South Beverly Drive   28 Banner Street
Beverly Hills, California 90212   London EC1Y 8QE

Printed in the United States of America
ISBN No. 0-8039-0340-5 (cloth)
ISBN No. 0-8039-0494-0 (paper)
Library of Congress Catalog Card No. 73-90713

THIRD PRINTING

CONTENTS

PART III: ANALYTICAL PERSPECTIVES

THE USES OF MASS COMMUNICATIONS

Current Perspectives on
Gratifications Research

ABOUT THE CONTRIBUTORS

LEE B. BECKER is an Assistant Professor in the Newhouse School of Public Communications at Syracuse University. His doctoral work was done at the University of Wisconsin (Madison). His research interests include the use and effects of political communication and the role of interpersonal communications in socialization.

JAY G. BLUMLER is Director of the Centre for Television Research and Reader in Mass Communications at the University of Leeds, England. In addition to writings on audience uses and gratifications, his publications reflect a range of political communication concerns, including especially the role of the mass media in election campaigns as well as their part in processes of political socialization, participation, and information transmission.

J. R. BROWN, a social psychologist, is Research Fellow in the Centre for Television Research, University of Leeds, England. He has conducted research into the gratifications sought by committed viewers of selected broadcast programs, the functions of local radio, and the role of television as an agent of child socialization. He is currently editing a volume of essays in the latter field.

JAMES W. CAREY is Director of the Institute of Communications Research and Professor of Journalism at the University of Illinois at Urbana-Champaign. His interests include the history of communications technology, communication systems, and popular culture.

JEAN CAZENEUVE has written widely in French in the fields of anthropology, ethnography, and mass communication. He is Professor of Sociology and Director of the French Press Institute at the Sorbonne, a member of the Academie des Sciences Morales et Politiques, and an advisor on many aspects of policy and programming to the ORTF.

[9]

J. K. CRAMOND, a psychologist, has served as Research Assistant in the Centre for Television Research, University of Leeds, England, since 1972. She has conducted research into children's attitudes to alcohol and drinking habits and is currently preparing a review of the literature of the impact of television on children's daily activities.

PHILIP ELLIOTT has been a Research Fellow at the Centre for Mass Communication Research, Leicester University, since 1967. He is the author of *The Making of a Television Series* (1972); *The Sociology of the Professions* (1972); and co-author of *Demonstrations and Communication: A Case Study* (1970). He is currently engaged in research on news broadcasting.

BRADLEY S. GREENBERG is Professor of Communication at Michigan State University. He has published extensively from his research on children and media impacts, minority portrayals in the media, and communication behaviors among the urban poor. He has co-authored two volumes of mass communication research, most recently *Use of the Mass Media by the Urban Poor.*

MICHAEL GUREVITCH is Senior Research Fellow in the Centre for Television Research, the University of Leeds, England, having previously served as Associate Director of the Communications Institute at the Hebrew University, Jerusalem. He received his Ph.D. in Political Science from the Massachusetts Institute of Technology. His current research interests lie in the fields of media uses and gratifications, political communication, and the study of communication networks.

JOHN W. C. JOHNSTONE is Professor of Sociology at the University of Illinois at Chicago Circle. He has conducted audience research for the Canadian Broadcasting Corporation and was formerly Senior Study Director for the National Opinion Research Center at the University of Chicago. He has written widely in the fields of mass communication, education, and the sociology of youth; and he recently completed a national study of practicing journalists in the United States.

ELIHU KATZ is Professor of Communication and Sociology at the Hebrew University of Jerusalem and Director of its Communications Institute. He has recently completed (with Michael Gurevitch) a study of the uses of leisure in Israel (Faber, 1974, in press) and is currently conducting a study (with E. G. Wedell) of the promise and performance of the mass media in nation-building.

F. GERALD KLINE is Chairman of the Interdepartmental Doctoral Program in Mass Communication Research and a member of the Journalism Department at the University of Michigan, where he is also a faculty associate in the Institute for Social Research. He is the editor of *Communication Research,* an international quarterly journal, and co-edited Volume I in this series, *Current Perspectives in Mass Communication Research* (1972).

ALBERT L. KREILING is Assistant Professor of Journalism and is affiliated with the Institute of Communications Research at the University of Illinois at Urbana-Champaign, where he received his Ph.D. His interests include popular culture, communication theory, and the black press.

WILLIAM J. McGUIRE is currently Professor of Psychology at Yale University. His research studies on attitude change, cognitive structure, and selective perception have been published in a variety of books and journals, including a chapter in the recent Schramm-Pool (eds.) *Handbook of Communication.*

JACK M. McLEOD is Professor of Journalism and Mass Communications and Chairman of the Mass Communications Research Center at the University of Wisconsin (Madison). He received his Ph.D. in Social Psychology at the University of Michigan. He is interested in research on political socialization and political communication.

DENIS McQUAIL is Reader in Sociology at the University of Southampton, England, and was formerly Television Research Fellow in the University of Leeds. His publications include *Television and the Political Image* (with Joseph Trenaman), *Television in Politics: Its Uses and Influence* (with Jay G. Blumler), *Towards a Sociology of Mass Communications,* and a selection of readings on the *Sociology of Mass Communications.*

HAROLD MENDELSOHN currently is Professor and Chairman, Department of Mass Communications, University of Denver. In addition he is the Director of the University of Denver's Communication Arts Center. As a member of the Surgeon General's Scientific Advisory Committee on Television and Social Behavior, he was a co-author of the Committee's monograph report, *Television and Growing Up: The Impact of Televised Violence.* He is the author of *Mass Entertainment* and co-author of *Polls, Television, and the New Politics* and *Minorities and the Police.*

PETER V. MILLER is a student in the Interdepartmental Doctoral Program in Mass Communication at the University of Michigan. He has been an Assistant Study Director at the Survey Research Center of the Institute for Social Research at the University for two years, and has served as a consultant to the Department of Communications, Canada.

ANDREW J. MORRISON is a student in the Interdepartmental Doctoral Program in Mass Communication at the University of Michigan. He has been an analyst in the Social Research and Media Divisions of Market Opinion Research, Detroit, Michigan, for two years. Mr. Morrison has also been an Assistant Study Director at the Survey Research Center of the Institute for Social Research.

TSIYONA PELED is a member of the faculty of the Communications Institute at the Hebrew University and a Senior Research Director of the Israel Institute of Applied Social Research. Her recent work has focused primarily on policy-oriented survey research on such topics as youth and drugs, family planning and fertility regulating behavior, psychosocial indicators of morale and social well-being, and uses of mass media.

KARL ERIK ROSENGREN received his *Fil.dr.* (Sociology) from the University of Lund, Sweden. At present, he is Associate Professor *(Docent)* and Senior Lecturer in the Department of Sociology of the same university. His publications include *Sociological Aspects of the Literary System* (Stockholm, 1968) as well as journal articles in the sociology of communications and literature.

R. J. WILDE, a psychologist, served from 1971-1973 as Research Assistant (at the Centre for Television Research, University of Leeds) in an investigation of television as an agent of child socialization, working especially on audiences' responses to children's magazine programs.

CHARLES R. WRIGHT is presently Professor of Communications and Sociology at the University of Pennsylvania's Annenberg School of Communications. He is the author of *Mass Communication: A Sociological Perspective* and co-author of four other books: *The Enduring Effects of Education; Inducing Change in Developing Communities; Applications of Methods of Evaluation;* and *Public Leadership.*

FOREWORD

THE PLAN UNDERLYING THIS VOLUME OF ESSAYS on the "uses and gratifications approach" to mass communication research is relatively straightforward and may be readily grasped by consulting the table of contents. In filling in the envisaged structure we, as editors, were happily afflicted with an embarrassment of riches. The opening chapter is a preliminary guidelines paper that was originally composed by ourselves and Michael Gurevitch in April 1973 with two aims in mind: first, to summarize the achievements of uses and gratifications inquiries to date; and second, to propose an agenda for discussion of the future direction of this approach in terms of a set of theoretical, methodological, and substantive issues that needed more systematic attention than they had been given in the past. Essays were solicited, then, according to the criterion of their likely contribution—through the presentation of new empirical evidence (Part II of the book) or the development of original analytical argument (Part III)—to a clarification of some of the problems posed in the opening overview. It was never our intention, however, to lay down the prospectus or philosophic foundations of a single and closely articulated school of thought. The reader of the ensuing pages will soon discover that they contain, and do not pretend to resolve, many of the vigorous controversies that have been provoked by this lively tradition of mass communication research.

One conclusion that we would firmly draw from the writings we have commissioned is that the uses and gratifications approach is well and truly launched on a third major phase of its development: a sort of coming of age. Perhaps it is not overly simple to suggest that, in its "childhood" of the 1940s and 1950s, the core emphasis of much work in this vein was on insightful *description* of audience subgroup orientations to selected media content forms. The outcomes of this early research seemed mainly to illuminate vividly something of the "feel" and quality of audience attachment to mass communication in its own right. Then, in the "adolescence" of the late 1960s, the core emphasis of many studies was switched to an *operationalization* of the social and psychological variables presumed to give rise to differentiated patterns of media consumption. And the outcomes of such work mainly held out the promise that the tendencies for audience members to seek certain satisfactions from media content could be measured and deployed in quantitative analysis. If we are not mistaken to discern an entry into maturity in the 1970s, then its core tendency probably centers in turn on attempts to use gratifications data to provide *explanations* of such other facets of the communication process with which audience motives and expectations may be connected. Of course this route of progress is still incompletely mapped and explored, but it appears to have two major branches. The empirical section of this book provides several significant examples of both. Thus, several studies attempt to establish that an understanding of patterns of gratifications is prerequisite to an understanding of media effects. This idea is well supported by the findings of both Kline et al. and of McLeod and Becker. Some of Greenberg's evidence suggestively associates escape and arousal motives for TV use among children with the growth of aggressive dispositions and (in the latter case) a liking for violent content.

The other branch of explanatory study strives to anchor the motivations and gratifications associated with media consumption to more systematic formulations of social and psychological "needs." Brown et al., for example, taking a fresh look at the displacement effects of television, seek to place the gratifications of children in the middle of a complex chain involving external changes in the communication environment, internal changes in audience need states (such as those resulting from maturation), and the efforts of producers and merchandisers of media content to cater to new needs as well as to find new ways of serving old needs. Likewise, the paper by Peled and Katz explores media use in the light of sociological theory about the functions of mass media for society, and for a society in crisis in particular.

This newer preoccupation with communication theory, on the one hand, and with social and psychological theories of motivation, on the other, connects the empirical papers with many of the issues raised in the analytical section (Part III). Under what conditions, for example, do the media compensate for the inaccessibility of more traditional sources of gratification? This question is treated both in the empirical studies of Kline and Johnstone and in the analytic essays of Rosengren and Cazeneuve. Are media gratifications best explained by recourse to needs projected onto the media from "outside," or is there a set of needs more closely linked to the actual situation of media exposure? This challenge is set forth in the analytic paper by Carey as well as in the theoretical discussions of Mendelsohn, Rosengren, and McGuire, but it also figures, albeit more implicitly, in the empirical papers by Kline et al. and Greenberg. And what does it mean to characterize the audience as "active"? Compare the discussions of Elliott, Cazeneuve, and McGuire, and the empirical papers of Peled and Katz, Johnstone, and Kline.

The growing preoccupation with explanation and theory should not be read, however, as if there were consensus on these matters. It means simply that these problems are no longer being circumvented or taken for granted, and that the variety of positions is being aired in an essentially problematic spirit. Nor should the emphasis on theory be mistaken for a complacency about the thorny methodological problems of gratification research. Indeed, many of the empirical papers reflect an unease over the limitations of both respondent self-report and investigator inference from indirect evidence as sources of data concerning audience motivations and gratifications.

One of the more fascinating recurrent themes of dispute in the book revolves around a problem of identity, boundary fixing and definition: What in essence *is* this art of so-called gratification research? Is it simply an approach to data collection, a heuristic model relating audience dispositions to other elements in the mass communication process, or perhaps even a theory in its own right? Despite the different perspectives adopted by our contributors, we sense that they have collectively mangaed to provide the basis for a shared answer. The uses and gratifications approach, they seem to be saying, is a research strategy that can provide a home for a variety of hypotheses about specific communication phenomena and a testing ground for propositions about audience orientations stemming from more than one sociological or psychological theory.

The heart of the matter concerns the relationship of the uses and gratifications approach to functionalism, a topic that is spontaneously raised in many of the essays. This is no place to rehearse the arguments that they canvass, but by way of summary three points of emphasis may be mentioned. First, there is broad agreement that the uses and gratifications tradition developed (sometimes knowingly, sometimes unwittingly) on the shoulders of functionalist paradigms in sociology and psychology. Second, most of the contributors are wary or critical of this attachment. Functionalism receives a searching and largely critical scrutiny in this collection, and only Wright, revisiting his seminal essay of 1964, is prepared confidently to assert that functionalism is "alive and well." Third, there is a strong tendency to suggest that uses and gratifications work need not be wedded to functionalism and could with equal facility be rooted in other theoretical traditions. This case is explicitly developed by McQuail and Gurevitch. But even Wright, in proposing a fusion of uses and gratifications and functionalist concerns, seems to presuppose their logical distinctness, while Carey's plea for an accommodation with popular culture analysis evidently demands an abandonment of functionalist models.

The lack of a uses and gratifications theory as such could be regarded as a source of weakness: eclecticism never seems elegant. Nevertheless, many of the essays highlight one outstanding strength that probably stems from this tradition's porous theoretical boundaries. For this volume seems to depict uses and gratifications research as a line of inquiry that is capable of reaching out effectively to a wide range of new theoretical developments in other disciplines, rather than as an esoteric, self-contained, and highly specialized subarea of communication study on its own. For example, the possibilities of linkage to a host of modern developments in psychological theories of motivation are excitingly unfolded by McGuire; the sociological prospects are set out by McQuail and Gurevitch; Cazeneuve introduces the perspectives of anthropology, ethnography, and philosophy; Kline et al. work with co-orientation theories in social psychology; Rosengren relates his uses and gratifications paradigm to recent attempts to resolve the traits vs. situation controversy in personality theory.

Otherwise, the contents of this book offer a mixture of support and challenge to believers in the promise of the uses and gratifications approach. It is encouraging, for example, to discern the "active audience" so forcefully at work in the Peled and Katz study of communication during Israel's crisis of the Yom Kippur war; to follow McLeod and Becker's careful and ingenious attempt to validate measures of political communication gratifications; and also to learn that such measures do seem to clarify the incidence of communication effects. Doubts about the policy relevance of gratifications data and fears that they might supinely uphold the status quo are more difficult to override, but they have at least been substantially countered by the examples cited by Mendelsohn and by the Israeli case study itself. In addition, one unanticipated facet of the uses and gratifications approach has emerged from several of the pieces. From their different standpoints the studies of Peled and Katz, Brown et al., and Kline et al. all underline the strongly dynamic character of the relationship between audience needs and mass media provision. The fluidity of this association over time will evidently merit yet closer attention in the future.

Nevertheless, the challenges to the uses and gratifications position are formidably conceived and coherently stated. Readers will form their own impressions of the cogency of the critiques mounted by Elliott and Carey, respectively. The former maintains that the uses and gratifications approach rules out consideration of the differential distribution of power and opportunity in society, the conflicts of interest between different groups, and how the media propagate ideologies to sustain the advantaged. The latter argues that the utilitarian means/ends model of motivation espoused by the uses and gratifications tradition diverts attention away from more strictly cultural dispositions to seek symbolic experience that is at once immediately pleasing and conceptually plausible. In the end the validity of these attacks may well turn on the previously mentioned relationship of uses and gratifications research to functionalist theory. If, as has already been argued, the approach can be detached from its former functionalist moorings, then the way may be opened to relate the uses and gratifications approach even to conflict theory (as Rosengren suggests) and to ground it in non-utilitarian as well as utilitarian models of motivation (as McGuire's survey implies).

Jay G. Blumler
Elihu Katz

PART I

PRELIMINARY OVERVIEW

Chapter 1

UTILIZATION OF MASS COMMUNICATION
BY THE INDIVIDUAL

Elihu Katz, Jay G. Blumler and Michael Gurevitch

SUPPOSE THAT we were studying not broadcasting-and-society in mid-twentieth-century America but opera-and-society in mid-nineteenth-century Italy. After all, opera in Italy, during that period, was a "mass" medium. What would we be studying? It seems likely, for one thing, that we would find interest in the attributes of the medium—what might today be called its "grammar"—for example, the curious convention that makes it possible to sing contradictory emotions simultaneously. For another, we would be interested in the functions of the medium for the individual and society: perceptions of the values expressed and underlined; the phenomena of stardom, fanship, and connoisseurship; the festive ambience which the medium created; and so on. It seems quite unlikely that we would be studying the effects of the singing of a particular opera on opinions and attitudes, even though some operas were written with explicit political, social, and moral aims in mind. The study of short-run effects, in other words, would not have had a high priority, although it might have had a place. But the emphasis, by and large, would have been on the medium as a cultural institution with its own social and psychological functions and perhaps long-run effects.

We have all been over the reasons why much of mass communication research took a different turn, preferring to look at specific programs as specific messages

AUTHORS' NOTE: A more extended version of this essay was first prepared for presentation in May 1973 to a conference at Arden House, Harriman, New York, on Directions in Mass Communication Research, which was arranged by the School of Journalism of Columbia University and supported by a grant from the John and Mary Markle Foundation. It may be consulted in full in W. Phillips Davison and Frederick T.C. Yu (eds.) *Mass Communication Research: Major Issues and Future Directions* (New York: Praeger, 1974). The present text is a modified version of an abridgment that originally appeared in *Public Opinion Quarterly* (Winter 1973-1974).

with, possibly, specific effects. We were social psychologists interested in persuasion and attitude change. We were political scientists interested in new forms of social control. We were commissioned to measure message effectiveness for marketing organizations, or public health agencies, or churches, or political organizations, or for the broadcasting organizations themselves. And we were asked whether the media were not causes of violent and criminal behavior.

Yet even in the early days of empirical mass communication research this preoccupation with short-term effects was supplemented by the growth of an interest in the gratifications that the mass media provide their audiences. Such studies were well represented in the Lazarsfeld-Stanton collections (1942, 1944, 1949); Herzog (1942) on quiz programs and the gratifications derived from listening to soap operas; Suchman (1942) on the motives for getting interested in serious music on radio; Wolfe and Fiske (1949) on the development of children's interest in comics; Berelson (1949) on the functions of newspaper reading; and so on. Each of these investigations came up with a list of functions served either by some specific contents or by the medium in question: to match one's wits against others, to get information or advice for daily living, to provide a framework for one's day, to prepare oneself culturally for the demands of upward mobility, or to be reassured about the dignity and usefulness of one's role.

What these early studies had in common was, first, a basically similar methodological approach whereby statements about media functions were elicited from the respondents in an essentially open-ended way. Second, they shared a qualitative approach in their attempt to group gratification statements into labelled categories, largely ignoring the distribution of their frequency in the population. Third, they did not attempt to explore the links between the gratifications thus detected and the psychological or sociological origins of the needs that were so satisfied. Fourth, they failed to search for the interrelationships among the various media functions, either quantitatively or conceptually, in a manner that might have led to the detection of the latent structure of media gratifications. Consequently, these studies did not result in a cumulatively more detailed picture of media gratifications conducive to the eventual formulation of theoretical statements.

The last few years have witnessed something of a revival of direct empirical investigations of audience uses and gratifications, not only in the United States but also in Britain, Sweden, Finland, Japan, and Israel. These more recent studies have a number of differing starting points, but each attempts to press toward a greater systematization of what is involved in conducting research in this field. Taken together, they make operational many of the logical steps that were only implicit in the earlier work. They are concerned with (1) the social and psychological origins of (2) needs, which generate (3) expectations of (4) the mass media or other sources, which lead to (5) differential patterns of media exposure (or engagement in other activities), resulting in (6) need gratifications and (7) other consequences, perhaps mostly unintended ones. Some of these investigations begin by specifying needs and then attempt to trace the extent to which they are gratified by the media or other sources. Others take observed gratifications as a starting point and attempt to reconstruct the needs that are being gratified. Yet others focus on the social origins of audience expectations and gratifications. But however varied their individual points of departure, they all strive toward an assessment of media consumption in audience-related terms, rather than in technological, aesthetic, ideological, or other more or less "elitist" terms. The convergence of their foci, as well as of their findings, indicates that there is a clear agenda here—part methodological and part theoretical—for a discussion of the future directions of this approach.

SOME BASIC ASSUMPTIONS OF THEORY, METHOD AND VALUE

Perhaps the place of "theory" and "method" in the study of audience uses and gratifications is not immediately apparent. The common tendency to attach the label "uses and gratifications approach" to work in this field appears to virtually disclaim any theoretical pretensions or methodological commitment. From this point of view the approach simply represents an attempt to explain something of the way in which individuals use communications, among other resources in their environment, to satisfy their needs and to achieve their goals, and to do so by simply asking them. Nevertheless, this effort does rest on a body of assumptions, explicit or implicit, that have some degree of internal coherence and that are arguable in the sense that not everyone contemplating them would find them self-evident. Lundberg and Hultén (1968) refer to them as jointly constituting a "uses and gratifications model." Five elements of this model in particular may be singled out for comment:

(1) The audience is conceived of as active, that is, an important part of mass media use is assumed to be goal directed (McQuail, Blumler and Brown, 1972). This assumption may be contrasted with Bogart's (1965) thesis to the effect that "most mass media experiences represent pastime rather than purposeful activity, very often [reflecting] chance circumstances within the range of availabilities rather than the expression of psychological motivation or need." Of course, it cannot be denied that media exposure often has a casual origin; the issue is whether, in addition, patterns of media use are shaped by more or less definite expectations of what certain kinds of content have to offer the audience member.

(2) In the mass communication process much initiative in linking need gratification and media choice lies with the audience member. This places a strong limitation on theorizing about any form of straight-line effect of media content on attitudes and behavior. As Schramm, Lyle and Parker (1961) said:

> In a sense the term "effect" is misleading because it suggests that television "does something" to children. . . . Nothing can be further from the fact. It is the children who are most active in this relationship. It is they who use television rather than television that uses them.

(3) The media compete with other sources of need satisfaction. The needs served by mass communication constitute but a segment of the wider range of human needs, and the degree to which they can be adequately met through mass media consumption certainly varies. Consequently, a proper view of the role of the media in need satisfaction should take into account other functional alternatives —including different, more conventional, and "older" ways of fulfilling needs.

(4) Methodologically speaking, many of the goals of mass media use can be derived from data supplied by individual audience members themselves—that is, people are sufficiently self-aware to be able to report their interests and motives in particular cases, or at least to recognize them when confronted with them in an intelligible and familiar verbal formulation.

(5) Value judgments about the cultural significance of mass communication should be suspended while audience orientations are explored on their own terms. It is from the perspective of this assumption that certain affinities and contrasts between the uses and gratifications approach and much speculative writing about popular culture may be considered.

STATE OF THE ART: THEORETICAL ISSUES

From the few postulates outlined above, it is evident that further development of a theory of media gratification depends, first, on the clarification of its relationship to the theoretical traditions on which it so obviously draws and, second, on systematic efforts toward conceptual integration of empirical findings. Given the present state of the art, the following are priority issues in the development of an adequate theoretical basis.

Typologies of Audience Gratifications

Each major piece of uses and gratification research has yielded its own classification scheme of audience functions. When placed side by side, they reveal a mixture of shared gratification categories and notions peculiar to individual research teams. The differences are due in part to the fact that investigators have focused on different levels of study (e.g., medium or content) and different materials (e.g., different programs or program types on, say, television) in different cultures (e.g., Finland, Israel, Japan, Sweden, the United Kingdom, the United States, and Yugoslavia).

Unifunctional conceptions of audience interests have been expressed in various forms. Popular culture writers have often based their criticisms of the media on the ground that, in primarily serving the escapist desires of the audience, they deprived it of the more beneficial uses that might be made of communication (McDonald, 1957). Stephenson's analysis (1967) of mass communication exclusively in terms of "play" may be interpreted as an extension, albeit in a transformed and expanded expression, of this same notion. A more recent example has been provided by Nordenstreng (1970), who, while breaking away from conventional formulations, still opts for a unifunctional view when he claims that, "It has often been documented (e.g., during television and newspaper strikes in Finland in 1966-67) that perhaps the basic motivation for media use is just an unarticulated need for social contact."

The wide currency secured for a bifunctional view of audience concerns is reflected in Weiss' (1971) summary, which states that, "When ... studies of uses and gratifications are carried out, the media or media content are usually viewed dichotomously as predominantly fantasist-escapist or informational-educational in significance." This dichotomy appears, for example, in Schramm's (1949) work (adopted subsequently by Schramm, Lyle and Parker, 1961; Pietila, 1969; and Furu, 1971), which distinguishes between sets of "immediate" and "deferred" gratifications, and in the distinction between informational and entertainment materials. In terms of audience gratifications specifically, it emerges in the distinction between surveillance and escape uses of the media.

The four-functional interpretation of the media was first proposed by Lasswell (1948) on a macro-sociological level and later developed by Wright (1960) on both the macro- and the micro-sociological levels. It postulated that the media served the functions of surveillance, correlation, entertainment, and cultural transmission (or socialization) for society as a whole, as well as for individuals and subgroups within society. An extension of the four-function approach can also be found in Wright's suggestive exploration of the potential dysfunctional equivalents of Lasswell's typology.

None of these statements, however, adequately reflects the full range of functions, which has been disclosed by the more recent investigations. McQuail, Blumler and Brown (1972) have put forward a typology consisting of the following categories: diversion (including escape from the constraints of routine and the burdens of problems, and emotional release); personal relationships (including substitute companionship as well as social utility); personal identity (including personal reference, reality exploration, and value reinforcement); and surveillance.

An effort to encompass the large variety of specific functions that have been proposed is made in the elaborate scheme of Katz, Gurevitch and Haas (1973). Their central notion is that mass communication is used by individuals to connect (or sometimes to disconnect) themselves—via instrumental, affective, or integrative relations—with different kinds of others (self, family, friends, nation, etc.). The scheme attempts to comprehend the whole range of individual gratifications of the many facets of the need "to be connected." And it finds empirical regularities in the preference for different media for different kinds of connections.

Gratification and Needs

The study of mass media use suffers at present from the absence of a relevant theory of social and psychological needs. It is not so much a catalogue of needs that is missing as a clustering of groups of needs, a sorting out of different levels of need, and a specification of hypotheses linking particular needs with particular media gratifications. It is true that the work of Schramm, Lyle and Parker (1961) draws on the distinction between the reality and pleasure principles in the socialization theories of Freud and others, but more recent studies suggest that those categories are too broad to be serviceable. Maslow's (1954) proposed hierarchy of human needs may hold more promise, but the relevance of his categories to expectations of communication has not yet been explored in detail. Lasswell's (1948) scheme to specify the needs that media satisfy has proven useful, and it may be helpful to examine Lasswell and Kaplan's (1950) broader classification of values as well.

Alternatively, students of uses and gratifications could try to work backwards, as it were, from gratifications to needs. In the informational field, for example, the surveillance function may be traced to a desire for security or the satisfaction of curiosity and the exploratory drive; seeking reinforcement of one's attitudes and values may derive from a need for reassurance that one is right; and attempts to correlate informational elements may stem from a more basic need to develop one's cognitive mastery of the environment. Similarly, the use of fictional (and other) media materials for "personal reference" may spring from a need for self-esteem; social utility functions may be traced to the need for affiliation; and escape functions may be related to the need to release tension and reduce anxiety. But whichever way one proceeds, it is inescapable that what is at issue here is the long-standing problem of social and psychological science: how to (and whether to bother to) systematize the long lists of human and societal needs. Thus far, gratifications research has stayed close to what we have been calling media-related needs (in the sense that the media have been observed to satisfy them, at least in part), but one wonders whether all this should not be put in the broader context of systematic studies of needs.

Sources of Media Gratifications

Studies have shown that audience gratifications can be derived from at least three distinct sources: media content, exposure to the media per se, and the social context that typifies the situation of exposure to different media. Although recognition of media content as a source of gratifications has provided the basis for research in this area from its inception, less attention has been paid to the other sources. Nevertheless, it is clear that the need to relax or to kill time can be satisfied by the act of watching television, that the need to feel that one is spending one's time in a worthwhile way may be associated with the act of reading (Waples, Berelson and Bradshaw, 1940; Berelson, 1949), and that the need to structure one's day may be satisfied merely by having the radio "on"

(Mendelsohn, 1964). Similarly, a wish to spend time with one's family or friends can be served by watching television at home with the family or by going to the cinema with one's friends.

Each medium seems to offer a unique combination of (a) characteristic contents (at least stereotypically perceived in that way); (b) typical attributes (print vs. broadcasting modes of transmission, iconic vs. symbolic representation, reading vs. audio or audio-visual modes of reception); and (c) typical exposure situations (at home vs. out-of-home, alone vs. with others, control over the temporal aspects of exposure vs. absence of such control). The issue, then, is what combinations of attributes may render different media more or less adequate for the satisfaction of different needs (Katz, Gurevitch and Haas, 1973).

Gratifications and Media Attributes

Much uses and gratifications research has still barely advanced beyond a sort of charting and profiling activity: findings are still typically presented to show that certain bodies of content serve certain functions or that one medium is deemed better at satisfying certain needs than another. The further step, which has hardly been ventured, is one of explanation. At issue here is the relationship between the unique "grammar" of different media—that is, their specific technological and aesthetic attributes—and the particular requirements of audience members that they are then capable, or incapable, of satisfying. Which, indeed, are the attributes that render some media more conducive than others to satisfying specific needs? And which elements of content help to attract the expectations for which they apparently cater?

It is possible to postulate the operation of some kind of division of labor among the media for the satisfaction of audience needs. This may be elaborated in two ways: taking media attributes as the starting point, the suggestion is that those media that differ (or are similar) in their attributes are more likely to serve different (or similar) needs; or, utilizing the latent structure of needs as a point of departure, the implication is that needs that are psychologically related or conceptually similar will be equally well served by the same media (or by media with similar attributes).

To illustrate the first approach, Robinson (1972) has demonstrated the interchangeability of television and print media for learning purposes. In the Israeli study, Katz, Gurevitch and Haas (1973) found five media ordered in a circumplex with respect to their functional similarities: books-newspapers-radio-television-cinema-books. In other words, books functioned most like newspapers, on the one hand, and like cinema, on the other. Radio was most similar in its usage to newspapers, on the one hand, and to television, on the other. The explanation would seem to lie not only with certain technological attributes that they have in common, but with similar aesthetic qualities as well. Thus, books share a technology and an informational function with newspapers, but are similar to films in their aesthetic function. Radio shares a technology, as well as informational and entertainment content, with television, but it is also very much like newspapers—providing a heavy dose of information and an orientation to reality.

An illustration of the second aspect of this division of labor may also be drawn from the same study. Here, the argument is that structurally related needs will tend to be serviced by certain media more often than by others. Thus, books and cinema have been found to cater to needs concerned with self-fulfilment and self-gratification: they help to "connect" individuals to themselves. Newspapers, radio, and television all seem to connect individuals to society. In fact, the function of newspapers for those interested in following what is going on in the world may have been grossly underestimated in the past (Edelstein, 1973; Lundberg and Hultén, 1968). Television, however, was found to be less frequently used as a medium of escape by Israeli respondents than were books and films. And a Swedish study of the "functional specialities of the respective media" report′d that, "A retreat from the immediate environment and its demands—probably mainly by the act of reading itself—was characteristic of audience usage of weekly magazines" (Lundberg and Hultén, 1968).

Media Attributes as Perceived or Intrinsic

When people associate book-reading, for example, with a desire to know oneself, and newspapers with the need to feel connected to the larger society, it is difficult to disentangle perceptions of the media from their intrinsic qualities. Is there anything about the book as a medium that breeds intimacy? Is there something about newspapers that explains their centrality in socio-political integration? Or, is this "something" simply an accepted image of the medium and its characteristic content?

In this connection, Rosengren (1972) has suggested that uses and gratifications research may be profitably connected with the long-established tradition of enquiry into public perceptions of the various media and the dimensions according to which their respective images and qualities are differentiated (cf. especially Nilsson [1971] and Edelstein [1973] and the literature cited therein). A merger of the two lines of investigation may show how far the attributes of the media, as perceived by their consumers, and their intrinsic qualities are correlated with the pursuit of certain gratifications. So far, however, this connection has only been partially discussed in the work of Lundberg and Hultén (1968).

The Social Origins of Audience Needs and Their Gratifications

The social and environmental circumstances that lead people to turn to the mass media for the satisfaction of certain needs are also little understood as yet. For example, what needs, if any, are created by routine work on an assembly line, and which forms of media exposure will satisfy them? What motivates some people to seek political information from the mass media and others to actively avoid it? Here one may postulate that it is the combined product of psychological dispositions, sociological factors, and environmental conditions that determines the specific uses of the media by members of the audience.

At certain levels it should not prove unduly difficult to formulate discrete hypotheses about such relationships. For example, we might expect "substitute companionship" to be sought especially by individuals with limited opportunities for social contacts: invalids, the elderly, the single, the divorced or widowed living alone, the housewife who spends much time at home on her own, and so on.

At another level, however, it is more difficult to conceive of a general theory that might clarify the various processes that underlie any such specific relationships. A preliminary structuring of the possibilities suggests that social factors may be involved in the generation of media-related needs in any of the following five ways (each of which has attracted some comment in the literature):

(1) Social situation produces tensions and conflicts, leading to pressure for their easement via mass media consumption (Katz and Foulkes, 1962).

(2) Social situation creates an awareness of problems that demand attention, information about which may be sought in the media (Edelstein, 1973).

(3) Social situation offers impoverished real-life opportunities to satisfy certain needs, which are then directed to the mass media for complementary, supplementary, or substitute servicing (Rosengren and Windahl, 1972).

(4) Social situation gives rise to certain values, the affirmation and reinforcement of which is facilitated by the consumption of congruent media materials (Dembo, 1972).

(5) Social situation provides a field of expectations of familiarity with certain media materials, which must then be monitored in order to sustain membership of valued social groupings (Atkins, 1972).

The Versatility of Sources of Need Satisfaction

Before becoming too sanguine about the possibility of relating social situations to psychological needs to media/content gratifications, it is important to bear in mind that gratifications studies based on specific media contents have demonstrated that one and the same set of media materials is capable of serving a multiplicity of needs and audience functions. Presumably, that is why Rosengren and Windahl (1972) have drawn attention to "a growing consensus that almost any type of content may serve practically any type of function." For example, Blumler, Brown and McQuail (1970) have found that the television serial *The Saint* serves functions of personal reference, identification with characters, and reality-exploration, in addition to its more obvious diversionary function. Similarly, their study of the gratifications involved in news viewing referred not only to the expected surveillance motive but also to functions of social utility, empathy, and even escape. In summarizing the implications of their evidence, McQuail, Blumler and Brown (1972) point out that:

> the relationship between content categories and audience needs is far less tidy and more complex than most commentators have appreciated. . . . One man's source of escape from the real world is a point of anchorage for another man's place in it.

Gratifications and Effects

Pioneers in the study of uses and gratifications were moved chiefly by two aspirations. The first, which has largely been fulfilled, was to redress an imbalance evident in previous research: audience needs, they said, deserved as much attention in their own right as the persuasive aims of communicators with which so many of the early "effects" studies had been preoccupied. The second major aim of uses and gratifications research, however, was to treat audience requirements as intervening variables in the study of traditional communication effects. Glaser's (1965) formulation offers a typical expression of the rationale behind this prospect:

> Since users approach the media with a variety of needs and predispositions . . . any precise identification of the effects of television watching . . . must identify the uses sought and made of television by the various types of viewers.

Despite this injunction, hardly any substantial empirical or theoretical effort has been devoted to connecting gratifications and effects. Some limited evidence from the political field suggests that combining functions and effects perspectives may be fruitful (Blumler and McQuail, 1968). But there are many other foci of traditional effects studies for which no detailed hypotheses about gratifications/effects interactions have yet been framed.

One obvious example is the field of media violence. Another might concern the impact on inhabitants of developing countries of exposure to television serials, films, and popular songs of foreign (predominantly American) origin. Yet another might relate to the wide range of materials, appearing especially in broadcast fiction, that purport simultaneously to entertain and to portray more or less faithfully some portion of social reality—e.g., the worlds of law enforcement, social work, hospital life, trade unionism, working-class neighborhoods, and ways of life at the executive level in business corporations and civil service departments.

Hypotheses about the cumulative effects of exposure to such materials on audience members' cognitive perceptions of these spheres of activity, and on the individuals engaged in them, might be formulated in awareness of the likely fact that some individuals will be viewing them primarily for purposes of escape, while others will be using them for reality-exploring gratifications. In these circumstances should we expect a readier acceptance of portrayed stereotypes by the escape seekers—the thesis of Festinger and Maccoby (1964) on persuasion via distraction might be relevant here—or by those viewers who are trusting enough to expect such programs to offer genuine insights into the nature of social reality?

A similar body of recently analyzed materials may be found in the television soap opera, with its postulated capacity to "establish or reinforce value systems" (Katzman, 1972). In fact one cluster of gratifications that emerged from an English study of listeners to a long-running daytime radio serial *(The Dales)* centered on the tendency of the program to uphold traditional family values (Blumler, Brown and McQuail, 1970). This suggests that an answer to Katzman's "key question" ("to what degree do daytime serials change attitudes and norms and to what extent do they merely follow and reinforce their audience?") might initially be sought by distinguishing among the regular followers of such programs those individuals who are avowedly seeking a reinforcement of certain values from those who are not.

In addition, however, the literature refers to some consequences of audience functions that conventional effects designs may be unable to capture. First, there is what Katz and Foulkes (1962) have termed the "feedback" from media use to the individual's performance of his other social roles. Thus, Bailyn (1959) distinguished child uses of pictorial media that might "preclude more realistic and lasting solutions" to problems from those that, at one level, were "escapist" but that should more properly be categorized as "supplementation." Similarly, Schramm, Lyle and Parker (1961) maintained that child uses of the mass media for fantasizing might either drain off discontent caused by the hard blows of socialization or lead a child into withdrawal from the real world. And Lundberg and Hultén (1968) have suggested that for some individuals the substitute companionship function may involve use of the media to replace real social ties, while for others it may facilitate an adjustment to reality.

Second, some authors have speculated on the connection between functions performed by the media for individuals and their functions (or dysfunctions) for other levels of society. This relationship is particularly crucial for its bearing on evaluative and ideological controversies about the role of mass communication in modern society. Thus, Enzenberger (1972) suggests that the 8 millimeter camera may satisfy the recreational and creative impulses of the individual and help to keep the family together while simultaneously atomizing and depoliticizing society. Or news viewing may gratify the individual's need for civic participation; but if the news, as presented, is a disjointed succession of staccato events, it may also leave him with the message that the world is a disconnected place. Similarly, many radical critics tend to regard television as part of a conspiracy to keep people content and politically quiescent—offering respite, para-social interaction with interesting and amusing people, and much food for gossip—while propagating a false social consciousness.

IMPLICATIONS FOR RESEARCH POLICY AND MEDIA POLICY

In reviewing the state of the art of gratifications research, we have focused on issues—theoretical, methodological, and ideological—rather than on systematized findings. We have also tried to make manifest our assumptions. Thus, we have confronted the image of the beery, house-slippered, casual viewer of television with the notion of a more "active" audience—knowing that both images are true. We have asked whether a methodology based on respondents' introspection can be adequate. We have indicated the absence of satisfactory bridging concepts between the constraints arising from social situations and the gratifications sought from the media; or between particular patterns of use and likely effect.

These issues bear not only on the direction of future research, but also, echoing Nordenstreng (1970), on the relationship between research policy and media policy. Thus, we have raised the question of the extent to which the media create the needs that they satisfy. Even more fundamentally, we ask whether the media do actually satisfy their consumers—an assumption that radical critics of the media take more for granted than do gratification researchers (cf., Emmett, 1968-1969). To assert that mass communication is a latter-day opiate of the masses presupposes a media-output audience-satisfaction nexus that gratifications research treats as hypothesis rather than fact.

In other words, our position is that media researchers ought to be studying human needs to discover how much the media do or do not contribute to their creation and satisfaction. Moreover, we believe it is our job to clarify the extent to which certain kinds of media and content favor certain kinds of use—to thereby set boundaries to the over-generalization that any kind of content can be bent to any kind of need. We believe it is part of our job to explore the social and individual conditions under which audiences find need or use for program material aimed at changing their image of the status quo or "broadening their cultural horizons" (Emmett, 1968-1969).

From the point of view of media policy, then, we reject the view that an application of the uses and gratifications approach to policy questions must inevitably support or exonerate the producers of junk or the status quo of media content. That belief seems to require the acceptance of one or both of two other assumptions: existing patterns of audience needs support the prevailing patterns of media provision and no other; and audience concerns are in fact trivial and escapist. For reasons that should now be plain, we find both these propositions dubious.

Though audience oriented, the uses and gratifications approach is not necessarily conservative. While taking account of what people look for from the media, it breaks away from a slavish dependence of content on audience propensities by bringing to light the great variety of needs and interests that are encompassed by the latter. As McQuail, Blumler and Brown (1972) have argued, uses and gratifications data suggest that the mass media may not, after all, be as "constrained as the escapist theory makes out from performing a wider range of social functions than is generally assigned to them in western societies today." In other words, instead of depicting the media as severely circumscribed by audience expectations, the uses and gratifications approach highlights the audience as a source of challenge to producers to cater more richly to the miltiplicity of requirements and roles that it has disclosed.

REFERENCES

ATKIN, C. K. (1972) "Anticipated communication and mass media information-seeking." Public Opinion Quarterly 36.

BAILYN, L. (1959) "Mass media and children." Psychological Monographs 71.

BERELSON, B. (1949) "What 'missing the newspaper' means," in P. F. Lazarsfeld and F. N. Stanton (eds.) Communications Research, 1948-9. New York: Duell, Sloan & Pearce.

BLUMLER, J. G., J. R. BROWN, and D. McQUAIL (1970) "The social origins of the gratifications associated with television viewing." Leeds: The Univ. of Leeds. (mimeo)

BLUMLER, J. G. and D. McQUAIL (1969) Television in Politics. Chicago: Univ. of Chicago Press.

BOGART, L. (1965) "The mass media and the blue-collar worker," in A. Bennett and W. Gomberg (eds.) Blue-Collar World: Studies of the American Worker. Englewood Cliffs, N.J.: Prentice-Hall.

DEMBO, R. (1972) "Life style and media use among English working-class youths." Gazette 18.

EDELSTEIN, A. (1973) "An alternative approach to the study of source effects in mass communication." Studies of Broadcasting 9.

EMMETT, B. (1968-1969) "A new role for research in broadcasting." Public Opinion Quarterly 32.

ENZENBERGER, H. M. (1972) "Constituents of a theory of the media," in D. McQuail (ed.) Sociology of Mass Communications. Harmondsworth: Penguin.

FESTINGER, L. and N. MACCOBY (1964) "On resistance to persuasive communication." Journal of Abnormal and Social Psychology 60.

FURU, T. (1971) The Function of Television for Children and Adolescents. Tokyo: Sophia University.

GLASER, W. A. (1965) "Television and voting turnout." Public Opinion Quarterly 29.

HERZOG, H. (1942) Professor quiz: a gratification study," in P. F. Lazarsfeld and F. N. Stanton (eds.) Radio Research, 1941. New York: Duell, Sloan & Pearce.

KATZ, E. and D. FOULKES (1962) "On the use of the mass media for 'escape': clarification of a concept." Public Opinion Quarterly 26.

KATZ, E., M. GUREVITCH, and H. HAAS (1973) "On the use of mass media for important things." American Sociological Review 38.

KATZMAN, N. (1972) "Television soap operas: what's been going on anyway?" Public Opinion Quarterly 36.

LASSWELL, H. (1948) "The structure and function of communications in society," in L. Bryson (ed.) The Communication of Ideas. New York: Harper.

——— and A. KAPLAN (1950) Power and Society. New Haven: Yale Univ. Press.

LAZARSFELD P. F. and F. N. STANTON [eds.] (1949) Communications Research, 1948-9. New York: Harper.

——— (1944) Radio Research, 1942-3. New York: Duell, Sloan & Pearce.

——— (1942) Radio Research, 1941. New York: Duell, Sloan & Pearce.

LUNDBERG, D. and O. HULTEN (1968) Individen och Massmedia. Stockholm: EFI.

McDONALD, D. (1957) "A theory of mass culture," in D. M. White and B. Rosenberg (eds.) Mass Culture: The Popular Arts in America. Glencoe: Free Press.

McQUAIL, D., J. G. BLUMLER, and J. R. BROWN (1972) "The television audience: a revised perspective," in D. McQuail (ed.) Sociology of Mass Communications. Harmondsworth: Penguin.

MASLOW, A. H. (1954) Motivation and Personality. New York: Harper.

MENDELSOHN, H. (1964) "Listening to radio," in L. A. Dexter and D. M. White (eds.) People, Society and Mass Communications. Glencoe: Free Press.

NILSSON, S. (1971) "Publikens upplevelse av tv-program." Stockholm: Sveriges Radio PUB. (mimeo)

NORDENSTRENG, K. (1970) "Comments on 'gratifications research' in broadcasting." Public Opinion Quarterly 34.

PIETILA, V. (1969) "Immediate versus delayed reward in newspaper reading." Acta Sociologica 12.

ROBINSON, J. P. (1972) "Toward defining the functions of television," in Television and Social Behavior. Vol. 4. Rockville, Md.: National Institute of Mental Health.

ROSENGREN, K. E. (1972) "Uses and gratifications: an overview." Sweden: Univ. of Lund. (mimeo)

——— and S. WINDAHL (1972) "Mass media consumption as a functional alternative," in D. McQuail (ed.) Sociology of Mass Communications. Harmondsworth: Penguin.

SCHRAMM, W. (1949) "The nature of news." Journalism Quarterly 26.

——— J. LYLE, and E. B. PARKER (1961) Television in the Lives of Our Children. Stanford: Stanford Univ. Press.

STEPHENSON, W. (1967) The Play Theory of Mass Communication. Chicago: Univ. of Chicago Press.

SUCHMAN, E. (1942) "An invitation to music," in P. F. Lazarsfeld and F. N. Stanton (eds.) Radio Research, 1941. New York: Duell, Sloan & Pearce.

WAPLES, D., B. BERELSON, and F. R. BRADSHAW (1940) What Reading Does to People. Chicago: Univ. of Chicago Press.

WEISS, W. (1971) "Mass communication." Annual Review of Psychology 22.

WOLFE, K. M. and M. FISKE (1949) "Why children read comics," in P. F. Lazarsfeld and F. N. Stanton (eds.) Communications Research, 1948-9. New York: Harper.

WRIGHT, C. (1960) "Functional analysis and mass communication." Public Opinion Quarterly 24.

PART II

EMPIRICAL STUDIES

Chapter 2

SOCIAL INTEGRATION AND MASS MEDIA USE AMONG ADOLESCENTS: A CASE STUDY

John W.C. Johnstone

THIS CHAPTER PRESENTS results from an empirical study of audience behavior framed in what now would be referred to as the uses and gratifications tradition of media studies. The analysis focuses not on the effects of exposure to the media, but on the social and social-psychological factors that prompt media exposure in the first place. As such, the analysis assumes that the media can have little or no impact on persons who have no use for them, that media fare is selected rather than imposed, and that particular media offerings are chosen because they are meaningful to those who choose them.

The study, which was conducted during the late 1950s and which was the subject of the author's doctoral dissertation (Johnstone, 1961), sought to examine audience behavior as social behavior. For many years audiences had been approached with conceptual tools borrowed mainly from the study of crowd and mob behavior. Following Blumer (1946), they were often conceived as aggregates of anonymous, heterogeneous, spatially separated, and unorganized individuals. The point of departure in this study, on the other hand, was that members of mass audiences do not experience the media as anonymous and isolated individuals, but rather, as members of organized social groups and as participants in a cultural milieu. This perspective acknowledges that audience members may select their content under a good deal of pressure and guidance from their social environment. As Freidson (1953) had suggested in an early study, it is possible to describe the mass audience without reference to the organized groups that compose it, but one cannot explain the behavior of its members except by reference to the local groups to which they belong.

This view of the mass audience, and of the mass communication experience, poses an interesting dilemma. By their intrinsic nature the mass media carry an individual's focus of attention away from the local milieu and into contact with a much wider social reality. Yet at the same time, social pressures work to divert this focus back into the sphere of the immediate social setting. There would appear, in short, to be an inherent incongruity between the social forces in one's local environment and the fundamental quality of the mass communications experience.

These competing pressures had been documented in a pioneering study by the Rileys (1951). These investigators had found, though with a precariously small sample, that children who were not integrated into peer groups used the media quite differently from those who were well integrated—the former experiencing the media primarily as fantasy, the latter as a source of ideas for peer-group interaction. Non-integrated children, moreover, were attracted to action and violence themes more often than well-integrated children were. The Rileys explained these results in terms of differential strains emanating from the social structure, and concluded that when children are under strain they are highly productive of fantasies, and tend to select out media materials that foster such fantasies.

The possibility that patterns of mass media use might be regulated within wider social contexts than the primary group was the central problem tackled in the study to be reported here. Although the influence of primary-group processes on media use had been demonstrated previously, no previous empirical work had examined media behavior within the context of more extensive networks of social relations.

The data to be presented here were collected as part of a study of high school social climates conducted at the University of Chicago between 1957 and 1959, and reported subsequently by James S. Coleman in *The Adolescent Society* (1961). The central purpose of this project was to identify the effects of different kinds of high school value climates on the aspirations and achievements of students, and ten high schools were hand-selected to include those emphasizing different kinds of values—for example, academic versus athletic achievement. The subjects of the study, then, were the students of ten Illinois high schools. Of the ten schools, four were located in small towns, two were in medium-sized cities, two were located in Chicato suburbs, one was in the center of Chicago, and one was in a tiny farming community. The schools ranged in size from 169 to just under 2,000 students, representing a total student body of some 9,000. Nine of the schools were public and coeducational, while the tenth was a Catholic parochial boys' school. The communities represented in the study varied markedly in socioeconomic characteristics, the median incomes ranging between $5,200 and $11,400 per annum. One of the ten schools was Elmtown, made famous in an earlier sociological study of American youth (Hollingshead, 1949).

The data to be reported here were collected by means of questionnaires given to all students in these ten schools. Questionnaires were completed by the students both at the beginning and end of the 1957-1958 school year, and were administered by field workers during class periods. The field work was organized so that all students in a given school filled out questionnaires on the same day, and questionnaires were also left behind for absentees. In total, data were collected from well over 90% of the enrolled student body in each school. Because the schools were hand-picked rather than randomly selected, however, they are actually representative only of themselves, and for this reason as well as the fact that students within each school represent a universe rather than a sample, no efforts will be made here to evaluate the statistical significance of relationships.

The remainder of the chapter is organized into three sections. The first deals with the changing social setting of adolescence, and examines exposure to television within that frame of reference. The second section then picks up the theme developed by the Rileys in their research, and relates rates of television use and movie-going among adolescents to their integration into the peer culture and in the high school. The third section deals with a different theme, namely the symbolic significance of popular singing idols in relation to social differentiation within the adolescent world.

All estimates of television exposure reported here are based on students' self-reports of viewing frequency. Students were asked, "About how much time, on the average, do you spend watching TV on a weekday?" and filled in one of seven categories ranging from "none, or almost none" to "four or more hours a day."

TELEVISION AND SIGNIFICANT OTHERS

Perhaps the most relevant sociological aspect about adolescence is that it represents a period of the life cycle marked by important changes in social attachments. These changes involve, on the one hand, movement away from the family of orientation, and on the other, increasing interaction with peers and members of the opposite sex. Changing social attachments of this sort would be expected to have a bearing on mass media interests and uses: for example, we might well expect television consumption to decline among adolescents as they grow older, since this type of media exposure is confined largely to the home. A number of studies, in fact, have demonstrated just such trends in adolescent television viewing habits (Witty, 1951; Glick and Levy, 1962; Furu, 1971), and the data from Illinois high school students show a similar pattern.

Interpreting cross-sectional data longitudinally, the right-hand column of Table 1 reveals that television viewing declines sharply as adolescents move through the high school years. Among freshmen, who are mainly persons in their fifteenth year, more than half of both boys and girls reported viewing television at least two hours a day; among seniors, on the other hand, the proportions hover around a third. For boys, the sharpest drop (10.2%) occurs between the junior and senior years, while for girls it occurs somewhat earlier (drops of 8.2 and 8.1%, respectively, between the freshman and sophomore and sophomore and junior years). This pattern is consistent with other evidence that girls in our culture generally mature earlier than boys. In overview, television consumption is cut just about in half within this brief four-year period, from medians of 101.6

TABLE 1

TELEVISION VIEWING, BY GRADE IN SCHOOL, SEX AND
ORIENTATION TO PARENTS

(Percent who view television two or more hours a day)

	Scores on Index of Parent Orientation		
	High	Low	Total
Boys			
Freshmen	59.4	52.1	55.2
	(N-419)	(N-449)	(N-868)
Sophomores	57.6	49.8	52.9
	(N-555)	(N-711)	(N-1266)
Juniors	47.8	42.7	44.5
	(N-362)	(N-553)	(N-915)
Seniors	37.3	32.3	34.3
	(N-241)	(N-498)	(N-739)
Girls			
Freshmen	55.7	49.9	53.5
	(N-476)	(N-395)	(N-871)
Sophomores	49.2	41.4	45.3
	(N-648)	(N-666)	(N-1314)
Juniors	40.1	35.0	37.2
	(N-511)	(N-491)	(N-1002)
Seniors	37.1	27.6	32.3
	(N-385)	(N-435)	(N-820)

and 94.9 minutes per day among freshmen boys and girls, to 55.4 and 44.0 minutes, respectively, among those in their senior year.

Of greater significance to the present discussion is the fact that changes in television consumption during these years can be interpreted as much as a function of social maturation as a product of chronological, biological, or cognitive growth. This is demonstrated by the comparisons in Table 1 between the viewing habits of adolescents differentially oriented to their parents. The measure of parental orientation employed here was developed from students' responses to five questions which dealt with preferences for hypothetical activities involving interaction with either parents or peers,[1] and the students are subdivided into two groups based on the median values of scores on this measure in the sample as a whole. Those classified as "high" on this index for the most part prefer activities which they do with their parents rather than with their friends; while those classified as "low" more often prefer to do things with their peers. An examination of the numbers of students classified in each grouping confirms that levels of "parent orientation" are lower among those in the older age-grades.

More significantly, however, the results indicate that in all eight test cases—boys and girls in the four school grades—it is those more strongly oriented to their parents who show the higher levels of television consumption. Moreover, if the grade-to-grade changes can be interpreted as the result of chronological or biological maturation, and the within-grade differences as the effects of social-psychological maturation, then the two types of effects can be said to be roughly equivalent: the average variation attributable to parent orientations averages out to 6.7% across the eight test cases, while the grade-to-grade differences in the twelve conditions where these "effects" can be estimated average to 6.9%.

These patterns illustrate how the reception of mass-mediated messages is linked to social contexts, and why it is significant that in the case of television viewing media exposure means the context of home and family rather than friends and peers. More generally, the results suggest that when significant others change, patterns of mass media exposure are also likely to change so that they fit better within the milieu in which one interacts with significant others. As one moves through the teen years in American life, this milieu is decreasingly the parental home.

MEDIA USE AND STATUS DEPRIVATION

Given the increased salience of peer-group relations to the maturing adolescent, it would follow that failure to be accepted by one's peers or failure to gain aspired levels of recognition in the student culture would be of considerable discomfort to adolescents. If it is also true that exposure to the mass media may serve cathartic or restorative functions for audiences, then persons in these situations might be expected to reveal higher rates of media exposure, especially to so-called escapist fare. One prominent source of content of this type is television; therefore, we will now examine the relationship between adolescents' social integration and their rates of exposure to television.

Two dimensions of social integration—popularity and status—will be differentiated here, the former to refer to one's acceptance by immediate peers, and the latter to one's standing, visibility, or prestige in the wider social environment. One of the principal analytic tasks in the Study of High School Social Climates was to map out friendship networks among adolescents, and for this purpose sociometric data were collected from all students in the ten schools. The structure of these friendship networks is reported in *The Adolescent Society*. For present purposes, however, we are interested only in the *extent* of one's peer-group integration, the number of sociometric choices a student received. Peer-group integration, then, is measured here by the number of times a student was named by other students in answer to the question, "Who are the boys (or girls) you go around with most often here at school?" When these nominations were assigned to the designated individuals, a wide range of popularity levels was found: some students (8.2%) received no mentions at all, while a few (3.1%) extremely popular sociometric "stars" were named ten or more times. Just two levels of popularity will be differentiated here: those who received three or more choices and those receiving two or fewer. This divides the sample into fairly even halves, since the median number of choices received was 2.6.

Social standing in the adolescent culture is not delimited by peer-group acceptance alone, however, since there is also the dimension of prestige emanating from the wider social system of the adolescent world. Various skills, attributes, talents, or achievements may be of high salience to adolescents in a community, and persons who possess these valued traits are likely to be accorded recognition on the basis of them. In high school social systems, several different roles may be accorded high status—the "best student" role, the "star athlete" role, the "best-looking girl" role, or the "leader in activities" role—to mention just a few. Rather than focus here on the specific sources of differentiation in these status systems, we will work simply from the assumption that in most American high schools the student body is stratified in terms of prestige, and that some individuals and subgroups have a great deal more "status" than others.

This dimension will be measured here by students' own appraisals of their standing in the prestige system, and specifically, by their answers to two questions: first, "Would you say you are part of the leading crowd?" and second, for those who did not think that they were, "Would you like to be part of the leading crowd?" Responses to these questions allow us to classify three kinds of status: first, self-designated "leaders," those who feel part of the leading group in the school; second, "aspirants," those who would like to be leaders but are not; and third, "non-competitors," those who do not define themselves as members of the leading group and who would not care to compete for such status. In these terms, 32.0% of the students are "leaders," 18.7% are "aspirants," and 49.3% are "non-competitors." One might well argue that subjective appraisals of this type do not validly measure real status, and strictly speaking they do not. On the other hand, the subjective element in these measures does allow us to pinpoint an unambiguous condition of felt status deprivation: "aspirants" very clearly are adolescents who want something they do not feel they have.

The fact that both sociometric status and self-designated status in the wider social system affect how adolescents feel about themselves can be demonstrated empirically. Table 2, for example, examines the prevalence of positive self-images[2] among those classified along both status dimensions simultaneously.

TABLE 2

POSITIVE SELF-IMAGES, BY SEX, NUMBER OF SOCIOMETRIC CHOICES
RECEIVED, AND PERCEIVED STATUS IN THE HIGH SCHOOL SOCIAL SYSTEM
(Percent who scored high on the Index of Self-Conception)

| | *Received 3 or more choices* | | | *Received less than 3 choices* | | |
	Leaders	*Aspirants*	*Non-Competitors*	*Leaders*	*Aspirants*	*Non-Competitors*
Boys	43.0	26.4	34.0	39.8	16.0	31.6
	(N-776)	(N-314)	(N-829)	(N-450)	(N-374)	(N-910)
Girls	37.9	20.9	32.2	34.4	12.0	28.2
	(N-924)	(N-460)	(N-1327)	(N-189)	(N-216)	(N-539)

In all six conditions here where the "effects" of sociometric status can be estimated, positive self-images are more prevalent among those who received more choices; and in all four cases where the "effects" of status in the wider system can be examined, it is "leaders" who show the strongest self-images, and "aspirants" the weakest. Among boys these values range between 16.0 and 43.0%, and among girls between 12.0 and 37.9%; it should be noted that self-images as measured here are somewhat stronger among boys. This outcome is consistent with data reported by Rosenberg (1965), but only for adolescents in the upper echelons of the social class hierarchy. Table 2 also shows that the lowest levels of self-appraisal are found among those in positions of double deprivation, while it is those who are both popular with their peers and who see themselves as members of the leading crowd who are the most self-confident. In general, these results confirm that both types of integration into the adolescent status system are salient to high school students.

At this point, we will examine the relationship between television exposure and these two dimensions of social integration. Television viewing will again be measured by the percentages within categories who view more than two hours a day, and in Table 3 these rates of "heavy" exposure are shown for boys and girls in the four high school grades classified simultaneously by peer-group integration and by their perceived status in the high school. In this table there are 16 conditions in which to examine differentials that can be attributed to position in the high school status system, and 24 conditions where comparisons can be made between adolescents with higher and lower sociometric status. With regard to status in the school system, 13 of the 16 comparisons show the highest rates among the "aspirants," in two cases the "non-competitors" are highest, and in one case the "leaders" have the highest viewing rates. On the second dimension the differences are almost perfectly consistent: in 23 of the 24 comparisons the higher rates are found among those who received fewer sociometric choices. Both of these dimensions can be said to affect viewing habits; therefore, their relative impact appears to be roughly the same.

For example, if we overlook the "non-competitors" and compare only the differences, on the one hand, between "leaders" and "aspirants," and on the other, between those with higher and lower sociometric status, the difference attributable to prestige in the school at large averages out to 5.7%, while that attributable to sociometric status averages to 7.6%. Though neither of these values is large, their combined impact, estimated by comparing the fully secure with the twice deprived, averages to 17.5% among boys and 10.6% among girls. In combination, then, status deprivation emanating from peer relations and from the wider adolescent social system does make a sizable difference in rates of "heavy" television use. It would also appear that boys are more likely than girls to increase their television viewing in response to status rebuffs from the adolescent social environment.

In general these data confirm that television viewing is heavier among adolescents who experience status frustration. While this does not establish directly that television viewing functions to reduce tensions generated in the

TABLE 3

TELEVISION VIEWING BY SEX, GRADE IN SCHOOL, NUMBER OF
SOCIOMETRIC CHOICES RECEIVED, AND PERCEIVED STATUS IN THE
HIGH SCHOOL SOCIAL STRUCTURE

(Percent who view television two or more hours a day)

	Perception of Status Position		
	Feels part of leading crowd (Leaders)	Does not feel part of leading crowd but would like to belong (Aspirants)	Does not feel part of leading crowd and would not care to belong (Non-competitors)
Received more than two sociometric choices			
Freshman boys	54.0 (N-224)	52.3 (N-109)	51.5 (N-190)
Sophomore boys	47.4 (N-310)	50.9 (N-132)	52.2 (N-312)
Junior boys	42.1 (N-252)	50.9 (N-108)	44.4 (N-261)
Senior boys	30.5 (N-252)	34.8 (N- 69)	28.5 (N-172)
Freshman girls	51.4 (N-220)	54.1 (N-159)	53.3 (N-225)
Sophomore girls	41.9 (N-284)	41.4 (N-203)	46.1 (N-401)
Junior girls	35.5 (N-234)	38.8 (N-137)	33.2 (N-340)
Senior girls	22.1 (N-231)	35.7 (N- 84)	35.5 (N-293)
Received two or less sociometric choices			
Freshman boys	63.3 (N-177)	72.4 (N-152)	59.1 (N-286)
Sophomore boys	60.7 (N-176)	64.6 (N-175)	56.3 (N-371)
Junior boys	48.1 (N-135)	58.4 (N-118)	51.4 (N-208)
Senior boys	39.8 (N-118)	48.6 (N- 70)	39.9 (N-178)
Freshman girls	51.2 (N- 80)	56.7 (N- 97)	56.2 (N-105)
Sophomore girls	47.9 (N- 73)	46.5 (N-142)	51.7 (N-203)
Junior girls	39.6 (N- 53)	46.2 (N- 78)	45.3 (N-150)
Senior girls	24.4 (N- 41)	43.9 (N- 41)	41.3 (N-121)

social world, it does suggest at least that felt deprivations emanating from the social environment do lead people to turn to television to seek out emotional restoration.

Before leaving this theme, it should be noted that certain other types of media usage among adolescents—most notably movie-going, radio listening, and record collecting—are positively rather than negatively associated with the extent of one's integration into the peer culture. Table 4 illustrates this for movie-going by duplicating the format of analysis just examined for television viewing. These data show that in 12 of 16 comparisons the highest rates of movie attendance are found among "leaders," while in 16 of 24 comparisons those who received three or more sociometric choices go to the movies more often than those receiving fewer choices. Although the discrepancies here are not so clear-cut as in the case of television viewing, it should be noted that in *all* eight comparisons those integrated into the peer culture on both dimensions are more frequent movie-goers than those integrated on neither. The average difference between the twice-integrated and twice-isolated works out to 18.0% for girls and 7.8% for

TABLE 4

MOVIE-GOING, BY SEX, GRADE IN SCHOOL, NUMBER OF SOCIOMETRIC CHOICES
RECEIVED, AND PERCEIVED STATUS IN THE HIGH SCHOOL SOCIAL STRUCTURE
(Percent who go to the movies once a week or more)

	Perception of Status Position		
	Feels part of leading crowd (Leaders)	*Does not feel part of leading crowd but would like to belong (Aspirants)*	*Does not feel part of leading crowd and would not care to belong (Non-competitors)*
Received more than two sociometric choices			
Freshman boys	49.1 (N-224)	36.7 (N-109)	34.7 (N-190)
Sophomore boys	35.0 (N-311)	25.8 (N-132)	31.7 (N-312)
Junior boys	35.3 (N-252)	25.0 (N-108)	34.1 (N-261)
Senior boys	35.7 (N-252)	26.1 (N- 69)	25.6 (N-172)
Freshman girls	50.9 (N-220)	47.5 (N-160)	37.8 (N-225)
Sophomore girls	40.9 (N-283)	30.5 (N-203)	41.1 (N-401)
Junior girls	50.8 (N-234)	26.3 (N-137)	35.3 (N-340)
Senior girls	42.8 (N-231)	30.9 (N- 84)	46.4 (N-293)
Received two or less sociometric choices			
Freshman boys	41.0 (N-178)	35.3 (N-153)	29.9 (N-284)
Sophomore boys	36.9 (N-176)	25.1 (N-175)	28.0 (N-371)
Junior boys	36.3 (N-135)	30.5 (N-118)	27.4 (N-208)
Senior boys	30.5 (N-118)	32.8 (N- 70)	28.6 (N-178)
Freshman girls	47.5 (N- 80)	39.2 (N- 97)	37.1 (N-105)
Sophomore girls	37.8 (N- 74)	27.8 (N 144)	30.0 (N-203)
Junior girls	35.8 (N- 53)	29.5 (N- 78)	38.6 (N-150)
Senior girls	46.3 (N- 41)	17.1 (N- 41)	41.3 (N-121)

boys. Particularly for girls, then, movie-going can be interpreted as a peer-
centered form of mass communications exposure.

Propensities of this sort clearly cannot be interpreted as responses to status
frustration and demand quite different explanation. One general feature of this
class of media behaviors is that they are typically experienced with peers rather
than with members of the family. When adolescents go to the movies, for
example, they are much more likely to go with their friends or with dates than
with their parents or by themselves. Listening to records, moreover, is an activity
that high school students often do in groups, and while the same is not
necessarily true of radio listening, the dominance of teenage music on American
radio means that when an adolescent tunes in, he or she is exposed to content
that has high salience in the teen world. These patterns, in short, seem to
reinforce the generalization that media consumption is structured, at least in
part, by the social setting in which one is situated.

THE SOCIAL USES OF POPULAR CULTURE

Status positions in the adolescent culture are arranged horizontally as well as vertically, and in most American high schools there is more than a single clique or in-crowd: terms such as "socies," "hoods," "greasers," "freaks," "intellectuals," and "wild ones" illustrate the variety of groupings that are recognized and named by high school students. The nature of this differentiation has been most clearly described by Schwartz and Merten (1967) in a study of another Illinois high school:

> [The] status system is structured along two dimensions. First, there are horizontal social strata defined by differentially evaluated life styles, that is, modes of dress, speech, and interpersonal demeanor. . . . The vertical component of this status system locates an individual's rank within one of these horizontal strata.

In the high school studied by Schwartz and Merten, which was not one of the schools included in Coleman's earlier research, two ways of life—"hoody" and "socie"—were perceived as dominant by the students. Moreover, during the mid-1960s groups identified by these names were visible in many other high schools in the United States: they were clearly present in a school in the St. Louis area studied by the present author in 1965 (Johnstone and Rosenberg, 1968), and information provided subsequently from graduate students who attended high school during those years indicates that these were evidently recognized groupings in high schools all over the country. Schwartz and Merten also identified a third life-style, which they called "the conventional way of life" and which was made up of all those patterns that were neither clearly "hoody" nor "socie." All in all, Schwartz and Merten provided a valuable social mapping of the parameters of the social world of adolescence as seen from within.

Although the relationships are far from perfect, the "socie" and "hoody" styles of life tend to differentiate youth from upper-middle-class backgrounds and those from the working class or the lower-middle class. Groups known by these terms were not in evidence during the late 1950s, but there was no doubt from evidence collected in the Coleman study that social class was an important basis of differentiation within the adolescent world. That social class also provided a basis from which high school students selected their popular culture was also evident from data collected in the Coleman study. One manifestation of this was in the popular singers they named as favorites. At the time when these data were collected, rock-n-roll music was just beginning to gain ascendancy in the American youth culture, though it should be noted that the Beatles had not yet come on the scene. The primary rock-n-roll proponents of the time, at least in white America, were Elvis Presley and Tommy Sands. Yet in 1957 and 1958 most high school students still preferred more conventional singers, such as Pat Boone and Perry Como. When asked to name their favorite singer from a list of six, for example, 56% of the students selected either Boone or Como, and just 27% named Presley or Sands, the rock-n-roll stars.

Who the high school students were who were first attracted to this music,

TABLE 5

PREFERENCE FOR ROCK-N-ROLL SINGERS, BY SEX, INTEGRATION INTO
HIGH SCHOOL ACTIVITIES, AND FATHER'S EDUCATION
(Percent who liked rock-n-roll singers best)

	Location of Self in relation to School Activities	*Father's Education*		
		Grade School	*High School*	*College*
Girls	Center	19.0 (N-153)	20.9 (N-387)	7.6 (N-368)
	Middle	26.8 (N-272)	24.0 (N-563)	15.1 (N-344)
	Outside	39.8 (N-402)	29.4 (N-523)	22.8 (N-245)
Boys	Center	27.7 (N-231)	23.9 (N-373)	16.1 (N-279)
	Middle	28.4 (N-331)	31.1 (N-550)	21.0 (N-319)
	Outside	37.1 (N-528)	31.7 (N-754)	24.3 (N-354)

however, is extremely revealing. Table 5 indicates the numbers who chose these
singers when the students are classified by sex, by their father's education—an
indicator of social class position—and by a measure of their perceived
connectedness to the social activities of their high school. This last measure
asked students to mark a circle to indicate how close they felt to the center of
the activities that went on in their school, and Table 5 divides the respondents
into three levels of perceived connectedness. What is striking here, of course, is
that all three of these factors—sex, father's education, and connectedness to the
high school—serve to differentiate musical tastes. In the late 1950s, rock-n-roll
singers were more popular among boys than girls, among students who saw
themselves as distanced from the social activities of their high schools, and
among students whose fathers had obtained less formal schooling—and who
presumably therefore were employed in the blue-collar rather than the
white-collar sector of the labor force. Moreover, the spread in percentages
produced by the two social location factors is very large: the figures range from
7.6% among girls with college-educated fathers who felt in the center of things in
the high school to 39.8% among girls with grade-school-educated fathers who
felt outside of things in the high school.

These data very clearly identify a social basis of taste within the adolescent
society, and they suggest that recognizable life-styles not dissimilar to those of
"socie" and "hoody," which emerged during the 1960s, were already operative
during the 1950s. In the context of the present discussion, of course, the main
significance of the data is that they clearly illustrate a social basis governing the
selection of popular culture items out of the mass media.

THE FUNCTIONS OF MASS MEDIA FOR ADOLESCENTS

Two types of mass media uses have been identified in this analysis; on the one hand, uses where the individual takes into account the context of the social milieu, and on the other, uses that carry the individual's attention away from the exigencies of his or her everyday experience. These uses were identified in part by the social forms of media reception—individualistic or group—but mainly they reflect the perspectives that an individual brings to the media. The fundamental distinction between these patterns of usage rests on whether the individual uses the media to keep contact with or to escape from the realities of his social environment. These patterns of usage can be formally labeled as *transcendental* and *experiential* uses.

Throughout the chapter, television viewing has been interpreted as a form of media exposure that transcends the context of the youth culture. This interpretation can be justified by the fact that television demands that the individual be exposed within a family rather than a peer setting, while at the same time the pressures of the adolescent social context call for independence from parents and conformity to peers. In addition, there is very little television fare that specifically reflects the youth culture. It is especially significant, then, that high school students not well integrated into the youth culture were found to be the heaviest users of television. For the adolescent, then, television viewing is at least in part a deprivation-based mass media response that permits the user to escape from a context which generates feelings of inadequacy. Although virtually all teenagers watch some television, heavy consumption within this age group may function as a substitute for interpersonal gratifications.

Experiential media uses are those where one can rehearse, reconstruct, or simply maintain contact with one's own experiences and everyday reality. Experiential usage can take either a collective or an individualistic form. In collective forms, such as when adolescents go to the movies or listen to records with their friends, the media provide a commodity for social interaction. In individualistic forms, as when a teenager listens to popular music on the radio, the media provide a channel through which an adeolescent can remain linked to his own social role, or can reinforce his identification within a subgroup.

NOTES

1. The index combined responses of the following types: (a) ranking the goal "pleasing my parents" highly among competing goals; (b) choosing to go with parents on a trip to New York rather than go with friends to the state basketball finals; (c) choosing to go West on a trip with parents rather than go camping with friends; (d) indicating that disapproval from parents would be harder to take than either disapproval from teachers or breaking up with a friend; and (e) stating that they would not join a club at school if their parents disapproved of the club.

2. Self-images here are measured by responses to three questions. The first asked students how many things about themselves they would change if they had the opportunity; and the second and third asked them to agree or disagree with the statements, "If I could

trade, I would be someone different from myself" and "I am often not able to keep up with the rest." The percentages indicate the numbers who scored positively on all three of these indicators.

REFERENCES

BLUMER, H. (1946) "The crowd, the public and the mass," in A. M. Lee, Jr. (ed.) New Outline of the Principles of Sociology. New York: Barnes & Noble.

COLEMAN, J. S. (1961) The Adolescent Society: The Social Life of the Teenager and its Impact on Education. New York: Free Press.

FREIDSON, E. (1953) "The relation of the social situation of contact to the media of mass communication." Public Opinion Quarterly 17: 230-238.

FURU, T. (1971) The Function of Television for Children and Adolescents. Tokyo: Sophia University.

GLICK, I. and S. LEVY (1962) Living with Television. Chicago: Quadrangle.

HOLLINGSHEAD, A. B. (1949) Elmtown's Youth: The Impact of Social Class on Adolescents. New York: Wiley.

JOHNSTONE, J.W.C. (1961) Social Structure and Patterns of Mass Media Consumption. Ph.D. dissertation. University of Chicago, Department of Sociology. (unpublished)

--- and L. ROSENBERG (1968) "Some sociological observations on the privileged adolescent," in J. F. Adams (ed.) Understanding Adolescence. Boston: Allyn & Bacon.

RILEY, M. W. and J. W. RILEY (1951) "A sociological approach to communications research." Public Opinion Quarterly 15: 444-460.

ROSENBERG, M. (1965) Society and the Adolescent Self Image. Princeton, N.J.: Princeton Univ. Press.

SCHWARTZ, G. and D. MERTEN (1967) "The language of adolescence: an anthropological approach to the youth culture." American Journal of Sociology 72 (March): 453-468.

WITTY, P. A. (1951) "Television and the high school student." Education 72: 242-251.

Chapter 3

MEDIA FUNCTIONS IN WARTIME:
THE ISRAEL HOME FRONT IN OCTOBER 1973

Tsiyona Peled and Elihu Katz

THE USES OF THE MASS MEDIA—particularly of television—in a crisis of national integration were brought to the fore during the days following the assassination of John Kennedy (see Mindak and Hursch, 1965; Schramm, 1965). The Yom Kippur War in Israel, for all its obvious differences, provides a number of similar examples of the functions of mass communications. What follows is a report on a series of studies conducted during the war on behalf of the Israel Broadcasting Authority. Their object was to ascertain home-front expectations of broadcasting and to assess the extent to which the media were fulfilling them.

EXPECTATIONS AND PERFORMANCE OF THE MEDIA IN CRISIS

One of the criticisms often levelled against the tradition of research on media gratifications is that it postulates an active audience, people seeking to fulfill needs or to solve problems via exposure to mass communications. Whatever the merit of this argument in normal times, there is no doubt that in a crisis the

AUTHORS' NOTE: The research described in this chapter was conducted by a joint team of the Hebrew University and the Israel Institute of Applied Social Research under the direction of the authors. The surveys were designed and the implications of the findings were discussed in closest possible cooperation with Mr. Arnon Zuckerman, director of Israel Television. Regular reports were also made to Mr. Moshe Hovav, director of Radio. Miss Michal Caspi, researcher for the Israel Broadcasting Authority, served actively as go-between and collaborator. We are also indebted to Mr. Ari Avner of the IBA for his careful scrutiny of our research results and advice concerning their publication. Altogether, it is a pleasure to acknowledge the partnership of the IBA in this work. The reader, for his part, should be warned that there are better (and worse) conditions for designing audience research than during wartime.

audience for the mass media consists of just such people. Most of the literature on communication and crisis deals with the role of the media ·in natural disasters—earthquakes, tornados, hurricanes, and the like (Baker and Chapman, 1962; Barton, 1963). Here the emphasis is on the role of the media as warning systems, on the demands placed on the media for confirmation that the danger is real, and for direction as to how to behave.

Much thought, but only little empirical research, has been given to the uses of the media in situations of social disaster, where people are in conflict not with nature but with each other: revolution, communal strife, war. In the case of intra-societal strife, it is also proper to examine the performance of the media from the point of view of society's need for early warning, for interpretation, and for tension-reduction.[1] Such analysis presumes, perhaps, the existence of relatively free media in a democratic society committed to the peaceful resolution of conflict. In different situations, there is struggle, often violent, for control of the media themselves.

In a society at war, the media are even more carefully scrutinized—both by leaders and by scholars—from the point of view of content and control. Assumptions are made about the functions of the media in the maintenance of civilian morale, the bolstering of convictions about the justice of the cause, the countering of rumors, the strengthening of solidarity, and so on. Yet, curiously, more research seems to have been done on enemy propaganda than on the functions and effects of the domestic media during wartime (for example, Kris and Speier, 1944). Even the Vietnam war seems to have been little studied from the point of view of audiences compared with the attention that was given to content and control.[2]

In certain crises where leadership is absent, or in disarray, the media themselves may sometimes even be said to "govern." Czechoslovakia in 1968 may have been an example. There one caught a glimpse of an audience rallying around the media, first as the harbinger of the promise of change, then—when the Russians said no—clinging to the media for some sense of direction in the etiquette of receiving an invading army.

The weekend following the assassination of President Kennedy may have been another example of government by media. This was a period of crisis for Americans. It was characterized by emotional depression and anxiety over the stability of the political system. According to Mindak and Hursh (1965), television functioned during this period to restore faith in the stability of society; to confer status and legitimacy on the leadership who were attending to the succession; to discourage would-be demonstrators and activists by glueing them to their television sets; and to provide emotional catharsis. Examining this and other studies, Schramm (1965) concluded that crisis sharpens the need for (1) information, (2) interpretation of the why of what happened, and (3) assistance in shaking off the shock and expressing grief. Schramm connected these demands with a phase theory of the restoration of balance to a society in crisis.

COMMUNICATION IN CRISIS: YOM KIPPUR, OCTOBER 6, 1973

As in the case of the Kennedy assassination, the invasion of the Syrian and Egyptian forces in October 1973 took Israel—and its media—by surprise. Indeed, up until the sounding of the air-raid sirens, nobody in Israel that day had any expectations at all of mass communications. Yom Kippur is the one day of the year when the media are totally shut down. Nor is there any transportation; unlike the Sabbath and other traditional holidays, even owners of private cars stay close to home and synagogue. Communication is with God and with intimate associates.

When the sirens sounded at 2 P.M., people were preparing for the final hours of the Yom Kippur vigil. There had been signs during the morning that "something" was happening. The mobilization of several reserve units had begun in the early hours, and army vehicles were rushing nervously through the streets, their headlights lit. But there was not very much activity until the air-raid sirens were sounded. Almost immediately, the national radio and TV services went on the air, announcing the combined Egyptian-Syrian attack and repeating this bulletin every few minutes together with the reassuring information that the Israeli forces were repulsing the enemy. The broadcasts were punctuated with civil defense instructions and with the coded names of military units being called up. Many young men went home to don their uniforms and came back to the synagogue to say goodbye to their parents. By now the streets were full of army traffic. But there was no sign of panic.

To understand the relative calm with which Israelis received the news, one must know something of the absolute trust that had been invested in the Armed Forces. One must also know something of the experience of the Six Day War in which several nearly newsless days were followed by the story of triumph, and then by the revelation that the Israeli broadcasters, not the Arabs, had been telling the truth. People felt that, this time, it would only be a matter of hours, not days. By evening a full blackout was in force, lasting until the cease-fire.

Public opinion immediately rallied. Social indicators show that there may even have been a *rise* in mood (well-feeling "most of the time" or "all of the time") during the first few days.[3] There was a drop after the first few days, but the mood remained high and stable throughout the eighteen days of fighting, even when the news was at its worst. Criticism of government which had been very high prior to the war—centering largely on economic issues—dropped off completely. The credibility of government spokesmen and of the broadcast media remained very high throughout the war, despite unmistakable evidence that the news of the first days—what little there was of it—had been far too optimistic. The people were expressing unqualified support, and, despite an increasing concern for the well-being of the state and the army, they were saying, in effect, don't worry about me. Suddenly there were no more economic problems; even the national health improved, despite the presumably negative selection of those who stayed home.

After the beginning of the war and during the fighting, then, there was grave concern but very high morale. It was only with the cease-fire on October 22 that all this changed: mood moved steeply down, criticism of government went sharply up, media credibility dropped steadily.

BROADCASTING POLICY AND RESEARCH

Broadcasting immediately adapted its programming to what was happening. Radio was on around the clock (rather than signing off at 1 A.M.). Television broadcast all day by combining the daytime instructional service with the nighttime general service. News bulletins were broadcast every hour, and sometimes more often on radio, and five times a day (rather than twice) on television. Lengthy radio and television newsmagazines featured reportage from the front. News was heavily censored, and the selection of warm, human interest items in the newsmagazines contradicted—in spirit at least—the terse, uninformative news bulletins. "Regards" to friends and family were broadcast throughout the day to and from the front.

Many types of programs were cancelled. Talk shows and serious commentaries were taken off the air. Imported light entertainment was reduced; sports and radio commercials were removed. Radio and television featured Israeli music and homemade entertainment. More and more live shows were telecast as well as live coverage of news events, such as press conferences and Knesset debates. The number of American action-adventure series was increased. Action films and full-length comedies were shown daily on television.

On the sixth day of the war, the broadcasting authorities expressed a strong interest in studying the public response. The media had become central to people's lives; first, for whatever clues could be transmitted concerning the well-being of loved ones, and second, because people at home had to stay inside their blacked-out houses during the long evening hours. The Yom Kippur War was the first crisis of its kind since the advent of television in Israel, and it was important for policymakers to find out how the broadcasts were being received. Moreover, there was the special problem of the unique composition of the audience. The listeners and viewers at home were women, and children, and older persons, sitting in relative isolation. Younger men were at the front, and for many immigrant families it is the younger men who provide a primary link to the larger social structure.

The broadcasting authorities were aware of these facts. Indeed, they felt themselves responsible not only for the supply of information, but perhaps even more for the gratification of the social and psychological needs of the audience. While they were limited and controlled by the censors and ceded some part of their sovereignty to officials who were given charge of information policy during the war, the professional staffs of radio and television enjoyed complete freedom in the area of programming. Radio had to serve both the men at the front and those at home; television was concerned only with the home audience. Both media knew that the enemy was listening and viewing.

We were asked to conduct very quick studies on a number of highly practical issues with immediate implications for broadcasting policy. The following are some of the questions we were asked to answer:

(1) What needs are prevalent in the public at this time, and which of these are the media expected to serve?

(2) Which media and what contents best satisfy these needs? For example, do action-adventure programs serve to release pent-up tension or to exacerbate it?

(3) What social and psychological functions are attributed to different kinds of programming—reportage from the front, for example?

(4) Are certain types of programs dysfunctional or irritating under such circumstances? Specifically, were the broadcasters intuitively right in removing advertising, sports, discussions, etc.? Was the decision to keep radio on around the clock justified? Was it, as some of the information policymakers insisted, keeping people awake at night and preventing them from getting to work in the morning? Was the programming in Arabic language—a regular feature of Israel's one-channel system—irritating to the Jewish population?

(5) What was the credibility of Israeli broadcasting—especially after the misleading information of the first few days? Were people actively involved in rumor-mongering? Were they listening to foreign broadcasts? Were they believing them?

These and other topics, which were formulated as operative questions in a structured questionnaire, were studied in a series of four surveys carried out between October 12 and November 7. Random samples of the adult (aged 20 and over) Jewish population in the three large cities (Tel Aviv, Haifa, and Jerusalem) were selected from the post office area code registers. Within each household respondents were selected according to the Kish (1955) method. Personal interviews were held in the homes of the respondents. When the designated respondent was not available (mainly mobilized men), another adult member of the same household was chosen as a substitute. In comparison with regular samples of these cities, the war survey samples were biased by sex (more women) and slightly upwards in age and education, but as such they represented the population on the home front.

FINDINGS I:
FUNCTIONAL DIFFERENCES AMONG MEDIA IN CRISIS

While our studies were mainly focused on the functions of television, we set out to identify the extent to which the several media of mass communication gratified different audience needs. To do this, we asked respondents to assess the importance of each of four media (radio, television, newspapers, and conversation) with respect to three of the fundamental communication needs associated with crisis. Specifically, we asked which medium was most helpful for

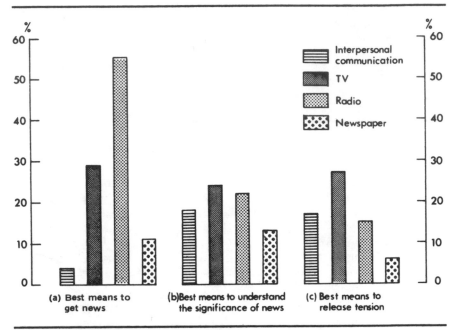

Figure 1: FUNCTIONAL DIFFERENCES AMONG MEDIA IN CRISIS

(1) obtaining information about the situation, (2) understanding the significance of what was happening, and (3) relieving tension. The results, which are given in Figure 1, show radio as the primary source of information and television as the medium that provides tension release. None of the media stands out as the predominant source of interpretation of the news: radio, television, and conversation were mentioned by almost equal numbers. Newspapers, surprisingly, were a little further behind, despite the fact that among the three functions interpretation is the one for which the newspaper is most often chosen.

There are certain differences among people at different educational levels. The more educated credited radio as the key source of information; television was more important as a news medium for the less educated. The helpfulness of radio and newspapers for understanding the significance of news was minimal among persons of low education; interpersonal communication was the medium that helped them most to understand what was going on. As for tension release, interpersonal communication was named more frequently by persons of highest and lowest education, while television was disproportionately effective for the middle educated. The particular importance of television for the middle classes and their lesser dependence on other people for gratifying both cognitive (interpretation) and emotional (tension-release) needs is noteworthy; a similar finding is reported in connection with the Kennedy assassination (Greenberg and Parker, 1965). It should also be noted—in connection with the management of crisis—that the lowest educated were less likely than the other two groups to find an outlet for mounting tension in *any* of the media, while measures of mood and worries showed that they were the most tense and anxious sector during the crisis. Greenberg and Parker (1965) also found that emotional involvement with the Kennedy assassination crisis was highest among the lower class.

On the whole, it is clear that the speed and ubiquity of radio make it the medium most capable of coping with the information needs of people in crisis, while television by comparison is a source of relief and release. But that does not mean, as we shall now see, that people did not want information and interpretation from television. They did and very much; but they "used" televised information in more complex ways.

FINDINGS II:
EXPECTATIONS OF TELEVISION IN A TIME OF CRISIS

Since television was the primary focus of our research, we asked respondents to indicate the proportion of television time which they would like to have devoted to each of three needs: (1) the provision of information and interpretation (taken together); (2) the reduction of tension; and (3) the strengthening of feelings of solidarity with army and nation.[4]

The ranking of these expectations over time is given in Figure 2. In the second week of the fighting (October 12), 53% of the home-front population expected television to devote "most of its time" to the need to know and understand. Over one-third wanted television to concentrate on tension release and the promotion of national solidarity.[5] Five days later, there was a small increase in the demand for all three functions, with a somewhat disproportionate rise in the demand for the non-informational ones. Immediately after the proclamation of the cease-fire on October 22, demand for all three functions dropped dramatically and the rank-order differences among them disappeared.

The maximal drop in the survey of October 23 occurred in the most important function. This could be a result of feelings that the cease-fire would bring with it alternative sources of information, such as interpersonal communication with people who had been at the front; it may be that it was an expression of fatigue, or satiety with the frequency of news bulletins and magazines. The drop in all three functions suggests, in fact, that people wanted relief from the medium itself. Indeed, the blackout was lifted, and people could get out of their homes more easily in the evenings or engage in alternative indoor activities such as reading. Yet during the next two weeks, when it became quite clear to everybody that the war had only just started on the political level and militarily the country was still engaged in a continuous war of attrition, the demand for the three TV functions increased again, and their hierarchy was reestablished. This is evident in the figures for November 7, a time when diplomatic activity and crisis fever were at a peak, and when the country was again frustrated by the absence of forthright statements from the government. In

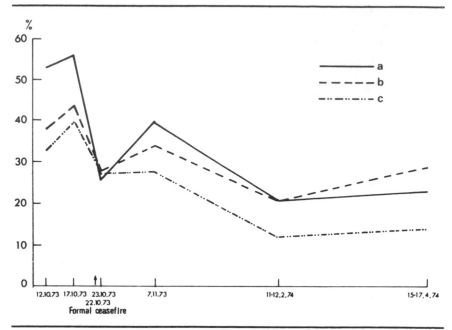

Figure 2: CHANGES IN PUBLIC DEMANDS OF TV

The portrayed percentages are of respondents who wished TV to devote most of its time to programs which help people to: a. know and understand the situation; b. release tension; c. feel proud for the state and the army.

two subsequent soundings on these same three items in mid-February and mid-April of 1974 (four and six months after the fighting, with ambiguity still high and internal affairs still unsettled in the wake of the war), there was a sharp drop in the demand for information and for reinforcement of national solidarity, and a relatively high level of constant demand for television to aid the reduction of tension.

In analyzing these data, it is important to keep in mind that our questions refer to respondents' expectations of television's role relative to the fulfillment of these needs. The changing levels of demand for each type of function, therefore, may not be taken as measures of the strength of the needs themselves. Thus, while there was probably a reduced level of *acute* demand for information during the later periods, a need for a full explanation of the so-called failure started to emerge; because this was not reflected in demands put on television, it might be inferred that there should have been a rising expectation for newspaper information as *compared* with electronic information. The available data, however, do not permit a test of this inference.[6]

Throughout the period, no significant relationships were found between socio-demographic variables, such as sex, age, and level of education, and the frequency with which television was expected to provide information and relieve tension. However, the desire for more television time for the expression of national solidarity was related to age and especially to level of education. Older people and those of lower education asked for more of this kind of content than did other groups.[7]

The wartime rank-ordering of TV functions was different for yet another age group: the children. According to their parents, tension release was the children's primary need. Help in obtaining and understanding information and the need to reinforce feelings of social solidarity were considerably lower in importance. But altogether, the baby-sitting functions of television deserve particular attention.[8]

FINDINGS III:
EXPECTATIONS AND THEIR FULFILLMENT

With respect to each of the major functions sought from broadcasting, an effort was made to examine the extent to which respondents actually found satisfaction when they switched the set on. How well did television meet their expectations? What sort of content is most associated with each kind of function? Here we shall consider the functions one at a time and attempt to report some of the evidence we collected on the questions we set out to answer.

The Need to Know and to Understand

Even in peacetime the media are the primary agents of "surveillance" and "correlation" as Wright (1959) and others have labelled these functional prerequisites of any social system. Israelis know these functions all too well; they, like their ancestors, have had to be on the alert continually. In times of tension the radio is ubiquitous. On the hour people will freely crowd round a car, stand under a balcony, or otherwise violate the "personal space" of others in order to listen to the news. Figure 3, which presents a selection of exposure to different sources of news, shows everybody listening to radio and television news during the weeks of war. It shows 68% of the population listening to radio all-day long (ten bulletins or more) during the second week of the fighting, and a sharp decline thereafter as the tide turned and the pace of significant events slackened. Note, however, the temporary return to intense radio listening during October 24 to 26, when the world was threatened with the possibility of a confrontation of the superpowers.

The demand for more—more news and more interpretation—during the first days of the war was expressed in a variety of attitudes and behaviors. People asked for more news bulletins and more reportage; they wanted the daily television newsmagazine to be lengthened from thirty to sixty minutes; they stayed up at night to listen to the radio. In considering the association between radio and crisis, it is interesting to note that 55% of the population reported turning on their radios for news while viewing evening television. As the war progressed, the viewing of the daytime television news bulletins sharply declined, as did listening to after-midnight radio news.

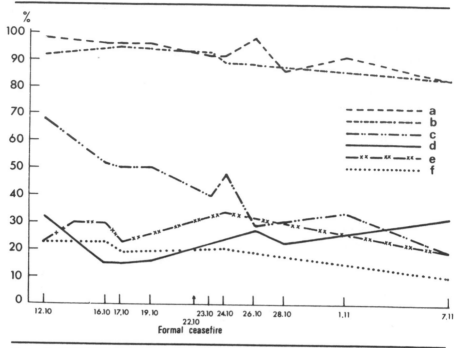

Figure 3: CHANGES IN THE CONSUMPTION OF INFORMATION FROM VARIOUS SOURCES

The portrayed percentages are of respondents who: a. listened to at least one news bulletin on radio; b. viewed the main newsmagazine on tv; c. listened to 10 or more news bulletins a day; d. received by word-of-mouth news not publicized in the mass media; e. listened to foreign radio news; f. viewed Arab tv news.

Ostensibly, the broadcast media seemed to satisfy the demand for news, reportage, and interpretation. Supply appeared to keep up with demand. People reported that the media satisfied their "need to understand." Assessing each of the broadcast media separately, about 90% of the population said that the commentaries and the reportage from the front were "helpful" or "very helpful" for satisfying their informational demands. Eighty-five percent graded the broadcast media as credible ("One can believe everything/most things which are broadcast").

And yet there was a problem. The country had been taken by surprise and so had the broadcasters. The first few days were marked by misleading information from national leaders about their foreknowledge of the attack, the army's degree of preparedness, the ease with which the surprise attack would be repulsed, and the damage already done to the enemy. It took two days to organize the flow of official information, and once the officials themselves knew what was happening, it took another day or so to begin to correct the misleading impressions that had been given to the public. Even then, no information was given over the air about Israel's losses in men or material, and the selection of eyewitness stories from the front gave the terse and colorless news a rosier tinge than it deserved. The commentators—and particularly General Haim Herzog—tried to paste the pieces together in order to give an overview of the situation, but it was not easy to counterbalance the patchwork of official bulletins and disconnected pieces of reportage. Moreover, the commentators, like everybody else, considered morale boosting to be part of their job.

Thus, the need "to know and to understand" was not altogether satisfied by the broadcast media. Admittedly, this was not immediately reflected in indices of satisfaction and credibility during the days of the fighting. But it was reflected, we believe, (1) in the sharp drop in credibility immediately following the cease-fire, (2) in the rate of rumor transactions, and (3) in the extent of listening and viewing to foreign stations.

As Figure 4 shows, the decline in the very high rate of credibility assigned to the broadcast media began on October 22. It continued on its downward course long after, and at the time of this writing (April 1974) was still at a low level. The curve of this decline corresponded to the sharp drop in other measures of support for and belief in leadership. With the outbreak of war, the populace rallied around the government in a dramatic display of unquestioned support and allowed doubt and criticism to emerge only when the fighting was over. The high level of credibility during the weeks of war has several sources: in part, it was due to the deservedly high reputations for credibility of the media and the Army Spokesman (the major source of official wartime news); in part, it was because people had learned from the Six Day War that "no news is good news" and assumed that the formula still held; and in part, it was due to a deliberate—often even conscious—repression of criticism and doubt while there was still fighting to be done. The need to know was not altogether satisfied by the media, and their loss of credibility is not easily repaired.

Access to alternative sources of information is not difficult in Israel. For a goodly portion of the population in a small, rather egalitarian country, word-of-mouth access to information sources, both civilian and military, is commonplace. Rumors, therefore, are not infrequent; many turn out to be correct (cf. Shibutani, 1966). Moreover, the radio dial is full of words and music from other countries. Almost half the population understands Arabic, but many of the Arab stations—and, of course, BBC, VOA, and other countries—broadcast frequently in English and occasionally in Hebrew. Television from Egypt, Lebanon, and Jordan is accessible in certain areas of Israel. And Jordan has a new Hebrew news program.

During the first days of the war the rumor rate (see Figure 3) was very high. Almost four in ten respondents indicated that they had received news that day from a personal source, news which they had not heard on the air or seen in the press. And during the same period a third of the population said that word-of-mouth had at least some degree of credibility (see Figure 4). Note that the curve of receiving information by word-of-mouth and the intensity of radio listening (both in Figure 3) were responsive to the same demand for information until October 26. After that date, both the frequency and credibility of rumor transactions increased simultaneously with the decline in media credibility

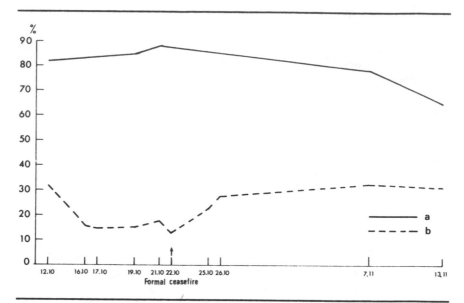

Figure 4: CREDIBILITY OF RADIO, TELEVISION AND WORD-OF-MOUTH NEWS

The portrayed percentages are of respondents who: a. think that all or most radio and tv news is believable; b. inclined to believe word-of-mouth news.

(Figure 4) and as a result of increased contact with family members and friends on leave from the front.

The search for information on foreign stations was equally frequent for radio and television, attracting about 25% of the population compared with lower levels of peacetime listening and especially viewing. Notice the return to the peacetime level of foreign viewing by November 7 (Figure 3).

The most salient motive for foreign radio listening (especially to the BBC, listening to which is positively related to education) was to learn about "how the world is responding to our situation." Frequency of exposure to Arab sources, which was negatively related to level of education, was motivated more often by a wish "to compare our version with the enemy's" and to see or hear Israeli prisoners of war in Arab captivity. The issues of "our losses," "our failings," and "our unpreparedness when the war started" were also the main topics around which the rumor industry flourished.

It should be noted that during the fighting the credibility of Israeli broadcasts was very high compared with that of Arab sources.[9] However, the credibility assigned to the several sources—Israeli broadcasting, foreign broadcasting, word-of-mouth—were intercorrelated.[10] Although the correlations were not high, they were consistent over time. Trust in foreign sources was positively related to belief in rumor and negatively related to various measures of credibility of Israeli media and Israeli leaders. The more people believed in rumors and in foreign sources, the less optimistic they were about Israel's stamina, the more criticism they voiced over government handling of the situation, and the more open they were in acknowledging the achievements of the Arabs in improving their image as warriors and in strengthening the credibility of their broadcasts.

The syndrome of decreasing credibility of Israeli broadcasting together with the inclination to accept information from alternative sources—mainly word-of-mouth—was more characteristic of the *higher* educated. It was also more characteristic of younger people. The lesser confidence in official sources of communication was related in turn to higher levels of criticism of the government's handling of the situation—which was also associated with the younger and more educated sectors of the population.

While it is true that these are the groups which are more likely to voice criticism of established authority even in peacetime, at first glance it seems surprising that they were the more active purveyors of rumor in war. Yet, in the present context, even this kind of behavior seems to fit, especially if one recalls Shibutani's (1966) definition of rumor as "improvised news." The syndrome is surely related to higher tolerance of ambiguity, that is, to a lesser "need" for closure. It probably reflects more active seeking among available sources of information and an ability to cope with the problem of selectivity. Indeed, rumor activity was directly related to level of education and inversely related to age during the Kennedy assassination crisis as well (Greenberg and Parker, 1965). But over and above these generalities, the Israeli situation suggests some additional dimensions. So far as word-of-mouth is concerned, the better educated is the group that is closest to first-hand information from centers of power. The younger people, naturally, also had maximal interaction with people who came home on leave from the front immediately after the cease fire. We found such interaction to be related to involvement with rumor and to heighten criticism of government and negatively affect morale. (On November 7, 55% of the respondents said that conversations with people on active duty influenced their mood for the worse, and 35% said that these contacts had lowered their confidence in the government's treatment of the situation.)

On a manifest level, then, the need to be informed and to understand might seem to have been well satisfied by the wartime broadcasts. Certainly, that is what most people said. But for certain groups at least Israeli radio and television were not enough; they looked elsewhere. And when the fighting was over, the credibility of broadcasting suddenly dropped.

The Need for Tension Release

Although it is no surprise that news bulletins, reportage, and commentary serve the needs of surveillance and correlation, it is less immediately evident—in the midst of a war—which media and what kinds of content help to relieve tension.

We have already seen that television exceeds the other media, by far, as a source of tension release. Moreover, its close link with the reduction of tension is reflected in the sizable number of respondents who saw this as television's major function.

Two complementary methods were employed for identifying the kinds of programs that gratify the need for relief from tension. One was a direct approach in which respondents were asked to assess the extent to which each of a variety of programs or program types was helpful for this purpose. The other method was more indirect; it is based on correlations between program preferences and the strength of respondent demand that television spend its time helping to reduce tension.

In both direct and indirect methods, it was found that action-adventure programs functioned to reduce tension. People said so; and the correlational analysis (see Table 1) shows that those who looked to television for help in tension management ("tension release" and "help in killing time") found it in this kind of show. Feature films and entertainment shows (domestic and imported) were also correlated with the desire for tension-reducing programming. A correlational analysis performed for each educational level separately showed that the more educated respondents were more consistent over time in their functional program preferences than were those with less education.

Although the catharsis theory of viewing action on the screen has been discredited with respect to violence, it does seem to be relevant in the present, more classical sense. At a minimum, these programs are gripping and thus distracting from reality-based tension. But perhaps more than this, they serve as vehicles that transport one's real-world strains into a fictional world where tension is escalated, brought to a climax, and resolved, with very little need to worry about what the likely outcome is going to be.

Surprisingly, news commentaries and reportage were also named as helpful in the area of tension release. This finding reconfirms, if it needs further confirmation, that a manifest analysis of the content of a message is not, in

TABLE 1

INTERRELATIONSHIP BETWEEN DEMANDS FOR TV FUNCTIONS AND
DEMANDS FOR TV PROGRAMS

Type of Demanded Program	The Demanded TV Function				
	Know and Understand	Tension Release	Pass the Time	Feeling of Pride	Trust in Leaders
Tension-action series		X	X		
Talk shows	X				X
Imported movies		X	X		
Imported entertainment shows		X	X		
Israeli movies		X		X	X
Israeli entertainment		X	X	X	X
Programs on Jewish tradition				X	X
Level of education				X	X
Age				X	X

NOTE: The entries marked X indicate cells where the monotonic relationship was consistently higher than .25 in three of the studies.

itself, an adequate basis for predicting how people will use it: between 60% and 70% of the respondents said that commentaries, radio and television reportage were each "helpful" or "very helpful" in reducing their feelings of tension. Thus, the handling of information, which was to reveal itself as dysfunctional in terms of credibility and the need to know, was apparently quite functional from the point of view of tension release. The cathartic use of informational material was most frequent among the low educated, who were—throughout the period of the fighting—the most tense and least critical sector of the population.

It is perhaps inevitable that there should be an inherent contradiction in the functionality of "good" news. If the news, in fact, is less rosy than its presentation, it will be dysfunctional in the long run for credibility and knowledge but functional in the short run for relieving tension. This, after all, is the risk that is entailed in managing the news with morale in mind; the managers believe that the short-term boosting of morale will outweigh the long-term disillusionment with the credibility of the source. In effect, they are betting on very brief crises and very short memories.

But this contradiction applies only to the *content* of information, not to its *frequency*. It is clear, our data confirm, that both needs—for knowledge and for tension release—are the better served the more frequent the news coverage. An additional piece of evidence relevant here is the fact that after-midnight news listeners reported that these broadcasts helped to reduce tension twice as often as to increase it.

It will be recalled that the effect of after-midnight news broadcasting was one of the concerns of the broadcasters and information policymakers. In fact, when the tide of the war turned, the issue began to be hotly debated, with one group arguing that news broadcasts after midnight kept people awake, increased tension and anticipation, and thus deprived people both of the tension-releasing functions of sleep and of the energy they would need for work the next morning. The other side of the argument, heard more frequently from the professional broadcasters, was that a steady supply of information, continually available on call, was essentially functional and served to reduce tension rather than to increase it. By the time we studied the question, only 20% of the population were tuning in their radios after 1 A.M.; the numbers were much greater during the early days of ambiguity. Among the listeners, half said the news at night did not affect their level of tension. The other half, as already reported, divided 2 : 1 in favor of the functional side.

Another aspect of our study of television programming concerned its potential dysfunctionality for tension release. This arose from the possibility that Israeli broadcasts in the Arabic language would be dissonant to the eyes and ears of the Jewish population. Israeli television operates on one channel only, and one-and-a-half hours per day of near-prime time are devoted to broadcasting in Arabic intended for Arab citizens of Israel and residents of the occupied territories. The Arabic programs were neither removed nor reduced during the crisis. Yet there was some concern that these programs might aggravate the feelings of Jews, who, seeking relief from television, encountered instead programs intended to show interest and respect for Arabic culture and traditions.

The results of our work in this area, however, show that a majority of the Jewish population did not think that the extent of programming in Arabic should be reduced during the war. Nevertheless, the proportion affirming the desirability of these programs dropped from the peacetime level of 80% to about two-thirds. People's tolerance for these programs and their willingness to forego these broadcast hours were expressed not only in terms of time but also with regard to content: the validity of programs of Arab folklore and tradition—those on which the concern of the professional broadcasters had especially focused— was affirmed by a majority of the population.

The Need for Social Integration

During the height of the fighting 40% of the population called for television programs that would contribute to their feeling of pride in state and army, solidarity with the leadership, and so on. A few months after the war—as Figure 2 shows—the proportion was down to 12% to 14%, the sharpest drop among the three functions studied.

While the need expressed for programs of information and tension release was equally frequent in all social groups, the demand for television to strengthen feelings of social solidarity was negatively related to education and positively related to age. That is, the older and less well-educated respondents especially looked to television for help in this area. Surely, this is an expression of a certain degree of relative marginality and a desire for vicarious participation, at least with respect to a crisis situation.

In seeking to identify the forms of program content used by respondents to heighten their feelings of social solidarity, we found that all types of broadcasts made in Israel, from the "heaviest" to the "lightest," served this function. This was also reflected in the intercorrelated preferences for such otherwise unrelated program types such as Israeli films, light entertainment, and programs on Jewish tradition (see Table 1).

Again, information programming of all kinds was thought to contribute to social solidarity. A very large majority (reaching 90%) of the population rated reportage and commentary on TV and radio as helpful in promoting feelings of national pride. They were referring, of course, to the dogged determination and heroic acts that characterized the Israeli effort to overcome and then repulse the surprise attack. In functional terms, then, media reportage—particularly that on TV—proved integrative as well as informative. Further evidence of the integrative functions of informational broadcasts is provided by the indication in the correlational analysis that the more people sought help from television for social integration, the greater their demand for television reportage and additional filmed material from the front, and the more likely they were to rate such material as helpful in strengthening their feelings of social solidarity. Coefficients of monotonicity between these variables range from .42 to .44.

Our research was not early enough or subtle enough to measure the extent to which the pronouncements of the leaders in the first days of the war strengthened or undermined feelings of social solidarity and confidence in government. There are many who would argue that these pronouncements heightened, rather than gratified, the need for reassurance that we encountered; that is, that they were actively dysfunctional from this point of view. By contrast, programs of Israeli entertainment—many of which were transmitted live, there having been no time to edit—appear to have made a major contribution to the feeling of national togetherness during the long evenings of relative isolation in blacked-out living rooms or shelters, and of anxiety over children, fathers and husbands at the front.

FUNCTIONS OF MEDIA IN CRISIS: SUMMARY AND CONCLUSIONS

Comparison of our findings with the analysis of the functions of television in the crisis following the Kennedy assassination suggests many points of resemblance. Considering the very different character of the two situations, it is perhaps surprising that there are resemblances at all. Of course, the differences in the role of the media in the two situations are of equal importance.

Reviewing the studies of the "integrative crisis" following the presidential assassination, Schramm (1965) sees television, first of all, as a focus for the expression of grief. He describes the compulsive fixation on television in therapeutic terms, and in terms of the need to participate vicariously in the events and the farewells and to learn the forms of expression proper to the occasion. He notes the demand for facts, for interpretation, and for help in shaking off the shock. He notes the compulsive need to talk to others, and the combined role of television and word-of-mouth in creating a collective experience of a magnitude hardly known even in the wired society of America. He credits the full news coverage and the frank and frequent appearance of national leaders with speeding the reassurance that was so eagerly sought and the consequent sense of national reintegration. By Saturday night, as Mindak and Hursh (1965) note, people were seeking means of escape from their television set, in order to resume the "normal" life of which television, for once, was not the symbol!

The civilian population of Israel turned to its media and to each other for some of the same reasons in October 1973. There was an urgent need for information and interpretation of the totally unexpected. People eagerly awaited the explanations of leaders. They sought relief from anxiety in the media and in conversation. They used the media to participate in the national grief when it came time for mourning. They found in the media a reinforcement of national solidarity.

Unlike the Kennedy crisis, the war in Israel spread over not days but weeks. It was a crisis of physical and social survival, not just of integration and succession. It was a time of high anxiety as well as grief.

In assessing the uses of the media in this crisis, we found an active audience with explicit expectations of the media and an apparent ability to assess the subjective utility of different kinds of content for different kinds of expectations. We found the demand for information and interpretation paramount. Radio was considered the most helpful source for information, although the demand for television news, reportage, and commentary was unrelenting, and the consumption of newspapers was higher than in regular days. Newspapers were especially used as an additional source of information and interpretation to the electronic media, which played the major role. Our findings confirm that the manifest analysis of message content is not in itself an adequate basis for predicting the use that will be made of the message. Thus, we found that televised information served not only the need to know but also the need for relief from tension and for a feeling of social connectedness. Because of the mismanagement of information policy in the first days of the war and the overconcern with immediate problems of civilian morale (and the problem of presenting an image of oneself which would make the enemy, and his potential allies, think twice), there developed certain frustrations in the process of satisfying informational needs via Israeli radio and television. Whereas Schramm (1965) shows that full news coverage and forthright statements of leaders speeded the process of reintegration, the Israeli media suffered a setback immediately after the cease-fire.

Instead of the phases of shock and reintegration described by Schramm, the Israeli situation was more complex. The initial reaction, abetted by the media, was one of an immeidate closing of ranks, a dramatic display of solidarity. The cohesiveness of the society, the "good" news, together with the frame of reference of the Six Day War, explain the initial response and the sustained high level of morale and credibility all during the weeks of the fighting. But during this second phase there were also gnawing doubts and a growing need for further information from unofficial sources, such as word-of-mouth and foreign broadcasts. And the result, in phase three following the cease-fire on October 22, took the form of lowered morale and credibility. Only in a fourth phase did the slow process of recovery begin, accompanied by frank and searching inquiry on the part of all the media.

Television and radio reportage brought the human side of the story into the living room; hence the attribution of functions of national solidarity to television reportage. Commentary gave perspectives on the enemy's plight which the news could not provide; hence the attribution of functions of tension release to programs of commentary.

Television was seen as the primary medium for relief of tension. Action-adventure programs served as agents of catharsis, distracting attention from the real-life tension by focusing it on fictional tension. Television programs on Israeli and Jewish themes gratified the demand for a heightened feeling of social solidarity. This demand was more characteristic of the older and the less educated—the more marginal members of the society—than of more integrated individuals.

Word-of-mouth was an important supplement to the mass media, rather more for the higher and lower educated than for those in the middle. One of the dilemmas implicit in our data is that interpersonal communication in crisis is at once functional and dysfunctional. It functions to interpret the news (especially among the less educated) and to reduce tension; but it also breeds rumor.

On the whole, the broadcast media in Israel are thought to have done a good job during the war. In its first test under fire, television discovered more of the potential of the medium than it had heretofore exploited. It realized that it is outside the studio where life goes on, and that the spontaneity of live programs may be preferable to the polish of edited ones. It appreciated something of the latent significance for viewers of programs that are made in Israel, and something of the rather sophisticated understanding of viewers of the functions of different kinds of programs (for example, nighttime radio, Arabic television, action-adventure series). Everybody appears to have learned something about the functions and dysfunctions of different sorts of information policy in crisis.

In this latter sense, it is fair to say that media executives (and researchers) also learned something of the policy potential of the study of uses and gratifications. The policymakers were sensitized to the relevance of defining situations from the point of view of the audience and to the ways in which audience members formulate their communication needs with respect to changing situations. Specifically, they (and we) learned that certain kinds of content answer to the needs of a society in crisis, and that both needs and their satisfaction should be monitored over time and with respect to subgroups in the society.

It is interesting to note that research of this kind is useful to broadcasters partly because they have a repertoire of responses—an armamentarium, as the medical profession calls it—readily available for use. That is, they have a supply of programs and programming ideas which can be rather easily drawn upon to meet the demands of their audiences. The researcher in turn can provide information to help "fit" supply to demand, or to anticipate the kind of supply that is likely to be lacking. Social prescriptions may not be much better than medical ones, but when they do not cure, they sometimes help to relieve the pain.

NOTES

1. The relationship between the performance of the media, media research, and research on indicators of social change is at issue here. See, for example, the work by Rivers (1971) which implicitly places part of the blame for the Watts uprising on the media's too narrow definition of news.

2. Interesting speculation about audience uses and effects, however, can be found in Michael J. Arlen (1969).

3. See the special war surveys conducted by the staff of The Continuing Survey, a joint project of the Israel Institute of Applied Social Research and The Communications Institute of the Hebrew University. A summary of some of these findings is reported in Guttman and Levi (1974).

4. The universe of media-related needs from which these questions ultimately derive is outlined in Katz, Gurevitch and Haas (1973). According to their paradigm, the content of the specific questions asked here would be summarized as follows:

Respondent (x) expects TV to devote *high/low* amount of time to programs which help people to

A	B		C
1. Strengthen	1. Information		1. Self
2. Weaken	2. Gratification	with respect to	2. Family
	3. Credibility,		3. Friends
	confidence		4. State,
	4. Contact		society
			5. Tradition,
			culture

The facet analysis of our questions is illustrated in the following examples: "What amount of time would you like TV to devote, these days, to programs which (1) "Help people know and understand the situation" $(A_1B_1C_4)$; (2) "Help people release tension" $(A_2B_4C_1)$; (3) "Help people to pass their time" $(A_2B_4C_1)$; (4) "Help people to feel pride in the state and the army" $(A_1B_3C_4)$.

5. These questions were not mutually exclusive. Respondents were asked to indicate how much television time should be devoted to each of the three types of needs. The reply "most of its time" should therefore be treated as a measure of the respondents' intensity of demand rather than their concern with whether total TV time adds up to 100%.

6. It is also possible that these stated expectations of television reflect not only needs but needs tempered by realities. Thus, a priori, the need "to feel pride in the state and the army" may have been no lower during this period, but replies may reflect the perceived inability of the media to cope with this task during a period of probing and re-examination of basic principles of philosophy and organization in army and government. On November 7, 33% of the respondents expressed an urgent need to get a full explanation of the "failure." At later dates, with the passing of time, the proportion was gradually increasing.

7. On October 17 when the demand for all TV functions reached its peak, 40% of the respondents wanted TV to devote most of its time to programs that could aid social integration. Subdivided by level of education, the figures of this request were 50%, 45%, and 33% for respondents of low, medium, and high levels of education, respectively.

8. Indeed, a specific question was repeatedly asked within our series to examine the expected role of TV as a baby-sitter. The results showed that in terms of time allocation, children were not perceived by the adult population as a group deserving high priority. However, the function of TV as a baby-sitter may best be discussed in terms of exposure behavior; a special survey conducted on behalf of the Israel Center for Instructional Television revealed that during the three first days of the war, when school was cancelled, about 50% of the 6 to 14 year olds viewed *all* the children's programs broadcast daily from 8 A.M. to 5:30 P.M.

9. In response to the following question, "When a news item is broadcast on Arab radio and TV which is not broadcast on our radio and TV, do you tend to believe it?" between 55% and 73% of the respondents said that during the fighting they did not believe *anything* that was broadcast on Arab radio. After the fighting, 57% of the respondents who were exposed to Arab radio broadcasts still said that they did not believe any of the Arab news. Those who are here classified as "believers" mentioned only partial trust. The reader is urged to keep this perspective in mind when reading the text.

10. In the four surveys that are the basis of this paper as well as in subsequent surveys in which these questions were incorporated.

REFERENCES

ARLEN, M. J. (1969) Living Room War. New York: Viking Press.

BAKER, G. W. and D. W. CHAPMAN [eds.] (1962) Man and Society in Disaster. New York: Basic Books.

BARTON, A. H. (1963) Social Organization Under Stress: A Sociological Review of Disaster Studies. Washington, D.C.: National Research Council.

GREENBERG, B. S. and E. B. PARKER (1965) "Social research on the Kennedy assassination," pp. 361-382 in B. S. Greenberg and E. B. Parker (eds.) The Kennedy Assassination and the American Public: Social Communication in Crisis. Stanford: Stanford Univ. Press.

GUTTMAN, L. and S. LEVY (1974) "The home front and the Yom Kippur War," in The 1974 Yearbook of The Encyclopedia Judaica (in press).

KATZ, E., M. GUREVITCH, and H. HAAS (1973) "The use of the mass media for important things." American Sociological Review 38 (April): 164-181.

KISH, L. (1955) Survey Sampling. New York: John Wiley.

KRIS, E. and H. SPEIER (1944) German Radio Propaganda. London: Oxford Univ. Press.

MINDAK, W. H. and G. D. HURSH (1965) "Television functions on the assassination weekend," pp. 130-141 in B. S. Greenberg and E. B. Parker (eds.) The Kennedy Assassination and the American Public: Social Communication in Crisis. Stanford: Stanford Univ. Press.

RIVERS, W. L. (1971) "The Negro and the news: a case study," pp. 151-168 in W. Schramm and D. F. Roberts (eds.) The Process and Effects of Mass Communication. Rev. ed. Urbana: Univ. of Illinois Press.

SCHRAMM, W. (1965) "Communication in crisis," pp. 1-25 in B. S. Greenberg and E. B. Parker (eds.) The Kennedy Assassination and the American Public: Social Communication in Crisis. Stanford: Stanford Univ. Press.

SHIBUTANI, T. (1966) Improvised News: A Sociological Study of Rumor. Indianapolis: Dobbs-Merrill.

WRIGHT, C. (1959) Mass Communication: A Sociological Perspective. New York: Random House.

Chapter 4

GRATIFICATIONS OF TELEVISION VIEWING AND THEIR CORRELATES FOR BRITISH CHILDREN

Bradley S. Greenberg

TO THE QUESTION, "Why do so many people spend so much time with the media?" advertisers say Hooray, social critics say Shame, the audience says Why Not, and social researchers say It's an Empirical Question.

The question was first studied by Herta Herzog (1944) in her effort to understand what needs radio soap opera fulfilled for its women listeners. That was a semi-clinical, intensive attempt to obtain expressions of media content needs.

This type of research has encompassed such overlapping concepts as needs, functions, motives, and gratifications obtained from mass media exposure. Yet, no major attempt to examine the television medium in a parallel way occurred until the late 1960s. Since then, extensive efforts in England, Sweden, and Israel (McQuail, Blumler and Brown, 1972; Rosengren and Windahl, 1972; Katz, Gurevitch and Haas, 1973) have contributed some significant new theoretical perspectives and findings, without, however, having as yet stimulated substantial counterpart efforts in the United States.

The particular study reported here turned to a specific issue of motives and gratifications for television watching among young people in England. It was undertaken concurrently with, but independently of, the other efforts in Europe and Israel and without prior shared knowledge among the investigators.

AUTHOR'S NOTE: This project was conducted with the financial and staff assistance of the Audience Research Department of the British Broadcasting Corporation. All control and decisions regarding the design and execution of the project remained with the principal investigator. Additional support was received from Michigan State University in the form of sabbatical funding for six months. In England, the BBC's Head of Research, Brian Emmett, was especially important to the completion of this project.

Obtaining information from young people about their motives and gratifications is crucial if one wishes to understand the evolution of adult orientations to the mass media. Similar or varied motives identified for pre- and post-adolescent children could be indicative of adult patterns.

For youngsters, television is the first major mass medium in all the developed nations. For them, television is the most pervasive, credible, consumed, and adored medium. To understand what they seek from that medium, and perhaps what they think they receive, is basic for understanding potential effects and social behaviors resulting from television and may be predictive of those behaviors.

In the United States, Greenberg and Dominick (1969) first examined television-watching reasons among lower-income white and black teenagers and middle-income whites. Although that study did not attempt systematically to isolate a comprehensive set of gratifications, it did demonstrate that such motivations differ strikingly among social class groupings. Lower-income black children were most dependent on television, followed by the lower-income whites and least by middle-income whites. This dependence manifested itself in certain motivations. The more disadvantaged youngsters sought more "school-of-life" gratifications; for example, learning about life, getting to see what people are like, learning how to solve problems. These same youngsters depended more on television for excitement and for thrills than their better-off counterparts. Functional differences were not found by social class or race in terms of such viewing motivations as escape, relaxation, or low-effort expenditures.

A similar approach was used in this study to identify the motives and gratifications that many young people seek and/or obtain from watching television 2.5 to 3.5 hours per day in England. The next section of this paper describes the methods of data collection that were adopted in the enquiry. The following section considers the evidence on functions in terms mainly of the structure of viewing gratifications it discloses. Thereafter the paper moves beyond the functions as such and examines each one in terms of a set of associated covariates, drawing on data also gathered from the respondents about their overall media use patterns, attitudes to media use, attitudes towards the use of aggression to solve problems, and some of their socio-demographic attributes. Since it enters a terrain rarely treated in the literature, this part of the discussion is relatively exploratory. It is concerned not so much with advance prediction of the kinds of behaviors that might accompany some media functions rather than others, as with beginning to describe just what the comingling of these might be. Each of the extracted television functions and gratifications was correlated against a larger set of variables, and emergent patterns of associations have been noted and described. In doing so our aim has been to determine whether the associations suggest a basis for the establishment or reinforcement of particular media functions.

METHODOLOGY

During the last week of February and the first week of March 1972, evidence was taken from 726 children in a school district in London, England, by means of a self-administered questionnaire.

The school district included some 100 schools. The district's chief administrative officer designated a subset of the schools as principally middle-class or working-class. In the nine schools visited, equivalent numbers of classes of 9, 12, and 15-year-old children were systematically selected to yield a representative pooling of respondents. The final stratified groups provided equivalent numbers of children in the three age segments specified, and equal portions of boys and girls. In terms of social class, two-thirds of the children were from working-class environments and one-third from a middle-class background. In terms of race, some 60% of the children were white, and most of the remainder were of Asian, African, or West Indian origin.

The questionnaire was administered by the principal investigator or by associates trained by him; classroom teachers were never used for this purpose. For 9-year olds, the investigator read out each questionnaire item, and the students followed the reading and then completed the item; for older students, the questionnaire was distributed in the classroom and individually completed.

Before considering the instruments of this project, it is necessary to describe the pretesting. Five months earlier we had acquired some preliminary evidence on the functions and gratifications of television viewing among London school children (Greenberg, 1972). In two classrooms each of 9, 12, and 15-year olds, the children spent 40 to 50 minutes writing an essay under our supervision on the subject, "Why I Like to Watch Television." This anonymous exercise was carried out with the understanding that what was written would not be read or graded by the teacher. This prior work was undertaken in order (1) to determine the language of the children in talking about television and particularly their motives for TV usage; (2) to gain some advance impression of what functions and motives might emerge in a larger-scale study; and (3) to determine an acceptable mode of testing within British schools.

In all, 180 essays were written and analyzed. Eight clusters of reasons for watching television were derived from them, and these provided the focal point for the present study:

(1) *To pass time.* This was a predominant response for all three age groups and did not appear to change with increasing age. Sample statements included the following:

> It gives you something to do when you haven't got anything to do.
>
> It fills up time.
>
> People really watch telly because there is not much else to do.

(2) *To forget, as a means of diversion.* The passing time statements and the ones below may both represent a use of television for escapist purposes, but there appeared to be a difference in terms of the

expressed motivation for such diversion. Whereas watching television to pass time appeared to be a more passive activity, the statements about forgetting seemed more goal-oriented. Here are some examples:

It helps me forget my problems.

I want to get away from the rest of my family.

To forget about school and homework.

(3) *To learn about things.* Here, the commonality among the statements reflected a desire for deliberate observational learning that might supplement school-type material. This form of learning was expressed in this way:

It teaches me things I don't learn at school.

I can learn how to do things I've never done before.

I want to know what's going on in the world, in other places.

(4) *To learn about myself.* This category of learning appeared to deal more directly with social learning, or wanting content that would aid the child in his social interactions with other people. Some examples:

So I can learn how I'm supposed to act.

I can learn about what could happen to me.

You can learn from the mistakes of others.

(5) *For arousal.* This is the notion of watching television for the expressed purpose of being stimulated in a variety of ways; for example:

It excites me.

It cheers me up.

It stirs me up.

(6) *For relaxation.* Virtually none of the youngest viewers, but a substantial number of the older ones, talked about how television served as a means of relaxation. One is tempted to contrast this motivation with the arousal category just described. To what extent relaxation is the antithesis of arousal, or merely something needed at a different point in time, however, could not be determined from the essays. The youngsters wrote:

It relaxes me.

It calms me down.

It's a pleasant rest.

(7) *For companionship.* For some children, television provided vicarious companionship, expressed thus:

It's almost like a human friend.

It helps me forget I'm alone.

It is very comforting if you're alone.

(8) *As a habit.* This was a catch-all category, useful in lumping a group of less specific reasons for watching television:

It's a habit.

I just like to watch.

I just enjoy watching.

These data were derived from content analyses of open-ended essays, and their generalizability was of course limited. However, the nature of the content served as the stimulus for developing an instrument which would help to answer a number of questions:

(1) To what extent are such motivations or functions independent of each other?

(2) How predominant is each of these in the motivational structure of the youngsters?

(3) With what other media-related behaviors and non-media behaviors are such motivations associated?

For each of the reasons outlined except one, four test statements were constructed that appeared to reflect that reason; for the arousal component, three items were used. The full set of 31 items is presented in the Appendix. The questionnaire format for the set of items was as shown in Table 1.

To determine the structure of the children's responses, and the consistency of those responses, endorsements of each of the items used were intercorrelated and factor analyzed. This procedure was repeated separately for the three age groups of youngsters. Principal axis factor analyses were performed, with varimax rotation, employing a Kiel-Wrigley criterion of two principal loadings per factor as a minimum.

VIEWING GRATIFICATIONS

The major analyses will reflect the basic factor structure of these reasons for watching television for the full age range of children, including the purity of the factors and the inter-item correlations constituting them. Then we examine the structure of these reasons for three age groups. Finally, we will look at the strengths of the factors in terms of how predominant these reasons for watching television were.

TABLE 1

QUESTIONNAIRE FORMAT

Instructions: WE'RE INTERESTED IN WHY PEOPLE WATCH TV. HERE ARE SOME REASONS THAT OTHER PEOPLE GAVE US FOR WATCHING TV. PLEASE TELL US HOW MUCH EACH REASON IS LIKE YOU. PUT A TICK FOR EACH ONE.

I watch TV . . .	*a lot*	*a little*	*not much*	*not at all*
1. because it relaxes me.	—	—	—	—
2. because it's almost like a real friend.	—	—	—	—
3. because it's a habit.	—	—	—	—
4. when I'm bored.	—	—	—	—

Overall Analysis of Motivation Items

Table 2 provides a summary of the data as factor analyzed across all the youngsters. For each of the factors that emerged, we have noted from which a priori motivation set the item came, and its factor loading. Only the largest factor loading is presented for each item; the magnitude of these individual loadings is such that few items overlapped significantly on any other factor. The complete factor loadings and correlation matrix are available on request.

From this analysis, we can identify the following major independent sets of reasons for watching television among British youngsters:

For Learning. What had been two separate a priori sets of items emerged as a single, consistent factor. No other items save those in the two learning sets—learning about things and learning about self—had any sizable loading on this factor. This factor accounted for 20% of the common variance among the items. The children did not differentiate those things that might be acquired from television in a school-like learning fashion from those that more often are identified as social learning items. If a child watched television to learn about things going on in the world, that child used television to a similar extent to find out how he should behave and how he should avoid mistakes. The correlations among this set of eight items averaged .37.

TABLE 2

ITEM FACTOR LOADINGS–8 FACTOR SOLUTION

Factor 1	Loadings	Factor 2	Loadings
Habit (2)*	.78	Learning-Self (3)	.70
Habit (4)	.72	Learning-Things (4)	.70
Habit (1)	.58	Learning-Things (1)	.65
Habit (3)	.48	Learning-Things (2)	.65
		Learning-Things (3)	.58
		Learning-Self (1)	.58
		Learning-Self (4)	.57
		Learning-Self (2)	.53
Factor 3		*Factor 4*	
Pass Time (3)	.60	Relax (1)	.70
Pass Time (4)	.50	Relax (2)	.61
Forget (2)	.49	Relax (3)	.51
		Companionship (1)	.47
Factor 5		*Factor 6*	
Forget (4)	.72	Arousal (1)	.79
Forget (1)	.69	Arousal (2)	.69
Forget (3)	.68	Arousal (3)	.40
Relax (4)	.52		
Factor 7		*Factor 8*	
Pass Time (1)	.77	Companionship (3)	.67
Pass Time (2)	.64	Companionship (4)	.60
		Companionship (2)	.51

*These numbers refer to item numbers in the Appendix.

As a Habit. The original set of habit items postulated as representing a unidimensional reason or motive for television watching emerged in that form. It is possible to regard it as referring to a general, non-specific enjoyment of television. All four items and only those four had their highest loading here, constituting 14% of the common variance. The children watched television because it was a habit, because it was interesting, and because it was enjoyable. The average inter-item correlation was .38.

For Arousal. This factor also consisted only of those items originally postulated as a single set. If a child watched TV for excitement, he also found thrills and was stirred up by it. And this pattern was unrelated to any other reason for watching television. This factor accounted for 13% of the common variance, and the average intercorrelation was .44.

For Companionship. Three of the original four items designed to reflect this need formed a single factor, accounting for 11% of the common variance. No other item loaded with this set of three. A singular motive in watching television, then, was to avoid being alone, when no one else was around to play with. This factor accounted for 11% of the variance and the average intercorrelation was .34.

To Relax. Here, three of the four original items were retained in a single factor. Children watched television because they wanted to calm down and because they found it a pleasant rest. One additional item from the companionship set—"because it's almost like a human friend"—also had its highest loading on this factor, but it was the weakest of the four loadings. In fact, whenever an item appeared in the results from another a priori set, it had the lowest loading. This relaxation factor accounted for 14% of the variance, and the items correlated .32.

To Forget. A final firm factor that emerged was the use of television as a means of diversion from problems primarily in the home. Three of the four items comprised this factor, plus a relaxation item—"because I don't have to do anything while I watch." The children said that television was useful as a means of getting away from the rest of the family and to get away from what they were doing (or were supposed to be doing). This factor accounted for 13% of the common variance, and the average intercorrelation was .30.

To Pass Time. The original set of items split into two independent factors for unknown reasons. One set of two items—"because it passes the time away" and "because it gives me something to do"—loaded together (Pass Time II). Another set of two items—"when I'm bored" and "when I have nothing better to do"—loaded together (Pass Time I), but separately from the other two. Even in lower-order factor solutions, these items split in this fashion. Each accounted for 5% of the common variance, with average intercorrelations of .29 and .33, respectively.

In summary of this overall analysis, six factors emerged cleanly as major reasons why children watch television. One of these encompassed two kinds of learning, social and formal learning, from the medium. The other five represented a disparate set of motivations for television watching. And although the data do not support the passing of time as a unidimensional motive for TV usage, in terms of our operationalism, the analysis did not disperse this boredom motive to other factors.

In all, these data accounted for 56% of the total variance.

Motivation Items by Age Groups

Although the overall solution is the most stable, given the number of subjects entered into the analysis, we also examined the motivational structure of each of the age groups separately.

For the 15-year-olds, the factors of Learning, Arousal, and Companionship emerged in almost identical fashion to that found across all the youngsters. In addition, the same two Pass Time components were identified.

For the 12-year-olds, the same factors of Learning, Arousal, To Forget, and Habit were identified. In this age group, the factors of Companionship and Relaxation melded onto a single factor with three of each of the original four items from these two components. Here one of the Pass Time sets also emerged.

Among the 9-year-olds, the factor system was least stable, but nevertheless, similar components of Learning, Forget, and Relaxation emerged. All four Habit items and three of the Arousal items came together to form a single factor.

Although we found some deviation from the overall pattern when the group was broken down into smaller age units (as might have resulted from stratification by sex or social class), there is sufficient similarity to lend face validity to the overall factor findings.

Factor Strength

Although we have already dealt with the relative prominence of these watching motivations in terms of the variance each of the factors accounts for, there is another way of evaluating their strength. This is in terms of the mean scores that were calculated for each of the factor items. Just how much was the child saying each of these reasons represented one of his personal reasons for gravitating to television? Table 3 presents average item means by factor. A mean

TABLE 3
FACTORS ORDERED BY ITEM MEANS

Motivation Factor	Average Item Mean
Habit	3.17
Pass Time II	3.11
Pass Time I	3.08
Companionship	2.91
Arousal	2.86
Learning	2.85
Relaxation	2.65
To Forget	2.39

score of 4.0 would indicate the child saying this reason is a "lot" like him, a score of 3.0 would mean it is a "little" like him, 2.0 that it is "not much," and 1.0 that it is "not at all" like him.

Almost all factors have means bordering on 3.0. The main exceptions are the use of television as a way of forgetting about one's problems and using TV to relax. For most of the motivations, the means are skewed toward the upper end of the scale, and to virtually the same extent. Not only are they independent of each other, then, most are equally salient to the youthful respondents. Further, these distributions contain no particular abnormalities. All the item standard deviations range from .87 to 1.16, with one exception.

One final examination is warranted, and that is of the mean factor scores for each of the different age groups. So that they could be compared on the same factor structure, we used the overall factor solution to provide a common reference point. These data are presented in Table 4.

Several generalizations may be drawn from this material. First, the three age groups are remarkably consistent in their ordering of motivations for watching television. Despite the fact that several means within an age group are not very different from each other, the overall correlation among the three age groups, in terms of ranking the motivations, is .83 (Coefficient of Concordance). Thus, the earlier finding of a consistent factor structure for the separate groups is reinforced by the finding that each of the motivations occupies approximately the same position in their hierarchy of reasons for watching television.

Second, there is a consistent difference between ages in just how strong the separate motivations are. For the 9-year-olds, each of the motives, with a single exception, is perceived as more regularly present than it is for the 12-year-olds. And for the 12-year-olds, each motivation has a higher mean score, with no exceptions, than the same motivation among the 15-year-olds. The consistency of this developmental pattern is beyond the .001 level (Friedman Two-Way Rank Order Analysis of Variance).

TABLE 4
FACTOR–ITEM MEANS BY AGE GROUPS

Motivation Factor	Age		
	9	12	15
Habit	3.34	3.28	2.88
Pass Time II	3.12	3.11	3.00
Relaxation	2.90	2.81	2.27
Pass Time I	3.11	3.20	3.00
Companionship	3.09	2.99	2.63
Arousal	3.13	2.94	2.47
Learning	2.98	2.95	2.61
To Forget	2.95	2.47	2.15

CORRELATES OF VIEWING GRATIFICATIONS

The next task was to determine how these functions were associated with—or predictive of—other behaviors and attitudes of the youngsters. For example, is one function more closely tied to one form of media behavior, and a second function to yet other media? Or does one function exist more often in homes where parents have certain attitudes than another function?

To undertake this analysis, function scores were computed on the basis of the factor structure in Table 1. For each factor, we summed the scores of the "legitimate" items on that factor. Thus, four scores were summed for the Habit factor, three items for Forgetting, and so on. The only exception was the use of a single Pass Time factor, rather than two, composed of three items (2, 3 and 4 in the Appendix) as identified on one of the age factor solutions. In total, seven function indices were constructed, with eight items representing the Learning factor, four the Habit factor, and three each for the other five factors. Four subsets of function correlates were examined. They dealt with media behaviors, media attitudes, attitudes toward aggression, and socio-demographic characteristics. Each of these will be outlined here with some indication of how they were operationalized.

Media Behaviors. Data were obtained from each respondent about the following media behaviors:

(1) The number of television shows watched regularly from a checklist of 18 shows, all of which regularly featured violence and violent acts as primary content ingredients.

(2) The number of television shows watched regularly from a checklist of 12 shows, which typically contained no violent content.

(3) The total of the 30 shows watched from the above two checklists.

(4) An index formed from three items that asked how many hours TV was watched on an average schoolday, on Saturday and on Sunday.[1]

(5) An index formed from three items which determined the frequency of reading a daily newspaper.

(6) Frequency of reading books and comic books for enjoyment.

(7) Frequency of going to the cinema and of listening to records.

(8) Frequency of radio listening.

The first of these variables—watching violent TV shows—also was subdivided into four content areas: western, action-adventure, science fiction, and variegated violence. Of the 18 shows, six represented action-adventure violence and four each for the other three areas. Subindices existed for these violence content areas and are included in a portion of the analyses.

Aggressive Attitudes. A central concern of this study was to examine the relationship between watching televised violence and possible increments in aggressive attitudes among viewers (Greenberg, 1975). For this purpose, five measures of aggressive attitudes were adapted from previous research (Dominick and Greenberg, 1972):

(1) The child's expressed approval of the use of violence in problem-solving situations.

(2) The perceived effectiveness of violence.

(3) The child's willingness to use violence.

(4) A summary measure across these three indices.

(5) The child's report of his parents' attitudes toward the use of aggression as an option in problem-solving situations, e.g., "Suppose one of your friends hit you. What do you think your parents would want you to do?"

TV Attitudes. The child's general orientation toward the medium was measured through four indices:

(1) The perceived reality of television, a three-item index tapping how true-to-life the child thought television entertainment content was.

(2) The intensity of the child's attachment to television, e.g., a e ment-disagreement on three items including, "If I had to give up the television, I don't know what I'd do."

(3) The frequency with which the child reported talking with friends and parents about things seen on television.

(4) The child's use of TV advertising, e.g., how often he saw things advertised he wanted and how often he got his mother or father to get something because he saw it advertised.

Socio-Demographic Attributes. Assessed were the child's race (white or non-white), social class (working- or middle-class), age (9, 12, or 15), and sex.

Results—Individual Correlations

Tables 5a-5d present the product-moment correlations between each of the learning functions and each of the covariates described above. With a sample size this large, quite small correlations achieve statistical significance. However, we prefer to be more conservative in interpretation and will deal primarily with correlates of .20 and above (significant at well beyond the .01 level). Using such a criterion for deciding which associations to point to, we shall try to identify both similarities in correlates across functions, and contrasts where some functions appear to distinguish certain types of viewers and their behaviors.

For a start, several of the television attitude measures correlated positively with most of the identified functions. Most consistently, talking about television with others and seeing things on television one wishes to talk about, correlated with each of the seven functions. As the child more often says he uses television to learn, because it is a habit, to relax, etc., that same child expresses a strong desire to talk about TV and says he does so frequently. The same is true about the intensity of his affinity for television. As a child indicates how dull life would be without television, he is more likely to claim more of the several gratifications available, save for the learning function. The child's susceptibility

TABLE 5a
FUNCTIONS BY MEDIA BEHAVIORS

Co-Variate	Learning	Habit	Relax	To Forget	Arousal	Companion's	Pass Time
#Violent shows	29	20	29	10	29	16	09
#Nonviolent shows	14	19	24	16	15	06	13
Total shows	27	23	32	15	27	14	12
Exposure to TV	14	31	16	13	21	11	19
Newspaper reading	07	-09	07	-01	-06	-04	-01
Book reading	20	14	17	09	27	17	06
Movies & Records	-06	-04	-07	-08	00	-01	-01
Radio listening	06	-02	06	-04	-01	00	-07

TABLE 5b
FUNCTIONS BY AGGRESSIVE ATTITUDES

Co-Variate	Learning	Habit	Relax	To Forget	Arousal	Companion's	Pass Time
Approval	09	09	-07	24	04	-02	14
Effectiveness	13	14	13	27	17	11	14
Willingness	06	14	13	21	19	04	07
Index	06	16	10	31	18	06	14
Parents' attitudes	09	-05	00	-21	-06	08	-04

TABLE 5c
FUNCTIONS BY TV ATTITUDES

Co-Variate	Learning	Habit	Relax	To Forget	Arousal	Companion's	Pass Time
Perceived reality	28	14	23	07	15	22	13
Intensity of TV	11	30	18	20	25	19	20
Talking re: TV	24	32	31	19	34	22	19
Advertising impact	27	24	23	10	30	20	10

TABLE 5d
FUNCTIONS BY DEMOGRAPHY

Co-Variate	Learning	Habit	Relax	To Forget	Arousal	Companion's	Pass Time
Race	–18	01	–09	21	–02	–06	06
Social class	–05	02	–03	10	01	01	03
Age	–19	–23	–25	–16	–33	–24	–10
Sex	00	07	04	–04	–04	02	03

to TV advertising content (available on only one of the three British channels) is also a general correlate, not confined to any particular gratification sought from television. The child who sees more things advertised that he wants, and who is more successful in getting these things out of his parents, has more of the TV motivations in his repertoire. Part, then, of the more general overriding motivation for watching TV may be the anticipated social interaction that will occur, the greater psychological dependency on that medium, and the desire for some goods shown in commercials.

As stipulated earlier, age is also a correlate of each of the functions. The younger child shows more identification with each of the gratifications than does the older child. In fact, age is the only consistent demographic correlate of the entire set of functions. Sex and social class do not differentiate and are unrelated to any of the identified functions. The role of race will be explored below.

The gratifications of using television to relax and as a matter of habit produce virtually identical sets of large correlates at the criterion level. Children who are more likely to indicate seeking these gratifications are more avid viewers of television in general—of both violence and nonviolence programming. They also express each of the attitudes cited above, i.e., they talk more about television, they love it more dearly, and they seek and get more of the advertised goods.

Learning as a motivation for television watching is not too dissimilar. Books, however, are more often read for enjoyment, television is perceived as very realistic in its entertainment content, and television watching is more oriented to violent content. This function predominates among non-white children, more so than among their white peers. No relationships exist with more aggressive behaviors.

For theoretical reasons, it is important to examine the contrast between youngsters who are higher in the use of television to escape, as compared with those who use it more for arousal. Correlates for children who say they want to get away from their problems include no media behavior variables—not television watching, nor book reading, nor anything else. These children are most likely to be white youngsters who say they talk a good deal about the television they watch. They are the children who, on each of the multiple indices of aggressive attitudes, express more aggression. Further, they believe their parents to be relatively tolerant of aggression as a means of dealing with problems. For them, seeking out television to get away from their problems carries with it an orientation to aggression not found with most of the other functions studied.

However, positive dispositions to aggression also characterize the children who go to television for arousal purposes, who say television excites them and stirs them up. Further, this arousal is well correlated with watching violence on television in particular, the correlation being twice as large with exposure to violent shows as to nonviolent ones. The particular subareas of violent content that are correlated with their arousal are action-adventure (detective) and science fiction shows. These youngsters also get arousal from reading books.

Thus, this analysis suggests that TV violence preferences and aggressive attitudes are more likely to be found among children who get/seek excitement from their viewing. The violent content does that for them. On the other hand, certain other children who also show aggressive tendencies, perhaps because of their attempt to evade personal problems, can satisfy their needs on a more content-free and even media-free basis.

Companionship is apparently a gratification that may be satisfied by any of the media, there being no particular correlate with any form of media behavior. In addition to some attitudes that are associated with most gratifications, however, those who seek companionship from television are more likely to believe that what they watch is realistic.

Multiple Correlations

The next step in the analysis was to compute the multiple correlations of a subset of the correlates with each of the functions. Some of the variables in Tables 5a-5d were dropped from this analysis, since they offered no independent relationships with the functions. These included newspaper reading, movie-going and record listening, radio listening, social class, sex, and parental attitudes toward violence. The index that summed the three measures of aggression (but not the individual measures themselves) was also eliminated. Included were the individual content categories of violent shows watched, e.g., westerns, action-adventure, time spent interacting with friends, and time doing homework.

As would be suggested by Tables 5a-5d, multiple correlation added little to our understanding of either the companionship or pass-time functions. We have not identified in this study variables that account for much of the variance in those two functions of television.

For the other five functions, however, each of the multiple correlations accounted for approximately 25% of the variance. And there was no reduction beyond a percent or two when the least squares deletion analysis was applied to the overall multiple correlation analysis. This analytic process removes from the multiple correlation equation all variables that fail to contribute independently to the dependent variables, the functions. The multiple correlations, after deleting non-contributing variables, ranged from .45 to .52 for the Learning, Habit, Relaxation, Forget, and Arousal functions.

For all five functions, two of the correlates persistently appeared in the final analysis—age and the propensity to talk about the television shows seen. One other—intensity of feelings about TV—remained for all five functions, save Learning.

In addition to these three correlates, the remaining significant correlates for each function were

Learning: Race (non-whites), the impact of commercials, and perceived reality. ($R^2 = .21$)

Habit: Total television watching, the watching of nonviolence, time spent with homework (negatively related), and watching science fiction violence. ($R^2 = .27$)

Relaxation: Perceived reality, and total television watching. ($R^2 = .22$)

To Forget: Race (whites), time spent with homework (negative), watching nonviolence, and beliefs that violence is both effective and approved in problem-solving. ($R^2 = .20$)

Arousal: Television exposure, watching science fiction violence, watching action-adventure violence, the impact of commercials, and expressed willingness to commit violence. ($R^2 = .26$)

These multiple correlation results parallel the findings for individual correlates, but reduce the sets. They do not alter the interpretation given the earlier results, but permit some more specific comments.

For the non-white children, watching television to learn about life subsumes greater perceived reality in television content and greater impact from TV commercials.

Watching television as a habit goes with watching anything available, and reduces time spent doing homework.

Relaxation also accrues with total television watching, not with specific content, and with the perceived reality of whatever television offers in the way of entertainment.

White youngsters often use television as a means of evading personal crises, while maintaining aggressive attitudes. Here there is one contrast from the previous discussion. Watching nonviolence is a significant correlate in the regression analysis, but its magnitude is not great. One element of forgetting personal problems may be the avoidance of schoolwork.

And children who want to be aroused by television do so through action-adventure programs, science fiction violence, and a strong penchant for advertised goods. This syndrome includes more apparent willingness to commit aggressive acts.

Age Differences

Given the consistency of the age relationships with each of the functions, one further analysis was undertaken. Multiple correlations of each of the functions with the sets of covariates were examined separately for the 9, 12, and 15-year-old age groups. This was done to determine whether the covariates differed by function along a developmental continuum. Given some space limitations, we shall summarize these findings without reference to the larger mass of supportive data examined.

The pattern of functional correlates for the 9-year-olds showed that Learning and Relaxation were accomplished through extended television watching. All four violence subcontent areas correlated with these functions for these younger children. The perceived reality of TV content was particularly important in these two functions. The relationship between watching violence and aggressive attitudes figured even more prominently in their Arousal gratification than in the entire sample of youngsters. Aggressive attitudes were also strongly associated with their use of television for Forgetting problems. Habit did not yield a set of correlates for this age group, nor did Companionship and Pass Time produce meaningful predictors.

The 12-year-old group represents youngsters who are at the peak of their television viewing, according to data from England, the United States, and Japan. Within this age group, the full set of seven functions was linked with larger sets of covariates. For these children, the use of television as a Habit emerged strongly, and was associated with watching all kinds of television content, both violent and nonviolent, and with the intensity of their attachment to television. Only for this age group did the use of television to Pass Time have a set of correlates. Further, for this age group, aggressive attitudes were more generally allocated to various functions; for example, aggressive attitudes served as correlates for Habit, To Forget, Arousal, and Pass Time.

For the oldest segment of the sample, the Habit function persisted, and the correlates for five functions—Learning, Habit, Relaxation, To Forget, and Arousal—were very similar to the overall solution presented earlier. These teenagers did not associate any of the behaviors studied with the function of Companionship and Pass Time.

Thus, the analysis of covariates of viewing gratifications by age groups has yielded some additional information. The full implication of such findings must await a more deliberative theoretical scheme for interpreting them.

SUMMARY AND DISCUSSION

The structure of the gratifications identified here is interesting in several respects. First, five of the factors—Habit, Arousal, Companionship, Relaxation, and Forget—are very similar in terms of the amount of variance each accounts for. Only the Learning factor appears to be a specifically more substantial factor. The roughly equal presence, then, of all six of these independent dimensions suggests that each has a unique role in the orientation of these adolescents to television. The specific nature of this orientation has only begun to be identified in this paper.

Another structural feature that bears summarizing is the similarity across age groups in the persistence of these factors. Although there is greater instability among the 9-year-olds than for the older age groups, the 12-year-olds do appear to be at an intermediate developmental structure which is continued through to the 15-year-old stage. Further, the 12-year-old structure contains some of the features of the 15-year-olds that were not apparent among the youngest age group. It may well be that there is a structural flow of motivations from 9 to 15 years of age for which the 12-year-old data identify a transitional period. One recalls that the age of 12 is a particularly critical one in television behaviors, representing an age of maximum viewing in several areas of the world.

The similarity in factor means parallels the loadings of individual gratifications and their equivalent contribution to variance among this set of motivation items. Except for the motivations of relaxation and forgetting, the remaining means were roughly equivalent with each other. The level represented by the average score meant that the child believed the factor did apply to his own viewing behavior to a considerable extent on the scaling system used. Primarily, though, the most interesting results obtained from the item means was the similar ordering of these factors by the three age groups studied. The ordering produced a cross-age group correlation of .83. Given relatively minor differences among some of the means, this level of relationship is very striking. There also was a levels difference which a correlation does not reflect. Each of the motivations was more strongly felt by the 9-year-olds than by the 12-year-olds, who in turn felt or described these motivations more strongly than did the 15-year-olds. We are uncertain to what extent this levels difference may be a function of differential scale usage by age, in contrast to more genuine differences in application of these gratifications to their viewing behaviors.

The last part of the paper was more exploratory. It took available data on media behaviors, attitudes, and other characteristics of these children and mingled them with the specific functions and gratifications data. Such findings are entirely descriptive at this point. All the functions emerged as associated with the children's general tendencies to talk with others about television programs, and seeing things that they wanted to talk about. Similarly, the child's overall intensity of affection for television was related to almost all the watching gratifications. Also part of the same system as the functions were perceptions of the reality of TV content and a desire for products engendered by television advertising. The former strikes us as an intervening variable in relation to other effects of exposure to television content, and the latter as one of those resultant effects. The results section has identified many of the other individual correlates that co-occurred with the individual functions or gratifications and these patterns need not be repeated here. It is now appropriate to turn to a more general discussion of the possible implications and extensions of this study's findings.

Perhaps the most critical discussion point is the generalizability of such findings. It cannot be claimed that these are the only motivations that exist for television watching, nor the only gratifications obtained. This set of six functions (or seven if the Pass Time component is a valid one) accounts for 56% of the common variance. Thus, a significant portion is unaccounted for. In the pretesting, which provided the origins of the principal functions elaborated in this study, we were surprised by certain omissions from the repertoire of responses obtained. For example, there was no spontaneous indication by the youngsters that a reason for watching television was to talk about the programs with peers, family, or anyone else. Believing strongly that this was nevertheless a reason for watching television, we developed an index of frequency of such conversation with others. As the findings have shown, this index emerged in strong relationship to each of the independent functions. So talking with others about television is interdependent: It pervades each of the motivations for watching.

Certain other notions, often invoked by both broadcasters and academics, were missing. Most noticeably, such words as "entertainment" or "information" did not appear among the children's reasons for watching television. Certainly, the information role may be subsumed by the learning functions, and entertainment may span several of the gratification categories. But these particular terms, pervasive for analysts, were not often used by the school children themselves.

We also doubt that these motivations are peculiar to British children. We would expect to find the same kinds of categories in similar studies of American children, or of any children, for that matter. Indeed, they may be generic across viewing audiences, differing only in emphasis and salience for adults as well as others. Such a major implication obviously requires verification, however, and a follow-up study on such an issue is in order.

Skirted entirely in this type of study is the question of whether the data referred to are motivations sought, gratifications received, or some combination of these. Surely what a child derives from television may well include some portion of what he sought, else he would turn elsewhere for these gratifications, but the specific extent to which this is the case remains unexamined. All previous approaches, including the present paper, appear to be confounding in this major regard. Consider the paradigm presented in Figure 1.

From such post hoc survey evidence, one cannot distinguish whether the response obtained from the viewer of the medium, or a fan of some specific content, is an accurate statement of what he wanted, or what he thinks he got. People go to the media to satisfy certain needs, or they go to specific content within the media for those needs. McQuail, Blumler and Brown (1972) refer to this as medium-person interaction. Yet that same interaction occurs on the righthand side of the paradigm. People come away from the medium or the program with something. No approach has so far dealt with the parallelism or discrepancy between what was sought and what was obtained. Furthermore, the issue of whether some gratification is obtained from the medium per se, or whether it is obtained from some programs more than others, also remains open.

A single medium, television, has been examined here. To what extent similar or different motivations are obtainable through other media has not been examined. More important, one should be able to conceptualize that certain media are more likely to provide more of certain gratifications or different gratifications than other media. Or that the receiver seeks whatever gratification

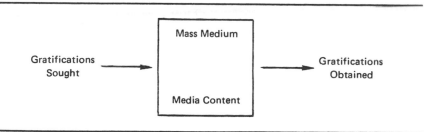

Figure 1.

he most requires at the moment from whatever medium is most accessible. This again poses the significance of the receiver-medium interaction.

Further, we have brushed only slightly with the issue of receiver-content interaction in obtaining certain gratifications. Are not certain content forms more likely to provide certain gratifications than other kinds of content? How might such content be categorized? In relating certain motivations more directly to violent fare and aggressive attitudes, the findings suggested that seeking Arousal and seeking To Forget one's problems were related to aggressive attitudes. However, the former motivation was also tied to watching violence, while the latter yielded few links to particular media behaviors except possibly watching nonviolent programs. Thus, one finds a theoretical tie between these data and Tannenbaum's findings that generalized arousal from media-watching is a strong predictor of post-viewing aggression (Tannenbaum, 1971).

One additional problem can be generated from the question of how frequent each of these motivations is. We have noted only that they are reported as probable reasons for watching television with more or less equal vigor. That is not necessarily isomorphic with how often they occur. One wonders just how often a typical child viewer wants to relax, in contrast to being aroused, or to learn, etc.

In exploring correlates of the identified functions, it is imperative to recall that only about one-fourth of the total variance in these concepts were explained by the multiple sets of variables studied. Thus, one might begin to speculate on what accounts for the remainder. Few data were collected about the child's life style, the nature of his interactions with peers and parents, his psychological make-up, or his intelligence and abilities. Perhaps these, among others, might begin to explain further the gratifications sought and obtained from television. Perhaps one needs to know more fully what use the child makes of his leisure and non-leisure time and what alternative behaviors to media usage are available to him. The psychological, cultural, and social bases of any given class of function or gratification seem to provide, then, a major part of the agenda for further research in this field.

In sum, we have presented a means of identifying a finite and similar set of motivations for turning to television among a wide age range of young people. The usefulness of this approach might well be tested in terms of its future ability to explain specific media choices, content selections, and post-viewing effects.

APPENDIX

Full set of items analyzed: *I watch TV* . . .

Relaxation

1. because it relaxes me
2. because it calms me down when I am in a temper
3. because it's a pleasant rest
4. because I don't have to do anything when I watch

Companionship

1. because it's almost like a human friend
2. so I won't be alone
3. when there's no one to talk to or play with
4. because it makes me feel less lonely

Learning about Things

1. so I can learn about things happening in the world
2. so I can learn how to do things I haven't done before
3. because it gives me ideas
4. because it teaches me things I don't learn at school

Habit

1. because it's a habit
2. because I just like to watch
3. because it's so much fun
4. because I just enjoy watching

To Pass Time

1. when I'm bored
2. when I have nothing better to do
3. because it passes the time away
4. because it gives me something to do

Learning about Myself

1. because it helps me learn things about myself
2. because it shows me how I'm supposed to act
3. so I could learn about what could happen to me
4. because it shows how other people deal with the same problems I have

Arousal

1. because it's thrilling
2. because it excites me
3. because it stirs me up

To Forget

1. so I can forget about school and homework
2. because it helps me forget my problems
3. so I can get away from the rest of the family
4. so I can get away from what I'm doing

NOTE

1. All indices were constructed after examining inter-item correlations and deleting some original items that had no consistent correlations with the others. The full set of items used in each index is available from the author.

REFERENCES

DOMINICK, J. and B. GREENBERG (1972) "Attitudes toward violence: the interaction of television exposure, family attitudes, and social class," in G. Comstock and E. Rubenstein (eds.) Television and Adolescent Aggressiveness. NIMH, 314-335. Washington, D.C.: U.S. Dept. of Health, Education and Welfare.

GREENBERG, B. (1975) "British children and televised aggression." Public Opinion Quarterly.

––– (1972) "Children's reasons for watching television." Audience Research Report VR/72/147. London: British Broadcasting Corporation.

––– and J. DOMINICK (1969) "Racial and social class differences in teenagers' use of television." Journal of Broadcasting 13 (Fall): 331-334.

HERZOG, H. (1944) "What do we really know about daytime serial listeners?" in P. F. Lazarsfeld and F. Stanton (eds.) Radio Research, 1942-43. New York: Duell, Sloan & Pearce.

KATZ, E., M. GUREVITCH, and H. HAAS (1973) "On the use of the mass media for important things." American Sociological Review 38, 2 (April): 164-181.

McQUAIL, D., J. G. BLUMLER, and J. R. BROWN (1972) "The television audience: a revised perspective," in D. McQuail (ed.) Sociology of Mass Communications. Harmondsworth: Penguin.

ROSENGREN, K. E. and S. WINDAHL (1972) "Mass media consumption as a functional alternative," in D. McQuail (ed.) Sociology of Mass Communications. Harmondsworth: Penguin.

TANNENBAUM, P. (1971) "Studies in film and television-mediated arousal and aggression: a progress report," in G. Comstock, E. Rubenstein and J. Murray (eds.) Television's Effects: Further Exploration. Washington, D.C.: Government Printing Office.

Chapter 5

DISPLACEMENT EFFECTS OF TELEVISION AND THE CHILD'S FUNCTIONAL ORIENTATION TO MEDIA

J. R. Brown, J. K. Cramond and R. J. Wilde

OTHER CONTRIBUTIONS TO THIS VOLUME will doubtless relate the history of uses and gratifications research and point to its demise in the 1950s and rebirth in the late 1960s. However valid in other respects, this pattern is not applicable to the study of younger audiences. Although several research workers have recently manifested a renewed interest in the functional orientations[1] of children to the mass media (Furu, 1971; Robinson, 1972; Brown, Cramond and Wilde, 1973; Dembo, 1973; von Feilitzen, forthcoming; Greenberg, 1974), the influence of the uses and gratifications approach was clearly present in several major studies of the 1950s and 1960s as well (e.g., Himmelweit, Oppenheim and Vince, 1958; Bailyn, 1959; Schramm, Lyle and Parker, 1961). In fact, if both waves of research are considered, it may be claimed that investigators of child media use have contributed a more varied set of conceptual and methodological tools to the uses and gratifications tradition than have students of the adult audience. In this chapter previous studies that have made use of the notion of functional linkage between the younger audience member and the mass media are first briefly reviewed. After identifying some of the assumptions that underpinned these studies, findings are presented from later work, including especially a small-scale before-and-after investigation of a Scottish community into which television was recently introduced, which suggests that some of the earlier assumptions stand in need of revision.

AUTHORS' NOTE: The research reported in this chapter was made possible by grants from the Television Research Committee and the Independent Television Authority to the Centre for Television Research of The University of Leeds in England.

REVIEW OF PAST RESEARCH

Many of the studies that have considered the relationship of children to the mass media from a functional standpoint may be subdivided into two broad categories of approach. One body of work focused on relationships between child characteristics and mass media behavior and interpreted detected associations in terms of certain gratifications that a given medium or body of content supposedly provided the individuals concerned. For example, from her discovery that boys, who were heavily exposed to the mass media and had an above average number of problems in their relations with peers or family, also showed a marked preference for "aggressive-hero" content, Bailyn (1959) drew the conclusion that "for certain children, under certain conditions, the mass media serve one function in particular—that of escape." Similarly, from her finding that upper-middle-class children with restricted home lives were heavier viewers than less restricted children (belonging to the same social class), Maccoby (1954) emphasized the escape function of viewing, arguing that heavy exposure is symptomatic of a need for vicarious satisfaction when the child is frustrated in his attempt to achieve satisfaction in "real life." Similar arguments appeared in other papers. Gans (1962), for example, ascribed the popularity of Hollywood films among British working-class youngsters to their provision of "adolescent aspiration fantasies." And Wolfe and Fiske (1949) related clearly demarcated and age-dependent preferences for different types of comic books to certain needs and behavior characteristics of growing children.

The other group of studies was interested in television as a new force on the mass media scene, competing with other pursuits and interests for the time and attention of children. Having found evidence, either through longitudinal investigation or through comparisons of communities with and without television at a particular point in time, that television makes unequal inroads into children's involvement with other activities, the authors sought to explain the unevenness of such displacement partly with reference to the principle of functional similarity. This expressed the thought that television better satisfied certain needs that had previously been met by the most displaced activities. Himmelweit, Oppenheim and Vince (1958) introduced this principle to explain their finding that the introduction of television was followed by a reduction in radio listening, comic reading and cinema attendance. It was also implicit in the interpretation by Schramm, Lyle and Parker (1961) of their similar pattern of displacement findings. Whereas Himmelweit, however, hesitated to define the particular function that had been transferred to TV from previous media uses, Schramm more explicitly maintained that television mainly provides escape from conflicts or, for the child who gives up the "challenge of life," entertainment and escape from boredom; other media, he argued, were functionally similar in the extent to which they too provided abundant "fantasy" materials.

It should be noted here that functional equivalence was not the only principle used by these investigators to interpret displacement effects. There was, in addition, Himmelweit's proposition that television tends to reduce the amount of time spent in relatively unorganized "marginal" activities. And Furu (1971) considered that certain disparities between Japanese and Western results (the fact, for example, that television caused a greater reduction in time spent on homework in Japan than in America or the United Kingdom) might be better explained by a principle of "psychological and physical proximity" between television and displaced activities.[2] Nevertheless, little attempt was made by any of the writers concerned to suggest exactly how these other principles related to the hypothesis of functional similarity (were they rival alternatives, for example, or complementary but compatible principles?). In practice most of the weight of interpretation fell on the principle of functional similarity.

The element common to most past research of this kind was its reliance on inference from other data when postulating the gratifications involved in children's media behaviors. In some respects this was a source of strength. It avoided the seeming ingenuousness of later studies in which the researcher baldly asked the child for what purposes he used various media. It meant that the studies could not be criticized for the transparency of the demands made on respondents. Above all else, the inferential approach offered parsimonious, even elegant, interpretations of some undeniably important data associations at other levels. Nevertheless, much of this work, and especially that which was concerned with the displacement by television of other leisure-time activities, rested on certain assumptions, the validity of which is not necessarily self-evident but probably could not have been adequately probed by reliance on inferential techniques alone. Three such assumptions were particularly central to the earlier research.

(1) One was that any given medium, or seemingly well-defined body of media content, tends to serve at most a limited number of needs and for some purposes may be treated as if its contribution to audience satisfaction were unifunctional. For example, much emphasis was placed by some authors on the escape function to the exclusion of other gratifications that might have been involved in children's uses of the same media.

(2) Another was that the observable characteristics of a given medium or body of content are an adequate guide to the satisfactions they are likely to offer devotees. This assumption is at work when Schramm, Lyle and Parker (1961) dichotomize television content between fantasy material and reality material; the former provides distraction, wish-fulfillment and an opportunity for vicarious problem solving, and the latter provides information for surveillance of the external world.

(3) A third assumption, which springs from the previous two, was that activities displacement in children is a relatively straightforward process. Certain activities are primarily suited to certain needs and, when a new medium becomes available, it tends to take over the job of catering to the needs it is best fitted for, pushing to the sidelines those media and activities that previously served them. Thus, the reductions in comic reading, radio listening and cinema attendance recorded by Schramm are all predicted by him on the basis of their classification as primarily "fantasy" oriented media.

Apparently, then, an impasse was reached in the early 1960s. The assumptions upon which inferential findings were based could not themselves be assessed using the inferential approach. Several studies in the late 1960s and early 1970s tackled these problems by asking the child direct questions about his uses of media and the satisfactions he typically gained from them. The remainder of this chapter presents findings from one study that employed a direct questioning technique to assess the functions served by the media before and after the introduction of television into a small village in Scotland.

DISPLACEMENT EFFECTS AMONG CHILDREN IN ARISAIG

Arisaig is a village on the northwest coast of Scotland, the inhabitants of which were unable for many years to receive television transmissions because of its location in a radio shadow. However, community action, inspired and directed by the local priest, led to the erection of an aerial on a nearby hill. Each household was wired to this aerial, and the village began to receive television and VHF radio broadcasts in the autumn of 1972.

Our decision to conduct research in Arisaig was not an easy one, since the sample of children available for study would inevitably be very small: 18 in Arisaig itself who would gain television; a further 11 from the neighboring district of Lochailort who would not (except for daytime broadcasts used for teaching purposes). Several other factors confounded the variables: the change children attended one school; non-change children attended a second school. Change children lived within the compact village; non-change children were spread over a wide area to the southeast of the village. Familiarity with the field enforced the acknowledgment that dramatic unidirectional change was highly unlikely and that clear-cut results could not be expected. However, the very fact that so few children were involved would allow the research team far more personal contact with their subjects than is usually possible. The study would also provide an opportunity to test certain hypotheses and, most important of all, perhaps, permit observation of a change in the communications environment that was unlikely to occur again in the British Isles.[3]

We selected, as a control area, the village of Furnace (located in Argyllshire, Scotland), which shared many characteristics with Arisaig, except that the children who lived there had been exposed to television all their lives. The following analysis draws on data collected in May 1972 and May 1973, four months before and eight months after the onset of television in Arisaig, respectively. The data were collected in interviews with three groups of children aged 5 to 11 years: the 18 residing in Arisaig (no TV-TV); 18 control children in Furnace (TV-TV); and the 11 children from Lochailort (no TV-no TV).

There is no doubt that, once it had become available, television quickly assumed a prominent place among the leisure pursuits of the Arisaig children, more so even than in those coming from Furnace. For the second round of interviews we prepared an instrument, based on random samples of broadcast programs, to compare the exposure to television of children in the two villages.[4]

A distinct difference between the groups was apparent, the Arisaig child having viewed an average of one hour and twenty minutes for every hour viewed in Furnace. Presumably this reflects a novelty effect that will eventually dissipate over time.[5]

Tables 1 and 2 provide data on the kinds of activity that were apparently displaced by the amount of time spent on television. They refer to the Furnace as well as the Arisaig children in order to draw attention to changes in activity that might have arisen from a year's growth and expanding experience. Changes in mass media exposure were based on the child's responses to relatively simple rating scales. Since time estimates by younger children would have been unreliable, all respondents were asked to answer questions of the type, "How often do you (listen) to (radio)," by using the scale points "every day," "most days," "once or twice a week," "hardly ever." (Comic usage was measured in terms of the number of comic books per week the child claimed to read.) In order to compress the data derived from such scales, a simple index of change in media use was calculated. The responses of each child to a media use scale in the pre- and post-interviews were coded: −1 for a decline in use (e.g., "every day" to "most days," "once or twice a week" to "hardly ever," etc.); 0 for no change; and +1 for an increase in use. Averaging these scores over children within media produces the index of change presented in Table 1. The findings for Arisaig clearly reproduce those recorded in the earlier studies that generated the functional similarity hypothesis—a decline in use of comics and radio and essentially no change in newspaper reading. A marginal decrease in the frequency of book reading in both communities reflects a change that might have been due not so much to the coming of TV as to a year's development. In addition, the year in Furnace yielded a slight increase in comic reading and more marked increases in radio and television patronage. Although the overall picture is straightforward enough and reminiscent of previous research, there is also evidence in the Furnace data of the influence of a dynamic that cannot be attributed to the onset of television.

Table 2 presents data about the number of activities undertaken in out-of-school time by the Arisaig children and their Furnace controls at the two different interview periods. Each cell entry represents the average number of

TABLE 1

INDEX OF CHANGES IN MEDIA USE BETWEEN
FIRST AND SECOND INTERVIEWS

	Arisaig	Furnace
Television	+ 0.9	+ 0.4
Books	− 0.2	− 0.1
Comics	− 0.4	+ 0.1
Radio	− 0.3	+ 0.3
Newspapers	+ 0.1	0.0

+ 1 = all children use medium more often
  0 = no change
− 1 = all children use medium less often

TABLE 2

AVERAGE NUMBER OF LEISURE ACTIVITIES UNDERTAKEN AT LEAST WEEKLY AT TIME OF FIRST AND SECOND INTERVIEWS

	Arisaig			Furnace		
	First Round	Second Round	Mean Change	First Round	Second Round	Mean Change
Indoor	5.72 (5.5)*	4.85 (3.83)*	−0.89 (−1.67)*	4.50 (3.61)*	5.94 (4.94)*	+1.44 (1.01)*
Outdoor rule	4.44	2.94	−1.50	2.28	2.67	+0.39
Outdoor other	4.06	3.00	−1.06	2.67	2.72	+0.05
Mean Total	14.22 (14.00)*	10.77 (9.77)*	−3.45 (−4.23)*	9.45 (8.56)*	11.33 (10.33)*	+1.88 (+1.44)*

*TV excluded

activities claimed to have been engaged in once a week or more often. Mean change scores are also given. The data show that before the coming of television Arisaig children mentioned many more leisure-time activities than did their Furnace counterparts; afterwards the Arisaig pattern resembled that of Furnace more closely. Overall the passage of a year had resulted in an average decrease of 4.23 activity mentions (not counting television viewing itself) by the Arisaig children compared with an increase of 1.44 among the controls. This suggests that in Arisaig the arrival of television had even suppressed some increasing involvement in other activity that might have occurred naturally otherwise.

This relatively clear picture becomes more complex when three different categories of activity are considered: indoor; outdoor rule governed; and outdoor non-rule governed.[6] The figures for Furnace show the change pattern for a stable communications environment. The 12-month period produces an increase in indoor activity, a slight increase in outdoor rule governed activities and no change in other forms of outdoor play. The figures for Arisaig show a decline over all categories, least pronounced in the outdoor non-rule governed category and greatest for indoor activities (other than television). Thus the greatest displacement of the coming of television undoubtedly fell on the range of indoor activities (measured by the figures in the table as −2.68 if the −1.67 mean change for Arisaig is combined with the +1.01 recorded for Furnace). This result is compatible with either the principle of functional similarity or that of physical proximity, but the nature of our checklist tends to rule out the "marginal unorganized activity" hypothesis.

A closer inspection of the table reveals, however, that rule governed outdoor behavior was more subject to displacement than were other outdoor activities (total mean score differences, taking account of change in both Arisaig and Furnace, of −1.89 and −1.11, respectively). This finding is difficult to explain in terms of any of the principles of displacement proposed by other authors. "Physical proximity" can be excluded at once, and "psychological proximity" or "functional similarity" would presumably be more consistent with a reverse result as would the assumption that television tends to displace more marginal and unstructured forms of activity. Of course, it may be argued that we are here dealing with frequency data and that measures of duration might have produced a different pattern. Nevertheless, a division of outdoor activities between rule governed and non-rule governed does create some difficulties in the attempt to apply previously formulated principles of displacement.

The above results were also more or less consistent with assessments secured from the Arisaig children of their degree of enjoyment of various activities before and after the coming of television. Although the differences were slight, they showed that indoor activity had become more enjoyable, while rule governed outdoor activity was regarded less favorably at the time of the second interview. In other words, there might have been some functional displacement from outdoor games to television.[7]

So far, then, the data are mainly in line with earlier results and their interpretation. Gross changes in levels of frequency of use of different media are consistent with past findings and the principle of functional displacement that was proposed to explain them. Only when subdivisions of activity according to the presence or absence of formal rules were involved was any difficulty experienced in explaining the results in terms of displacement principles set forth in previous writings. However, it was also possible in this study to test the functional similarity hypothesis more rigorously by using a direct questioning technique. Several ways of tackling the problem of directly assessing the satisfactions derived from different media and other activities were tried out in pilot work on children in Leeds. The instrument finally adopted was quite similar to one developed independently by Furu (1971). A set of seven cards, each bearing a sketch representing a medium, solitary activity, or accompanied activity was prepared. The child was familiarized with the cards before being asked a series of nine questions, for example, "Which of these things do you do if you're sad and want to be cheered up?" Figure 1 provides a full list of the questions, which were arrived at after culling the literature, discussion with other researchers, and contacts with children during piloting. The instrument was administered toward the end of a face-to-face interview. In addition to cards representing TV, books, comics, radio, records, solitary play, and accompanied play, the child was able to make a "nothing" response, signifying that none of the preferred alternatives gave him the designated satisfaction. The following results are based on the administration of this instrument at the two interviews not only to the Arisaig and Furnace children but also to those living in Lochailort who at year 2 were still exposed only to school broadcasts.

Table 3 shows the number of times that each medium was mentioned as a source of satisfaction for each of the nine needs at years 1 and 2. (The maximum possible entry is 162; this would occur only if each child chose the same medium as a preferred source for all nine functions.) Comparison of the three communities at year 1 predictably shows a closer resemblance between Arisaig

Bored:	Which of these things do you do if you are bored and want something to pass the time away?
Things in world:	Which of these things do you do if you want to find out about things that happen all over the world?
Talk about:	Which of these things gives you something to talk about with your friends?
No one talk:	Which of these things do you do if there's no one about to talk to or play with?
Exciting:	Which of these things do you do if you want something exciting?
Grown up:	Which of these things tells you about being grown up?
Sad/cheer up:	Which of these things do you do if you're sad and want to be cheered up?
Forget:	Which of these things do you do if you want to forget about nasty things?
Think about:	Which of these things gives you something to think about?

Figure 1: FUNCTIONS STATEMENTS USED IN STUDY AND LABELS USED IN TABLES

TABLE 3
TOTAL NUMBER OF FUNCTIONS BEST SERVED BY SELECTED
MEDIA AND ACTIVITIES IN YEARS 1 AND 2

	Total Year 1			Total Year 2		
	Lochailort	*Arisaig*	*Furnace*	*Lochailort*	*Arisaig*	*Furnace*
TV	13	15	39	17	66	59
Book	29	26	22	40	24	31
Comic	18	17	13	18	11	23
Radio	21	25	8	28	11	11
Records	23	14	17	18	18	19
Self	15	16	9	12	9	3
Others	14	16	22	21	17	12
Nothing	31	33	32	10	6	4
Totals	164	162	162	164	162	162

and Lochailort children than the Arisaig and Furnace respondents. Excluding the "nothing"[8] category, books are the source of greatest satisfaction in the no-TV group, followed fairly closely by radio; television is the source of satisfaction mentioned most often by the Furnace children. Furthermore, satisfactions are more evenly spread over media in the no-TV groups when compared with Furnace, where there is a distinct peaking for television. Perhaps a greater discrepancy between the groups on comic reading would have been expected if television was a partial substitute, but the figures for radio are certainly in line with functional displacement predictions. Comparing year 1 with year 2, there is an expected change for Arisaig in terms of the number of satisfactions provided by television (15 allocations rising to 66), but there is also an increase for Furnace (39 to 59). There are decreases among the Arisaig children in finding satisfaction especially from radio as well as from comic reading and solitary activity. In contrast to these declines, the table suggests that books, records, and accompanied play had withstood the encroachment of television. On the other hand, an inspection of changes in the Lochailort group's functional orientations reveals, in an otherwise relatively stable pattern, a marked increase in the satisfactions recorded from book reading. Once again, then, at this level of gross analysis the functional similarity hypothesis is apparently upheld, although there is a disturbing discrepancy to be found in the implication from Lochailort that the impact of television, while not reducing the children's enjoyment of books, had perhaps suppressed some of the increase in book-reading satisfactions that might have otherwise taken place.

Gross change, however, is not necessarily an accurate guide to individual change. A more direct test of the functional similarity hypothesis would depend on the number of times the functions served by a particular medium or activity were displaced specifically by television. Table 4 presents evidence on this point as well as showing the number of times that the respondents consistently nominated a particular medium or activity as best for gratifying a particular need at both interviews. The totals at the bottom of the table show that the number

TABLE 4

FUNCTIONS OF SOURCES AFTER ONE YEAR:
DISPLACED BY TV AND CONSISTENCY OF NOMINATION

	Displaced by TV			Consistent		
	Lochailort	Arisaig	Furnace	Lochailort	Arisaig	Furnace
TV	–	–	–	2	6	17
Book	–	12	14	16	4	2
Comic	5	10	2	3	2	4
Radio	3	12	2	10	1	2
Records	2	5	2	10	4	6
Self	–	5	1	2	3	–
Others	–	4	8	8	6	5
Nothing	5	12	13	6	2	–
Totals	15	60	42	57	28	36

of displacements by television was greatest among the Arisaig children and least for those living in Lochailort. In addition, consistency over time in the nomination of sources of satisfaction was predictably reversed, with Lochailort children proving most stable in this respect and Arisaig children least so. However, it was less predictable that many functions of other activities and media should have been displaced by television in Furnace and also that the total number of consistent choices recorded in Lochailort was only 57 out of a possible 162.[9] It was as if a considerable amount of displacement could occur even without the stimulus of a major change in the respondents' communications environment.

A further difficulty for the functional similarity hypothesis as originally propounded arises from the fact that, of the 60 displacements effected in Arisaig by television, only 22 (approximately three-eighths) concerned functions previously served by comics and radio. In fact books were displaced equally as often as the other two media (on 12 occasions in Arisaig and as many as 14 in Furnace), a finding that reinforces the previously mentioned suggestion that television may have inhibited an expansion of the child's functional orientation to book reading.

Yet another important point may be extracted from Table 4. Had there been only two kinds of development over time—consistent nominations plus displacement by television—summating within a group, the column totals would have equalled 162. In fact the totals are Lochailort 72, Furnace 78, and Arisaig 88. In other words, there was considerably more functional displacement between years 1 and 2 in all three communities than could have been ascribed to the influence of television alone; other media must have been "displacers" as well as "displaced." Table 5 summarizes the functional displacement picture from this point of view.

It can be seen that in Arisaig and Furnace the major single source of functional displacement is television, but within these villages and in Lochailort as well, there is overall a confused picture created by a general shuffling around of functions. In all three groups, books displace a number of other media, thus explaining why, although often displaced by television, they still managed to maintain a functional importance in year 2 at least as great as in year 1 (see Table 3). In Lochailort both radio and comics quite often serve as displacers of other media as do comics in Furnace. Our data are taken from too few respondents to look more closely at patterns of displacement between specific media, but one or two tendencies may be mentioned. In Furnace, books displaced satisfactions gained from television on eight occasions. In Arisaig, they displaced radio on seven occasions. Comics displaced television on six occasions in Furnace; they also provided choices on six occasions where no source of satisfaction had previously been mentioned.

Yet another source of complexity is introduced when we consider the differential vulnerability of various functions to influence by the appeal of a particular medium like television, whether newly injected into the community or long established there. In preceding tables we have presented data within media, summating over functions. In Table 6 we present data for functions, summating over media. These are consistency data showing the number of times that a medium was selected as a source of a given satisfaction on both occasions. Each cell entry has a maximum of 18. The three communities represent three conditions under which a year's growth has taken place: a stable communications environment with television; a stable communications environment without television; and in Arisaig, a changing communications environment. We may argue, therefore, that television is not a necessary condition for any result that obtains throughout all three communities. This seems to apply to two sets of functions. First, there is a group showing uniformly low consistency, that is, a high rate of change as a consequence of a year's further experience and growth, and not necessarily influenced by television. In this group are information about being grown-up; helping the child to forget unpleasant experience; and companionship. Second, at the other extreme, there is a mood control function, "Cheers me up when I'm feeling sad," that shows relatively high consistency across the three groups. Again, the fact that this result applies across different conditions suggests that television is not influential for this function. The remaining functions show a similar pattern,[10] least consistency in the change condition, highest consistency in Lochailort. Moreover, assuming that a changing communications environment is more complex than a stable one, then the column totals reveal a clear trend: the more complex the communications environment, the less the consistency in functional orientation over time.

TABLE 5
NUMBER OF TIMES EACH SOURCE OF SATISFACTION
DISPLACES THE FUNCTION OF ANOTHER

	TV	Book	Comic	Radio	Records	Self	Others	Nothing
Lochailort	15	24	15	18	8	10	13	4
Arisaig	60	20	9	10	13	6	11	3
Furnace	42	29	19	9	8	3	8	3

TABLE 6

NUMBER OF CONSISTENT MEDIA (AND OTHER SOURCE)
NOMINATIONS FOR EACH FUNCTION

	Lochailort	*Arisaig*	*Furnace*
Bored	5	1	4
Things in world	11	—	5
Talk about	5	6	6
No one talk	3	3	1
Exciting	8	2	5
Grown up	2	1	2
Sad/cheer up	8	8	7
Forget	3	3	1
Think about	8	1	5
Totals	53	25	36

Min = 0, Max = 18

Despite its seeming plausibility, then, when applied to interpret gross changes following the introduction of television into a community, in how children spend their time and what they use mass media for, there are too many developments that the rather simple principle of functional similarity cannot readily explain. These include the impact of TV on book reading; the incidence of much displacement after one year even among children living in stable communities (whether they had had television all along or had never been exposed to it); evidence that, even when TV comes for the first time to a locality, other media do not merely lose functions to its appeal but also take over some that they had not previously served; and the fact that different functions vary in their susceptibility to the impact of a new medium. The overall impression conveyed by the evidence is that functional similarity, if retained, should be subsumed under a principle with a greater explanatory potential and a wider range of application. The following section discusses, with the help of new data, some of the considerations overlooked by the functional similarity hypothesis and proposes a new principle of displacement.

FUNCTIONAL SIMILARITY OR FUNCTIONAL REORGANIZATION?

One of the root difficulties with the principle of functional similarity arises from its implicit dependence on the assumption that particular media serve at most only a limited set of functions, tending, perhaps, even to virtual unifunctionality of performance. By and large this assumption has been undermined by more recent research with adult audiences (cf. McQuail, Blumler and Brown, 1972; Katz, Gurevitch and Haas, 1973). So far as our own respondents are concerned, its unsuitability may be confirmed by noting the range of functions served by the main media used in year 2 by the 36 children from Arisaig and Furnace combined. At that time television was mentioned by 16 respondents as best for serving at least four of the nine functions included in our instrument. The equivalent figure for books was 18 respondents mentioning at least two functions; for comics 8 respondents mentioning at least two functions; and for records 12 respondents mentioning at least two functions. The point is that when multifunctionality prevails, the impact of a new medium is less likely to be restricted to the absorption of a limited set of functions from a limited set of media. Instead it is more likely to trigger off a complex chain reaction of functional reallocation all around.

Yet other weaknesses may be highlighted by the introduction of findings from another study conducted in Leeds concurrently with the Arisaig research (Brown, Cramond and Wilde, 1973). This investigation sought to plot age trends in children's functional uses of various media. The study was based on a sample of 800 school children, equally split on age (160 children each at ages 7, 9, 11, 13, and 15), and equally distributed between the sexes within age and by social class within age and sex. Figure 2 shows the age trends for four selected sources of satisfaction—records, books, television, and peers—on four selected functions—arousal (excitement), mood control (forgetting unpleasant experience), social utility (having things to talk about), and information (about different places).

Two main points emerge from these data of relevance to the present argument. One concerns the age trend for book reading, which is characterized by a gradual decline in claimed functional use over time. This is consistent with the finding embedded in Table 4, showing that satisfactions gained from books had been displaced by television in both Arisaig *and* Furnace, although Table 3 had revealed an apparent stability in the total satisfactions provided by books over the year. Books, it seemed, had lost out on some satisfactions (for some children) in favor of television but had gained other satisfactions from the remaining available sources. However, the Lochailort data showed a marked increase in satisfactions provided by book reading in the course of a year. And all of this change had occurred within an apparent stability of exposure to books (the reason why previous investigators had supposed no functional impact of TV on book reading).

In terms of exposure, then, television does not displace books. Taken as a whole, however, our data strongly suggest that the satisfactions gained from reading, the "uses" of books, are modified by television. Could it be that in functional terms television displaces books to an even greater extent than either radio or comics? The idea is attractive; television is, for the average child, a multifunctional medium, and in part this must be due to its wide range of content. Only books can match that range to the same extent. Other media (with the possible exception of radio) tend to be characterized by a somewhat narrower span of content and are perhaps less able to cater to several kinds of need simultaneously. On this basis we can argue that exposure to books is little affected by the onset of television, not, as Himmelweit and Schramm have implied, because books serve a functions alien to television, but because some of the functions they continue to serve, although more limited, are still salient to children, while television takes over the book's role as the predominant

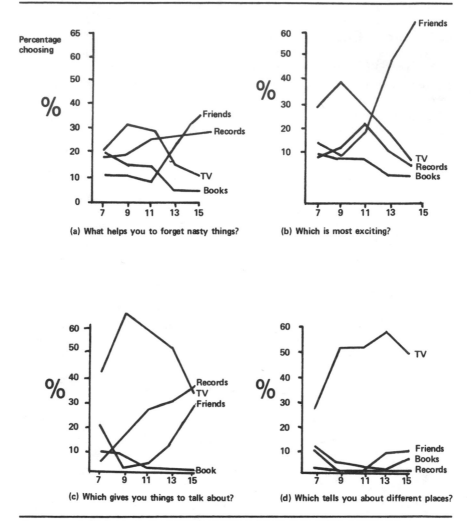

Figure 2: AGE TRENDS FOR FOUR SATISFACTIONS AND FOUR SOURCES OF SATISFACTION

multifunctional medium in the child's communications environment. The Leeds results show that functional dependence on books tends overall to decline with age. Nevertheless, for three statements, this decline was delayed. These concerned relief from boredom, provision of food for thought, and involvement (operationalized as, "Which of these things do you get so lost in that you're not interested in anything else when you're doing it?"). Are these, then, the residual functions served by book reading which, when combined with school and parental encouragement, explain the failure of most previous studies to find a decline in book reading following the introduction of TV?

The second main weakness of the thesis of functional similarity, as highlighted by the Leeds evidence, is its failure to take account of the fact that any repercussions from the introduction of a new medium will inevitably interact with developments attributable to the on-going process of growing up itself. For example, after a slight decline from seven to nine years there is a dramatic increase in the extent to which children regard their peers as a source of excitement (Figure 2b). In terms of the functions sometimes labelled "coin of exchange" (having things to talk about), records are nominated increasingly with age (an increase that is even more evident if girls only are considered); peers initially decline and then increase their importance, while television, the most important source at seven years of age, begins a steady decline at age nine until the mid-teens when there is little or no difference between the three main sources of this satisfaction (Figure 2c). Among children especially, then, media-related needs tend to evolve with the passage of time and also tend to be directed with a certain amount of fluidity to different media at different phases in their development.

All the results seem to point to the influence of a process which for obvious reasons we shall call *functional reorganization.* The introduction of a new medium, instead of provoking a piecemeal displacement, creates a change in the communications environment to which the child reacts by a more comprehensive restructuring of his functional orientations to media (and other elements of his environment). But over and above the special cases in which new media become available, there seems to be a continuing pattern of reorganization during childhood and adolescence that leads to the more stable functional orientations of the adult audience member.[11] In other words, media use may be regarded as adaptive behavior characterized by an on-going process of reorganization, the dynamic of which is provided by changes in the communications environment and developments in the audience member's unfolding experience.

SOME FURTHER IMPLICATIONS OF
FUNCTIONAL REORGANIZATION

In this final section some further implications of this concept of functional reorganization are considered from two perspectives. First, a way of tracing the sources of such reorganization back to certain stages in childhood development that may give rise in turn to altered media orientations is outlined. Second, some repercussions of functional reorganization among audience members on equivalent developments in media content are explored.

The interplay between three fairly straightforward conceptual distinctions may help to explain age trends in mass media use—both exposure patterns and functional orientations. The first of these refers to the gratifications involved in mass media use and distinguishes among them between those that represent *continuous requirements* and those that may be termed *cyclical requirements.* An example of a continuous requirement found in childhood is the growing individual's evident need constantly to monitor new information and process new experience. A cyclical requirement par excellence is mood control, reflecting a need that is experienced more spasmodically than continuously.

A second notion may be summarized by the phrase, *access to suitable content and control over its selection.* That is, with respect to a particular requirement, a child will turn to that medium which provides the appropriate stimulation—he seeks access to suitable content. If the requirement is one that tends to fluctuate (cyclical), then he will also need greater control over the selection of content; if, on the other hand, it tends to be more continuous, then it will be sufficient to have access to a source of suitable content, one which over a period of time can be counted on to provide a fair amount of what he desires, thereby relieving the individual of any need to take special steps to get what he is seeking. Of course the relationships involved here are more complex than has so far been implied. A given requirement, for example, may at one time be continuous and at another time more cyclical in character. The need for information, for example, may often be served by a fairly continuous source of sensations with cognitive import. On occasion, however, this requirement may "peak." If, say, the child is obliged to find out all he can about the Roman Empire, then it is highly unlikely that one evening's viewing will be in any sense functional; instead he will turn to a source that provides access to and control over the selection of content—to books, perhaps, or authoritative people.

A third factor in the development of functional involvement concerns the child's ability to make optimal use of a medium. This capacity may be termed *reading the medium* because it is so clearly exemplified by what is involved in responding to print. Before the child has learned to read, print can be of little consequence to him. Once he has mastered the skill of reading, including of course the ability to interpret what is written and to relate it to his own experience, then print is available for him to draw on in gratifying his various needs. In a similar way, before the individual can make optimal use of television, or any other medium, he must learn to "read" it, to understand its grammar and conventions, and be able to interpret and make real its typical contents.

Can these notions add anything at all to our understanding of mass media usage? First, it seems evident that the interplay of changing need states, differential access to content and its control and a developing ability to "read" available media must provide much of the dynamic for the processes of change that underlie functional reorganization. Second, these concepts may help to explain and interpret certain empirical findings. Figure 3 offers an illustration, bringing together evidence from the aforementioned Leeds study of children's media functions by age and television exposure figures for British children collected by the BBC in 1971 (Greenberg, 1973). Whereas the latter show an exposure to television peak in early adolescence, the equivalent peak for its functional use (averaging over 13 satisfactions) occurs two to three years earlier. Why should there be such a discrepancy? An answer may be attempted in terms of the foregoing discussion. The peak for functional use is seen as occurring at that moment when the child has mastered the medium—when he has learned fluently to read its content. At this time he probably even gets some satisfaction

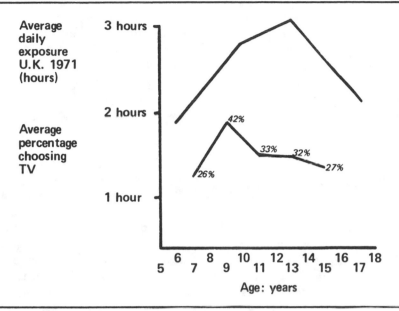

Figure 3: CHOICE OF TV AS A SOURCE OF THIRTEEN SATISFACTIONS (SUMMATED) AND AVERAGE EXPOSURE TO TV

out of the sheer act of mastery itself. (Think, for example, of the pleasure that a child can derive from explaining to his parents the mechanics of a plot that is just within his capacity to comprehend.) Moreover, his skills will enable him to use television as a multifunctional instrument of satisfaction. But at the same time peer pressures, internal changes, and a curiosity about the wider aspects of his environment will encourage him to explore the possibility of using other media to gratify some of his needs. For a while television is the safe standby; he will carry on viewing while trying to forge new functional links with other media and activities.

Thus an explanation can be offered for the puzzling discrepancy between functional and exposure peaks in children's uses of television. But why should such a dramatic decline in exposure occur during later adolescence? In order to explain this we must reintroduce the notions of need state and content suitability. If we can show that the dominant need states change over time, then this might link up with changing exposure patterns via the provision of suitable content. And that is exactly what seems to happen. The stage that coincides with increasing functional use of television has been termed the latency period. During this time the child is moved chiefly by relatively continuous need states; that is, he processes prodigious amounts of information, internalizes the rules and values of his society, and seeks excitement, entertainment, and some relaxation. Since for all these requirements it is inessential to have a high degree of control over the selection of media content, television is a suitable medium for their satisfaction. But as the heavy weather of puberty sets in, intense new feelings and more volatile fluctuations of mood are experienced. Mood control becomes a more salient requirement. And in order to maintain a measure of stability, the adolescent now needs more than suitable content: he needs it at the right time; he must have control over the selection of content. In television this control is in the hands of broadcasters rather than audience members; therefore, the adolescent tends to turn his back on television in favor of records, magazines, and, of course, interaction with his peers. Much of the decline in TV use, then, could arise from the dramatic upsurge of mood control requirements in adolescence.

Access to and control over the selection of suitable content are seen, then, as important elements in the process of functional reorganization. But reciprocally, functional reorganization may also precipitate a number of changes in the forms and styles of mass media content. As the introduction of a new medium upsets existing functional relationships between the previously established media and their audiences, pressures are exerted on executives and producers working in the latter to try out content innovations capable of serving new needs and of rebuilding thereby a sizable and loyal audience. Sometimes an attempt is made to locate and cater for needs that have been relatively neglected by the insurgent medium; at other times a market first opened up by the newcomer will be more or less imitatively exploited by the others. Repercussions of this kind may have been partly responsible, then, for some of the output trends in other media that followed the growth of television during the last 20 years: content changes in comic books (e.g., the inclusion of information pages about sports and hobbies); the introduction of inexpensive books aimed at 5- to 8-year-old children; the establishment of specialist magazines for teenagers; the provision of continuous popular music on radio; and generally the dramatic expansion of "pop" as the basis of an international industry.

Teasing out the many lines of evolving interaction between different media and their content cannot be an easy task. According to this analysis, some of their sources are embedded in patterns of audience exposure, behavior and response that will have been "read" by a wide range of less than perfect indicators, such as readership surveys, circulation figures, direct feedback from audience members (letters, competition entries, etc.), and, of course, that form of intuition that underlies so much of the practice of mass communication. The Arisaig data have disclosed some of the complexity of functional reorganization that may be provoked by the onset of a new medium. Such a reorganization may lead in turn, through devious and sometimes distorting channels of feedback, to the gradual reshaping of content provided by media. The thrust of this final speculation may be captured by the parting thought: "Old media never die; they only change their functions."

NOTES

1. Few students of mass communications now use the term "function" in its original sense (see, for example, Walsh, 1972). Unfortunately, this means that the potential utilities

of linking an area of study to an existing body of theory have been neglected. In our own work some distinction has been made between satisfactions (for example, "to be cheered up," or "to forget" unpleasant experiences) and functions (for example, "mood control," which would cover both the aforementioned satisfactions). However, for the present paper, in line with many authors, no distinction is made between function, satisfaction and gratification.

2. Physical proximity refers to two activities that share the same physical context, for example, homework and viewing in the case of Japan. Psychological proximity can be given one or both of two interpretations: (a) phenomenological, applying to two activities that experientially are similar, and (b) the condition that obtains when the child can easily think of the satisfaction to be derived from some activity.

3. In fact, after much publicity in the British press we failed to find any other community not served by television. However, it is likely that when VHF broadcasting is stopped in favor of UHF, some communities in mountainous areas will *lose* their TV signal.

4. The children were asked whether or not they had seen any of a preselected list of 50 programs screened in the week before interview. These were derived from a random designation of three units, each lasting an hour, from each of seven daily program logs. Any program that was wholly or partly broadcast during the chosen hour was listed. Since the Furnace interviews were held a week after those in Arisaig, the resulting program lists, drawn from the same time periods, were not entirely identical. Nevertheless, there was an overlap of 41 programs between the two groups of 50 programs.

5. It is difficult to explain this difference by the influence of extraneous factors. Interviews were conducted in consecutive weeks when meteorological conditions were similar. In fact Arisaig enjoyed somewhat more daylight at the time, being located some 60 miles north of Furnace. Furthermore the two groups of children shared similar social and geographical environments and were, of course, matched for age and sex.

6. Some examples of outdoor rule governed activities include football, hide-and-seek, country dancing. Outdoor non-rule governed activities included cycling, fishing, playing on swings, and so forth.

7. If so, this might reflect some social trends affecting children's leisure-time pursuits in which modern mass media could be implicated. In a paper analyzing trends in American children's play, as revealed by studies conducted in 1896, 1898, 1921, and 1959, Sutton-Smith and Rosenberg (1971) record among their conclusions, "The increasing preference of children is for informal group activities. . . . Formal games are vestiges of an earlier and more hierarchically arranged society, and they may pass out of spontaneous play as the formalities which they represent become increasingly meaningless to new generations of children. We would not expect such games to disappear completely, but we would expect them to become relatively less important parts of a child's development in this culture." From this perspective television is seen as an almost inevitable *element* and *consequence* of rapid change in the social ethos, technology, and ecology of this century; as media researchers we are inclined to neglect too often the wide angle lens in favor of the tight close-up.

8. There is a more or less consistent decrease in use of the "nothing" category for all three communities. Presumably this results from one year's growth; the child has become more able to locate sources of satisfaction.

9. It is possible that the table is measuring "noise"; that is, that our instrument is unreliable. We are inclined to reject this explanation since the data are not random but reveal patterns that are consistent over a number of tabulations and that together form the basis of an argument in line with data from other sources. Certainly our subjective impression when interviewing the children was that they understood the task presented and responded to it seriously and thoughtfully.

10. The social utility satisfaction, "talk about," was somewhat peculiar inasmuch as Arisaig children at year 1 sometimes nominated TV because they talked about its imminent arrival; in addition, at year 2 some Lochailort children nominated TV because they discussed it at school.

11. However, changes in media provision themselves probably do give rise to some forms of reorganization in adulthood as do changes in the mature person's social and psychological circumstances. Panel studies of adult audiences would throw light on the applicability or otherwise of the concept of functional reorganization to their patterns of mass media use.

REFERENCES

BAILYN, L. (1959) "Mass media and children: a study of exposure habits and cognitive effects." Psychological Monographs 73, 1: 1-48.

BROWN, J. R., J. K. CRAMOND, and R. J. WILDE (1973) "Children's use of the mass media: a functional approach." Paper presented to the British Psychological Society, Leeds. (mimeo)

DEMBO, R. (1973) "Gratifications found in media by British teenage boys." Journalism Quarterly 50, 3.

FURU, T. (1971) The Function of Television for Children and Adolescents. Tokyo: Sophia Univ. Press.

GANS, H. (1962) "Hollywood films on the British screen: an analysis of the functions of American popular culture abroad." Social Problems IX: 324-328.

GREENBERG, B. S. (1974) "Gratifications of television viewing and their correlates for British children," in J. G. Blumler and E. Katz (eds.) The Use of Mass Communications: Current Perspectives on Gratifications Research. Beverly Hills: Sage.

——— (1973) "Viewing and listening parameters among British youngsters." Journal of Broadcasting 17, 2.

HIMMELWEIT, H., A. N. OPPENHEIM, and P. VINCE (1958) Television and the Child: An Empirical Study of the Effect of Television on the Young. London: Oxford Univ. Press.

KATZ, E., M. GUREVITCH, and H. HAAS (1973) "On the use of the mass media for important things." American Sociological Review 38: 164-181.

MACCOBY, E. (1954) "Why do children watch television?" Public Opinion Quarterly 18 (Fall): 239-244.

McQUAIL, D., J. G. BLUMLER, and J. R. BROWN (1972) "The television audience: a revised perspective," in D. McQuail (ed.) Sociology of Mass Communications. Harmondsworth: Penguin.

ROBINSON, J. P. (1972) "Toward defining the functions of television," pp. 568-603 in E. A. Rubenstein, G. A. Comstock and J. P. Murray (eds.) Television and Social Behavior, Vol. 4. Rockville, Md.: National Institute of Mental Health.

SCHRAMM, W., J. LYLE, and E. B. PARKER (1961) Television in the Lives of our Children. Stanford: Stanford Univ. Press.

SUTTON-SMITH, B. and B. G. ROSENBERG (1971) "Sixty years of historical change in the game preferences of American children," in R. E. Herron and B. Sutton-Smith (eds.) Child's Play. New York: John Wiley.

von FEILITZEN, C. (forthcoming) "The functions of media for Swedish children," in J. R. Brown (ed.) Children and Television. London: Cassell & Collier-Macmillan Ltd.

WALSH, D. (1972) "Functionalism and systems theory," in P. Filmer, M. Phillipson, D. Silverman and D. Walsh (eds.) New Directions in Sociological Theory. London: Collier-Macmillan.

WOLFE, K. and M. FISKE (1949) "The children talk about comics," pp. 3-50 in P. Lazarsfeld and F. Stanton (eds.) Communication Research 1948-1949. New York: Harper.

Chapter 6

ADOLESCENTS AND FAMILY PLANNING INFORMATION: AN EXPLORATION OF AUDIENCE NEEDS AND MEDIA EFFECTS

F. Gerald Kline, Peter V. Miller and Andrew J. Morrison

RESEARCH INTO THE EFFECTS OF MASS COMMUNICATION, as Katz, Blumler, and Gurevitch point out in this volume, has neglected the role of audience motivation in the effects process. Rather, the audience has been regarded for all practical purposes as a homogeneous, passive mass that is acted upon by the media. Although a concern with the effects of mass media is not unreasonable, the absence of a consideration of the needs of audience members has limited our understanding of how effects come about. The uses and gratifications model suggests that individual uses for media content act as an intervening variable: mitigating or enhancing the ultimate effects of a media message.

Apart from this theoretical shortcoming, effects research has been encumbered with various methodological problems. While laboratory conditions afforded investigators the means to isolate the effects of experimental manipulations, these same conditions hampered researchers in their ability to generalize their findings to the effects of mass media in natural settings. On the other hand, cross-sectional surveys seeking to explore media effects are inevitably constrained from drawing the desired causal inferences.

Even survey panel studies face problems in parceling out effects, because, although they allow for analysis with temporally prior independent variables, they often do not provide the researcher with adequate control to enable him to isolate with assurance the causal agent. Thus, in relating media exposure to

AUTHORS' NOTE: The authors are indebted to the John and Mary R. Markle Foundation for the bulk of the funds supporting this study and to the Population Program Development Fund of The University of Michigan for supplementary support.

change in some attitude, knowledge, or emotional state, we are unsure generally what it is in the media that is causing changes in the state. Without even a facsimile of a "control group," it is not strictly justifiable to attribute changes in audience states to media alone. It may be that the media interact with some other variable to produce effects, or that the relationship between media exposure and effects is spurious—the product of some extra-media agent. A further confounding factor is pretest sensitization, the interaction of the effect of the measurement experience on the respondent with the experimental (communication) variable.

What has been lacking in effects research, then, is theoretical consideration of audience motivation, the needs of audience members, and the uses they make of the media, as well as a research method that seeks an optimum blend of laboratory control and survey generality.

A DESIGN FOR EFFECTS RESEARCH

In an attempt to overcome the methodological problems outlined above, the authors have been conducting a field experiment in two midwestern American cities which were matched on important media characteristics.[1] The design of the study provides for an experimental and control group, with additional controls for pretest sensitization. One of the matched cities serves as the experimental group, receiving a campaign of radio messages on a particular topic designed to reach a target audience of adolescents. The other city serves as a control group, the purpose of which is to isolate the cause of any changes in knowledge or communication activity that may occur in the experimental city with regard to the topic addressed in the media campaign.

To illustrate, the design calls for interviews with a random subsample of respondents in each city at Time I. Following this wave of interviews, a month-long family planning radio campaign is directed at the audience of the experimental or "media" city, while the other city receives no campaign.[2] Interviews then take place after the campaign, involving both the original subsamples and two other subsamples, one in each city, which did not receive interviews before. In this way, we can control for confounding extra-media effects on the dependent variables that might result from pretest sensitization. The resulting scheme is the familiar Solomon "Four-Group" design as explicated in Campbell and Stanley (1966).

The respondents for the study are adolescents, sampled on a geographic probability basis from the two cities. A sample of approximately 300 was drawn in each city, with each sample randomly divided into subgroups to meet the requirements of the experimental design.[3]

The model being examined here encompasses some of the major components of the uses and gratifications approach; namely, that we posit need states in the audience which are associated with differential effects from mass media messages. These effects are seen to be gratifications of the need states and are further defined by the control over availability of information that our experimental design provides.

CONCEPT DEVELOPMENT AND OPERATIONALIZATION

Need States

Typically, uses and gratifications studies derive measures of the needs served by media content in an inductive manner; questioning respondents directly concerning their perceived wants and the media that gratify those wants best (Katz, Gurevitch and Haas, 1973). These need statements are then clustered empirically or according to some category system derived from the structure of the responses.

Katz, Blumler and Gurevitch (1974) emphasize the methodological dependence of the users and gratifications approach on self-report as a valid and effective means of measuring media-related needs. It is assumed that respondents are sufficiently self-aware to be able to depict the type and extent of their needs as well as the relative contribution of various media toward their gratification. As inductive empirical methods (such as cluster analysis) improve, they imply, the ascertainment of need becomes more accurate.

It is clearly possible, however, to envisage sources of bias in self-report that may mitigate our belief in the validity of the "needs" measured in this way, particularly in the case of a sensitive topic like family planning. An adolescent may be somewhat reluctant to admit the need for family planning information, especially information about birth control methods if he or she is not married or contemplating marriage. Such bias would seriously hamper attempts to discover the motivations of adolescents for seeking family planning information. Also, younger adolescents may not be able to estimate accurately their need for this type of information because of their general ignorance of the topic area. (Elliot echoes these reservations elsewhere in this volume.) We therefore chose unobtrusive measures for ascertaining need.

Central to our model, then, is the conceptualization of needs for information in an adolescent, derived, on the one hand, from the pressures of biological and chronological maturation, and on the other hand, from the individual's orientation toward those people who compose a primary group around him or her. The age and sex of an adolescent, quite clearly, should bear strongly upon the amount and type of information required about the topic of family planning. Females, although in biological development similar to the males in the age range we have sampled, usually have matured earlier and are about two years ahead in awareness of sexuality and sexual activity. The males will also feel the pressure of information needs as they progress through adolescence.

A different but complementary conceptualization of need is derived from the social comparison literature (Festinger, 1954). Unlike the biological-maturational character of the first need description, this second one is rooted in the social network that surrounds the adolescent. Here the focus is on the adolescent's comparison of his perceived knowledge about family planning with his perception of the knowledge of important persons surrounding him or her—the parents and peers. This comparison, also considered in the co-orientation literature as a congruency concept (Chaffee and McLeod, 1973), produces an information dependence typology with which we may characterize adolescents (Jones and Gerard, 1967).

If the adolescent perceives that his or her knowledge about family planning is equal to a particular primary group referent, we may say that he or she is *congruent* with that person with regard to perceived knowledge on the topic. Conversely, there are two potential conditions of perceived knowledge *incongruency* that may exist with any one partner. The adolescent may perceive that he or she knows more about family planning than a partner; this person may be termed in an *incongruent (ahead)* state. The adolescent may also perceive that he or she knows less than a partner. This condition would represent an *incongruent (behind)* state.

It is expected that persons in these different conditions of congruency or incongruency would tend to perceive messages in the mass media differently and to obtain different types of information therefrom. A person in the incongruent (ahead) condition may use the media more than those in the other conditions, for example, because he or she cannot rely on the referent "other" for new information. Moreover, if the heavy exposure to media hypothesis holds for the incongruent (ahead) adolescent, he or she may glean from the media relatively unique pieces of information. If the knowledge self-perception of such an adolescent is accurate in reality, furthermore, commonplace media information may be ignored because it has little utility for one who already knows a good deal about the topic.

What of the other congruency types and their relation to media message perception and knowledge? The congruent adolescent, unlike his incongruent (ahead) counterpart, may rely less on the media for information about the topic because the interpersonal channels around him or her are viable sources of information. That is, if knowledge held in the interpersonal environment is perceived as equal to the adolescent's knowledge, the interpersonal sources may be seen as able to provide some information (which would not be the case for the incongruent [ahead] adolescent). Information gain associated with media use for congruent adolescents might be expected to include the more redundant types of information presented in media channels, if these adolescents actually use the media less and actually know less than the incongruent (ahead) teenagers. Further, the congruent adolescent may gain information which, while not presented in media, may be gained through interpersonal discussion as a "spin-off" of media use.

Predictions with regard to media exposure and knowledge for the incongruent (behind) adolescent follow the logic of the previous arguments. This adolescent should rely still less on media sources of information about the topic. Since others in the environment are perceived by the adolescent to know more than himself or herself, it is reasonable to think of these others as probable sources of information. Too, the kind of knowledge to be gained from media for this adolescent would be similar to that for the congruent adolescent: redundant media information and other information of the "spin-off" variety.

Thus, major differences in both media message perception and knowledge gain can be predicted from this social information need concept of congruency and incongruency. But when we speak of a greater reliance on media sources by the incongruent (ahead) adolescents, we do not mean to imply that no interpersonal communication is undertaken by this person. To the contrary, an adolescent in the ahead condition may talk about the subject frequently with others. The fact that he perceives himself as knowing more than a particular significant other about family planning does not exclude the possibility of his learning something from that other or sharing an idea with him. In fact, to the extent that the topic is something that is discussed in the social environment, we would expect an accentuated amount of media message perception and knowledge within any congruency type. That is, if we consider adolescents who fit into the incongruent (ahead) category in comparison with a particular other, the adolescents who engage in conversation would, we expect, perceive more messages and hold more knowledge than their nontalking counterparts. The reason for this expectation is the belief that talking about a topic raises its salience to the conversants and may also give information about the topic the character of "social currency." Thus, talking may be said to increase awareness of the topic and to attach a social value to information concerning it. The more topic-related messages one perceives in the media, and the more knowledge one holds, the more social rewards are available in conversation.

We can conceive, then, of another social information need that we would expect to complement or enhance in most cases the congruency concepts explicated above. Just as adolescents in different congruency types may be expected to need different amounts and kinds of information, so too do adolescents who are in *talking* or *nontalking* conditions with regard to the topic. Within any particular congruency type, talking should enhance media message perception and knowledge.

Criterion Variables

Having discussed the independent variables (need states), let us now consider the criterion variables, which we place under the general rubric of *gratifications.* Two different types of dependent variables are considered. First, we wish to elucidate a *communication activity* which we argue is activated by the need states above. Next, we examine various types of *knowledge* measures which should be associated with the need states and the communication activity.

Message discrimination is the term used to describe the communication activity above. In this concept, we attempt to assess the amount of information in the media about a specific topic (family planning in this case) that is attended to by respondents during a specified time period. Through open-ended questioning with probes, we elicit messages perceived by the respondent about the subject, and the number of messages mentioned by a person with regard to a specific medium is counted. Then, we sum all of the messages perceived in all of the media to get a total message discrimination score for each respondent (see Clarke and Kline, 1974; Miller, Morrison and Kline, 1974).[4] Message discrimination is employed here, rather than media time-use measures, because we believe that it more realistically measures what is obtained from media exposure, and does not confound the "amount" of media used with the distribution of number and type of messages recalled by the audience in the media over time.

The *knowledge* measures are three: knowledge of family planning *information sources* (i.e., help centers and clinics in which family planning information is disseminated); knowledge of *birth control methods;* and knowledge of the *correct fertility time* of a female.[5]

The two types of dependent variables, message discrimination and knowledge, should be related to the independent variables as elucidated above. But they are also related to one another, according to our argument. That is, message discrimination should be positively related to all three types of knowledge; knowledge gratification may be seen as a product of mass media behavior on the part of the audience member, as the uses and gratifications model would predict.

While message discrimination and knowledge should be directly related to the need states and to each other, their relationship to each other should be mediated by the types of need states in which an adolescent exists. So it is that we expect message discrimination to be related to the holding of relatively unique pieces of knowledge available in media in the case of an adolescent in the incongruent (ahead) condition. Female fertility time knowledge fits this character of uniqueness, and we would therefore expect message discrimination to be related to holding this knowledge among adolescents in the ahead condition. On the other hand, message discrimination should be related to more commonplace knowledge-holding among adolescents in the congruent and behind states.

These general remarks about how the various concepts fit together guide the presentation of our analysis, the form of which is presented more schematically in the next section.

ANALYSIS DESIGN AND HYPOTHESES

First, we wish to ascertain whether our two general conceptions of need for information are interrelated or perhaps surrogates for one another. We might hypothesize that age and sex (maturational needs) and congruency and talking typologies (social information needs) might be so highly related as to represent the same need phenomenon. We address this question in our first analysis, using cross-sectional data from Time I only. With this test performed, we assess the impact of age and sex and the congruency and talking typologies on message discrimination and knowledge of information sources, birth control methods, and female fertility time, again using the Time I data. We conclude the cross-sectional analysis with an examination of the correlational links between the discrimination of messages and family planning knowledge measures, controlling for the maturational and social information need states. This analysis is a precursor of the longitudinal analysis in which we attempt to assess the effects of a media manipulation on knowledge gain, controlling for the various types of information need.

The longitudinal analysis that follows, then, will address first the gross effects of the media campaign by examining city differences in the criterion variables over time. The analysis of covariance (as suggested by Campbell and Stanley, 1966) or an equivalent will be utilized to assess these results. Next, we perform a more sensitive analysis of the effects of the media campaign on respondents within the media city by examining the effects while treating the information need types as contingent conditions.

We will test the following hypotheses:

(1) The criterion measures of message discrimination and knowledge increase in value with age and are higher for girls within each age category.

(2) Perceived knowledge congruency is related to message discrimination such that adolescents in the incongruent (ahead) state perceive the most messages, followed by the congruent adolescents and the incongruent (behind) adolescents.

(2a) Message discrimination is higher for adolescents in the talking condition than for those in the nontalking condition, within each congruency condition.

(3) There is a positive relationship between perceived comparative knowledge and actual knowledge. That is, ahead adolescents know more information sources and birth control methods than do congruent adolescents and the congruent adolescents know more than behind adolescents. The relationship will also hold for female fertility time knowledge.

(3a) Adolescents in the talking condition score higher on the three knowledge measures than those in the nontalking condition, within each congruency condition.

(4) Mass media message discrimination is positively related to knowledge of family planning sources of information, birth control methods, and correct female fertility time.

(4a) The relationships between message discrimination and knowledge measures are *not* affected contingently by maturational information needs (age and sex), in that there is a concomitant growth of message discrimination and knowledge as age increases, and in that females attain higher levels of each within age categories.

(4b) The relationships between message discrimination and knowledge *are* affected contingently by perceived knowledge congruency. The relationship between message discrimination and knowledge of birth control methods and information sources is strongest for adolescents in the congruent and behind conditions. The relationship between message discrimination and knowledge of correct female fertility time is strongest for adolescents in the ahead condition.

(4c) The relationships between message discrimination and knowledge measures are stronger for adolescents in the talking condition than for those in the nontalking condition.

(5) Message discrimination is greater in the media city subsequent to the experimental media manipulation.

(5a) The knowledge measures are higher in the media city subsequent to the media manipulation.

(6) The effects of the mass media campaign on knowledge gain are mediated by the congruency and talking information needs as elucidated in Hypotheses 4b-4c.

In these hypotheses, then, we offer a systematic examination of various conceptions of information need as they relate directly to media exposure and knowledge, and as they act contingently to specify the relationship between media exposure and knowledge gain. Both cross-sectional and longitudinal tests are performed in our attempt to understand the interface between audience needs and media effects.

CROSS-SECTIONAL DATA ANALYSIS

Tables 1a-b display data used to assess the relationship between our maturational and social information need measures. That is, we are concerned here with whether age and sex are related to perceived knowledge congruency and talking with father, mother and peer. An examination of Table 1a reveals significant differences by sex but not by age in the amount of talking done with peers and with the mother. Within each age category, the females undertake significantly more interpersonal communication than males with their friends and mothers about family planning. The adolescent-father dyad, however, reveals no significant differences in talking behavior by sex or by age.

Table 1b reveals that perceived knowledge congruency, the other social need state, does not relate significantly to sex or age at all, except for the congruency relationships with father and mother for 14-year-olds. Here we find significant sex differences, with males perceiving themselves significantly more "behind" each parent in family planning knowledge than do females. And while there does appear to be a tendency for older adolescents to perceive themselves as more in the congruent and ahead states with respect to parents and peers, the tendency does not satisfy the criterion of statistical significance.

A few tenuous relationships, then, do exist between the two general types of information need states. Sex is related to talking behavior with two of the three referent others and with congruency perceptions within one age category. Overall, one gets the impression that females do exhibit more social needs for information, and that older adolescents of either sex also tend in this direction. But the evidence is not strong enough to justify treating the maturational need state as a surrogate for the social need state or vice versa. Instead, we will treat the two types of information need as separate for analytic purposes, and simply note here that the relationships that do exist between the two concepts lend some validity to the notion of using talking and perceived congruency states as measures of information need. The links between them and age and sex are what

TABLE 1a

PERCENT TALKING ABOUT FAMILY PLANNING AS A
CONSEQUENCE OF AGE AND SEX

	14		15		16		17	
	M	F	M	F	M	F	M	F
N =	(56)	(53)	(83)	(55)	(85)	(77)	(75)	(51)
With:								
Peers**	11	23	7	35	9	26	9	26
Father	38	35	35	30	40	37	46	44
Mother*	50	75	42	82	47	72	52	71

*Sex is significant with p $<$ .05.
**Sex is significant for all but 14-year olds with p $<$ .05.

TABLE 1b

PERCENT INTERPERSONAL KNOWLEDGE CONGRUENCY ABOUT
FAMILY PLANNING WITH FATHER, MOTHER AND PEER AS A
CONSEQUENCE OF AGE AND SEX

	14		15		16		17	
	M	F	M	F	M	F	M	F
N =	(56)	(53)	(83)	(55)	(85)	(77)	(75)	(51)
With Peer:								
Ahead	14	12	8	10	12	11	16	27
Congruent	80	74	81	83	78	71	74	61
Behind	6	14	11	7	10	18	10	12
Father:*								
Ahead	0	9	6	4	7	7	13	16
Congruent	26	46	31	49	33	46	46	53
Behind	75	46	63	46	61	47	41	31
Mother:*								
Ahead	2	4	6	4	5	8	7	8
Congruent	20	44	30	41	32	40	53	55
Behind	78	52	64	55	63	52	41	37

*Sex is significant for the 14-year old age group with p $<$ .05.

we would expect intuitively given the face validity of the need of older
adolescents, and particularly females, for family planning information.

We test the face validity of age and sex (maturational need) as measures of
information need in our next analysis. In Table 2, the impact of the
maturational need on perception of media messages and knowledge of
information sources, birth control methods and correct fertility time is assessed.
Arrayed are the mean number of messages, sources, and methods, as well as the
percentage of respondents correct on fertility time for each age group by sex.
The effect of age and sex on knowledge of sources and methods is obvious. For
each, knowledge is lowest for 14-year-old boys and highest for 17-year-old girls.
This finding supports our prediction in Hypothesis 1 that knowledge increases
with age and is higher for females than males. Sex alone significantly

TABLE 2

FAMILY PLANNING MESSAGES DISCRIMINATED, INFORMATION SOURCES,
BIRTH CONTROL METHODS AND CORRECT FEMALE FERTILITY TIME
AS A CONSEQUENCE OF AGE AND SEX

	14		15		16		17	
	M	F	M	F	M	F	M	F
N =	(56)	(53)	(83)	(55)	(85)	(77)	(75)	(51)
(Mean)								
Messages	2.4	1.9	2.5	2.7	1.5	3.4	2.6	3.2
Sources*	1.3	1.8	1.5	1.9	1.6	2.2	1.7	2.3
Methods*	1.0	1.7	1.4	2.5	1.5	2.6	2.0	2.6
(%)								
Time**	25	25	25	39	25	49	32	53

*Age and Sex are significant with $p < .05$.
**Age is significant for girls and there is a Sex difference with $p < .05$.

discriminates on knowledge of the correct fertility time, with females once again holding more knowledge than males. Within the female sex, age is a significant factor with regard to knowledge of fertility time—the older girls, naturally, knowing more than the younger ones.

The only case where maturational need structure does not perform as predicted is that of messages discriminated. Here, neither age nor sex is related, although the mean number of messages is higher for girls than boys in the 15 to 17 age range, lending partial support for the hypothesis. There is also a weak monotonic relationship between age and messages discriminated within the female group.

But in the statistical sense, we have a null finding with regard to messages—for which we can only suggest an explanation. It could be that the messages perceived by younger males belong more in the "public affairs" category (e.g., overpopulation), where boys are usually a year or two ahead in information-holding, than in the "sexuality" category, where girls are usually a year or two ahead.

Given that higher knowledge implies a greater need for that knowledge, we have demonstrated, with but one exception, that the biological maturation process creates a need for information about family planning matters. Message discrimination provides the exception to the rule, but even in this case the pattern of relationships fits the hypothesis.

Now we need to look at the same criterion variables—messages and the three kinds of knowledge—in relation to the social information needs. Hypotheses 2 and 2a predict that message discrimination should be greater for those in the ahead condition than for those in the congruent (next highest) or behind states. Moreover, adolescents who talk with significant others about the topic should perceive more messages than those who do not talk. Table 3a allows us to assess the tenability of those hypotheses.

The perceived knowledge congruency typology significantly predicts message discrimination in the hypothesized pattern, as does talking. It makes no

TABLE 3

CRITERION VARIABLES AS A CONSEQUENCE OF TALKING AND PERCEIVED
INTERPERSONAL KNOWLEDGE CONGRUENCY ABOUT FAMILY PLANNING
WITH FATHER, MOTHER AND PEER

	Talking			Not Talking		
	Ahead	Congruent	Behind	Ahead	Congruent	Behind
(a) Message Discriminations						
With:						
Peer*	(12)5.42	(60)4.05	(18)3.50	(53)3.08	(311)2.28	(38)2.24
Father*	(16)4.06	(76)3.59	(92)2.43	(20)3.35	(115)2.85	(153)2.04
Mother*	(19)3.32	(133)3.51	(154)2.54	(9)2.78	(65)2.40	(124)1.85
(b) Family Planning Sources						
With:						
Peer**	2.75	2.30	2.11	1.94	1.70	1.74
Father**	2.56	2.07	2.00	1.90	1.68	1.59
Mother**	2.11	2.09	1.92	2.22	1.59	1.54
(c) Birth Control Methods						
With:						
Peer**	2.42	2.60	2.28	2.25	1.82	2.00
Father*	2.38	2.51	1.73	2.90	2.13	1.52
Mother***	2.21	2.47	1.88	2.00	2.08	1.49
(d) Percent Correct Fertility Time						
With:						
Peer	30	38	39	35	35	36
Father	40	28	37	35	38	35
Mother	39	34	36	33	38	31

NOTE: Cell sizes for Tables 3a-d are in parentheses in Table 0a.
  *Talking and Congruency are significant with $p < .05$.
 **Talking is significant with $p < .05$.
***Congruency is significant with $p < .05$.

difference which significant other is paired with the adolescent for the perceived knowledge comparison; if the adolescent perceives himself or herself ahead of a referent in this regard, more messages are discriminated. Congruent adolescents perceive fewer messages than aheads and more than behinds, except for one case (adolescent-mother dyad, talking condition) in which the congruents perceived more messages on the average than the aheads. Talking also produces message discrimination in the predicted direction, with those who engaged in conversation with any partner higher across the board than those who did no talking. These marked consistencies provide strong support for our hypotheses.

One further observation may be made on the evidence in Table 3a. There is greater media message perception or reliance on nonsocial sources of information when we look at an adolescent-peer knowledge comparison than when we examine the adolescent-father dyad. Similarly, more messages are discriminated when we consider the adolescent-father dyad than when the adolescent-mother knowledge comparison is observed. These findings hold with a couple of exceptions whether the adolescent is ahead, congruent with, or behind the referents in perceived knowledge, and in both talking conditions.

This finding, paradoxical at first blush, may be interpreted as follows: the number of messages discriminated is a measure of *distance* between the adolescent and the referent—the more reliance on nonsocial sources by the adolescent when a particular other is considered, the more distant is that other from the adolescent in providing information about the topic. According to this interpretation, the peer is most distant, followed by the father and mother. The fact that the mother is closest to the adolescent in these terms has some intuitive appeal, since she is a likely source of information about this delicate subject for both girls and boys. The father, on the other hand, is less likely to be approached for information, and the peer is least likely. This is not to say that fathers necessarily know less than mothers about family planning (although this is true) or that no family planning discourse takes place within the peer group (although the future orientation of family planning makes the topic less likely for conversation than immediate sexual relationships). But the mother, because of her availability to the adolescent for conversation as well as her knowledge of the topic area, is likely to be "closer" than the other two referents.[6]

In Table 3b, we note that the mean number of family planning information sources named follows the same general pattern as that of messages. In this case the effect of the perceived knowledge typology is not statistically significant; but talking does significantly predict higher source knowledge. Following the logic of Hypotheses 3 and 3a, we would argue that there is some support for the notion that the social information need predicts higher knowledge. Hypothesis 3a is clearly supported, while Hypothesis 3 is somewhat substantiated by the pattern of means (although statistical significance is not attained).

The outcome of Table 3c is less clear. The perceived knowledge typology works to differentiate knowledge of birth control methods only when comparisons for the adolescents with the parents are made. Moreover, the congruent adolescents in this instance appear to know more than their incongruent (ahead) counterparts. In this case, we find that perceived knowledge is not related monotonically to actual knowledge as posited in Hypothesis 3. A further complicating factor is the fact that talking only predicts greater knowledge when the peer and father-adolescent dyads are considered. The overall impression we gain from an examination of this table is that the two social information need states do not predict well when birth control knowledge is considered.

Similarly, Table 3d reveals no relationship between the perceived knowledge typology or talking state and knowledge of the correct female fertility time. Clearly, the maturational needs of age and sex are stronger predictors of methods and fertility time knowledge than the social information need states. The power of the two general types of need states is thus differentiated by the types of knowledge predicted by them. Maturational needs prevail when less commonplace knowledge (methods and fertility time) is considered. The social information needs, on the other hand, are strong predictors of message discrimination and knowledge of information sources. In later analyses, we will examine how the maturational needs and social needs mediate the relationship between media exposure and knowledge, and thus apply a stronger test to the efficacy of the two general types of need states.

First, however, let us look at the relationships between message discrimination and knowledge without controlling for any of the need measures. Table 4 presents product-moment correlations between the number of messages discriminated and the three family planning knowledge measures. Clearly, perception of messages is related to family planning knowledge in the case of information sources and birth control methods. There is no relationship, however, between fertility time knowledge and messages. We would attribute the lack of a relationship in this latter case to the fact that fertility time knowledge is so unique and scarce in the population (as evidenced by Table 2) that it varies independently of any message recall about the general topic of family planning. For information sources and birth control methods, however, we can interpret the relationship with message discrimination as an indicator of *gratification* from media exposure.

To sum up our knowledge to this point: (1) two types of information need have been discovered—maturational needs and social information needs—that differentially predict media message discrimination, as well as various types of knowledge about family planning; (2) in the case of maturational needs (age and sex), we find that knowledge of information sources, birth control methods, and female fertility time is strongly predicted, but message discrimination is not; (3) the social information needs (perceived knowledge congruency and talking) are related to message discrimination and knowledge of information sources, but knowledge of birth control methods and female fertility time is not systematically predicted; (4) message discrimination is related to knowledge of birth control methods and information sources, but not to knowledge of fertility time. These analyses have been aimed at establishing the viability of our unobtrusive measures of information need through their ability to differentiate certain kinds of message recall and knowledge. Further, we wished to present evidence linking message discrimination to knowledge. The thrust of the findings presented so far is that, by and large, we have useful measures of information need and that the preliminary work of linking these to message discrimination and knowledge justifies their further exploitation. This we do next in an attempt to judge how different types of information need affect the relationship between media messages and knowledge. In this analysis, and the experimental analyses to follow, we address the core of uses and gratifications theory; testing the proposition that audience needs are an important contributor to whatever effects occur as a result of media exposure.

TABLE 4

CORRELATIONS BETWEEN FAMILY PLANNING MESSAGE DISCRIMINATION
AND CRITERION MEASURES OF FAMILY PLANNING KNOWLEDGE (N=535)

Family Planning Sources	.36*
Birth Control Information	.46*
Correct Fertility Time	−.06

*Correlations are significant with p < .05.

Turning, then, to Table 5, we present evidence germane to the proposition (in Hypothesis 4) that maturational information needs do not act contingently to modify the relationship between messages and knowledge. The correlations between the media exposure variable and knowledge measures are sustained across all age categories for both males and females, except for the additional evidence for no correlation between media messages and fertility time knowledge. The lack of any systematic pattern in the correlations across the contingent conditions suggests that the conditions do not affect the relationship between messages and knowledge. Since age and sex did not significantly relate to message discrimination in Table 2, it is understandable why the maturational need measure does not work to mitigate the media-knowledge relationship in this case. Although age and sex are appealing measures of need from the point of view of simplicity and parsimony, and despite the results of earlier analyses, their failure to predict differences in this case is good cause for turning to other measures of need.

Do the social information need concepts do any better in making sense of the relationships between message perception and knowledge? That is, can we find different relationships between media exposure and knowledge when we consider people with different needs for information? Table 6 indicates that we can, to a degree. First looking at Table 6a, we find some support for our prediction that a stronger relationship should exist between messages and knowledge of information sources when the congruent people are considered. Significant correlations exist between message discrimination and knowledge of sources in each case where the adolescent perceives himself to know the same amount about family planning as does a significant other. We can also see that when adolescents perceive themselves behind significant others in knowledge there are significant correlations between messages and knowledge of sources (although not as many). Although this pattern is inconsistent, it lends some support to the idea that, for people in the behind condition, the message perception—knowledge relationship should be stronger than for those in the ahead condition.

It would appear, then, that people who rely less on nonsocial sources of information (the congruent and behind adolescents) gain from media the more

TABLE 5
CORRELATIONS BETWEEN FAMILY PLANNING MESSAGE DISCRIMINATION AND FAMILY PLANNING SOURCES, METHODS, AND CORRECT FERTILITY TIME FOR AGE AND SEX

	14		15		16		17	
	M	*F*	*M*	*F*	*M*	*F*	*M*	*F*
N =	*(56)*	*(53)*	*(83)*	*(55)*	*(85)*	*(77)*	*(75)*	*(51)*
Sources	.36*	.28*	.29*	.34*	.24*	.43*	.29*	.41*
Methods	.64*	.42*	.37*	.44*	.42*	.30*	.56*	.34*
Time	−.20	.17	−.12	.13	−.06	−.03	−.11	−.06

*Correlations are significant with p < .05.

commonplace information. But now let us look at some paradoxical features of Table 6a. In the first place, it seems that the salience of the topic, as measured by adolescent conversations with others about it, does not seem to make much difference to the impact of message perception on knowledge. Contrary to prediction, the relationships are just as strong (or stronger) in the nontalking condition as in the talking condition. Salience does not contribute to our understanding of how media exposure and knowledge relate.

One further complication is the significant correlation between message perception and knowledge of sources in the peer, no talking, ahead condition. That is, when considering people who perceive themselves as ahead of their peers in knowledge about family planning and who do no talking about the topic, we find that message discrimination and knowledge of sources are related significantly. This finding goes counter to our expectation, since we hypothesized that message perception and knowledge would be related for aheads only in cases of unique knowledge, like correct fertility time.

A similar pattern appears in Table 6b, where we once again observe the significant correlations in the congruent and behind conditions—this time for a different type of knowledge, birth control methods. We note again that the salience of the topic, as gauged by talking and nontalking, seems to make no difference to these relationships. And again we find an unpredicted correlation between messages and knowledge for people who perceive themselves ahead of their peers in knowledge, this time in the talking condition. These findings bear

TABLE 6

Correlations Between Family Planning Message Discrimination and Criterion Measure of Family Planning Information Within Contingent Conditions of Talking and Perceived Interpersonal Knowledge Congruency About Family Planning

	Talking			Not Talking		
	Ahead	*Congruent*	*Behind*	*Ahead*	*Congruent*	*Behind*
(a) Family Planning Sources						
With:						
Peer	(12).30	(60).35*	(18).14	(53) .32*	(311).34*	(38)−.08
Father	(16).18	(76).38*	(42).17*	(20)−.01	(115).47*	(153) .46*
Mother	(19).06	(133).40*	(154).17*	(9) .49	(65).28*	(124) .36*
(b) Birth Control Methods						
With:						
Peer	.57*	.46*	.78*	.18	.43*	.16
Father	.26	.48*	.34*	.42	.50*	.36*
Mother	.16	.52*	.34*	.56	.54*	.31*
(c) Correct Fertility Time						
With:						
Peer	.13	−.12	−.15	−.05	−.01	−.01
Father	.43	−.12	.00	.04	.03	−.03
Mother	.53	−.07	−.05	.40	−.05	.01

NOTE: Cell sizes for Tables 6a-c are found in parentheses in Table 6a.
*Correlations are significant with p < .05.

out, for the most part, our ideas about how the social information typology should affect the connection between message perception and knowledge.

The only interpretation we can make about the two unpredicted significant correlations in the ahead of peer condition is that the proposed asymptotic character of the message-knowledge relationship is not as straightforward as we first believed. Instead of persons who perceive themselves ahead of *any* referent being more knowledgeable, it appears that this holds only for people who believe they are ahead of their parents. The adolescents who perceive themselves as ahead of their peers, on the other hand, have not reached the point where the media can tell them very little that is new, and so they are able to gain information about information sources and birth control methods. Those who are ahead of the parents in perceived knowledge, on the other hand, already know so much about the topic that they can gain only the most unique pieces of information.

The test of this latter proposition, in Table 6c, does not conform to our expectations, at least by the standard of statistical significance. No significant relationships exist at all between message discrimination and knowledge of correct female fertility time. The strongest of these nonsignificant correlations, however, are found in the case where the adolescent perceives himself or herself as ahead of the parents in knowledge about family planning.

To highlight the findings in this complex table: (1) in the case of congruent and behind adolescents, message perception and knowledge of information sources and birth control methods are related for the most part, supporting Hypothesis 4b; (2) contrary to prediction, the salience of the topic (measured by talking) makes no difference to these relationships; (3) contrary to prediction, no relationship exists between message discrimination and knowledge of fertility time; (4) contrary to prediction, relationships do exist between message discrimination and knowledge of information sources and birth control methods in the ahead-of-peer condition.

This last finding we have attributed to the character of the peer referent. Being ahead of the peer does not mean the same thing as being ahead of the parents. If one perceives onself as ahead of the parents, this seems to preclude learning from the media all but the most unique pieces of information. Being ahead of the peer, however, does not imply this knowledge position.

Before moving on, however, it should be noted that, according to Table 6c, there does seem to be a tendency for message perception and knowledge of fertility to be related among the ahead-of-parent adolescents, even though this has not quite attained statistical significance.

The longitudinal data analysis is next, in which the relationships discussed above will this time be examined as functions of the experimental manipulation carried out in the "Media City." We have used the samples from both the media and control cities in our previous analysis, but now we will concentrate on each city separately.

EXPERIMENTAL DATA ANALYSIS

First, let us look at the gross effects of the media campaign in Table 7. We can see that the manipulation was successful in that there were significantly more messages discriminated in the media city than in the other. To measure message discrimination in this case, we asked the respondents if they had heard any family planning commercials on the radio during the period when the commercials were being played. If they said yes, and 46% said they did in the experimental city versus 23% in the control city, we asked what they had heard and on which stations. We then coded as many messages as we could obtain with probes. On the average, .72 messages were heard in the media city, and only .18 in the non-media city. So far as the knowledge variables were concerned, however, the table shows (in line with the negative outcomes of much media effects analysis) no differences by city.

In this instance (and all further between-city comparisons presented below), the statistical significance of any differences found was checked by use of a covariance analysis technique.[7] In the case of the message variable, we used as a covariate the number of radio messages discriminated at Time I. For the other measures, we used the number of information sources or birth control methods known or the percentage of persons correct on fertility time at Time I as the covariates.

Although information sources were a predominant part of our messages, we found no differences in their knowledge after the experiment. Birth control methods were not mentioned in the commercials, but might have been obtained through "spinoff" information-seeking; they apparently were not. Finally, although one radio station carried messages on correct fertility time, we detected no gain in knowledge here either.

Given these findings, our task is now to see whether the introduction into the analysis of measures of information need alters the impression of null media effects conveyed at the gross level. If so, we could state on the basis of experimental evidence that the uses and gratifications model contributes significantly to our understanding of how audience outlook and media use are related to each other.

TABLE 7
FAMILY PLANNING KNOWLEDGE DIFFERENCES AS
A CONSEQUENCE OF MEDIA MANIPULATION

	N =	Media City (90)	Non-Media City (95)
(Mean)			
Number of messages*		.72	.18
Sources		1.44	1.40
Methods		1.61	1.65
(%)			
Fertility time		32	28

*Differences between cities is significant at p < .05.

Adopting a similar approach in this analysis to that which was followed in the correlational examination of message discrimination and knowledge, we ask the question: How are the effects of media messages on knowledge mediated by different information needs? We consider this question by examining the responses of those within the media city, where message effects have been demonstrated. Following our previous argument, we would expect higher mean knowledge of information sources and birth control methods for those people who heard messages during the radio campaign and were in the congruent or behind conditions. The percentages for correct fertility time should be higher for those who heard messages and were in the ahead condition.

Perhaps the most likely candidate for a significant finding would be knowledge of information sources, a prime feature of all radio messages; then fertility time, which was mentioned in a few messages; and lastly, birth control methods, which were not mentioned in any messages. In Tables 8a-c, we present evidence germane to these predictions, separating for the first time the two types of information need. Table 8 refers only to relationships mediated by the knowledge congruency typology; Table 9 presents the same relationships when controlled for talking. We separate knowledge congruency and talking because there were no interactions between the two variables in previous analyses, and we wish to keep as large a cell size as possible.

TABLE 8

FAMILY PLANNING KNOWLEDGE AS A CONSEQUENCE OF MASS MEDIA
CAMPAIGN AND INTERPERSONAL KNOWLEDGE CONGRUENCY FOR
FATHER, MOTHER AND PEER WITHIN MEDIA CITY

	Ahead		Congruent		Behind	
	Messages Heard		Messages Heard		Messages Heard	
	0	1+	0	1+	0	1+
(a) Mean Information Sources						
With:						
Peer	(5)1.40	(4)2.25	(46)1.10	(22)2.00*	(6)1.00	(7)2.00*
Father	(3)2.00	(6)2.17	(21)1.10	(18)1.78*	(32)1.09	(10)2.30*
Mother	**	**	(22)1.09	(17)2.05	(31)1.16	(16)2.06*
(b) Mean Birth Control Methods						
With:						
Peer	1.00	3.25	1.39	2.05	.33	2.57
Father	2.00	3.33	1.38	2.44	1.13	1.50
Mother	**	**	1.36	2.71	1.23	1.94
(c) Percent Correct Fertility Time						
With:						
Peer	20	75	30	31	17	28
Father	100	60	29	44	18	10
Mother	**	**	27	52	25	18

NOTE: Cell sizes for Tables 8a-c are found in parentheses in Table 8a.
  *Significant difference between 0 and 1+ messages, p < .05.
**No adolescents in ahead mother cell.

Looking, then, at Table 8a, we see that the predictions made in the case of knowledge about information sources are supported. Adolescents who consider that they know the same or less than a referent other, and who had heard one or more of the radio messages, do know more sources of family planning information (with one exception). This finding lends considerable credence to the uses and gratifications approach: although no knowledge effects were found from the media campaign, such effects do appear when account is taken of the needs of the audience for information.

The evidence on the other two foci of Table 8, however, is not so positive. Neither birth control methods nor correct fertility time are differentiated by message perception, controlling for the knowledge congruency states. The finding for birth control methods is not surprising, since the radio commercials presented no information about such methods. The finding for fertility time is also understandable, since messages concerning it received little "play" during the campaign (the single station carrying this commercial also had the smallest audience).

Before examining Table 9, we should recall our hypotheses concerning the mediating effect of talking. We supposed that since the presence of a talking partner would tend to give the topic some salience, those in the talking condition should be more likely to gain information from messages heard. The evidence of Table 6 should also be recalled, however. There, no clear function of talking in mediating the relationship between message perception and knowledge was discerned.

In Table 9a, the effect of talking is the opposite of what was predicted. That is, message discrimination is related to knowledge for those who have *no* talking partners. Why should persons who know of no one with whom they can share information learn more (in effect) than those who have talking partners? We must once again point to the asymptotic character of the message-knowledge relationship. People who had talking partners knew more than those who did not at Time I, as evidenced in Table 3. In order to gain more information from the campaign, they probably would have had to learn something that was not in the messages themselves. The nontalkers, on the other hand, had no where to go but up (as was the case with the congruent and behind adolescents). Thus, when the effects of messages are considered using the covariance technique (which controls for the Time I level of knowledge) the nontalkers can readily attain statistical significance; while the talkers, who were much higher in knowledge to begin with, were hard pressed to reach still higher levels of knowledge on the basis of the message campaign.

So it is that the significant relationships in Table 9 come about on the "nontalking" side. We should be careful not to miss the point that audience need satisfaction through media may not be possible, if the audience members already know a good deal about the topic. In that event they would be better advised to seek out experts or to read thick tomes than to listen to the radio.

To complete our examination of Table 9, we can see that there are practically no significant relationships for birth control methods or fertility time. Having

TABLE 9

FAMILY PLANNING KNOWLEDGE AS A CONSEQUENCE OF MASS MEDIA
CAMPAIGN ON TALKING WITH FATHER, MOTHER AND PEER WITHIN MEDIA CITY

	Talking		*Not Talking*	
	Messages Heard		*Messages Heard*	
	0	*1+*	*0*	*1+*
(a) Mean Information Sources				
With:				
Peer	(5) .80	(7)2.57	(54)1.14	(27)1.85*
Father	(27)1.29	(12)2.25	(31) .93	(22)1.86*
Mother	(33)1.33	(22)2.18	(25) .80	(12)1.66*
(b) Mean Birth Control Methods				
With:				
Peer	1.40	2.57	1.18	2.26*
Father	.96	2.25	1.45	2.36
Mother	1.15	2.45	1.32	2.08
(c) Percent Correct Fertility Time				
With:				
Peer	20	28	27	38
Father	25	41	29	31
Mother	27	40	28	25

NOTE: Cell sizes for Tables 9a-c are found in parentheses in Table 9a.
*Significant difference between 0 and 1+ messages, $p < .05$.

recited our interpretation of this null phenomenon in connection with Table 8, we will not bore the reader with more of the same here.

We might, however, offer some further evidence in nontabular form that will give the reader a fuller picture of the experimental effects of the media campaign. Approximately 57% of the radio messages discriminated in the media city concerned sources mentioned in the campaign or some aspect of the scenarios embodied in the messages. None of these messages was perceived in the control city. Moreover, the fact that an adolescent said that he heard "something" on the radio did not produce differences in knowledge acquisition when analyses were carried out. Rather, it was the adolescent's ability to recall one or more of the *messages* that he or she heard which provided the additional power to add knowledge to the adolescent's repertoire. It is message discrimination, rather than mere exposure, that seems to bring about gains in information holding.

To sum up the results of the experimental analysis, we may say that many of our ideas about how media effects and audience needs relate have been borne out. We also find strong compatibility between this analysis and the cross-sectional analysis. Those in the congruent and behind states, as well as those in the nontalking condition, gained information from the campaign. This seems to be the case because the adolescents in these conditions had not reached the point where it was difficult to add *new* information from media sources. The aheads and the talkers had reached this asymptote, and could not gain at the same rate as the others.

More generally, the experimental analysis suggests that some reports of "no significant effects" in traditional mass communication research findings may have been inaccurate or incomplete. If the investigators concerned had studied different dependent variables (knowledge gain rather than attitude change) and taken account of those needs of people that were liable to enhance or inhibit effects, their conclusions might have been different. After all, no significant knowledge effects were detected in this study at the gross level of analysis, but once certain, possibly influential, contingent conditions were spelled out in detail, evidence of the occurrence of such mediating effects became apparent. It is at the interface of audience need and media provision, then, where mass communication is most likely to have an impact on some of its consumers.

SUMMARY AND CONCLUSIONS

One way of summarizing the implications of this study is to note that although media use may not always be premeditated in the sense suggested by Katz, Blumler and Gurevitch, it may reflect a relatively unconscious process of "planning" that is influenced by characteristics of the social system in which the audience member is situated. For example, only 6% of our respondents claimed that they had actually "sought" family planning information in the month before the initial interview. Nevertheless, striking differences in message perception and knowledge were detected when different kinds of adolescents were considered—that is, those who held different positions according to the knowledge congruency and talking typologies. *Gains* in knowledge as a result of the campaign were also made by those who knew the same or less in relation to others around them, rather than by those who knew more. Since these congruent and behind adolescents actually knew less than their ahead counterparts at Time I, there is some evidence here against the "knowledge gap" hypothesis proposed by some authors (Tichenor, Donohue and Olien, 1970) to suggest that information inequalities are actually widened by mass media exposure. At any rate, those taking part in this experiment who originally knew less managed to learn more from the campaign than did the others. Presumably the usefulness of this information to those who acquired it should be investigated in subsequent research, but it might entail pulling oneself ahead of, or even with, significant others in knowledge perception. To the extent that this happens, another effect of media exposure would be highlighted—changing the character of the information need state that led to the original media use. Thus, needs could be seen as continually shifting, not only changing in response to media exposure but also giving rise in turn to new patterns of media use.

Although this experiment was conducted in two cities in the American Midwest, some of its implications may have a wider applicability than just to the population included in the study. The utility of the unobtrusive measurement of information need seems to have been demonstrated here, as has been the need to consider the place of the individual in his *communication* environment rather than the usual profile of his demographic characteristics.

Furthermore, in concentrating on a particular topic, we have been able to elucidate a number of factors that are relevant to the acquisition of knowledge about it. We have made such distinctions as "commonplace" and "unique" information, which, though not highly discriminating, have shed some light on the kind of information that is gained from media by persons with different kinds of need. A similar approach will eventually be adopted with regard to three other topics under investigation in our wider study—job aspirations and drug and alcohol use.

We might expect different factors to prove influential when these other subjects become the focus of study. Certainly the taboo character of family planning information and its relative paucity in the media contributed to the findings presented here. Whereas few adolescents thought they knew more than their parents about family planning, the relationship could be different in the case of drugs, where many teenagers can draw on personal experience and some parents can only state truisms. The prevalence of drug information could reduce the impact of any set of transmitted commercials. The combination of social system changes and difference of information availability could drastically alter the size of the gains likely to be achieved by a campaign. Perhaps in the case of drugs virtually all teenagers are near the highest levels of knowledge that can be supplied by the media. In that event, null effects would be explained by the lack of a need for the information that the media provide.

To conclude, we have been told for years that mass communication research must take account of the audience member's social context when assessing effects. Our attention has also been repeatedly directed to the characteristic shortcomings of studies conducted in laboratories (due to their artificiality) and in the field (due to their cross-sectional character and lack of control). More recently, the literature has reflected issues posed by the uses and gratifications approach, for example, that effects cannot be understood without an examination of audience needs. In this study an attempt has been made to encompass these major trends of thought in the field. In future publications, we will further develop the ideas set forth here and, hopefully, promote a better understanding of the relationship between audience gratifications and mass media effects.

NOTES

1. The middle-sized cities were chosen on the basis of having isolated local media environments, in that messages produced in one city would not reach the audience of the other (ascertained through commercial audience data). This condition would ensure that a media campaign in one city would not contaminate the control group. Moreover, the two cities have similar demographic characteristics. Data reported here encompass only one of the four experimental manipulations in this study, the others dealing with occupational, alcohol, and drug information. Each of these campaigns entailed a research design similar to the one outlined in this paper, so that we have four separate experiments, each with controls for external effects and sensitization. Data from these later experiments will be reported in future publications.

2. The messages were presented on the three radio stations in the media city that had

large teenage audiences, based on commercial audience rating figures. They presented scenerios encouraging adolescents to seek further information about family planning, and included names and telephone numbers of information sources on the topic. In addition, these components were combined with a further piece of information—the time of each month when a woman is most likely to get pregnant—in three of the scenarios carried by one station only. National surveys have shown that adolescents are quite ignorant of this most basic piece of family planning information.

It is typically assumed in experimental research that nothing happens in the control group when the experimental manipulation takes place in the experimental group. This assumption may be challenged in many instances, and especially so in a field experiment such as ours, where external influences may impinge upon the control group even though the experimental manipulation cannot. In order to account for such an occurrence, we performed a content analysis of the media in both cities during the media campaign. This analysis revealed no significant differences between the cities in terms of the information environment about family planning, except for the additional information provided by our campaign in the media city.

3. In actuality, the sample in each city was divided into three subgroups, those mentioned in the text and one group that served as a means to measure the *maturation* effects of the media messages. That is, we have two groups in each city which are interviewed immediately after the experimental manipulation and one group which is not interviewed until several months after the media campaign to test for long-range effects of the messages. Data from this group will not be reported in this paper.

4. The message discrimination measure was produced by asking the respondent what he or she had seen in each of seven media about the topic of family planning within the previous month. The responses were coded and summed within and across media to provide the measure of total message discrimination about the topic. The media included newspapers, books, magazines, television, film, billboards, and radio.

5. Knowledge of family planning information sources was measured by asking the respondent to name places he knew about where information or services regarding family planning could be obtained. The responses for each adolescent were summed to yield this measure of knowledge. Likewise, the knowledge of birth control methods consists of the sum for each respondent of all the birth control methods that could be named. The measure of knowledge of the correct fertility time of a female was derived by asking the respondent when a woman would be most likely to get pregnant, and asking the adolescent to choose the correct answer from four alternatives: immediately before her monthly menstrual period, during her menstrual·period, immediately after her monthly period, or about two weeks after her period. This item, developed in conjunction with family planning experts, is answered correctly by choosing the last response, although the assumption of a regular 28-day menstrual cycle is built into the answer. The item has been used in several national studies of family planning knowledge.

6. To quantify this notion of distance between the adolescent and the three referent others, we performed a *conjoint measurement analysis* of the data in Table 3a. In this analysis, the message discrimination scores for each cell of the table are input into a scaling algorithm which produce row and column scores for the matrix. That is, scores are produced for the peer, father, and mother rows, and the ahead, congruent, and behind columns. We found that *in the talking condition*, the row scores produced by the program were: peer, 1.96; father, 1.08; and mother, .03. Thus, the peer was most distant, followed by the father and mother. In the *nontalking condition*, row scores obtained were equal for all three referents. Thus, talking was found to be the major component of distance. See Luce and Tukey (1964), Krantz (1964), Tversky (1964), and McFarland (1968) for technical details of the measurement procedure.

7. The cell entries in the covariance analysis tables are mean scores unadjusted for the covariate scores. Significance test indications are therefore of more substantive value in assessing the difference between means.

REFERENCES

CAMPBELL, D. T. and J. C. STANLEY (1966) Experimental and Quasi-Experimental Designs for Research. Chicago: Rand-McNally.

CHAFFEE, S. H. and J. M. McLEOD (1973) "Interpersonal approaches to communication research." American Behavioral Scientist 16: 469-499.

CLARKE, P. and F. G. KLINE (1974) "Media effects reconsidered: some new strategies for communication research." Communication Research 1, 2 (May).

FESTINGER, L. (1954) "A theory of social comparison processes." Human Relations 7: 117-140.

JONES, E. E. and H. B. GERARD (1967) Foundations of Social Psychology. New York: John Wiley.

KATZ, E., J. G. BLUMLER, and M. GUREVITCH (1974) "Utilization of mass communication by the individual: an overview," in J. G. Blumler and E. Katz (eds.) The Uses of Mass Communications: Current Perspectives on Gratifications Research. Beverly Hills: Sage.

KATZ, E., M. GUREVITCH, and H. HAAS (1973) "On the use of the media for important things." American Sociological Review 35 (April): 164-181.

KRANTZ, D. H. (1964) "Conjoint measurement: the Luce-Tukey axiomatization and some extensions." Journal of Mathematical Psychology 1: 248-277.

LUCE, D. R. and J. W. TUKEY (1964) "Conjoint measurement: a new type of fundamental measurement." Journal of Mathematical Psychology 1: 1-27.

McFARLAND, D. D. (1968) "An extension of conjoint measurement to test the theory of quasi-perfect mobility." Mighican Studies in Mathematical Sociology. Paper 3: 10.

MILLER. P. V., A. J. MORRISON, and F. G. KLINE (1974) "Approaches to characterizing information environments." Paper presented to the session in analytical technique and methodology in communication research, International Communication Association, New Orleans.

TICHENOR, P. J., G. A. DONOHUE, and C. N. OLIEN (1970) "Mass media flow and differential growth in knowledge." Public Opinion Quarterly 34: 159-170.

TVERSKY, A. (1964) Additive Choice Structures. Ph.D. dissertation. University of Michigan, Ann Arbor.

Chapter 7

TESTING THE VALIDITY OF GRATIFICATION MEASURES THROUGH POLITICAL EFFECTS ANALYSIS

Jack M. McLeod and Lee B. Becker

THE "HYPODERMIC" PERSUASION MODEL OF MASS MEDIA EFFECTS is by now well buried under a mound of rhetoric—topped off by a layer of supportive data. Null findings from media campaign studies have testified to the inadequacy of this simple learning model, which predicts that repetitive exposure of media messages is sufficient to change the attitudes and behaviors of large numbers of people in important ways.[1] At its worst, this model makes the tacit assumption that media content equals audience effect.

While the hypodermic thesis is deficient in many respects, the antithesis to this model may be no less flawed. The "limited effects" model, by making the audience member so active and selective that any effect can be obtained from any message, comes close to substituting the fable of the omnificent audience for what Bauer and Bauer (1960) have called the "myth of the omnipotent media."[2] If the receiver can get anything he or she wants out of any message, then the content of the media does not really matter. Whatever the implications of this conclusion might be for public policy, it is a deceptive guide for communication research. In rejecting the hypodermic effects model, we should avoid developing an unwarranted disregard for the effects of communication.

AUTHORS' NOTE: The research reported here was supported in part by grants from the John and Mary R. Markle Foundation and the Social Science Research Council of Great Britain and by the University of Wisconsin Graduate School. The authors thank various members of and visitors to the Centre for Television Research, University of Leeds, England, where the senior author spent the spring of 1973 as a Visiting Research Fellow. Jay G. Blumler, Michael Gurevitch and Ray Brown deserve particular thanks. The authors also acknowledge the assistance of Dean Ziemke in preparation of the paper.

USES AND GRATIFICATIONS RESEARCH

The uses and gratifications research tradition may be seen as a reaction to the simplicity of the hypodermic model and to its overstatement of media effects. It is our contention that this reaction should not lead away from a concern with effects; rather, that systematic relationships between gratifications sought and effects represent an important and perhaps necessary step in the development of gratifications research. It is true that the early gratification studies in, the Lazarsfeld-Stanton series (1942, 1944, 1949) were concerned with functions for the person rather than with the broader issues of social effects, but the more recent revival of interest in this research tradition here and throughout the world makes the link with effects research more feasible (see Katz, Blumler and Gurevitch, 1974). It should no longer be thought of as coterminous with the limited effects model.

The designs of the early gratifications studies did not permit easy combination or comparison with other research strategies. As summarized by Katz and his colleagues (1974), the limitations of these studies included their dependence upon open-ended statements of needs that make comparisons difficult; classification of these statements in a qualitative manner without respect to their prevalence in the population; their failure to tie gratification statements to their social or psychological origins; and their lack of attention to the interrelationships among the various media functions.

Studies in the recent renaissance of gratification research have overcome most of these difficulties, but have by no means solved the host of conceptual and methodological problems inherent in any new research program of broad scope.[3] Major difficulties arise from the conceptualization of media gratifications sought as specific secondary motives derived from the underlying need structure of the person.[4] This "discovery" of motives may come a bit late in that motivation as a research area in social psychology has shown a steady decline in popularity during the past decade. Invariant trait notions of motives have given way to situationally determined motive states; cognition, rather than motivation or personality, seems to be the most promising area of research.

At least three conceptual problems have hindered the development of gratifications research. First, if there is to be a link between media gratifications and underlying motives, more satisfactory classification systems of motives must be used. Invariant trait conceptualizations unresponsive to social situations, such as need achievement, seem ill-suited to any theoretical linkage to media gratifications.[5] Second, it appears that media behavior may be motivated at several different levels of specificity. For example, at one extreme, a person might be viewing television for a precise piece of information, such as who won an election and by how many votes, and at the other extreme a person might be listening to the same program because "it was on" or he was too tired to turn it off. Bogart (1965) would term the latter "pastime" activity as contrasted to motivated behavior, but it is scientifically consistent to say that all of these are motivated but at rather different levels. The problem becomes one of how to develop a conceptual, motivational scheme that handles all levels in a logical manner. Third, it seems reasonable to assume that a person may be oriented to a given type of media fare not by a single motive but rather by a set of motives simultaneously or in sequence over time. Fortunately, recent developments in multivariate statistics make such analyses more feasible.

Solutions to these conceptual problems are dependent upon attention to the proper operationalizations of gratifications sought from media use.[6] Some have approached measurement by inferring needs and media gratifications from the requirements of a person's status and role rather than from more direct methods.[7] There are obvious weaknesses to this approach, including the inability to deal with more than one need at a time. More direct approaches, such as self-report measures, seem preferable, *if* their validity can be established with some certainty. Self-report measures, of course, are dependent on the individual's ability and willingness to tell the researcher why he does what he does with the media.

Unfortunately, little attention has been paid to formal validation of self-report gratification measures. The Blumler and McQuail (1969) research using gratifications sought from political party broadcasts in the 1964 British general elections does provide some evidence relevant to validation. A set of eight items representing reasons for watching party broadcasts and nine items listing reasons people have for avoiding such broadcasts were developed prior to the election from extensive discussions with and questioning of groups of voters residing in the city of Leeds. In the 1964 questionnaire, respondents were then asked to indicate which of these items applied to them. Strength of motivation, indexed by the number of reasons the respondent gave for watching political broadcasts relative to the number of reasons given for avoiding such political fare, was found to be related to the number of broadcasts the voters reported viewing during the campaign, despite a negative association between this motivation index and customary time spent with television. This finding, coupled with data showing strength of motivation to interact with campaign exposure in affecting knowledge gain and shift in party attitudes during the campaign, can be interpreted as validating evidence of the self-report measures. Blumler and McQuail also looked at the relationship between two specific gratifications and a series of dependent variables. Those respondents who said they watched political broadcasts "to remind me of my party's strong points" showed greater levels of selective exposure and sensitivity to campaign issues than did voters who said they watched political broadcasts "to help (me) make up my mind how to vote in an election."

Recent research by McLeod, Becker and Byrnes (1974) found support for the Blumler and McQuail assertion that the gratifications sought from the media can serve as a deterrent of media content effects. Respondents who read political news to make voting decisions and/or to keep up with campaign events showed little tendency to adjust their perceptions of the salience of issues to the content of the newspaper they read, while those not so motivated did show such an agenda setting effect. The Blumler and McQuail and McLeod, Becker and Byrnes findings do give some evidence of the validity of self-report measures; they were not intended, however, as a systematic examination of validity.

FORMAL VALIDITY PROCEDURES

There are four basic approaches to the validation of self-report media gratification items. The first does not involve validity per se, but rather reliability as a necessary condition for validity. If the various gratification items can be shown to have stable correlations across periods of time, we can begin to have some faith that the responses are not merely capricious or so highly tied to the immediate situation that they have no predictive power. Similarly,, if equivalence reliability can be demonstrated by the intercorrelations of items that are theoretically connected, there is evidence of the nonrandomness of responses to the items. This test is even stronger if the two related items differ in measurement, for example, one using close-ended self-report categories and the other using projective techniques or open-ended responses. If either of these types of reliability, test-retest or equivalence, can be established, then we have a much better chance of finding validity in more direct tests.

Pragmatic validation through demonstration that some known criterion group is higher or lower than a control group on the self-reported gratification also increases the strength of the technique. For example, if we can identify a group of lonely people, such as a chapter of Parents Without Partners, we should be able to show that they are more likely to endorse "companionship" as a gratification sought from the media than would a cross section of the public. Alternately, we might take a large sample of older married people or marginally but currently employed people and reinterview them some time later, after some change in their status, such as loss of spouse (in the case of the older sample) and employment (in the case of the marginally employed), to validate change in gratifications.

Construct validity differs from pragmatic validity in that it deals with the theoretical connection between two or more variables. This third approach to validity, then, depends upon establishment of a significant relationship between various antecedent, causal conditions theoretically linked to specific gratifications and the measures of those gratifications. The difficulty here appears to be a lack of theoretical sophistication concerning the social and psychological origins of media gratifications, although some attention has been given to this problem (Blumler, Brown and McQuail, 1970).

The final approach, construct validation through the study of gratification effects, is the strategy we have adopted here. Since the inception of the concept, studies of media gratifications have implied that they have subsequent effects or consequences even though they have not often been measured or studied. It even can be argued that the uses and gratifications approach has its strongest justification in the specification of these effects. Although we have focused on the validation of gratifications measured by self-report responses to lists, it is also true that adequate conceptualization of such variables would permit their experimental manipulation as well as measurement. This is a strategy never tried in uses and gratifications research. If the effects produced by the induced gratification are the same as those indicated by the measured variable in a correlational study, then we have very powerful validation evidence.

THE TRANSACTIONAL MODEL

Validation of media gratification measures through analysis of effects requires the use of a proper model for such evaluation. A reasonable synthesis of the hypodermic and limited effects models, in which the exposure characteristics of the message *combine with* the orientations of the audience member in producing an effect, may be able to escape the unwarranted simplicities of each of the parent models. Such a transactional model could recognize the erroneousness of the "content equals effect" approach to media studies as well as the inadequacy of the "audience intention equals effect" position. Instead of such an either/or position, the transactional model would argue for inclusion of both exposure and orientations (such as gratifications sought); the two types of variables would then be pitted against each other in analysis and their relative importance for a given effect identified. Effects analysis according to this model could either proceed additively (the gratification contribution supplementing that due to exposure) or interactively (an exposure effect being contingent on the pressence of a gratification condition).

In addition to placing emphasis on measurement of gratifications, such a transactional model also has implications for operationalizations of media use variables. Although time spent with a given medium is the most frequently used media exposure variable, it is less than satisfactory in most instances. Not only does time lump together exposure to widely varying types of content, but its measurement is confounded by such extraneous factors as leisure time available to the person (Samuelson, Carter and Ruggels, 1963). Stronger results are likely to come from using exposure to specific content categories within a medium. These categories political news, situation comedies, and the like—are researchers' concepts, however, that may or may not correspond to the psychological categorizations of the audience. Receiver-based content categories remain an unexplored possibility. Another approach for television and other visual media is categorization based on the auditory and visual *form* rather than content (Watt and Krull, 1974).

We have occasionally used the term audience *orientations* rather than the more specific *gratifications* because the latter is only one of several possibilities that could fulfill the requirements for what the person brings to the exposure situation. While most of the work to date has dealt with positive orientations such as gratifications sought from media, it is no less logical to suppose that the aversive reactions of audience members to various aspects of media content may also determine the effects of exposure. Such negative *avoidances* will be given attention equal to that of positive gratifications in the research presented here. In terms of measurement, orientations may be indexed directly through self-report or indirectly as inferred from the receiver's position in the social structure. Credibility and other attitudes toward the media might also be considered orientational variables in the model; McLeod, Rush and Friederich (1968-1969), however, found that credibility was unrelated to knowledge gain either as a direct effect or through its interaction with exposure. Another possibility is dependence upon a particular medium for a given type of content, a variable found to act as a contingent condition for agenda setting (McLeod, Becker and Byrnes, 1974).[8]

The legacy of both the hypodermic and limited effects models indicates an overemphasis on the persuasive, attitudinal consequences of communication. As has been argued more elaborately elsewhere, this represents an overly restrictive view of media effects (Blumler and McLeod, 1974; McLeod, Becker and Byrnes, 1974). It may be helpful in articulating these more subtle media effects to make certain distinctions about their types. As has been mentioned, certain main effects may be anticipated but others may be interactive with orientations serving as contingent or contributory conditions. By adapting the McGuire (1968) model of social influence, we can divide effects into those stemming from message *reception,* including attention and comprehension, and those involving *organization* of the message through cognitive restructuring and overt behavior. Since types of responses may be interrelated, it is desirable to study patterns of several effects to understand the operation of the transaction model.

Finally, we should distinguish direct effects anticipated by the audience member from indirect effects unanticipated by the receiver. An example of the former type of effect is the person who watches television news in order to keep up with the world and who shows effects from both exposure and his motivational orientation in terms of increasing knowledge. The latter type of effect might be shown by the person who reads news for human interest reasons. Even though he is not directly motivated to avoid learning, his learning might be impeded nonetheless if human interest serves as a distractive force in the communication process.

STUDY DESIGN

The American presidential campaign of 1972 provided an opportunity to conduct a preliminary validity test of the television gratification and avoidance items used by Blumler and McQuail (1969) and Blumler, McQuail and Nossiter (1971) through analysis of political effects. As such, it should be thought of as an illustrative rather than definitive study; as stated earlier, effects analysis is only one among the various possible validation strategies. Our particular study is limited in several ways: it deals only with one area of subject matter, politics; it uses a set of gratification and avoidance measures from the British political situation rather than items elicited from an American sample; and it studies effects taken from a multipurpose design rather than tailoring measures of effect to fit specific gratifications. Since the last two limitations should act to make it more difficult to obtain evidence of validity, the analysis provides at least a reasonable evaluation of self-report gratifications procedures. In addition, the analysis presented here deals only with gratifications and avoidances associated with one medium—television.

During September and October of 1972 personal interviews were conducted with 389 potential voters whose addresses were selected from registration lists for the city of Madison, Wisconsin. The systematic probability sample was stratified according to voter age; individuals aged 18 to 24 were oversampled because the primary purpose of the study was to examine the communication and political behavior of people being given the opportunity to vote in a presidential race for the first time. Those 25 years and older serve as a comparison group and are kept separate in all analyses. The non-student areas of the city were also oversampled to increase the proportion of the lesser educated respondents. When the person whose name was selected from the registration list was living at the address, he or she was interviewed; if the person had moved, a person then living at the sampled address was selected to be interviewed. As a result, there was a small proportion of respondents who were not registered to vote although eligible to do so.

Hour-long interviews were conducted by graduate students and advanced undergraduates enrolled in a communications research methods course at the University of Wisconsin and trained in interviewing techniques. A wide range of political and communication topics was covered, including media exposure measures; lists of media gratifications, avoidances and related attitudes; effects criteria such as perceptions of voting issues and outcomes, interest and activity in the campaign, and probability of voting; and various measures used as controls.

During the week following election night of 1972, telephone interviews were conducted with 356 of the previously interviewed respondents. Questions from this round included additional effects variables: reports of campaign and election night viewing, voting intent, and interpersonal discussion late in the campaign.

Television Exposure Measures

The transactional model requires independent measures of media exposure, gratifications and effects. Media exposure may be further divided into measures of time spent with a given medium and attention to various kinds of content. Measures used were

> *Television time:* "On the average weeknight, how many hours do you usually watch television after 5 p.m.?"

> *TV entertainment content:* "About how often do you watch the following kinds of TV shows: Do you watch . . . *frequently, sometimes, rarely,* or *never?*" Responses to the following categories were summed: crime and adventure shows, movies, and situation comedies.

> *TV public affairs content:* "About how often do you watch the following kinds of TV shows: Do you watch . . . *frequently, sometimes, rarely,* or *never?*" Responses to the following categories were summed: national news broadcasts, local news broadcasts, and news specials and documentaries.

Television Gratification and Avoidance Measures

The Leeds gratification and avoidance measures were pretested and found to be suitable for use after only minor wording changes. The following sets of reasons for using political content in television and for avoiding such political material were used:

> *Television gratifications:* "Here is a list of statements that different people have made when asked why they watch television shows that feature political candidates. For each statement on the list, please tell me whether it applies to you *a lot, a little,* or *not at all.*"
>
> (1) To judge what political leaders are like. (Surveillance)
> (2) To see what a candidate would do if elected. (Surveillance)
> (3) To keep up with the main issues of the day. (Surveillance)
> (4) To help make up my mind how to vote in an election. (Vote Guidance)
> (5) To use as ammunition in arguments with others. (Anticipated Communication)
> (6) To judge who is likely to win an election. (Excitement)
> (7) To enjoy the excitement of an election race. (Excitement)
> (8) To remind me of my candidate's strong points. (Reinforcement)

The use of three levels of response categories represents a deviation from the Leeds procedures that used only a dichotomous "applies" versus "does not apply" response. The items were placed in a different order from the one specified above. The order indicated here represents a grouping of the eight items on five dimensions indicated by the size of correlations between items and according to the dimensions used by Blumler and McQuail (1968). Labels given the dimensions are indicated in parentheses.

> *Television avoidances:* "Here is a list of statements that different people have given for avoiding television shows that feature political candidates. For each statement on the list, please tell whether it applies to you *a lot, a little,* or *not at all.*"
>
> (1) Because I am not much interested in politics. (Partisanship, negative item)
> (2) Because my mind is already made up. (Partisanship)
> (3) Because I prefer to relax when watching television. (Relaxation)
> (4) Because you can't always trust what politicians tell you on television. (Alienation)
> (5) Because some candidates talk down to the audience. (Alienation)
> (6) Because some candidates talk over one's head. (Alienation)
> (7) Because they hardly ever have anything to say. (Alienation)

Three dimensions emerged from our factor analysis of the reasons for avoidance of political television materials. One large "alienation" cluster developed, as did a "partisanship" dimension (opposing the first two items on the above list). The final item produced a unique "relaxation" factor.[9]

Political Effect Measures

As discussed earlier, most communication research has focused rather narrowly on the persuasive effects of media exposure. For political communication research this has meant that direction of voting has been the dominant dependent variable. We attempted to expand this focus to include a variety of cognitive as well as attitudinal variables as political effects. Also included were subsequent communication outcomes, with the premise that among the most likely effects of communication is further communication.

Eight effect variables were selected from among the many possible measures administered during the September-October interviews. The selection was made so as to maximize variety among these dependent variables. To various degrees, these measures raise questions about the direction of causation—that is, do media exposure and gratifications cause them or are they actually antecedent to the media variables in causal order? In order to answer the causal direction question more thoroughly, six measures dealing with the latter part of the presidential campaign were used from the post-election telephone interview. Of course, reliance on the telephone limited the type and intricacy of the questions that could be used.

The time one effect measures included

Issue Accuracy: Indexed by the number of stands of the two major presidential candidates correctly identified across ten campaign issues. The possible range was from 0 to 20 with a mean of about 8 correct. Some sample issues: We should pass a federal law legalizing abortion in every state; we should go ahead with plans for development of a new strategic bomber. On three issues, Nixon was for the issue and McGovern was against it, and on three other issues the reverse was the case. Both candidates were for two other issues and both were against the two remaining issues.

Probability of Voting: "Unanticipated problems often prevent people from voting. It may be too early to tell, but would you say you *definitely will vote, probably will vote, don't know, probably will not vote,* or *definitely will not vote?*" This five point scale was used rather than actual vote/not vote because it reflects a finer gradation of the person's commitment to the act of voting.

Interest in Campaign: "Would you say you have been *very interested* in this campaign, *interested* in this campaign, *indifferent, disinterested* in this campaign, or *very disinterested* in this campaign?"

Campaign Activity: Indexed by the number of "yes" responses to five types of campaign activities since the party conventions: passed out leaflets or other campaign material; worn a campaign button or displayed a sign or bumper sticker; tried to convince someone to vote as you plan to vote; attended a political dinner or rally, and contributed money to a party or candidate.

Convention Viewing: Indexed by the sum of viewing of each of the two party's conventions, as measured on a four-point scale: *most of it, some of it, only a little of it,* or *none of it.*

Advertisement Viewing: "If a paid political advertisement were on television for George McGovern (Richard Nixon), about how much attention do you think you would give to it? Would you pay *close attention, some attention,* or *no attention*?" An index was formed by summing the responses to ads for each of the candidates.

Selectivity in Vote Prediction: Indexed by the degree of overestimation of own candidate's vote percentage in comparison with the actual vote in November.

Perceived Differences Between Candidates: "Some people have said that in this campaign there is very little difference between the two candidates, George McGovern and Richard Nixon. Would you *strongly agree, agree, are neutral, disagree,* or *strongly disagree* with that statement?"

The six post-election telephone survey effect items were

Vote Outcome Accuracy: Indexed by the inverse of the discrepancy (regardless of direction) between the respondent's recall of the proportion of the total vote received by Nixon and the actual vote he received in November (61%).

Political Discussion: The estimate of the number of times the respondent discussed the election during the last week of the campaign with friends.

Election Night Media Use: The number of hours the respondent reported watching or listening to voting results on election night.

Campaign Special Viewing: The number of hours the respondent reported watching or listening to broadcast specials paid for by each party during the closing weeks of the campaign. This was asked separately for each party and included Nixon radio specials that had no counterpart in the McGovern campaign.

Selectivity in Special Viewing: Indexed by the degree of discrepancy between the number of times the respondent viewed his own candidate's specials compared to the number of times he or she watched the specials of the opposition candidate.

Voting Intent Change: The level of change in vote position regardless of direction between the September-October interviews and the November telephone reinterviews. Vote direction was a three point scale from McGovern to Nixon with undecided-didn't vote in the middle position.

Control Variables

Two other threats to the validity of a relationship found between gratifications and avoidances and political effects can be dealt with through the use of certain control variables. The first of these threats is spuriousness, or the existence of a relationship between the effect variable and the media orientation because of common, prior, causal variables. The second of these threats exists if the gratifications and avoidances are not media-connected enough, so that the effect results not from media content but from the more general variable tapped by the gratification measure. Variables included in the analysis to control for these alternative explanations were General Political Interest, Non-campaign Political Activity, Political Alienation, Education of Respondent, and Political Media Dependence (the extent to which the respondent relies on a given medium for political information).

RESULTS

Item Comparisons

Since the list of television gratifications and avoidances had not been used in the United States previously, close examination was given to the level of endorsement of the various items in our groups of younger and older voters. This analysis (not presented in tables) shows that while the older adults spend considerably more time with television and pay more attention to television entertainment content, they do not differ very much from those under 25 years old in the reasons they give for seeking and avoiding television programs focusing on political candidates. While the younger voters are more likely to use television to help them make up their minds and to use it for ammunition in arguments than are the older voters, the two groups were found to be strikingly similar on almost all other measures.

It was also found that Surveillance is a dominant type of gratification sought by both age groups. All three items on that dimension showed means above two on the three-point scale. The single Vote Guidance item received a similarly high level of endorsement, while less enthusiasm was shown for the two Excitement items and Anticipated Communication. None of the seven avoidance items was strongly endorsed, and their mean acceptance levels were well below that of the eight gratification items.

An empirical examination of the various gratification and avoidance dimensions was undertaken to answer three types of challenges to their logical status: (1) Were these dimensions merely surrogates for the more standard television exposure measures? (2) Were the avoidance dimensions simply the mirror images of the corresponding gratifications? and (3) Were the intercorrelations of dimensions within the gratification and avoidance blocks so high as to prevent their separation in subsequent analyses of effects?

Evidence relevant to these questions is presented in Table 1. Since media exposure and gratifications seldom have been studied in the same research, the first question challenges validity by asking whether gratifications are merely another way of measuring television exposure. If this were the case, then we would expect to find strong correlations between the exposure and gratification dimensions. There is clearly little connection in either age sample between time spent with television and the five gratification dimensions. When exposure to specific content is examined, a few stable associations are found: those viewing higher levels of news and public affairs programming tend to use the medium for Surveillance while the heavy entertainment users tend to seek Reinforcement in

TABLE 1

CORRELATIONS BETWEEN TELEVISION EXPOSURE VARIABLES, GRATIFICATIONS, AND AVOIDANCES FOR YOUNG AND OLDER VOTERS[a]

	Television Exposure			Gratifications					Avoidances		
	Viewing Time	Public Affairs	Enter- tainment	Surveil- lance	Vote Guidance	Anticipated Comm.	Excite- ment	Reinforce- ment	Partisan- ship	Relax- ation	Alien- ation
Exposure											
Viewing Time	—	.34	.57	.01	-.10	-.08	.04	.04	.11	.34	.23
Public Affairs	.30	—	.32	.14	-.01	-.00	.03	.11	-.03	-.03	-.03
Entertainment	.50	.29	—	.20	.12	.04	.05	.18	-.03	.26	.23
Gratifications											
Surveillance	.03	.20	.06	—	.46	.24	.36	.45	.00	-.18	-.02
Vote Guidance	-.06	.07	-.00	.52	—	.24	.24	.39	-.30	-.11	-.10
Anticipated Comm.	-.00	.10	-.04	.30	.23	—	.17	.23	.03	.03	.00
Excitement	.05	.10	.08	.38	.22	.31	—	.44	.06	.01	.08
Reinforcement	.03	.09	.12	.37	.28	.28	.35	—	-.05	-.09	.02
Avoidances											
Partisanship	.13	.08	-.10	.10	-.02	.16	.11	.12	—	-.14	.08
Relaxation	.19	-.09	.26	-.13	-.02	.01	.06	.03	-.13	—	.49
Alienation	.10	-.14	-.04	-.12	-.01	.11	.04	.05	-.09	.41	—

a. Correlations below the diagonal are for young voters (18-24); correlations above the diagonal are for older voters (25 and older). N for the young voters is 223; N for older voters is 166.

their political programs. But none of these relationships is overwhelmingly large, and the general finding is one of relative independence of television exposure and the gratifications sought from political television programming.

The same question can be asked about the connection between exposure and the avoidances expressed regarding political broadcasts. Here there is some indication of an association: heavy television users tend to be high on all three avoidance dimensions and, not unexpectedly, the entertainment fans are more likely than others to prefer to relax rather than watch political material. Even here, however, the correlations are not so strong as those between the two specific content exposure measures. The findings do argue for the need to control exposure while studying avoidances (and other orientations) and vice-versa.

Since there is little comment in the research literature on media avoidances, it is important to consider whether these avoidances are merely negative restatements of the positive gratification dimensions. Table 1 shows that this is not the case. Only 4 of the 30 avoidance-by-gratification comparisons are statistically significant and only the tendency for the Relaxation avoiders to be low on Surveillance is consistent across the two age groups. Clearly, the avoidances can be discriminated from the gratifications and merit study in their own right.

The third question was whether the inter-dimension correlations of gratifications and avoidances would be so high as to preclude proper interpretation of individual dimensions in their relationship to effects. The answer to this question is somewhat ambiguous. The average intercorrelation of the gratification dimensions is .32 for each age group and is even more substantial for particular pairs: Surveillance-Vote Guidance, Surveillance-Reinforcement, and Excitement-Reinforcement. The avoidance intercorrelations tend to be lower, except for the very strong association between Relaxation and Alienation. In general, the gratification and avoidance inter-dimension correlations are low to moderate and argue for cross-dimension controls and for a cautious approach in assigning estimates of importance to specific dimensions.

Validity Tests

The basic validity question is whether the clusters of gratification and avoidance dimensions add anything to the prediction of the 14 political effect variables beyond the variance accounted for by the more standard time and exposure measures. In the linear regression analysis model used, the exposure items were introduced as a first block of variables. Then, the gratification and avoidance dimensions were added as a block and F tests were conducted to see if the additional variance accounted for by the gratification-avoidance block was statistically significant relative to the variance left unaccounted for by both blocks. This procedure maintains the individuality of the specific variables but sums their effects into either the exposure block or the gratification-avoidance block; each variable within a block is introduced into the equation simul-

TABLE 2

MULTIPLE CORRELATION COEFFICIENTS BETWEEN TELEVISION EXPOSURE
VARIABLES, GRATIFICATIONS, AND AVOIDANCES AND VARIOUS
POLITICAL EFFECTS VARIABLES FOR YOUNG AND OLDER VOTERS

Political Effect	*Age*	*Exposure*	*Exposure Plus Gratifications and Avoidances*
Time 1			
Issue Accuracy	Young	.21[b]	.40[a]
	Old	.28[a]	.39
Probability of voting	Young	.13	.32[a]
	Old	.20	.37[b]
Interest in campaign	Young	.12	.44[a]
	Old	.18	.42[a]
Campaign activity	Young	.29[a]	.44[a]
	Old	.24[b]	.49[a]
Convention viewing	Young	.33[a]	.44[a]
	Old	.35[a]	.50[a]
Advertisement viewing	Young	.16	.46[a]
	Old	.18	.47[a]
Selectivity: Vote Prediction	Young	.07	.19
	Old	.23[a]	.36
Perceived differences between candidates	Young	.14	.38[a]
	Old	.12	.33[b]
Time 2			
Vote outcome accuracy	Young	.08	.33[a]
	Old	.13	.28
Political discussion	Young	.22[b]	.37[b]
	Old	.24[b]	.49[a]
Election night media use	Young	.18	.25
	Old	.16	.51[a]
Campaign special viewing	Young	.24[a]	.30
	Old	.18	.31
Selectivity: Specials	Young	.17	.25
	Old	.13	.34
Voting intent change	Young	.09	.25
	Old	.19	.40[a]

NOTE: The multiple Rs presented in the exposure column are for the equation when the political variables are regressed only on the exposure variables. The Rs presented in the gratifications and avoidances column are for the final equation in which all exposure variables and all gratification and avoidance items are used. Probabilities presented for the exposure column are for the F tests for the amount of variance explained in the effect variable by only the exposure variables. Probabilities presented for the gratifications and avoidances column are for the F tests for the ratio of the additional variance accounted for by this group of variables to the unaccounted for variance. For the young voters, N at Time 1 is 223, and at Time 2 it is 209. For the older voters, N for Time 1 is 166, and for Time 2 it is 147.
a. $p < .01$
b. $p < .05$

taneously with other variables in the block. By combining all gratification and avoidance dimensions into one block, regardless of specific expectations as to the roles of the individual items, we were able to test the general hypothesis that the gratifications and avoidances explain variance in the political effects over and above that explained by the exposure variables (see Table 2).[10]

The multiple Rs for the effect variables by the block of three television exposure measures (Television Time, Public Affairs Viewing, and Entertainment Viewing) are shown in the first column of Table 2. The second column presents the multiple Rs for the combination of the three exposure variables and the block of gratifications and avoidances (five gratification and three avoidance dimensions). The results for the exposure variables alone are not overly impressive; only 10 of the 28 comparisons are statistically significant. More important is the test of gratification and avoidance dimensions. Table 2 shows that in 18 of the 28 tests, the introduction of these dimensions adds a significant amount of variance to that accounted for by the exposure items.

The gratifications and avoidances are particularly powerful in predicting the extent of individual participation in the election campaign, as indicated by the Campaign Activity and Probability of Voting findings. In addition, the gratification and avoidance dimensions contribute significantly to Campaign Interest and such related media activity as convention and advertising viewing. The voters' perceptions of the distinctiveness of the candidates also seem to depend in part on the reasons they have for watching and avoiding political television materials.

For the most part, the late campaign effects are not predicted as well by either the simple exposure measures or the gratifications as are the Time 1 effects, though political discussion as the campaign nears its end is clearly related to both groups of variables. The lack of consistent findings for the late campaign media variables (Election Night Media Use and Campaign Special Viewing) may indicate that such behavior is less predicted by what the individual is seeking or attempting to avoid than by other relevant variables such as a realistic assessment of election outcome, timing of the programming, and late campaign interest. The lack of significant effects for either of the selectivity measures may be due to the fact that clear predictions for these variables could be made only for two of our gratification and avoidance dimensions (Reinforcement and Partisanship). In addition, the expected relationship between television use and selectivity is unclear.

One of the interesting findings in Table 2 is the lack of strong differences between the younger and older voters for all effects except those dealing with accuracy. Only for the young voters are both issue and election outcome accuracy predicted by the gratifications and avoidances, and exposure predicts accuracy only for the Time 1 measures. Another interesting difference between the two age groups surfaces for the Voting Intent Change variable. For the older voters only, change in vote is predicted by the motives for television use.

In general, the regression results provide impressive arguments for both gratifications and avoidances. Further analyses not in Table 2 show that on the average, both sets of orientational variables add about equally to the variance accounted for and tend to produce as strong or stronger relationships to political effects than do the customary media exposure measures.[11]

The transactional model discussed earlier leaves ambiguous the relationship between the media exposure variables and the orientational variables as they induce the various types of effects. The regression analysis shown in Table 2 assumes a simple additive model that sums the effects of the two sets of elements. On the other hand, it is possible to propose an interactive model that predicts that the effect will be multiplicative, the product rather than the sum of exposure and orientation. For example, it is plausible that the effect per unit time of exposure would be greatest for learning for persons sensitized through seeking of gratifications such as Surveillance and Vote Guidance and least for those distracted because they prefer to relax.

To test for the possible added prediction of an interactive model, a multiplicative term was developed by multiplying the level of each gratification and avoidance dimension for each respondent by the level of his or her media exposure measures. For example, a respondent who felt the Surveillance items applied to him "a lot" and who also watched news and public affairs programming regularly would receive a considerably higher score relative to other respondents in the multiplicative model than in the additive model.[12]

Whereas it would be more conclusive to the validity of the gratification and avoidance dimensions if the multiplicative model had shown stronger multiple correlations than those of the additive model, our preliminary analysis (not in the tables) indicates that this is not the case. More often than not the additive model produced at least somewhat better prediction. There is no evidence here for the interactive effects of exposure and gratifications or avoidances reflected in the multiplicative model.

Gratification and Avoidance Dimension Analysis

Since Table 1 has shown several examples of strong associations between certain gratifications and avoidances within each medium, inferences about the contribution of individual dimensions should be made with considerable caution. The partial correlation coefficients generated for each dimension, controlling for all other exposure items and gratification and avoidance dimensions, are unstable to the extent that the given dimension correlates with these other measures. When two or more measures are highly correlated and each is related to the criterion variable, the finding that one variable remains high while the others drop out of the regression equation can be unreliable from a statistical point of view. This is the multicollinearity problem discussed by Blalock (1972).

While the zero-order correlations of the dimensions with the effect variables also may be misleading, they do provide the ground work for subsequent analyses. Two major impressions were gained from a review of the zero-order matrices. First, it appears that no single dimension dominates the relationships with the effect variables, and the explanation of any given effect seems to be shared by several dimensions. Virtually every dimension shows at least moderate associations with one or more effect variables. Second, although the majority of attention has been placed on gratifications sought, the avoidance dimensions seem on average to be at least as closely related to political effects. The avoidances seem to predict better than gratifications such relatively passive effects as election night media use and campaign interest as well as different types of accuracy. The gratifications predict better to more active effects, such as general campaign activity, probability of voting, and frequency of discussion, and to both varieties of selectivity. In other words, the avoidances suppress passive activity while the gratifications increase more involving activity.

Another approach to empirical explication was to analyze the strongest effect predictions for each dimension treated individually, partialing for relevant exposure and control variables. The other gratification and avoidance dimensions were not included as controls in order to reduce the possibility of instability. For each dimension, two or three effect variables were selected that reflected strong prior predictions, variety in their content and, where possible, included both a September-October and a post-election measure. Three other variables were included in each model: in keeping with the transactional approach, the most relevant exposure variable was included along with a political control variable and the respondent's educational level. Controlling for education and the political variable represented an attempt to guard against the possible alternative explanation of spuriousness from a prior causal variable affecting both the gratification-avoidance dimensions and the effect variables. The education control helps to protect against the possibility that the more highly educated respondents might give socially acceptable answers to both the gratification and effect questions. For each model the political variable conceptually closest yet logically prior to the effect variable was chosen. For example, political interest was used as a control where campaign interest was the effect variable.

The individual gratification-avoidance analyses for television are shown in Table 3. The zero-order correlations with the effect variable are indicated for each of the four predictor variables in the analysis along with the third-order partials controlling for the other three variables in the set. It is apparent that the respondent's education is not a good predictor of most effect variables, although other analyses had shown that it was related to several gratification and avoidance dimensions. Consistent relationships are shown only in the more educated respondent's being more likely to discuss the campaign and in perceiving the candidates' stands more accurately. The various political control variables used—interest, activity, and alienation—produce stronger effect results, most of which remain significant after partialing out the other three variables. It is probable, then, that the political control variables will be the most important source of reduction of the key gratification and avoidance partials. The television exposure partials underscore the earlier inference that time and content viewed are surprisingly weak predictors of political effects.

The results of partialing on the crucial gratification and avoidance effect

TABLE 3

ZERO-ORDER AND PARTIAL CORRELATIONS BETWEEN SPECIFIC GRATIFICATIONS AND AVOIDANCES AND POLITICAL EFFECTS CONTROLLING FOR ANTECEDENT VARIABLES FOR YOUNG AND OLDER VOTERS

Political Effect	Age	Education		Political		Exposure		Gratifications	
		Zero	Partial	Zero	Partial	Zero	Partial	Zero	Partial
Probability of voting (T1)	Young	.00	−.01	.09	.10	.08	.02	.23[a]	.23[a]
	Old	.07	.04	.09	.09	.16[b]	.14	.25[a]	.23[a]
		(Years Completed)		(Political Activity)		(Public Affairs TV)		(Surveillance)	
Interest in campaign (T1)	Young	.08	.00	.47[a]	.45[a]	.08	−.11	.31[a]	.28[a]
	Old	.17[b]	.02	.59[a]	.55[a]	.15[b]	.15	.24[a]	.10
		(Years Completed)		(Political Interest)		(Public Affairs TV)		(Surveillance)	
Political discussion (T2)	Young	.15[b]	.12	.22[a]	.19[a]	−.02	−.10	.19[a]	.17[b]
	Old	.32[a]	.29[a]	.24[a]	.17[b]	.00	−.03	.11	.06
		(Years Completed)		(Political Interest)		(Public Affairs TV)		(Surveillance)	
Advertising viewing (T1)	Young	−.03	−.06	.20[a]	.20[a]	.01	.05	.13	.12
	Old	.07	.05	.19[b]	.16[b]	.08	.07	.20[a]	.19[b]
		(Years Completed)		(Political Interest)		(Public Affairs TV)		(Vote Guidance)	
Campaign special viewing (T2)	Young	−.06	−.10	.17[b]	.15[b]	.16[b]	.13	.12	.09
	Old	−.09	−.09	.07	.07	.06	.06	.12	.10
		(Years Completed)		(Political Interest)		(Public Affairs TV)		(Vote Guidance)	
Campaign activity (T1)	Young	.02	.01	.27[a]	.26[a]	.09	.03	.20[a]	.19[a]
	Old	.18[b]	.14	.31[a]	.26[a]	−.03	−.01	.34[a]	.31[a]
		(Years Completed)		(Political Activity)		(Public Affairs TV)		(Anticipated Comm.)	
Political discussion (T2)	Young	.15[b]	.12	.22[a]	.19[a]	−.02	−.08	.10	.05
	Old	.32[a]	.28[a]	.24[a]	.17[b]	.00	−.02	.17[b]	.10
		(Years Completed)		(Political Interest)		(Public Affairs TV)		(Anticipated Comm.)	
Advertising viewing (T1)	Young	−.03	−.04	.20[a]	.19[a]	.01	.07	.22[a]	.21[a]
	Old	.07	.03	.19[b]	.15	.08	.07	.12	.08
		(Years Completed)		(Political Interest)		(Public Affairs TV)		(Excitement)	

Variable	Age								
Political discussion (T2)	Young	.15[b]	.13	.22[a]	.20[a]	-.02	-.08	.08	.08
	Old	.32[a]	.30[a]	.22[a]	.10	.00	-.03	.38[a]	.34[a]
		(Years Completed)		(Political Interest)		(Public Affairs TV)		(Excitement)	
Advertising viewing (T1)	Young	-.03	-.06	.20[a]	.20[a]	-.15[b]	-.19[a]	.22[a]	.19[a]
	Old	.07	.06	.15[b]	.13	-.13	-.12	.28[a]	.28[a]
		(Years Completed)		(Political Interest)		(Public Affairs TV)		(Reinforcement)	
Selectivity: vote pred. (T1)	Young	-.04	-.02	-.04	-.06	.04	.05	.08	.08
	Old	.00	.02	.05	.04	-.17[b]	-.19[b]	.13	.15
		(Years Completed)		(Political Interest)		(Public Affairs TV)		(Reinforcement)	
Perceived differences between candidates (T1)	Young	.09	.04	.22[a]	.14[b]	.13[b]	.08	.17[b]	.10
	Old	.23[a]	.20[a]	.14	.03	.10	.11	.24[a]	.20[a]
		(Years Completed)		(Political Interest)		(Public Affairs TV)		(Partisanship)	
Vote outcome accuracy (T2)	Young	.22[a]	.17[b]	.28[a]	.17[b]	.05	.03	.27[a]	.19[a]
	Old	.14	.09	.33[a]	.29[a]	.03	-.05	.19[b]	.11
		(Years Completed)		(Political Interest)		(Public Affairs TV)		(Partisanship)	
Voting intent change (T2)	Young	-.04	-.05	.02	.05	-.01	-.01	-.05	-.06
	Old	-.07	-.03	-.15[b]	-.08	-.07	-.08	-.25[a]	-.23[a]
		(Years Completed)		(Political Interest)		(Public Affairs TV)		(Partisanship)	
Campaign activity (T1)	Young	.02	.06	.27[a]	.24[a]	-.22[a]	-.16[b]	-.19[a]	-.14[b]
	Old	.18[b]	.10	.31[a]	.27[a]	-.23[a]	-.18[b]	-.16[b]	-.02
		(Years Completed)		(Political Activity)		(Entertainment TV)		(Relaxation)	
Election returns (T2)	Young	-.04	.01	.19[a]	.17[b]	-.12	-.10	-.12	-.10
	Old	.17[b]	.13	.31[a]	.26[a]	-.24[a]	-.23[a]	-.24[a]	-.19[b]
		(Years Completed)		(Political Interest)		(Entertainment TV)		(Relaxation)	
Issue accuracy (T1)	Young	.39[a]	.34[a]	.01	.06	-.18[a]	-.10	-.23[a]	-.17[a]
	Old	.35[a]	.31[a]	-.06	-.03	-.26[a]	-.21[a]	-.11	.02
		(Years Completed)		(Alienation)		(Entertainment TV)		(Alienation)	
Interest in campaign (T1)	Young	.08	.04	-.23[a]	-.18[a]	-.05	-.02	-.23[a]	-.17[a]
	Old	.17[b]	.11	-.31[a]	-.25[a]	.00	.03	-.22[a]	-.13
		(Years Completed)		(Alienation)		(Entertainment TV)		(Alienation)	

NOTE: The partial correlations presented here are between the political effects variables and the column variables controlling for the remaining three variables in the row. N for the young voters is 223 for the pre-election questionnaire effects (T1) and 209 for the post-election telephone questionnaire (T2); for the older voters the Ns are 166 and 147 respectively.

relationships were generally to reduce but not to eliminate the zero-order correlations. Of the 24 significant zero-order correlations with political effects shown in Table 3, 18 remain significant after removing the effects of the relevant exposure, education, and political variables. Among the dimensions, it appears that Partisanship and Alienation are the most likely to be reduced by these controls.

Specific explication of the individual dimensions is perhaps best approached through a synthesis of inferences from the several types of analysis that have been discussed: the partial coefficients from specific dimension analysis of Table 3, the zero-order correlations, and the tenth-order partials for each dimension remaining when all exposure and other gratification-avoidance dimensions were controlled (tables not shown). Of course, the three sources of inference produce some inconsistencies as do the age comparisons within each. As a result, the synthesis should be taken not as incontrovertible evidence but rather as a source of hypotheses for future research using more intensive designs.

Television Gratifications

Surveillance. It appears that using television to judge candidates and to keep up with issues, independent of general political interest, level of exposure, and other gratifications, is tied to increased campaign acitivity in the form of interest, watching of advertising and election night results, and more active forms such as voting and campaign activity. To a lesser degree, it is associated with accurate perceptions of issues and vote results. It is generally unrelated to shifting of voting preferences during the campaign or to selective retention of information that is gained.

Vote Guidance. In some respects, the pattern of effects connected to Vote Guidance resembles that shown by Surveillance. Those using political television to make voting decisions watch more campaign advertising, develop more interest in the campaign, and are likely to vote in the election; however, these tend to drop out when Surveillance is brought into the regression equation. This results from the strong association between these two gratifications, and the greater strength of Surveillance may reflect its greater reliability due to multiple measurement (three items versus one for Vote Guidance). Whatever the conceptual status of Vote Guidance is, it clearly does not share with Surveillance a tendency to lead to gains in political knowledge during the campaign. None of the analyses for either age group showed any evidence of a gain in accuracy among the Vote Guidance seekers.

Anticipated Communication. Respondents who used political television as a source of ammunition for arguments with others tend to take a greater interest in the campaign than other people, to be more politically active than other respondents, and to use advertising and special programs as sources of information. They do not tend to learn more than others about the issues, and their frequency of campaign discussion is largely explainable by their generally higher level of political interest. One reason for their unimpressive knowledge gain may be that they show a slight tendency to be selective in the information they hold. This dimension is an exception to the general finding of a few age differences in the strength of television gratification-effect relationships. Considerably stronger relationships are found for the older anticipators, although their level of endorsement of this gratification tends to be somewhat less than among younger voters.

Excitement. Viewing of candidate programming on television for excitement and to see who is likely to win produces mixed and rather unimpressive results. When other variables are controlled, the relationship of this variable to campaign interest and activity reduces to zero. The only substantial findings after partialing indicate that older Excitement voters discuss the election more frequently and watch more election returns, while the younger group reflect their enthusiasm through advertising and campaign special viewing. Clearly, spectator excitement is not translated into knowledge or campaigning activity.

Reinforcement. Respondents who use political television to remind themselves of their candidates' strong points are, not surprisingly, more likely than others to be politically active and have strong intentions to vote. Their most emphatic tendency, however, is reflected in their interest in campaign advertising, where perhaps their candidates' strong points are presented most distinctly. Their tendency to selectively view political communication may be manifested in the modest tendency to selectively cognize information that appears when other gratifications and exposure are controlled. The selective retention of information may account for the slight tendency for this group to be below average in accurate perceptions of the presidential candidates' stands on issues, despite their above average attention to public affairs.

Television Avoidances

Partisanship. Conceptually, this factor represents the most complex situation among the dimensions in that it combines a positive and a negative loading for two avoidance items: my mind is already made up (positive) and I'm not much interested in politics (negative). In addition, there is a close parallel to general political disinterest except that here the tie is specifically to television. This means that political interest should be controlled, and, in fact, introduction of this variable does reduce the effect of Partisanship in several instances.

Despite, or perhaps because of, the conceptual complexity of Partisanship, it is the best predictor among all gratification and avoidance dimensions across the effect variables. Those high on Partisanship tend to be highly accurate on the knowledge measures and to be interested in the campaign. Much of the knowledge may come from newspapers in that they are high in news viewing and tend to be frequent readers of public affairs content in the newspaper. The two age levels differ somewhat in other patterns shown, with the young partisans being politically active in the campaign and discussing the campaign with others while the older partisans tend to exhibit their motivation by spending a long time viewing results on election night. As might be expected, the older partisans tend to see larger differences between candidates than do other respondents and to be less likely to change their voting positions during the campaign.

Relaxation. Those who say they avoid political television broadcasts because they prefer to relax are characterized by a lack of interest in all kinds of political media content later in the campaign. They also tend to discuss politics less and to be somewhat less interested and less likely to vote. Most of the high zero-order correlations of Relaxation with effects disappear when control variables are introduced. Interestingly, much of the reduction occurs because these relaxers spend a great deal of time watching television and particularly entertainment content. It appears that this is not an artifact of low education causing both high soft content exposure and the effect variables. Possibly, motivation to relax and exposure to the numbing admixture of murder and comedy interact to reduce political interest, knowledge, and activity.

Alienation. Respondents were classified as alienated to the extent they agreed that they avoided political programs because you can't trust politicians, that candidates talked over or under people's heads, and that politicians hardly ever had anything new to say. Independent of exposure, other avoidances and gratifications, and other controls, this alienation orientation led to a lack of interest in the campaign and less attention to political advertising. The younger alienated respondents also tended to be inaccurate in their understanding of campaign issues and to fail to see any difference between Nixon and McGovern.

CONCLUSIONS

Considerable evidence was presented for the validity of the self-report measures of gratifications and avoidances developed by the Leeds research group (Blumler and McQuail, 1969; Blumler et al., 1970, 1971). Even after the effects of television time and content exposure on 14 political effect variables were held constant in regression analyses, the gratification and avoidance dimensions were able to explain significant amounts of additional variance in over half the comparisons. Although political effects, such as campaign issue accuracy and campaign interest, were chosen that previously have been theoretically linked to media exposure, the gratifications and avoidances accounted for considerably more variance than did the exposure variables. Even after controlling for education and for political variables that could be considered to be causally prior to the effects examined, individual gratifications and avoidances explained significant amounts of variance.

The analysis of the individual gratification and avoidance dimensions does indicate the need for finer conceptualizations, with particular attention devoted to the active avoidance items. While research in the past has focused on what the individual seeks from media content, our analysis suggests that it is at least as important to consider what the individual wants to avoid, since these "negative" orientations also seem to delineate media effects.

The avoidance of television political content because of a preference for relaxing fare is particularly interesting from a theoretical standpoint in that it produces some unanticipated consequences. For example, this particular kind of avoidance leads to a low level of accuracy—a result that may be dysfunctional to and unexpected by the individual voter. These and other findings suggest that voters have open to them at least two mechanisms to "protect" themselves from unwanted political materials broadcast on television: (1) they can avoid the content by turning off the set or leaving the room, or (2) they can "avoid" the content by deflecting the impact of that message.

Explication of the gratification and avoidance dimensions and their role in mediating the effects of communication exposure presents a notable dilemma: focusing on specific items aids in clarifying the concept and its particular importance, but it may lead to a misunderstanding of its relative importance when other gratifications and avoidances are considered. For example, analysis of Vote Guidance independent of other gratifications shows its strength in predicting to probability of voting and campaign interest. But Vote Guidance is highly related to Surveillance, and the former variable seems to predict to voting and interest primarily because of this covariance. Our analysis does show, however, that the individual gratifications and avoidances do not lead to the same effects, and that differences in such motives should be considered. Increasing reliability through intensive analysis of particular dimensions and adding items to these dimensions should improve the conceptualization of these dimensions.

Analyses of gratifications and avoidances should not be confined to their additive effects in a linear regression model. It would be useful to examine possible interactive effects of combining two gratification dimensions or a gratification and an avoidance dimension in the same model. It is also likely that certain gratifications have their strongest impact under certain circumstances in the person's situation. For example, the effects of Anticipated Communication should be quite different if the person's family and friends are homogeneous on political attitudes than if they are heterogeneous in this respect. This strategy calls for crossing the gratification with the social situation in the examination of effects.

It is clear from the low correlations between the various exposure measures and the gratification-avoidance dimensions, as well as from the evidence of independent political effects, that gratifications and avoidances are not merely surrogates for media use or exposure. This argues as much for improving the conceptualization and measurement of media exposure as it does for similar further efforts regarding gratifications and avoidances. The weakness of time-spent measures of media use was clearly illustrated by the generally low predictive power of television time for the examined political effects. While the content measures of media exposure indicated stronger relationships than did the time variables, they generally accounted for less of the political effect variance than did the gratifications and avoidances. In addition, the television exposure analyses showed that the negative impact of entertainment television was at least as strong as the positive effects of public affairs viewing.

Some clues to the weakness of the media exposure variables were found in some subsequent analyses not reported in our results. The respondents were partitioned according to the individual's dependence on either television, newspapers, or other people as the major source of political information. This variable, Media Dependency, was found by McLeod, Becker and Byrnes (1974) to limit the agenda setting effects of the media such that those persons dependent on newspapers for their political news were more likely to reflect the agenda of that medium. Here we found that the effects of television exposure variables were stronger for those dependent on television. The data also showed a high level of media specificity in the form of distinctions between content types (low correlations between public affairs and entertainment viewing) for only those dependent upon television. These findings argue for the inclusion of media dependency as an orientational variable in future research using the transactional model.

Our results give strong encouragement to a transactional model of *additive* media effects. Both exposure and gratification-avoidances made independent and noninteractive contributions to political effect variance. It would be unwise, however, to abandon prematurely the possibility of *interactive* effects of exposure and gratifications. The most potent theoretical formulation suggests that the interaction might take place between a specific message and the gratification sought at that time for that message. Our design dealt only with broad classes of message exposure (public affairs and entertainment viewing) and a roughly focused set of gratifications and avoidances. If uses and gratifications researchers can abandon the historical antipathy of nonexperimentalists to experimental research, more adequate and precise tests of interactive effects can be made. It is even possible that a portion of existing research in experimental social psychology could be reconceptualized as having manipulated exposure and a gratification (or at least the respondent's intent or orientation) without recognizing it as such.

We recognize that validity is a much broader and more complex concept than is implied in our effect analysis here. Only one medium, television, was examined, although subsequent political effect analyses not reported tend to show evidence for the validity of gratifications sought from newspapers. We have used only effect analysis while additional evidence and insights regarding validity could be gained from the analysis of antecedents to gratifications and from other procedures discussed at the start of this chapter. In addition, we have investigated only self-report measures of gratifications and avoidances, while the transactional model implies a host of other person-orientational variables and less direct measures as well. At least, we have applied effects analysis to show that there is no reason to abandon the use of self-report measures of gratifications and avoidances. We hope, too, the results indicate to those working in the uses and gratifications tradition that they should incorporate into their research the analysis of media effects rather than artificially separate the two areas.

NOTES

1. This is not to say that the mass media do not change the attitudes and behaviors of smaller numbers of people in important ways. Douglas, Westley and Chaffee (1970) show that under certain, specified conditions media campaigns can affect community attitudes regarding important issues. It also does not imply that large numbers of people cannot be changed in less important ways. Repetitive exposure to unfamiliar stimuli have been demonstrated to produce affective change by Rajecki and Wolfson (1973), Becker and Doolittle (1973), and others.

2. For a more extended critique of the limited effects model and its unfortunate consequences for political communication research, see Blumler and McLeod (1974) and McLeod, Becker and Byrnes (1974).

3. Some of the more recent studies done in the United States focusing in whole or in part upon gratifications include: Schramm, Lyle and Parker (1961); Gans (1962); Katz and Foulkes (1962); McLeod, Ward and Tancill (1965-1966); and Lyle and Hoffman (1971). The most important recent work, however, has been conducted outside this country; in addition to the work cited elsewhere in this paper, see: Furu (1971) [Japan]; McQuail, Blumler and Brown (1972) [Great Britain]; Rosengren and Windahl (1972) [Sweden]; and Katz, Gurevitch and Haas (1973) [Israel]. Outside the United States, uses and gratifications studies constitute the most active and rapidly growing research area today.

4. Some confusion also arises from the distinction between gratifications sought and gratifications gained. Both the discussion here and the findings presented below are concerned with the former.

5. We should not assume that the gratifications sought are invariant across social situations nor that their origins are inherently intrapersonal. As Merton (1949) argues, "Gratifications derived from mass communications are not merely psychological; they are also a product of the distinctive social roles of those who make use of those communications." For examples of information seeking as a motive state generated from interpersonal social situations, see Atkin (1972), Chaffee and McLeod (1973), and Clarke (1973).

6. We are taking the position that media gratifications result from more general motives, which can be either intrapersonal (psychological) or interpersonal (social) in origin. Media responses are only a subset of a larger set of possible responses to these general motives. The gratification sought follows from the general motive but it is temporally prior to the media behavior. In short, it is the reason the individual chooses the particular response to the general motive or set of motives.

7. The inferential approach is illustrated by Kline, Miller and Morrison (1974). Unmeasured informational needs are inferred from the person's sex and age and through his reports of the presence of talking partners and others' information levels relative to those of the person. McCombs and Weaver (1973) and Cole (1974) similarly infer individual needs from other measured variables, such as voting record and political interest.

8. Chaffee (1973) discusses the role of orientations derived from personal needs and wants along with those derived from position and role in the social structure; primary group relationships; content of previous media presentations; and the medium itself. He suggests that the effects of political communication stem from media exposure as an independent variable in combination with these "contingent orientations." The term contingent orientation may be misleading since it implies that orientations serve only as boundary conditions for the effects of exposure. It would seem that they also could serve as contributory conditions affecting but not delimiting the effect, or as main effects given some minimal level of exposure.

9. Note that the "interest" item loads negatively on the partisanship factor, so the factor groups those high in interest who have already made up their minds about the election.

10. The gratification and avoidance column of Table 2 shows the unique contribution of

these variables. A simple subtraction of the exposure column entries from the gratification-avoidance column entries, however, grossly underestimates the power of the gratifications and avoidances, which share some of their predictive power with the exposure counterparts. Findings for issue accuracy illustrate this point well. The multiple R for the television exposure items with this variable is .21 for the young voters and .28 for the older voters. Adding the gratification and avoidance items increases the R for the young to .40 and the R for the old to .39. But the multiple R for the gratifications and avoidances without the exposure items in the equation for the young is .38; for the older voters, the multiple R for the gratifications and avoidances alone is .30.

11. Another indication of the predictive power of the gratification and avoidance items comes from reversing the order of entry of the blocks of variables in the equation. By introducing television gratification and avoidance items into the equations first, 18 of the 28 multiple Rs resulting from this block of variables alone are significant. But the addition of the television exposure variables results in unique contributions reaching significance levels in only 8 of the 28 possible cases. It is important to keep in mind when interpreting these equations that the ability of a block of variables to explain a *statistically* significant amount of incremental variance is a function of its correlation with the first block entered in the equation, the amount of variance explained by the first block (since the error terms are reduced by the accounted for variance), and its own strength.

12. For several of the gratifications and avoidances, the multiplicative prediction is not represented by a straight-forward multiplication of the exposure and gratifications variable, but rather by the inverse of exposure multiplied by the gratification variable. In the following interactive models, those who are low on public affairs exposure and high on the gratification receive the highest score: Excitement, Reinforcement, Partisanship, Relaxation, and Alienation. See Blalock (1972) for a discussion of additive and interactive models.

REFERENCES

ATKIN, C. K. (1972) "Anticipated communication and mass media information seeking." Public Opinion Quarterly 36: 188-199.

BAUER, R. A. and A. BAUER (1960) "America, mass society and mass media." Journal of Social Issues 16: 3-66.

BECKER, L. B. and J. C. DOOLITTLE (1973) "The effects of mere exposure to political advertisements." Paper presented to the Association for Education in Journalism, Ft. Collins, Colo.

BLALOCK, H. M. (1972) Social Statistics. New York: McGraw-Hill.

BLUMLER, J. G. and J. M. McLEOD (1974) "Communication and voter turnout in Britain," in T. Leggatt (ed.) Sociological Theory and Survey Research. Beverly Hills: Sage.

BLUMLER, J. G., J. R. BROWN, and D. McQUAIL (1970) "The social origins of the gratifications associated with television viewing." Leeds: University of Leeds, Centre for Television Research. (mimeo)

BLUMLER, J. G. and D. McQUAIL (1969) Television in Politics. Chicago: Univ. of Chicago Press.

――― and T. NOSSITER (1971) "Political communication and the young voter: a progress report." Leeds: University of Leeds, Centre for Television Research. (mimeo)

BOGART, L. (1965) "The mass media and the blue-collar worker," in A. Bennett and W. Gomberg (eds.) Blue-Collar World: Studies of the American Worker. Englewood Cliffs, N.J.: Prentice-Hall.

CHAFFEE, S. H. (1973) "Contingent orientations and the effects of political communication." Paper presented to the Speech Communication Association, New York.

――― and J. M. McLEOD (1973) "Individual vs. social predictors of information seeking." Journalism Quarterly 50: 237-245.

CLARKE, P. (1973) "Teenagers' coorientation and information-seeking about pop music." American Behavioral Scientist 16: 551-566.

COLE, E. B. (1974) "Surveillance and voter decision making: a dynamic model of need for orientation." Paper presented to the International Communication Association, New Orleans.

DOUGLAS, D. F., B. H. WESTLEY, and S. H. CHAFFEE (1970) "An information campaign that changed community attitudes." Journalism Quarterly 47: 479-487, 492.

FURU, T. (1971) The Function of Television for Children and Adolescents. Tokyo: Sophia University.

GANS, H. (1962) "Hollywood films on the British screen: an analysis of the functions of American popular culture abroad." Social Problems 9: 324-328.

KATZ, E., J. G. BLUMLER, and M. GUREVITCH (1974) "Utilization of mass communication by the individual: an overview," in J. G. Blumler and E. Katz (eds.) The Uses of Mass Communications: Current Perspectives on Gratifications Research. Beverly Hills: Sage.

KATZ, E., M. GUREVITCH, and H. HAAS (1973) "On the use of mass media for important things." American Sociological Review 38: 164-181.

KATZ, E. and D. FOULKES (1962) "On the use of media for 'escape': clarification of a concept." Public Opinion Quarterly 26: 377-388.

KLINE, F. G., P. V. MILLER, and A. J. MORRISON (1974) "Adolescents and family planning information: an exploration of audience needs and media effects," in J. G. Blumler and E. Katz (eds.) The Uses of Mass Communications: Current Perspectives on Gratifications Research. Beverly Hills: Sage.

LAZARSFELD, P. F. and F. STANTON [eds.] (1942) Radio Research, 1941. New York: Duell, Sloan & Pearce,

——— [eds.] (1944) Radio Research, 1942-43. New York: Duell, Sloan & Pearce.

——— [eds.] (1949) Communications Research, 1948-49. New York: Harper.

LYLE, J. and H. R. HOFFMAN (1971) "Children's use of television and other media," pp. 129-256 in E. A. Rubinstein, G. A. Comstock and J. P. Murray (eds.) Television in Day-to-day Life: Patterns of Use. Washington, D.C.: Government Printing Office.

McCOMBS, M. E. and D. WEAVER (1973) "Voters' need for orientation and use of mass media." Paper presented to the International Communication Association, Montreal.

McGUIRE, W. J. (1968) "Personality and susceptibility to social influence," pp. 1130-1187 in E. F. Borgatta and W. W. Lambert (eds.) Handbook of Personality Theory and Research. Chicago: Rand-McNally.

McLEOD, J. M., L. B. BECKER, and J. E. BYRNES (1974) "Another look at the agenda setting function of the press." Communication Research 1, 2: 131-166.

McLEOD, J. M., R. R. RUSH, and K. FRIEDERICH (1968-1969) "The mass media and political information in Quito, Ecuador." Public Opinion Quarterly 32: 575-587.

McLEOD, J. M., L. S. WARD, and K. TANCILL (1965-1966) "Alienation and uses of the mass media." Public Opinion Quarterly 29: 583-594.

McQUAIL, D., J. G. BLUMLER, and J. R. BROWN (1972) "The television audience: a revised perspective," pp. 135-165 in D. McQuail (ed.) Sociology of Mass Communications. Harmondsworth: Penguin.

MERTON, R. K. (1949) "Patterns of influence," in P. F. Lazarsfeld and F. N. Stanton (eds.) Communications Research 1948-49. New York: Harper.

RAJECKI, D. W. and C. WOLFSON (1973) "The ratings of materials found in the mailbox: effects of frequency of receipt." Public Opinion Quarterly 37: 110-114.

ROSENGREN, K. E. and S. WINDAHL (1972) "Mass media consumption as a functional alternative," pp. 166-194 in D. McQuail (ed.) Sociology of Mass Communications. Harmondsworth: Penguin.

SAMUELSON, M., R. F. CARTER, and W. L. RUGGELS (1963) "Education, available time, and use of the mass media." Journalism Quarterly 40: 491-496.

SCHRAMM, W., J. LYLE, and E. B. PARKER (1961) Television in the Lives of Our Children. Stanford: Stanford Univ. Press.

WATT, J. H. and R. KRULL (1974) "An information theory measure for television programming." Communication Research 1: 44-68.

PART III

ANALYTICAL PERSPECTIVES

Chapter 8

PSYCHOLOGICAL MOTIVES AND
COMMUNICATION GRATIFICATION

William J. McGuire

ANY INQUIRY INTO THE GRATIFICATIONS that people derive from mass communications requires us to know something of the unfulfilled needs of the person and something of the potential rewards offered by the media. This double intellectual demand is not an overwhelming challenge, since there are few people in today's world, whatever their profession or avocation, who do not consider themselves quite expert in the areas of human psychology and mass media.

Still, while most people feel possessed of a natural expertise in both areas, any inquiry into the topic must take one or the other term, motivation or gratification, as its initial point of departure (Katz, Blumler and Gurevitch, 1974). The authors of most of the other chapters in this *Annual Review,* being more identified with communications or sociological research than with psychology, have taken the gratifications offered by the mass media as their starting point, in that they begin by analyzing the potential rewards offered, whether by the media content, or by exposure per se, or by the social settings in which exposure to the media typically occurs (Katz, Gurevitch and Haas, 1973).

In this chapter, on the other hand, we shall take the opposite pole as our point of departure. As a card-carrying psychologist with an assignment to review the psychological foundations of audience gratification, we shall focus initially on the nature of human motivation. Then, from an analysis of the person's needs and characteristic modes of satisfying them, we shall examine the possible gratifications that an individual may obtain from the mass communication available in our society.

PRELIMINARY ISSUES

The main body of the chapter is devoted to a consideration of how each of a series of fundamental human motives is relevant to mass media consumption. But before turning to this main task, two preliminary questions should be considered. First, there is the issue of the extent to which media exposure is motivated as opposed to being an almost random or externally-determined tuning in on what happens to be available. The second preliminary issue has to do with whether a "cafeteria" display of human motives such as the one laid out in this chapter (or various other catalogs of needs that have been proposed) constitutes a useful approach to the problem.

Is Mass Communication Consumption Motivated?

Some astute observers consider any answer regarding what motivates mass communication exposure to be a question-begging exercise. Doubt that audience motivation and gratification form any great part of the forces which determine media consumption stems from at least three considerations. First, it is argued that media exposure is not so much a deliberate process stemming from inner drives as rather haphazard, an outcome of chance and external circumstances. Second, it is argued that the gratifications offered by the media are so paltry compared to the audience's real needs that the motivational factor could hardly loom large in determining exposure. Third, it is argued that even where media gratifications are available, we would exaggerate the rationality of the audience and the indexing of the media to suppose that these gratifications could be efficiently found. Each of these three objections deserves some discussion here.

External determination of communication consumption. Bogart (1965) has cautioned enthusiasts of the uses and gratifications approach to consider whether exposure to the mass media might not be so determined by external circumstance that choice among the smorgasbord spread by one's culture is not so much a purposeful activity as the outcome of chance or extrinsic forces. For example, one's newspaper purchasing and reading may be more determined by the available delivery systems and one's television viewing more by the mealtime resulting from one's spouse's work schedule, than by one's own personal motivations or the gratifications available.

While admitting that external circumstances play a large part in determining one's media exposure, we should remember the cautionary tale of the scientist who believed so strongly in Boyle's Law that he could never accept Charles's Law: that external circumstances are an important determinant of mass media exposure does not rule out the possibility that personal needs are also a factor. People show clear and loyal preferences among equally accessible mass communications. Such characteristic persistence cannot be viewed as mere continuation of a chance habit, if we remember learning theory's fundamental law of effect that repetition does not stamp in a response unless there is reinforcement; without reinforcement, repeated exposure would have the opposite effect of extinguishing the habit. Furthermore, individual choices tend to distribute themselves over equally available mass communication alternatives in a pattern too far from random to be attributable to chance.

Triviality of media gratifications. A second argument against explaining mass communication exposure in terms of human motivation is that the gratifications to be obtained from the media appear to be highly illusory and inadequate relative to the more compelling needs that grip the individual. When one considers the dire privations, the destitution and failure, the pangs of unrequited love, and all those other tragedies of the human condition whose actualities, bad enough, are exaggerated by our fears, it does seem that any solace offered by a daytime television serial, the sports page of the newspaper, or a broadcast symphony is pitifully inadequate.

Still, the extent of mass communication consumption suggests that the media must be doing something right. A formidable portion of the public's time in the developed nations is spent in media consumption, as documented in the United Nations' time budget studies of a dozen countries (Szalai, 1972). However unpromising media contents seem for meaningful fulfillment of deep human needs, people are voting with their time massively in the media's favor. Before we dismiss the gratifications to be found in the media, we should (like the person asked how his or her spouse is) hesitate and ask back, "Compared to what?" Perhaps the satisfactions that mass communication can offer to the person, pitiful though they may be, are better than the alternatives offered in the real life of quiet desperation which many members of the public endure. The large proportion of their time that people choose to devote to media consumption is evidence that however illusory the gratification offered, it may exceed the more tangible but inaccessible or unsatisfying satisfactions available in their actual world.

Poor indexing of media gratifications. A third argument against the utility of a motivational approach to media exposure is that, even granting that there are potential gratifications to be found in mass communication, there remains the difficulty that people are not very effective at finding gratifications and the media do not index well these potential rewards. To purge the uses-and-gratifications approach of any exaggerated "rational man" component, it is useful to distinguish between forces that determine our initial exposure to a given television (or other mass media) program and forces that maintain exposure to the medium or program once it occurs. We might grant that the initial search and exposure to alternative mass communication material may be rather haphazard and controlled by external circumstances, but still contend that for continuing exposure it is necessary that there be motives and gratifications to maintain this response. Perhaps we concede too much if we grant that motivational factors are completely inoperative in the initial discovery of appropriate materials. Studies of perception of the media (such as Katz, Gurevitch and Haas, 1973) indicate that people do have some reasonable grasp of what functions might be served by exposure to one medium as compared with another. (It would be of interest to know more about the extent to which their perceptions are similarly structured and perspicacious as regards within-media materials.) But while personal needs may have some impact on search and initial exposure to the media, it must be granted that external circumstances and chance are compelling in most instances. One has little opportunity to watch television or read a newspaper, as compared with listening to one's car radio as one drives home from work. The discovery of a favored book or television program often depends on accidental exposure or a casual remark.

Where the uses-and-gratifications approach seems more powerful is when we turn to the question of maintaining continued exposure once one has found appropriate mass communication material. While the initial tuning in to a television program (or newspaper column or magazine feature or whatever) may have been largely haphazard and unmotivated, behavioral theory's "law of effect" reminds us that such exposure would soon extinguish in the absence of reinforcement to maintain the habit. Hence our subsequent discussion of the motivational aspects of communication consumption focuses more on what maintains continued exposure to certain kinds of material rather than on what precipitates initial exposure.

Classifications of Human Motives

Previous classifications. In this chapter the question of human motivation and communication gratification is approached from the former, motivational term. That is, we begin by outlining a system of human motives and then consider what implications each motive has for gratifications to be obtained from the mass media. Any attempt to choose a list of human motives confronts us with an embarrassment of riches. In their Stakhanovite analysis of an unabridged English language dictionary, Allport and Odbert (1936) found about 18,000 words that described trait-names. While not all of these could be considered terms for human motives in any strict sense, many thousands did fall under the motivational rubric. Theorists have offered many alternative distillations of this linguistic richness in the form of a manageable listing of human motivations, sometimes with an attempt at organization. For example, to mention only a few of the better known classifications, Murray (1968) describes 28 basic psychogenic needs and groups them into six classes; Erikson (1963) lists eight, reflecting increasing psychological maturity; and Maslow (1970) considers a longer list and organizes them into a seven-step hierarchy ranging from basic physiological needs to self-actualizing needs. Moreover, classifications of the "motives" must sensibly be expanded to include lists of "instincts" like McDougall's (1923) or "emotions" such as Bridges' (1932); of "values" as proposed by Allport, Vernon and Lindzey (1951) or by Rokeach (1973); of "temperaments" as proposed by Sheldon (1942); and of motivation-connoting personality dimensions such as those suggested by Jung (1933), Cattell (1957), and Eysenck (1953), among many others.

Any attempt here to compile still another list of basic motives risks simply adding other plausible but noncompelling classifications to those already available. There seem to be virtually innumerable ways of slicing up conceptually the reality space of human motives. Any given classification is perhaps best done for the specific purpose for which it is intended to be used, thus maximizing the likelihood that our attention will be directed to all the gratification aspects important to the given domain of inquiry. We shall try to present here a classification of human motives that is sufficiently inclusive, relevant, and heuristically provocative so that it will direct our thinking to as many as possible of the gratifications to be obtained from mass communication.

A classification system to reflect recent trends in motivation theory. An *Annual Review* chapter naturally should stress recent developments. Since science has its fashions, oscillating between opposite poles in its momentary emphases, a stress on recency risks neglecting some perennial truths that happen temporarily to be out of style. On the other hand, science is a cumulative, evolving intellectual enterprise, so stress on recency has the excuse that in general the newer understanding is superior to the older, if we stand on the shoulders of giants (or even of pygmies).

Fortunately for our purposes here, the two most dominant recent trends in motivation theory both serve to stress aspects of human needs that are likely to be particularly relevant to mass communication consumption. One of these is the emphasis on "humanistic" rather than physiological motives and the other is the stress on the "cognitive" component of motivation. Illustrative of the popularity of the humanistic approach is the current enthusiasm for Maslow's (1970) hierarchical theory of human motivation with its emphasis on cognitive, aesthetic, and self-actualization needs, and for Erikson's (1963) extension of the Freudian theory of psychosexual development to more mature stages that stress such needs as developing an identity and ego integrity. Illustrative of the second trend, an emphasis on cognitive factors, is Dember's (1974) analysis of the cognitive revolution in motivation and the heavy stress on cognitive approaches in the two most recent comprehensive books on motivational theory (Weiner, 1972; Madsen, 1974). The recent work has focused not only on the cognitive needs of the individual, but even on the cognitive components of the basic physiological drives such as thirst and pain (Zimbardo, 1969).

In recognition of these two recent advances, we shall stress cognitive, as well as the more traditional affective, factors as we generate a system of human motives and shall deal also with motives that stress self-growth as well as self-preservation as the object of human endeavor. To these two dimensions, cognitive versus affective and growth versus preservation, we shall add two further dimensions to our system for generating communication-relevant human needs. As a third dimension for classifying human motives we shall use the classic polarity of active versus passive initiation of human striving. The fourth dimension to be used is the equally prevalent distinction between internal and external goal orientations of human motives.

Selecting bipolar opposites on each of these four dimensions as our system for generating motives, it is possible to construct a matrix of 16 cells, each of which constitutes a basic, pervasive human need. The four-dimensional system of

TABLE 1

A STRUCTURING OF 16 GENERAL PARADIGMS OF HUMAN MOTIVATION

(In terms of the possible mass communication gratifications discussed in this chapter)

Mode	Stability	Initiation / Orientation →	Active	Active	Passive	Passive
			Internal	External	Internal	External
Cognitive	Preservation		1. Consistency	2. Attribution	3. Categorization	4. Objectification
Cognitive	Growth		5. Autonomy	6. Stimulation	7. Teleological	8. Utilitarian
Affective	Preservation		9. Tension-Reduction	10. Expressive	11. Ego-Defensive	12. Reinforcement
Affective	Growth		13. Assertion	14. Affiliation	15. Identification	16. Modeling

16 motives is illustrated in Table 1. Each of these 16 concepts of human motivation can be regarded as a "model of man" or a basic paradigm of human nature, emphasizing a particular aspect of human complexity and a particular motivational orientation. One could extend the system by adding more dimensions (the next bipolar addition would double to 32 the number of motives) or by increasing the levels within each dimension (for example, one might add a third level, "conative" to the "cognitive" versus "affective" dimension; and to the "preservation" versus "growth" dimension, we might add a catabolic "destructive" category). However, we shall forgo such extensions here because we feel that the 16 types of needs used in this chapter may already err on the overly complex side. The 16-motive system used here seems sufficiently powerful heuristically to call our attention to a very wide range of possible gratifications from mass communication, and emphasizes adequately those needs that have received the major attention of motivational researchers in recent years.

THE COGNITIVE MOTIVES:
THEIR RELEVANCE TO MEDIA GRATIFICATION

Our major division among the motives is that between the cognitive and the affective. By way of clarifying this distinction, this cognitive-affective polarity might be contrasted as stressing the directive aspects of motives versus their dynamic aspects, that is, forces that orient, as contrasted with those that energize, the individual. The cognitive motives stress the person's information processing and attainment of ideational states, while the affective motives stress the person's feelings and attainment of certain emotional states.

When the cognitive orientations are divided on the basis of three further dimensions (see Table 1), we arrive at a total of eight cognitive motives. Each of these will be discussed below by mentioning the fundamental concept of human motivation that it stresses, some theorists who have dealt with it, and its implications for possible gratifications offered by mass communications.

Cognitive Motives Stressing Preservation of Current Equilibrium

Four of the cognitive motives that have received attention of late treat the individual's cognitive needs as essentially conservative, directed toward maintaining achieved orientations. Two of these conservative motives regard the individual as active: the *consistency* theories that stress the attainment of an internal equilibrium and the *attribution* theories that stress the individual's maintenance of his external orientation to the environment. The other two cognitive preservation motives depict the individual more as a passive responder, including the *categorization* theories that emphasize our attempt to make sense of the world in terms of our internal categories and the *objectification* theories that stress our attempt to make sense of our experiences in terms of externals.

We shall now consider each of these four cognitive preservation motivations in turn, touching upon the fundamental concept of the person which they encapsulate, some recent proponents, and their implications for communication gratifications.

Consistency theories. The theorists who stressed the person's need for consistency dominated personality and social psychology during the 1960s. The numerous viewpoints represented here have in common that they regard the person as beset by numerous conflicting forces among which one must be an honest broker, coming up with a modus vivendi in the form of a compromise solution that minimizes the extent to which any single force remains out of line in the conflict resolution that the person achieves. The conflicting forces include one's own needs, one's information, the views of significant other people with whom one wishes to retain good relationships, one's own past and present behavior, etc. Somehow the person must find compromise attitudes and behavior that resolve this complex situation by a "least-squares deviation" or "minimax" solution that minimizes the extent to which any one consideration is left with a large discrepancy from the achieved compromise.

Many variants of consistency theory have been put forward, particularly during the 1960s, differing somewhat among themselves as to the weights they ascribed to the conflicting forces, the processes by which the person arrives at a resolution, the assumptions made regarding which solution is most satisfying, etc., but all agreeing that the person is an interconnected system pushed in many directions by inner and outer forces and tending toward a resolution that maximizes psychological coherence within the system. These consistency formulations include Heider's (1958) balance notion, Osgood and Tannenbaum's (1955) congruity, Festinger's (1957) dissonance, Newcomb's (1953) inter-personal symmetry, McGuire's (1960) probabilogic, Abelson and Rosenberg's (1958) psycho-logic, Cartwright and Harary's (1956) graph theoretical approach, etc. Useful reviews are found in McGuire (1966) and Abelson, Aronson, McGuire, Newcomb, Rosenberg and Tannenbaum (1968).

These consistency theories, which depict the person as striving to maintain a complex and precarious connectedness and coherence among his or her inner experiences, suggest that mass communications present a potential danger in that any new information might well be upsetting to the delicate balance one has achieved. But considering that the person has considerable latitude in selecting media content and in perceiving and retaining it selectively, these consistency theories suggest that mass media content also offers numerous opportunities for gratifying the need for consistency. The person in conflict regarding a life issue—be it a political attitude, a parent-child relationship, or whatever—can find almost any material needed to suggest or bolster an incipient resolution from among the mass communication content offered by news and public affairs programs, newspapers of known editorial slant, the dramatic fare of daytime television serials or novels, etc. These materials can help the individual to live with any compromise resolution to complex issues by presenting various rationalizations, or suggesting helpful distinctions or syntheses, or at least by offering the comparative consolation that other people have more serious problems or have arrived at even less happy solutions. Resolutions are worked out more easily and securely through exposure to the media than in dialogue with other persons because the one-way communication involved in media use does not entail a challenge to such resolutions as one works them out.

Attribution theories. If the consistency theories dominated personality and social psychology during the 1960s, the 1970s belong to the attribution theories. Both types of theory deal with the cognitive-preservation motive and both imply an active stance by the person, as shown in Table 1; but while the consistency theories stress the person's internal orientation toward maintaining an inner balance, the attribution theories stress an external orientation toward maintaining an interpretation of one's environment. By "attribution theories" we are referring to the family of notions that depicts the person as an implicit theorist attributing causes and motives to occurrences in his experience, and responding to any occurrence, not so much in terms of its appearance as in terms of the causal interpretations that one makes of it. According to this view of human nature, we are implicit personality theorists, implicit physicists, etc., and our perception of our world involves an imposition of our prior theory of reality on the external events that we experience. How one responds to a favorable or unfavorable outcome to oneself or to another depends on whether one attributes this outcome to an internal or external force. For example, the gratifications one receives from another person's praise depend on whether one attributes that praise to the constraints imposed by the person's role (as, for example, when it comes from one's mother) or constitutes an attempt at ingratiation or is apparently based on an objective appraisal of oneself (as when it comes from an independent stranger).

These attribution theories which have become so popular during the past several years in the personality and social psychology areas have precursors in perceptual theorists extending back over a century, for example, in Helmholtz's doctrine of unconscious inference and, more recently, Michotte's (1954) work on perception of causality. It entered the personality and social psychology areas largely through the influence of Heider's (1958) naive psychology, though there were relatively independent substreams such as that from Rotter (1966) and Phares' (1957) work on inference of internal versus external control of outcomes. Important landmarks of this movement are Jones and Wortman's (1973) work on ingratiation and other factors in person perception and Kelley's (1967) attempt to weave together the various strands into a generic attribution theory. The most recent compendium along these lines is Jones, Knouse, Kelley, Nisbett, Valens and Weiner (1972).

Insofar as mass communication presents a culturally stereotyped and sanitized oversimplification of an untidy and unsatisfying reality, it offers the recipients an opportunity for the gratification of bolstering their implicit theories of the world. For example, Lerner (1970) has dealt with the average person's notion of a just world, such that people tend to get what they deserve, resulting in a tendency to blame the victim. Correspondingly the fictional

contents of mass communication use certain supportive formulae and conventions by custom (and until recently, often by explicit industry regulation),
such as that crime does not pay and that in the end things turn out well for the
good guys in the white hats. By immersing themselves in such depictions that
follow the approved formulae, the public can obtain a gratifying bolstering of
the theories by which they live. There are some recent trends, reflecting changes
in taste and easing of moral censorship, which allow more departures from the
formulae and permit evil occasionally to triumph and good to go unrewarded;
also, traditionally there has been an audience for tragedy in which things do not
turn out well and for comedy which casts derision at certain cherished values.
But theorists of tragedy and comedy have suggested various possible ways in
which such seeming threats to our reassuring theories of the world can actually
bolster these outlooks on a deeper and purer level.

Categorization theories. Continuing our consideration of cognitive-preservation paradigms, but here turning to conceptualizations that depict the person
as somewhat more passive than did the consistency and attribution theories
discussed above, we consider first the views that portray the individual as a
categorizing or classifying machine. The person is viewed as confronting an
overly complex world with a need to sort his experiences into an ever-ready set of
categories, striving to find a place for everything and to put everything in its
place. Because one is cognitively limited, the infinite variety of the world that
impinges upon us must be fitted into general categories that oversimplify one's
experience but also allow one to cope with it more effectively than if one tried
to encode each occurrence completely. In the course of our phylogenetic and
ontogenetic development, humans have evolved rough and ready categories that
allow them to classify experience by selecting out certain characteristics for
noticing while ignoring other aspects, so that they are able to cope fairly well
with ordinary experiences in a world that is too much with them. These
categories have evaluative and behavioral tags that guide one's responses to one's
experiences.

This categorizing concept of human nature traces back at least to Külpe's
(1922) Würzburg School. It is found also in Bartlett's (1932) work on the
remembering of stories, showing how we attempt to fit these into preconceived
categories or schemata. The categorization concept is used powerfully by Sherif
(1935) in his demonstration of people's need for and use of frames of reference
and by Luchins (1942) in his work on rigid adherence to sets in our thought
processes. Asch's (1952) work on attitude change as involving not so much a
changed evaluation of the original target object as a change in the perception of
which target object we are evaluating, also falls within this theoretical
framework, as does the work of Levi-Strauss (1958) and the other structuralists.
Perhaps the most provocative utilization of this concept of our need to sort
experiences into preconceived categories is Piaget's (1968) work on how the
child confronts reality with gradually developing cognitive structures, finding
gratification both from assimilating experiences to these structures and from
accommodating the structures slightly toward the new experiences.

These categorization theories view the person as receiving gratification insofar as he is able to sort experiences among his preconceived categories and as being distressed by any experiences that cannot be fitted into his preconceptions. A slightly more elegant version of the theory holds that experiences that fit perfectly are gratifying, but even more gratifying are experiences which just fail to fit but which one is able to handle with one's preformed categories by slightly reinterpreting the experience or slightly modifying one's preconceived structures. This viewpoint suggests that characteristic mass communication fiction, involving stock characters in formula plots, is easily assimilated to one's preexisting categories. And even the news and public affairs programs tend repetitiously to present standard disasters in a ritualized manner, familiar figures taking expected public stances, etc., which probably can easily be fitted into the preexisting conceptual categories of the public which chooses to be exposed to this material. Perhaps the slight variations on the themes that are introduced by skillful scriptwriters or enterprising reporters involve just enough novelty to present a manageable challenge to one's preconceived categories which, after some slight stress due to this initial challenge, prove in the end to be, like the good guys in the white hats, adequate to the task. Such manageably challenging material meets the ideal prescription for a gratifying exercise of our cognitive categories.

Objectification theories. While the categorization theories represent an internally oriented version of the passive type of cognitive-preservation paradigms, the objectification theories to which we now turn are an externally oriented subtype. This view of human nature represents the person as rather passive and deficient in ideational life, tending to infer one's own attitudes, feelings, satisfactions, etc., from observations of such externals as one's own overt behavior or that of other people and various situational factors. The person is viewed as typically nonreflective and deficient in internal cognition, developing a conceptual viewpoint only when externally challenged to do so and then looking for external cues as a basis for forming a conceptualization. For example, the likes and dislikes on which we seem to act have never been articulated to ourselves, so that when suddenly asked whether we like to listen to the radio, we are momentarily taken aback and then make an inference from our own behavior that, since we are always listening to it, yes, we must like it. This viewpoint has been called "radical behaviorism" in that it depicts us as learning about even our own mental states from our overt behavior, quite similarly to the way we make inferences about other people's internal states from their overt behavior.

Early proponents of the objectification viewpoint would include William James' (1884) theory of the emotions and the early behaviorists who viewed thought as implicit speech, if not an epiphenomenon to be disregarded altogether. Among the more recent theorists, an element of this paradigm lies behind Festinger's (1954; Latane, 1966) social comparison theory. The idea is used provocatively in Schachter's (1971) cognitive-physiological theory of the emotions which depicts the individual as interpreting his generalized arousal state as being any of a wide variety of emotions depending on situational factors. Perhaps the most explicit and creative user of this viewpoint is Bem (1972). These objectification theorists are often grouped with the attribution theorists. In our scheme here, both are classified as being external preservation subtypes of cognitive theories of human nature, but are usefully distinguished in that the attribution theories depict the person as more active in the initiation of this interpretive gratification while the objectification theories depict the person as rather passive, making inferences mainly in response to external demands.

These objectification theories regard the person as inadequately directed by internal cues and thus in chronic need of external guidelines. Our lack of a developed ideology (or even of specific attitudes) presents a constant potential for embarrassment. Exposure to mass communications, whether of the entertainment or of the informational variety, can supply a plethora of predigested and easily assimilable viewpoints. Since one is deficient even in cues for interpreting one's own tensions and anxieties, exposure to media content provides labels and interpretations for one's own vague feeling states. When one is unable to evaluate the adequacy of one's own performance, these depictions provide social comparisons that serve as a yardstick for measuring its suitability. Again, by selective exposure to the appropriate mass communication material, the person can find a gratifying interpretation for personal anxiety and guilt by attributing negative feelings to external factors and even find some reassurance regarding the adequacy of his or her own behavior by contrasting it with the even more heinous behaviors of people portrayed in the media.

Cognitive Growth Theories

The four theories which we considered in the previous section (consistency, attribution, categorization, and objectification) all stress the cognitive mode of gratification, as do the four theories to which we turn here. But while the first four viewpoints stressed the preservation of an initial cognitive status quo as the motivational goal, the four theories to which we turn here (autonomy, stimulation, teleological, and utilitarian—as listed in the second row of Table 1)—all stress growth or development of one's present state as one's cognitive goal. The first two of these cognitive-growth paradigms, *autonomy* theories and *stimulation* theories, stress the individual as active in the initiation of gratification sequences, while the third and fourth paradigms, the *teleological* and the *utilitarian,* depict the individual as more passively responding to environmental demands.

Autonomy theories. The viewpoints we consider here constitute the epitome of the humanistic trend that has become increasingly prominent in recent psychological thought. They depict the person as seeking self-realization by developing an integrated, autonomous identity. Some of these theorists have started with Freudian or Marxian notions of developmental stages but extended these into far more mature levels than those on which Freud focused and in more individualistic and ideational directions than did Marx. Growth through the various stages is depicted as marked by crises and one's response to them as often characterized by crucial challenges and peak experiences. The ultimate aim of this personal growth is an integrated *weltanschauung* and a feeling of personal autonomy and meaning.

Advocates of this view of individual striving include Allport's (1961) individualism and Tillich's (1952) notion of the individual's ultimate concern. Erikson's (1963) concept of stages of human development and the search for autonomy and identity represents a development from the Freudian viewpoint, and Fromm's (1964) dialectic humanism is a version that integrates Freud and Marx along these lines. Maslow's (1970) self-actualization theory is another popular example. Somewhat more specific in stressing only part of this total paradigm is Dichter's (1971) view of motivation research as applied to advertising and Brehm's (1966) reactance theory and Steiner's (1970) work on the illusion of freedom, both of which stress the autonomy needs of the individual, that is, one's need to feel that one controls one's own destiny.

At first glance it might seem that mass communications offer little gratification for the kind of humanistic need stressed by these autonomy theories. The daily fare of our newspapers and television programs seems not to offer much help toward becoming an integrated, autonomous personality, secure in the knowledge that one is captain of one's fate and master of one's soul. However, it may be that the average member of the public has a somewhat more modest identity aspiration. Keeping up with the current scene in the world of politics, entertainment, sports, or whatever, through the newspaper, radio, or television set, probably gives one some feeling of participation and control in things larger than oneself. Such a feeling might arise either because knowledge is indeed power or because it gives the illusion of power, as in Spinoza's saying that if a thrown stone took thought in flight, it would think it was moving of its own volition. The factual material of the media serves to develop the individual's interests and aspirations and provides integrating themes and an opportunity to identify, in fact or at least in fantasy, with movements that transcend one's own personal affairs. Even the entertainment material in the media provide potential gratification for one's autonomy and integration needs. Popular fiction, with its stress on the ultimate victory of virtue, does help to suggest that one is ultimately the master of one's fate. In their early study of the daytime radio serial, Warner and Henry (1948) stressed that the fans of these programs developed a characteristic weltanschauung that was reflected in the "big sister" plot and character development; furthermore, the heroine of that serial shared the role of many of the listeners, but her masterly performance in it gave the role a power, importance, and meaningfulness that could strengthen the listener's own sense of worth.

Stimulation theories. The viewpoints to which we turn here, like the autonomy theories just considered, are cognitive paradigms that stress the active growth needs of the individual; but while the autonomy theories concerned an internal goal of these strivings, the stimulation theories emphasize an external orientation. They view the person as having a stimulus hunger, a need for varied experience constituting an exploratory drive that makes the individual characteristically curious, seeking after novelty, rather capricious, playful and prone to fads. Besides bread, the person needs food for thought (or at least circuses) to escape from the aversive state of boredom.

Among the more developed views of this aspect of the person are Berlyne (1969) on complexity, arousal, and curiosity and Fiske and Maddi (1961) on the need for varied experience. Lest it be thought that such theorists vastly overestimate the human being's needs to know and to experience everything, it should be remembered that a number of "comparative" psychologists (for example, Harlow, 1953; Hebb, 1955; Fowler, 1965) have stressed that lower animals also exhibit exploratory drives and curiosity needs. For example, rats tend spontaneously to alternate their behavior and monkeys show willingness to work for no other reward than a chance to look out of their cage into a lively laboratory scene. The need for stimulation has even been given a physiological basis in theories that the limbic system requires a certain amount of activity in reverberating circuits in order for the individual to respond adequately and discriminatingly to outside stimulation, and in such exotic observations as the detrimental effect of dream deprivation (Foulkes, 1966).

While critics complain that mass communications are not sufficiently stimulating, for many members of the public living a "life of quiet desperation" there is probably much more action, excitement, and stimulation in the contents of a newspaper or a television program than in their quotidian experience in the real world. Most people tend to associate primarily with individuals of their own age, sex, socioeconomic class, etc., so that mass communication content is a vastly broadening experience, putting them in touch with a much wider range of people than do their daily lives. In terms of the world's total diversity, television and newspaper fare may be narrow, repetitious, and stereotyped; but they are probably less so than one's own direct experiences with the world. The distance from one's own experience of so much of what is presented in mass communications (indeed, its distance from anyone's experience in that it is often so unrealistic) can only have the effect of providing stimulating novelty. Insofar as there is a human need to be stimulated, mass communications furnish a wealth of actualities and fantasies that provide its recipients with something to think about and an escape from boredom.

Teleological theories. We turn here to the first of two cognitive growth theories that depict the individual as somewhat more passive as regards initiation of behavior than did the autonomy and stimulation theories just considered. The first of these passive theories, the one that stresses a more internal orientation, we call the "teleological" paradigm. This title has in the past connoted theological and vitalistic assumptions, but the views under consideration here stem more from a computer analogy for information processing. The person is viewed as a pattern matcher, who contains internal representations of desired end states to which one matches one's perception of the present situation, receiving feedback as one changes one's orientation toward the outside world which indicates whether one's changes are increasing or decreasing the match between the current actual and the desired end pattern. This partial depiction of the person uses concepts like internal representation, information search, pattern matching, cybernetics, and feedback. It stresses acts rather than responses and plans rather than stimuli.

Early precursors of this viewpoint include Brentano, Husserl, Stumpf, and others of the "act psychology" school, but it came fully into its own only as the computer became familiar as a model for the human brain and for our conscious experience and behavior. The idea is developed in Wiener's (1961) notion of cybernetics, in Ashby's (1952) design for a brain, and Von Neumann's (1958) suggestions regarding the computer as an analog for the brain. It is stated more fully in the volume by Miller, Galanter and Pribrum (1960) on plans and the structure of behavior, and receives its fullest recent account in Powers' (1973) theory of behavior as the control of perception.

This depiction of people as carrying within their heads patterns of end states that they strive to match with their current perceptions of the external world suggests that mass communications can be a fertile source of gratification. The fictional material often—all too often, according to some arbiters of artistic taste—encapsulates a conventional morality that fits nicely the viewpoint of the "silent majority" of the public. Such material provides constant reaffirmation of the wisdom and ultimate vindication of one's choice of and persistence in a respectable life-style by showing that those who cling to it tend to be rewarded, while those who adopt unconventional life-styles that flaunt the rules of propriety or conventional morality tend to come to an evil end. But even for the unconventional segments of the public, mass communications offer some fits to their own deviant conceptual patterns, if they choose the less orthodox media content. Moreover, the conventional stories, in order to achieve dramatic tension, frequently show deviant forces temporarily prevailing until the final denouement; hence, those outside the conventional ranks can receive some gratification by observing that their way of life is fun while it lasts. Turning from the entertainment content to the "factual" media content, the latter also tends to match the eternal verities by which people live, stressing themes like loyalty to one's country, helpfulness to other people, etc., depicting deviations in a somewhat softened form or as rather reprehensible. And where advocacy journalists present unsavory aspects of reality, those who find such verisimilitude disturbing to the internal pattern to which they are trying to fit the outside world can tune out, while others who already have developed a jaundiced view of the world can find a welcome confirmation in this debunking of the all-is-well theme.

Utilitarian theories. The final cognitive growth paradigm, like the teleological theories just discussed, depicts the person as rather passive. Unlike the teleological theories, it stresses the external rather than the internal orientation of the person. These "utilitarian theories" view the individual as a problem solver who approaches any situation as an opportunity to acquire useful information or new skills for coping with life's challenges. These theories stress the person's view of life as an endeavor containing challenges which require considerable skills to meet but which, with effort, can be surmounted. They also depict the individual as taking an essentially positive stance toward the outside world, including communications from it, because they view it as a valuable source of helpful and relevant information.

This notion of people as somewhat plodding, pragmatic, and positive thinking, constantly improving their repertory of coping mechanisms, is a fundamental assumption in such superficially disparate approaches as Lewin's (1951) field theory and Tolman's (1932) theory of purposive behavior. It also informs the thinking of a long line of needs-instrumentality theorists, extending at least from Woodruff and DiVesta (1948) and Smith, Bruner and White (1956) through Peak (1955) and Rosenberg (1956) to Fishbein and Ajzen (1972). In the communications field, it has inspired Bauer's (1964) notion of persuasion as problem solving; Leventhal's (1970) idea that communications in order to be persuasive should stress, not so much convincing the recipient to share the source's viewpoint, but rather prescribing just how the recipient can comply; and McGuire's (1969) notion that under a wide range of circumstances communications are persuasive to the extent that their intent is explicit rather than disguised.

While professional educators have often looked askance at the teaching role of the mass media, their negative appraisal may be based on professional disdain and snobbery as much as on any demonstrated educational deficiency in the media as compared to the other teaching institutions of our society. The informational content of mass communication probably accounts for as much of the individual's sophistication in public affairs and grasp of social and psychological phenomena as do those other two educational institutions of our culture, the home and the school. Even the entertainment content (such as the daytime television serial and the novel) conveys a great deal of information to viewers or readers about taste in clothes and furnishings, styles of life, and appropriate interpersonal relationships. Studies going back to the Lazarsfeld-Stanton (1941, 1949) period of communication research have demonstrated that even the daytime radio serial was considered by its audience to be a valuable source of information on how to cope with life's problems (Herzog, 1944). The sophisticated educator might wonder whether what the soap operas teach is the best lesson; but from the preoccupation with audience gratification that concerns us here, the important point is that the audience believed to a poignant extent that they were learning how to live and cope from these radio dramas. From this partial point of view of the person as a striving problem solver, mass communications offer a wide range of gratifications in the form of content that is perceived as instructive regarding how to live, how to manage, what is happening, and what it means.

THE AFFECTIVE MOTIVES:
THEIR RELEVANCE TO MEDIA GRATIFICATION

The eight motives that were considered in the previous section all came under the "cognitive" rubric. Here we turn to the second major division, the "affective" motives, including the eight shown in the lower half of Table 1. As mentioned earlier, these affective motives deal more with the dynamic energizing aspects of human motivation, characterized by feeling states, while the cognitive motives deal more with the directive or orienting forces, involving information-processing tendencies.

Affective Motives Stressing Preservation of the Current Equilibrium

Four of the perennially popular motivational paradigms belonging to the affective family stress needs that are essentially conservative, being directed toward maintaining one's equilibrium rather than toward any kind of personal growth. Of these preservation motives, two stress the person's active initiative in obtaining gratification, namely, tension-reduction theories and expressive theories. The *tension-reduction* theories focus on more internally oriented goal states, while the *expressive* theories stress aspects of our motivation that are directed toward the external environment. The other two motivational paradigms that stress affective preservation, the *ego-defensive* and the *reinforcement* theories, focus on aspects of human motivation that involve more passive reacting rather than active instigation. We shall first consider the two affective preservation paradigms that stress active initiation and then the two that focus more on passive reaction tendencies.

Tension-reduction theories. We consider here the "nirvana" model of human motivation, prevalent at many times and places, that views the person as a tension system such that any reduction of arousal is gratifying and any increase aversive. Theorists deriving their inspiration from fields as far apart as mysticism and physics have felt at home with this notion that the ultimate goal of the individual is a zero state of arousal that approximates personal annihilation. In some cases the theorist's guiding idea seems to be a theological one, involving reunion with an all-embracing unitary infinite. At the opposite extreme, the point of departure is a mechanistic one, with the person perceived as driven toward compliance with the second law of thermodynamics.

Among the many important proponents of a tension-reduction viewpoint one must include Freud (1933) and most of his followers in the psychoanalytic schools. The dominant Hullian behavioristic school (Hull, 1952; Dollard and Miller, 1950; Miller, 1959) has also taken as a fundamental postulate the notion that reward involves drive reduction. Behind them all lies Aristotle who, while not a member of the American Psychological Association, is not to be completely discounted for that reason. The Philosopher's use in *Ars Poetica* of the catharsis concept to explain the appeal of fearsome tragedy introduced the notion of tension-reduction through vicarious expression.

This Aristotelian cathartic theory of drama indicates a particular relevance of the tension-reduction theory to possible gratifications of mass communication, namely, relief through vicarious expression of one's pent-up emotions through fantasy. To Aristotle's mention of pity and fear, the modern preoccupation with violence in life and drama compels us to add aggression, all being negative emotions needing release according to the tension-reduction view. A corollary of these theories is that these emotions are convertible as to target and mode of expression, such that if one does not gain release by expressing them externally, one may turn them against oneself; and if not released in fantasy, then in reality. Apologists for the growing level of violence in the print and electronic media often use the catharsis concept to argue that presentations of aggressive materials are beneficial to the individual and society by allowing expression in external fantasies of destructive tendencies that might otherwise be turned inward against the self or outward against other persons. In the U.S. Surgeon General's Report (U.S. Surgeon General Scientific Advisory Committee, 1972), five volumes of research results include very little support for this notion, although there are still some who adhere to it .(Feshbach and Singer, 1971). Leaving aside this controverted area of the effects of television violence, the tension-reduction paradigm of motivation suggests that one may obtain release from other emotional tensions through identifying with and abreacting one's own pent-up feelings in fantasies facilitated by the factual and fictional materials presented in mass communication. Failing this, the theory suggests one might at least be afforded some rest and relaxation by the distractions offered by the media.

Expressive theories. Among the affective preservation paradigms that view the person as actively initiating behavior, the tension-reduction theories just considered deal with an internally oriented goal state, while the expressive theories to which we turn here deal with the person as more externally oriented. The gist of this notion is that the person gains gratification by self-expression and acting out. Just as the exercise of one's physical skills and strenuous exertion in sports and recreation is rewarding, so also is expressing or acting out one's feelings and beliefs. Attesting to one's existence by leaving one's mark in the form of an achievement, a trivial graffiti or even a destructive act are all considered within this partial view of the person as being rewarding in their own right, independent of any utilitarian return that they may occasion.

Some theorists argue for the importance of the expressive need by pointing out that human play (Huizinga, 1939; Leont'ev, 1965) or creativity (Peckham, 1965) shows our need for self-exertion and self-assertion. The idea seems also to force itself on developmental psychologists from K. Bühler's (1918; C. Bühler, 1928) notion of "functional pleasure" (a delight derived from exercising a function) to Piaget (1968). Various arousal and activation theorists (Peak, 1968; Arnold, 1960; Berlyne, 1969) have also suggested, though not so emphatically, the reward value of acting out. Stephenson (1966) has stressed the play factor in mass communications.

The expressive paradigm is heuristically provocative as regards gratification from mass communication. There is the possibility that it facilitates fantasy whereby one can, through identification with the characters depicted, vicariously express one's feelings rewardingly (along the lines that "it is lovely to be in love," or "the man you love to hate"). One can also "do high deeds in Hungary to pass all men's believing" through fantastic identification with heroic characters and even cartoon animals, possibilities to which our attention has already been called by students of the effects of exposure to comic books, television, etc., (Singer, 1971). Existential theorists have stressed the need for activity in order to gain an identity: until one utilizes one's existence by making choices and acting on them, one lacks an essence. It might seem that action through vicarious participation in events depicted in mass communications is a rather pitiful way of asserting one's being and so developing an essence, but perhaps these opportunities are more gratifying through their richness than one's real-life possibilities are through their actuality. Even where this acting out involves vicarious participation in seemingly disturbing events (the Gothic novel, the terror film, the frightening television drama, etc.), Freud and the other psychoanalysts, in their discussion of the utility of nightmares and of seemingly disturbing symptoms, have suggested ways in which these can be gratifying considering the total situation of the person. By acquainting the person with issues, whether in the passing political scene or the perennial human condition, mass communications facilitate the person's developing an attitude or point of view, which ideological development itself can be a gratifying, self-enhancing activity besides furnishing the basis for subsequent action in word or deed that might constitute a further rewarding self-expression. This play concept of the person also reminds us of the perennial popularity of the game features in mass communication: crossword puzzles in newspapers, contests even in literary magazines, mystery novels, daytime TV quiz programs and—turning from participant to spectator play—the sports news.

Ego-defensive theories. Among the affective preservation notions of human motivation, two which depict the person as rather passive include the ego-defensive and the reinforcement. The two differ in that the ego-defensive paradigm, which we consider in this section, focuses on internally oriented aspects of the person's drives while the reinforcement theories stress externally directed aspects. The gist of the ego-defensive notion is that through the life span we develop a certain image of ourselves that we are highly motivated to maintain because it allows us to live with ourselves and our world. The person clings tenaciously to this self-concept because it is formed with difficulty. Its formation requires a creative synthesis and distillation of a great deal of conflicting information and divergent considerations; its development requires a considerable amount of rationalization and costly rejection of attractive alternatives. To maintain it, the person uses the "defense mechanisms" described by the psychoanalysts such as denial, reaction-formation, displacement, personification, etc.

Theorists who have used this point of view creatively have typically adhered to a psychoanalytic outlook. The classical work on the "authoritarian personality" by Adorno, Frenkel-Brunswick, Levinson and Stanford (1950), somewhat adumbrated by Sartre (1948), is perhaps the best developed presentation. It depicts anti-minority attitudes, such as anti-Semitism, as part of a larger syndrome typically involving idealization of authority figures and the in-group accompanied by disdain and hostility toward the powerless, the minorities, and those who deviate from the norm. This personality structure is derived in turn from a resolution of the Oedipal complex where the boy learns early to repress hostile feelings toward his father in order to avoid punishment, bolstering the repression with a reaction formation idealizing the father matched by a hostility to those outside the power structure and differing from the cultural norm. This approach is worked out further in Smith, Bruner and White (1956) and most fully by Katz (1960) and his students of the "functional" school of attitude change (Sarnoff, 1960; Stotland, Katz and Patchen, 1959). Cooper and Jahoda (1947) have also used this ego-defensive notion to account for response to mass communication material.

The ego-defensive theories lie implicitly or explicitly behind much of the discussion of selective attention and distorted perception of media contents by the audience motivated to maintain its preconceptions. The average person is presented with a range of materials by the newspaper, the television set, etc., that is far wider than one could possibly obtain in one's ordinary life which is typically spent with persons much like oneself. From this material one can extract information to construct one's self-concept, one's view of the world and of human nature and social relations as needed; and when one has already formulated such concepts, then mass communications allow one to bolster this image of oneself and one's world. And in desperate times where one's rationalizations and self-image are tottering or shattered, one can at least immerse oneself in the distractions offered by mass communication and so win at least temporary escape from one's anxieties.

Reinforcement theories. Ego-defensive and reinforcement theories are alike in depicting people as passive in achieving their affective preservation needs; the reinforcement theories conceptualize the individual as more externally directed in defining the desired end state than do the ego-defensive theories we have just considered. The central theme of the reinforcement paradigm is that the person in any given situation behaves in ways which have led to reward when in the past one was in a comparable situation. The theory also postulates that experiences which have accompanied rewards in the past themselves acquire secondary reward value. Behavioristic theories of this type usually specify in considerable detail (with more quantitative precision and empirical basis than is typically found in psychology) the degree to which a strengthening of such habits is affected by various factors in the situation (for example, the intensity of the drive state at the time, the amount of reward, its immediacy, and the periodicity at which it was received).

Such reinforcement theorists dominated scientific psychology during the first half of this century. Names like Pavlov and Thorndike, J. B. Watson and Guthrie, Hull and Skinner, N. E. Miller and Estes, and a multitude of other "Hullians" such as K. Spence, E. Hilgard, O. H. Mowrer, R. Sears, and C. I. Hovland remind one that this view until recently constituted the establishment, hard-headed school of general experimental psychology. While these reinforcement theorists no longer dominate basic research, the viewpoint is still used creatively by attitude change researchers such as Janis, Staats, A. J. and B. E. Lott, R. F. Weiss, W. Weiss, R. M. Baron (see Greenwald, Brock and Ostrom, 1968), and in the behavioral therapy school of clinical psychology (Bandura, 1969; Wolpe, 1969).

Since exposure to mass communication is almost invariably voluntary, the content is typically designed to be intrinsically rewarding to the receivers, whether by conveying needed information, providing entertainment, bringing one into contact with other people, or whatever. The content for which the recipients may feel no need (such as some commercial and political messages) is typically interlarded with more rewarding material. Aside from the attractive contents, some exposure habits tend to be rewarding in themselves; for example, watching television during mealtime or during the relaxed part of the evening in the company of one's family and friends, or reading a newspaper or book while sitting in a quiet and comfortable environment free from one's daily cares. For all these reasons the mass media tend to be directly rewarding, and to acquire constantly increasing secondary reinforcement value, so that they become habituating.

Affective Growth Theories

Like the four theories just considered (tension-reduction, expressive, ego-defensive, and reinforcement), the four to which we turn here all fall under the "affective" rubric (rather than the "cognitive" which included our first eight theories). While the four affective theories just considered all stress the person's motivation as directed toward preservation of a current equilibrium, the four affective theories to which we now turn stress people's motivation to grow or improve their present states.

These four affective growth theories constitute the last row in Table 1. Two of them stress the individual as active in the initiation of behavior, namely, the *assertion* and the *affiliation* theories. The other two, *identification* and *modeling*, depict the individual as more passive. We shall discuss the four in sequence, in each case following the previous organization of describing the essence of the theory, then identifying some of its proponents, and finally considering its implication for mass communication gratification.

Assertion theories. Of the two affective growth paradigms which view human motivation in the active mode, the assertion theories are those which stress the internal orientation of the person's drives. They view the person as a competitive achiever, seeking success, admiration, and dominance. Humans are regarded as striving to develop their potentials in order to enhance esteem by self and others. Human society is conceived as an organized struggle in which the individual's aim is personal aggrandizement and surpassing other people.

This view of human society as a war of each against all receives explicit articulation in Hobbes and Nietzsche among the philosophers and in one of sociology's founding fathers, Herbert Spencer, as well as in the social Darwinists such as Bagehot, Gumplowicz, and Sumner. Alfred Adler (1927) split with Freud by maintaining that the will to power is a more important part of human motivation than is sexuality. McClelland (1961) and Weiner (1974) have emphasized achievement motivation, and both they and Winter (1973) have stressed power needs in human personality. Lorenz (1966) and other ethologists, together with allied social commentators such as Morris (1967) and Tiger and Fox (1971), have also stressed the basically aggressive facet of human motivation.

The assertion theories might seem to be focusing on an aspect of human motivation which calls for so aggressive and domineering a stance that mass media consumption would be too passive an enterprise to offer any appreciable gratification. However, in at least two ways mass media consumption can satisfy these assertive needs. For a large part of the adult public, mass communications constitute the main educational provision of society, offering information, indicating needed skills and even supplying some of them, depicting ways of coping, and suggesting new worlds to conquer. All of these elements can contribute realistically to a gratification of the individual's need for power and achievement. In the domain of fantasy also, mass communications give opportunities to identify with powerful figures of public life and fiction. It is likely that to large sections of the public lacking any real power or competence or even hope of attaining them, these fantasies, which are greatly enriched by the media, offer the main possibility for obtaining gratification for the assertive aspects of their personalities.

Affiliation theories. Continuing our discussion of affective growth paradigms that stress active initiation we turn, with the affiliation theories, to those that emphasize the externally oriented aspect of this motivational mode. These theories view people as being basically altruistic and cohesive, seeking acceptance and affection in interpersonal relations. The affiliative concepts stress that aspect of human motivation that drives the person to establish with other people connections that are characterized by mutual helpfulness and reciprocated positive affect.

Theories that focus on altruism and cooperativeness have at least as old a history as the more egotistical assertion theories, stressing interpersonal competition and subordination, which we just considered. At the beginning of scientific psychology and sociology at the turn of the twentieth century, this side of human personality was stressed by Ribot in his notion of sympathy, by Kropotkin in his concept of a mutual aid need, and by Giddings in his emphasis on consciousness of kind. During the middle period of the century, theorists like Sorokin (1950) with his notion of altruism and Lewin (1951)—and the group movement to which his theories and personality gave rise (Back, 1972)—kept the idea the central one within social and psychological thought. Currently, the notion of affiliation needs and the bases of interpersonal attraction and helping behavior is receiving a vast amount of detailed research attention (for example, Byrne, 1971; Aronson, 1970; Berscheid and Walster, 1969; Rubin, 1970).

The implications of the affiliation paradigm for mass media gratification are numerous. Among the communication theorists, Katz, Gurevitch and Haas (1973) have particularly emphasized the usefulness of mass communication in connecting the individual with various human networks. Media contents serve to reaffirm for the recipients their sense of participating in the events and institutions depicted, of being part of the human drama on a broader stage than their own personal concerns. Media contents also provide the individual with a conversation piece that can serve as common ground for interaction with other people whom one meets in daily life in like circumstances. Again, some of the fictional content like that of the daytime television or radio serial bring the faithful audience into more daily contact with the characters portrayed than the audience attains with any of the real people in their lives except possibly for a few members of their nuclear family. The extent to which the audience experiences substitute socialization by interacting with the almost-real characters in the daytime serials is poignantly exhibited in a study of the British public's reaction to the termination in 1969 of the long-time radio serial, *The Dales* (Blumler, Brown and McQuail, 1970).

Identification theories. Turning to the passive subclass of affective growth models, we start with the identification theories as the paradigm stressing the person's internal goal orientations. Included here are concepts of people as role players or identity adopters, seeking ego enhancement through the addition of satisfying roles to their self-concepts. One gains self-acceptance and pleasure through acquiring additional role identities and by increasing the perceived significance of those roles that are already a part of one's self-concept.

This partial view of the person as a constellation of roles derived from his social statuses and fantasies and individualized by his personality idiosyncracies has been central to the theory of the person used by Linton (1945) and Newcomb (1943) and has been developed in detail by Sarbin and Allen (1968). This view of the person as a role adopter and player has been used particularly creatively by Goffman (1959) with his concepts of self presentation, encounters, altercasting, etc., and lies behind much of the theorizing of the growing schools of ethnomethodology (Garfinkle, 1967) and symbolic interactionism (Blumer, 1969).

Since the mass media, obviously in their fictional presentations and to an appreciable extent even in their factual ones, present people playing recognized and stylized roles, these identification theories have considerable relevance to the gratifications to be obtained from media consumption. Even where the content is not explicitly designed to present characters in attractive roles (for example, in news stories), the media tend to portray people in a myriad of dramatic situations involving interesting responses that acquaint the audience with a variety of roles and life-styles, thus supplying material for possible role identities to add to one's own self-concept. The fictional content explicitly presents people in roles, typically stylized for prompt recognition and often quite glamorous, allowing the easy adoption in fantasy of ego-enhancing roles through identification with the characters. Even where the persons depicted are presented in pedestrian roles (as in the case of the inevitable "housewife and mother" in the daytime serials), the presentation is such as to emphasize and enhance the significance of these roles which in fact are shared by most members of the audience (Katzman, 1972).

Modeling theories. This final paradigm of human motivation, like the identification theories just considered, views the individual as seeking affective growth in a rather passive manner. But these modeling theories differ from the identification theories in emphasizing the more external orientations of gratification seeking. They focus on the suggestible aspect of human proclivities, our automatic tendency to empathize with the feelings of the people we observe and to imitate their actions, matching our behavior to that of observed others who serve as models for how we are to react, and to take pleasure in interpersonal similarity.

A number of social theorists have stressed this tendency of the person to model behavior on that of other people. LeBon with his stress on suggestibility falls into this group as do Binet and other Parisian psychologists who came under the intellectual influence of Charcot and later Janet at the Salpêtrière clinic. The imitation tendency has been stressed also by students of infants' speech acquisition and by behaviorists (Miller and Dollard, 1941). Some researchers have recently come to stress the tendency of children and adults to imitate scenes they see depicted in mass communication or in their individual experience (Bandura, 1970; Berkowitz, 1969). While the earlier theorists thought of the imitative need as innate, the more recent behaviorists regard the tendency as an acquired disposition, so that interpersonal similarity is a secondary rather than a primary reinforcement; but this distinction between phylogenetic and onto-genetic acquisition (Byrne, 1971) is not terribly critical to the present question of media gratification through modeling.

Mass communications present numerous models for easy and gratifying imitation. The print media through articulate writers and interpreters are frequently able to present models of thought patterns that are more explicit and comprehensible than any that the average person is likely to receive from his or her peers. The pictorial media such as television, motion pictures, and comic books, present vividly and dramatically models of physical behavior from which the individual can obtain gratification by imitation in fact or fantasy. Students of mass communication fiction have stressed the prevalence of gratifying daydreams of oneself acting like the fantastic hero or the prototypic housewife and mother. This gratifying modeling extends beyond the dramatic content that is being intentionally presented. Daytime television serial viewers are reported to dress in idiosyncratic styles and to furnish their homes in the characteristic fashions that reflect those of the characters and actors presented. Again, the five volumes of studies in the U.S. Surgeon General's Report (1972) indicate the audience's tendency to imitate the undesirable aggressive behavior of people depicted in violence shows and news programs, even where such scenes are presented with seeming disapproval. But whether it is an innate or learned reward, and whether the material presented is or is not intended as a model, this modeling tendency of the human personality makes it likely that the audience will obtain gratification from interpersonal similarity and matching one's feelings, thoughts, and behavior to that of the models depicted in mass communications.

CONCLUDING COMMENTS

Our assignment is this *Annual Review* devoted to the uses and gratifications approach to mass communication research called for us to take psychological motives as our point of departure, which explains in some degree our emphases and omissions. In a preliminary discussion of the reasonable objection that mass media exposure is so situationally determined that recipient motivation has little to do with it, we granted that initial exposure might be largely the outcome of chance and situational factors. However, on the basis of a postulate that for a behavior to be maintained it must be reinforced, we argued that human needs and gratifications are significant determinants of the typical continued exposure to given types of materials.

To call attention to as many as possible of the gratifications offered by mass communications, we generated a broad and inclusive system of 16 basic human motives, each of which approximated a "model of man" or partial view of human nature. Each motive was then discussed briefly as regards its basic concept, its representative proponents and its implications regarding the gratifications to be derived from mass communications. The 16 motives were generated by a procedure designed to be inclusive of the significant aspects of human needs and gratifications, efficient by limiting the list to minimally overlapping motives, and heuristically provocative as regards suggesting the nature of media gratifications. The most important criterion to be met by such a system is that it be creatively stimulating to the user. Hence, other students of the topic might well have started with alternative dimensions for generating the motives or might have filled the cells of our matrix with motives different from the ones we identified.

To exploit fully this system of motives (or any other comparably inclusive set of motives that one finds more comfortable to one's own thought patterns) would require a fuller consideration of the media structure and past findings and theories about uses and gratifications than was employed here. One should, for example, list the numerous uses and gratifications to the individual that have been suggested in the writings on this topic since the Lazarsfeld-Stanton work in the early 1940s, adding up to 35 years of thinking by a number of very insightful persons (though admittedly the uses-and-gratifications approach was heavily used only at the beginning and the end of this 35-year period). This list of purported gratifications could then be related to the 16 general motivational paradigms, with the likelihood that pairing a certain set of gratifications with a given motive might be provocative regarding how other motives might be used to suggest still other gratifications. A motivational matrix such as the one presented here could also be made more useful for present purposes by analyzing mass communication into its meaningful subparts (such as lists of media types and lists of content types). Each motive might then be confronted with each of the elements in the several lists for increased suggestions of possible media gratifications.

REFERENCES

ABELSON, R. P., E. ARONSON, W. J. McGUIRE, T. M. NEWCOMB, M. J. ROSENBERG and P. H. TANNENBAUM [eds.] (1968) Theories of Cognitive Consistency. Chicago: Rand-McNally.

ABELSON, R. P. and M. J. ROSENBERG (1958) "Symbolic psycho-logic." Behavioral Science 3: 1-13.

ADLER, A. (1927) Practice and Theory of Individual Psychology. New York: Harcourt, Brace & World.

ADORNO, T. W., E. FRENKEL-BRUNSWICK, D. J. LEVINSON and R. N. STANFORD (1950) The Authoritarian Personality. New York: Harper.

ALLPORT, G. W. (1961) Pattern and Growth in Personality. New York: Holt, Rinehart & Winston.

——— and H. S. ODBERT (1936) "Trait-names: a psycholaxical study." Psychological Monographs 47, 1 (Whole No. 211).

ALLPORT, G. W., P. E. VERNON and G. LINDZEY (1951) A Study of Values. Rev. ed. Boston: Houghton Mifflin.

ARNOLD, M. (1960) Emotion and Personality. New York: Columbia Univ. Press.

ARONSON, E. (1970) "Some antecedents of interpersonal attraction," pp. 143-173 in W. J. Arnold and D. Levine (eds.) Nebraska Symposium of Motivation. Lincoln: University of Nebraska Press.

ASCH, S. E. (1952) Social Psychology. Englewood Cliffs, N.J.: Prentice-Hall.

ASHBY, W. R. (1952) Design for a Brain. New York: Wiley.

BACK, K. W. (1972) Beyond Words. New York: Russell Sage.

BANDURA, A. [ed.] (1970) Theories of Modeling. New York: Atherton.

——— (1969) Principles of Behavior Modification. New York: Holt, Rinehart & Winston.

BARTLETT, F. C. (1932) Remembering. New York: Macmillan.

BAUER, R. A. (1964) "The obstinate audience." American Psychologist 19: 319-328.

BEM, D. (1972) "Self-perception theory," pp. 1-62 in L. Berkowitz (ed.) Advances in Experimental Social Psychology. New York: Academic Press.

BERKOWITZ, L. (1969) Roots of Aggression. New York: Atherton.

BERLYNE, D. E. (1969) "Laughter, humor and play," pp. 795-852 in G. Lindzey and E. Aronson (eds.) Handbook of Social Psychology. Reading, Mass.: Addison-Wesley.

BERSCHEID, E. and E. WALSTER (1969) Interpersonal Attraction. Reading, Mass.: Addison-Wesley.

BLUMER, H. (1969) Symbolic Interactionism. Englewood Cliffs, N.J.: Prentice-Hall.

BLUMLER, J. G., J. R. BROWN, and D. McQUAIL (1970) "The Dales: a 'uses and gratifications' investigation of a daytime radio serial." Leeds: University of Leeds, Centre for Television Research. (mimeo)

BOGART, L. (1965) "The mass media and the blue-collar worker," in A. Bennett and W. Gomberg (eds.) The Blue Collar World. Englewood Cliffs, N.J.: Prentice-Hall.

BREHM, J. W. (1966) A Theory of Psychological Reactance. New York: Academic Press.

BRIDGES, K.M.B. (1932) "Emotional development in early infancy." Child Development 3: 324-341.

BUHLER, C. (1928) Kindheit und Jugend. Leipzig: Hirsch.

BUHLER, K. (1918, German edition) The Moral Development of the Child. Rev. ed., 1930. New York: Harcourt-Brace.

BYRNE, D. (1971) The Attraction Paradigm. New York: Academic Press.

CARTWRIGHT, D. and F. HARARY (1956) "Structural balance." Psychological Review 63: 277-293.

CATTELL, R. B. (1957) Personality and Motivation Structure and Measurement. New York: World Book.

COOPER, E. and M. JAHODA (1947) "The evasion of propaganda." Journal of Psychology 23: 15-25.

DEMBER, W. N. (1974) "Motivation and the cognitive revolution." American Psychologist 29: 161-168.

DICHTER, E. (1971) Motivating Human Behavior. New York: McGraw-Hill.

DOLLARD, J. and N. E. MILLER (1950) Personality and Psychotherapy. New York: McGraw-Hill.

ERIKSON, E. H. (1963) Childhood and Society. 2nd ed. New York: Norton.

EYSENCK, H. J. (1953) Structure of Human Personality. New York: Wiley.

FESHBACH, S. and R. D. SINGER (1971) Television and Aggression. San Francisco: Jossey-Bass.

FESTINGER, L. (1957) A Theory of Cognitive Dissonance. Evanston, Ill.: Row, Peterson.

––– (1954) "A theory of social comparison processes." Human Relations 7: 117-140.

FISHBEIN, M. and I. AJZEN (1972) "Attitudes and opinions," pp. 487-544 in P. H. Mussen and M. R. Rosenjweig (eds.) Annual Review of Psychology. Palo Alto, Calif.: Annual Reviews.

FISKE, D. W. and S. R. MADDI (1961) Functions of Varied Experience. Homewood, Ill.: Dorsey.

FOULKES, W. D. (1966) Psychology of Sleep. New York: Scribner.

FOWLER, H. (1965) Curiosity and Exploratory Behavior. New York: Macmillan.

FREUD, S. (1933, German edition) New introductory lectures on psycho-analysis. Rev. ed., 1964. London: Hogarth.

FROMM, E. (1964) The Heart of Man. New York: Harper & Row.

GARFINKLE, H. (1967) Studies in Ethnomethodology. Englewood Cliffs, N.J.: Prentice-Hall.

GOFFMAN, E. (1959) Presentation of self in everyday life. New York: Doubleday.

GREENWALD, A. G., T. C. BROCK, and T. M. OSTROM [eds.] (1968) Psychological Foundations of Attitudes. New York: Academic Press.

HARLOW, H. F. (1953) "Motivation as a factor in the acquisition of new responses," pp. 24-49 in Current Theory and Research in Motivation. Lincoln: University of Nebraska Press.

HEBB, D. O. (1955) "Drives and the C.N.S. (conceptual nervous system)." Psychological Review 62: 243-254.

HEIDER, F. (1958) The Psychology of Interpersonal Relations. New York: Wiley.

HERZOG, H. (1944) "What do we really know about daytime serial listeners?" in P. F. Lazarsfeld and F. N. Stanton (eds.) Radio Research 1942-1943. New York: Duell, Sloan & Pearce.

HUIZINGA, J. (1939) Homo Ludens. Amsterdam: Pantheon.

HULL, C. L. (1952) A Behavior System. New Haven: Yale University Press.

JAMES, W. (1884) "What is emotion?" Mind 9: 188-205.

JONES, E. E., D. E. KNOUSE, H. H. KELLEY, R. E. NISBETT, S. VALENS, and B. WEINER (1972) Attribution: Perceiving the Causes of Behavior. Morristown, N.J.: General Learning Press.

JONES, E. E. and C. WORTMAN (1973) Ingratiation: An Attributional Approach. Morristown, N.J.: General Learning Press.

JUNG, C. G. (1933) Psychological Types. New York: Harcourt, Brace & World. (Reprinted in Collected Works, Vol. 6. Princeton: Princeton University Press, 1971.)

KATZ, D. (1960) "The functional approach to the study of attitude." Public Opinion Quarterly 24: 163-204.

KATZ, E., J. G. BLUMLER, and M. GUREVITCH (1974) "Utilization of mass communication by the individual: an overview," in J. G. Blumler and E. Katz (eds.) The Uses of Mass Communications: Current Perspectives on Gratifications Research. Beverly Hills: Sage.

KATZ, E., M. GUREVITCH, and H. HAAS (1973) "On the uses of the mass media for important things." American Sociological Review 38: 164-181.

KATZMAN, N. (1972) "Television soap operas: what's been going on anyway?" Public Opinion Quarterly 36: 200-212.

KELLEY, H. H. (1967) "Attribution theory in social psychology," in D. Levine (ed.) Nebraska Symposium on Motivation. Lincoln: University of Nebraska Press.

KULPE, O. (1922) Vorlesungen über Psychologie. 2nd ed.

LATANE, B. [ed.] (1966) "Studies in social comparison." Journal of Experimental Social Psychology 2 (Monograph Supplement).

LAZARSFELD, P. F. and F. N. STANTON [eds.] (1949) Communications Research 1948-1949. New York: Harper.

——— (1941) Radio Research, 1941. New York: Duell, Sloan & Pearce.

LEONT'EV, A. N. (1965) Problems of mental development. 2nd ed. Moscow: Mysl',

LERNER, M. J. (1970) "The desire for justice and reactions to victims," pp. 205-229 in J. Macauley and L. Berkowitz (eds.) Altruism and Helping Behavior. New York: Academic Press.

LEVENTHAL, H. (1970) "Findings and theory in the study of fear communications," pp. 119-186 in L. Berkowitz (ed.) Advances in Experimental Social Psychology. New York: Academic Press.

LEVI-STRAUSS, C. (1958) Anthropologie structurale. Paris. (Trans. New York: Basic Books, 1963.)

LEWIN, K. (1951) Field Theory in Social Science. New York: Harper.

LINTON, R. (1945) The Cultural Background of Personality. New York: Appleton-Century-Crofts.

LORENZ, K. (1966) On Aggression. New York: Harcourt, Brace & World.

LOTT, A. J. and B. E. LOTT (1972) "The power of liking: consequences of interpersonal attitudes derived from a liberalized view of secondary reinforcement," pp. 109-148 in L. Berkowitz (ed.) Advances in Experimental Social Psychology. New York: Academic Press.

LUCHINS, A. S. (1942) "Mechanization in problem solving: the effect of Einstellung." Psychological Monographs 54, 6 (Whole No. 248).

MADSEN, K. B. (1974) Modern Theories of Motivation. New York: Wiley-Halsted.

MASLOW, A. H. (1970) Motivation and Personality. 2nd ed. New York: Harper & Row.

McCLELLAND, D. C. (1961) The Achieving Society. Princeton: Van Nostrand.

McDOUGALL, W. (1923) Outline of Psychology. New York: Scribner.

McGUIRE, W. J. (1969) "Suspiciousness of experimenter's intent," pp. 13-57 in R. Rosenthal and R. Rosnow (eds.) Artifact in Behavioral Research. New York: Academic Press.

——— (1966) "Current status of cognitive consistency theories," in S. Feldman (ed.) Cognitive Consistency. New York: Academic Press.

——— (1960) "Cognitive consistency and attitude change." Journal of Abnormal and Social Psychology 60: 345-353.

MICHOTTE, A. E. (1954, Belgian ed.) The Perception of Causality. Rev. ed., 1963. New York: Basic Books.

MILLER, G. A., E. GALANTER, and K. H. PRIBRUM (1960) Plans and the Structures of Behavior. New York: Holt.

MILLER, N. E. (1959) "Liberalization of basic S-R concepts: extensions to conflict behavior, motivation and social learning," in S. Koch (ed.) Psychology: A Study of a Science, Vol. 2. New York: McGraw-Hill.

——— and J. DOLLARD (1941) Social Learning and Imitation. New Haven: Yale University Press.

MORRIS, D. (1967) The Naked Ape. New York: McGraw-Hill.

MURRAY, H. A. (1968) "Components of an evolving personological system," pp. 5-13 in D. L. Sills (ed.) International Encyclopedia of the Social Sciences. New York: Macmillan.

NEWCOMB, T. M. (1953) "An approach to the study of communicative acts." Psychological Review 60: 393-404.

——— (1943) Personality and Social Change. New York: Dryden.

OSGOOD, C. E. and P. H. TANNENBAUM (1955) "The principle of congruity in the prediction of attitude change." Psychological Review 62: 42-55.

PEAK, H. (1968) "Activation theory," pp. 218-239 in R. P. Abelson et al. (eds.) Theory of Cognitive Consistency. Chicago: Rand-McNally.

——— (1955) "Attitudes and motivations," pp. 149-188 in M. R. Jones (ed.) Nebraska Symposium on Motivation. Lincoln: University of Nebraska Press.

PECKHAM, M. (1965) Man's Rage for Chaos. Philadelphia: Chelton.

PHARES, E. J. (1957) "Expectancy changes in skill and chance situations." Journal of Abnormal and Social Psychology 54: 339-342.

PIAGET, J. (1968) La Structuralisme. Paris: Presses Universitaires de France. (Trans. New York: Basic Books, 1970.)

POWERS, W. T. (1973) Behavior: The Control of Perception. Chicago: Aldine.

ROKEACH, M. (1973) Nature of Human Values. New York: Free Press.

ROSENBERG, M. J. (1956) "Cognitive structure and attitudinal effect." Journal of Abnormal and Social Psychology 53: 367-372.

ROTTER, J. B. (1966) "Generalized expectancies for internal vs external control of reinforcement." Psychological Monographs 80, 1 (Whole No. 609).

RUBIN, Z. (1970) "Measurement of romantic love." Journal of Personality and Social Psychology 16: 265-273.

SARBIN, T. R. and V. L. ALLEN (1968) "Role theory," pp. 488-567 in G. Lindzey and E. Aronson (eds.) Handbook of Social Psychology. Reading, Mass.: Addison-Wesley.

SARNOFF, I. (1960) "Psychoanalytic theory and social attitudes." Public Opinion Quarterly 24: 251-279.

SARTRE, J. P. (1948) Portrait of an Anti-Semite. London: Secker & Warburg. (Reflections sur la Question Juive. Paris: P. Morhien, 1947; New York: Partisan Review, 1946.)

SCHACHTER, S. (1971) Emotion, Obesity and Crime. New York: Academic Press.

SHELDON, W. H. (1942) The Varieties of Temperament. New York: Harper.

SHERIF, M. (1935) "A study of some factors in perception." Archives of Psychology 187.

SINGER, J. L. (1971) Control of Aggression and Violence: Cognitive and Physiological Factors. New York: Academic Press.

SMITH, M. B., J. S. BRUNER, and R. W. WHITE (1956) Opinions and Personality. New York: Wiley.

SOROKIN, P. A. [ed.] (1950) Explorations in Altruistic Love and Behavior. Boston: Beacon.

STEINER, I. D. (1970) "Perceived freedom," pp. 187-248 in L. Berkowitz (ed.) Advances in Experimental Social Psychology. New York: Academic Press.

STEPHENSON, W. (1966) The Play Theory of Mass Communication. Chicago: University of Chicago Press.

STOTLAND, E., D. KATZ, and M. PATCHEN (1959) "The reduction of prejudice through the arousal of self-insight." Journal of Personality 27: 507-531.

SZALAI, A. [ed.] (1972) The Use of Time. The Hague: Mouton.

TIGER, L. and R. FOX (1971) Imperial Animal. New York: Holt, Rinehart & Winston.

TILLICH, P. (1952) The Courage to Be. New Haven: Yale University Press.

TOLMAN, E. C. (1932) Purposive Behavior in Animals and Man. New York: Century.

U.S. Surgeon General Scientific Advisory Committee on Television and Social Behavior (1972) Television and Social Behavior. 5 volumes and introductory volume. Washington, D.C.: Government Printing Office.

VON NEUMANN, J. (1958) The Computer and the Brain. New Haven: Yale University Press.

WARNER, W. L. and W. E. HENRY (1948) "The radio daytime serial: a symbolic analysis." Genetic Psychology Monographs 37: 3-71.

WEINER, B. (1974) Achievement Motivation and Attribution Theory. Morristown, N.J.: General Learning Press.

——— (1972) Theories of Motivation: From Mechanism to Cognition. Chicago: Markham.

WIENER, N. (1961) Cybernetics. 2d edn. New York: John Wiley.

WINTER, D. G. (1973) The Power Motive. New York: Free Press.

WOLPE, J. (1969) The Practice of Behavior Therapy. New York: Pergamon.

WOODRUFF, A. D. and F. DiVESTA (1948) "The relation between values, concepts and attitudes." Educational and Psychological Measurement 8: 645-659.

ZIMBARDO, P. G. (1969) The Cognitive Control of Motivation. New York: Scott-Foresman.

Chapter 9

FUNCTIONAL ANALYSIS AND
MASS COMMUNICATION REVISITED

Charles R. Wright

SOME FIFTEEN YEARS AGO, drawing heavily upon the theoretical orientation of Merton (1957), I attempted to specify a functional perspective for the study of mass communication (Wright, 1959, 1960). The resultant paradigm provided a useful framework (labelled a functional inventory) for the classification of many alleged and some documented consequences of mass communication activities for individuals, groups, societies, and cultural systems. The essay also considered problems in the specification and codification of the kinds of communication phenomena that lend themselves to functional analysis, the need to formulate new hypotheses in terms of functional theory, and a variety of difficulties in inventing research designs and in finding research sites suitable for conducting functional analyses of mass communication. It was noted that various studies during the immediate preceding years had explicitly or implicitly used a functional framework for examining different aspects of mass communication (some were cited by way of illustration) and, therefore, the paper was not a call for something novel; rather, it was a preliminary first step toward explicit consideration of certain theoretical and methodological issues relevant to the future growth of a functional theory of mass communication.

However preliminary the statement was, it has not been superceded. Both the promise of functional analysis and the difficulties inherent in its application to problems of mass communication, which were foreshadowed there, remain timely a decade and a half later. In a recent survey of the historical development of mass media studies, Brown (1970: 55) observes that "there has recently been something of a vogue for the use of Merton's paradigm of functional analysis in the mass media field." Even more recently, F. Gerald Kline (1972), in a

AUTHOR'S NOTE: I am grateful to Professors Mary E. W. Goss and Herbert H. Hyman for their helpful comments on an earlier draft of this paper.

constructive review of theory in mass communication research, states: "It would appear that, in general, the major *leitmotif* of communication research has been functionalist from the beginning . . . [and] we are using functional analysis as described by Merton and cited by Wright (1960)."

Among the recent theorists whose writings display, in varying degrees of explicitness and acceptance, a concern with a functional approach to an understanding of mass communications are De Fleur (1970), Edelstein (1966), Gerbner (1967), Halloran (1964), Katz, Gurevitch and Haas (1973), Klapper (1960, 1963), Kline (1972), Larsen (1964), McQuail (1969), Mendelsohn (1966), and Meyersohn (1969). These several examples of functional perspectives, together with others both theoretical and empirical (it is not our intention here to survey these developments), are testimony to the intellectual attractiveness and viability of a theoretical orientation coming into its time. As the field of mass communication research enters the last quarter of the twentieth century, functional analysis appears alive and well.

The opportunity provided by the editors of this volume to reflect upon the earlier formulation of theoretical and methodological points relevant to a functional theory of mass communication is, therefore, highly welcome. Although this essay is self-contained, the reader may wish to compare certain points with the original article (Wright, 1960) which the current essay neither repeats nor replaces. The theme here is functional analysis *revisited* not necessarily revised! The reflections center on the three main topics discussed in the earlier essay (and summarized below) plus consideration of the relation between functional analysis and the uses and gratifications approach to the study of mass communication. Emphasis will be given to functional analysis of the consequences of mass communication for society, rather than for the individual, a challenging but difficult research focus.

SUBJECTS SUITABLE FOR FUNCTIONAL ANALYSIS

Functional analysis is primarily concerned with the consequences of standardized, patterned, and repetitive social phenomena, such as social roles and institutional patterns (see Merton, 1957). The original essay suggested the need "for specification and codification of the kinds of phenomena in mass communication which have been, or can be, clarified by means of the functional approach, together with formal statements of the basic queries which are raised in each instance." This need persists today, together with a pressing need for the development of research designs and strategies for the functional analysis of various kinds of communication phenomena, especially with regard to their consequences at the societal level. Four kinds of communication phenomena were specified in the earlier essay, which will be commented upon now in the light of research possibilities.

Functions of the Total Mass Communication System

Mass communication in toto, or the very existence of mass media, is one kind of standardized social phenomenon whose consequences need to be examined. What difference does it make, especially for a society, to have a mass communication system? Can one design research to answer such a macro-sociological question? I (Wright, 1960: 607) concluded pessimistically that one cannot and that functional analysis at this level "appears currently to be dependent primarily on speculation, and holds little immediate promise for the development of an empirically verifiable theory of mass communication." I think now that this view was unduly pessimistic because it couched the question unrealistically (for purposes of contemporary research) in terms of all or nothing, that is, the presence or absence of mass media in a society. Recent research and theory have been both more realistic and more promising of obtaining a purchase on this macrosociological issue.

Imagine a society in which all communication was interpersonal. There were no media for mass communication. Everything that its members sought to find out about events in their environment (social and physical), everything they needed in order to discover the socially shared interpretations about these matters and prescriptions for reacting to them, everything about the values, rules and expectations of members of their society, everything that might serve as social lubricant—jokes, stories, songs, etc.—all these things were available only through direct communication between individuals. All communication needs had to be met in this way. One could conduct research to determine the extent to which individuals, or categories of individuals, made use of interpersonal communications to gratify their needs for information, guidance, and entertainment, but there would be no question about the mode of communication employed; everything had to be interpersonal.

Consider now the opposite type of imaginary society, one in which no one could communicate directly with anyone else, but all had access to mass communicated materials. One could conduct research to determine the extent to which individuals, or categories of individuals, made use of mass communication (in general, or various media in particular) to gratify their needs for information, guidance, and entertainment, but there would be no question about the mode of communication employed; everything had to be mass communication.

Societies of the first type (limited to interpersonal communication) are increasingly difficult to imagine, let alone find, except on a small scale of remote villages and exotic places. As national types they hardly exist. Societies of the second type (limited to mass communication) are entirely imaginary. In today's world, most societies have a total communications system that includes both capabilities—interpersonal and mass communication. Three questions of significance emerge: (1) What is the communication mix that characterizes a society? (2) What difference does this make? and (3) What are the conditions (both external and within the media systems) which affect the kinds of social consequences that the media have? Among the significant external conditions are other social institutions in the society (for example, forms of government);

internal conditions include the pattern of media ownership and control, degree of centralization, and standardization of media content, among others.[1]

One can argue that the intrusion of any amount of mass communication into a social system creates a qualitative change that results in a society different from one solely dependent upon interpersonal communications. Beyond this, most macrosociological treatments consider variations in the facilities for mass communication. Students of modernization and development, for example, classify societies according to the quantity of various media for mass communication; for example, number of newspapers published, television transmitters in operation, cinema seats, radio transmitters, or in terms of some ratio of such facilities to total population (e.g., radio receivers per 100 persons). The assumption is usually made that increased facilities for mass communication are accompanied by an increase in their usage by more members of the population. This seems reasonable, although it is seldom documented by research.

Attempts to document the social consequences of a heavier or lighter mix of mass communications/personal communications are all too rare. Theorists of modernization argue that the intrusion and expansion of the mass media lead to changes in the members of the society and in social institutions which make both the population and the society more receptive to social change, more "modern," more "developed." The intervening mechanisms and processes by which such changes come about vary from theorist to theorist and include such psychological factors as the development of empathy and such sociological factors as the ability to move ideas, goods, records, and other commercial items about with dispatch. Examples of theoretical and empirical efforts to come to grips with the study of the role of mass communication in social change and especially in social development can be found in the works of Hyman, Levine and Wright (1967), Lerner (1958, 1963), Lerner and Schramm (1967), Pye (1963), Rogers and Svenning (1969), and Schramm (1964). Since an excellent recent summary and analysis of various theories and research on the role of mass communication in social development is presented by Frey (1973), these will not be reviewed here.

One theorist, George Gerbner (1967, 1972), takes the view that mass communication (which he defines as the mass production and distribution of messages) provides the *main* thing that members of the "audience" share and that, in this sense, mass communication creates its own *public.* Societies lacking in such facilities are also lacking in massive publics. This viewpoint suggests one macrosociological function of mass communication, namely, the creation of new publics.

Not only does mass communication provide a common stream of messages (message system) for its public, but also, in Gerbner's theory, these messages *cultivate* the images of society shared by its public. These message systems provide their audience with an interpretation of the world in terms of what *is,* what is *important,* what is *right,* and what is *related* to what else. In this manner they cultivate the audience's images of reality. This is difficult to prove, but research is now under way at The Annenberg School of Communications under a program of studies on "cultural indicators" directed by George Gerbner and Larry Gross. The program at present consists of two prongs. The first is a continuing monitoring and analysis of the content of various mass media. In particular the project has included a systematic analysis of prime time network television drama. The second prong involves research on the public, aiming at discovering the extent to which their views about social facts correspond more to the televised presentation or more to reality. For example, are heavy viewers of television more likely than light viewers to believe that violent crimes are a common occurrence (an image of the world presented in many television dramas), and are the latter viewers more likely to have an image that corresponds more with the actual incidence of violent crimes as reflected in official statistics? To the extent that heavy viewers of television give answers more characteristic of the world as portrayed by biased television content than by life, the inference is made that their world view has been cultivated by the media. Cultivation, then, is a function of mass communication. One *social* consequence of these mass communicated latent messages could be the creation of widespread "cultural false consciousness" (Gross, 1974).

An ingenious and illuminating series of studies of the sometimes subtle consequences of mass communication, especially television, on the political process has been conducted during the past two decades by Kurt Lang and Gladys Engel Lang. In their view (Lang and Lang, 1969: 19), "the mass media structure issues and personalities. They do this gradually and over a period of time, and thus this impact seems less spectacular than the shift or crystallization of a particular vote decision." They consider, among other social effects, the ways that public events, especially political, are structured and influenced by the presence of mass media, and the ways in which mass communication helps to shape the image of public events for individuals, with related social consequences for the political process. Although the focus is on television and politics, their research has broader implications for the functional analysis of mass communication in general; it demonstrates that such studies can be made through imaginative research designs exploiting contemporary social events covered by the mass media [2]

Modes of Mass Communication

A second type of functional analysis considered in the earlier essay dealt with each particular method of mass communication (e.g., newspapers, television) as a subject for analysis. The basic research question posed was what functions (and dysfunctions) can be attributed to each medium and how can these be isolated through research. One research strategy suggested was to conduct studies in societies in which a particular medium is absent or when the normal operation of a medium is disturbed, for example, by a strike, providing one can account for the influence of other factors in the situation.

This research strategy still seems promising to me, although in practice it appears to have been more beneficial in illuminating the functions of particular media for individuals than for the social system. Kimball (1963), for example, conducted an instructive longitudinal study of the impact of a prolonged newspaper shutdown on the residents of New York City. This study was especially informative about the alternative modes of communication which people turned to for substitutes for the missing newspapers as the shutdown continued over time. It became clear that for many individuals these alternative modes were not functional equivalents for newspaper reading. The study also demonstrates the value of a research design that allows one to trace a changing awareness of functions over time. (But it was not designed to provide data on the impact of the press on the society and its social institutions.) Research opportunities need not await the total disappearance of a particular medium. Lyle (1962), for example, studied the impact of a double newspaper merger, which greatly reduced the number of daily newspapers available to residents of the Los Angeles metropolitan area. And Steiner (1963) provides some interesting qualitative data on what people did when their television set was broken, reactions which gave indirect clues as to the possible functions that television was having when in operation. Other research opportunities come to mind: the closing of a neighborhood movie house; the termination of a major mass magazine such as *Life;* a near breakdown in a total communications system such as during a natural crisis.[3] These are, admittedly, atypical situations, but that is precisely why they are potentially useful as research sites. The purpose of such research is not to study the impact of the crisis per se (or other change in the communication facilities), but rather to use this moment of increased sensitivity to the missing (or changed) medium in order to cull clues as to the functions that it normally performs.

An alternative strategy is to search for occasions in which a new medium of communication is being introduced into a society, or in which an older medium is being augmented in scope or is reaching new segments of the society. Examples of studies of what happens when television is introduced into a community are found in the work of Campbell (1962), Himmelweit, Oppenheim and Vince (1958), and Schramm, Lyle and Parker (1961). The major emphasis in these studies is on the consequences of television for the individual, but some consideration is given to the larger social implications. The introduction of cable television, especially insofar as it provides for new local channel program origination, should provide research opportunities for the study of its functions for both the individual and the community. An example of a new mode (if not medium) of communication for some people is brought about through the development of literacy. An example is a recent study by Heli de Sagasti (1972).

De Sagasti explored the social implications of newly acquired adult literacy in the context of an "underdeveloped" society. Intensive interviews were conducted with adult women, migrants working as domestic servants in Lima, Peru, who had recently learned to read. Prior expectation, based upon prevailing theories about the impact of literacy upon members of developing societies, was that literacy would open the world horizons for these individuals, enhance their interest in and exposure to national and international issues, and expand their uses of the mass media. Change their lives it did; but not exactly in the ways anticipated.

De Sagasti (1972: 2) found that the major impact of newly acquired literacy was upon the private and social skills of the individual. "Newly developed adult literacy facilitates interpersonal communication, both spoken and written; this constitutes a dominant advantage of literacy for the respondents." As literate persons, the respondents now could enjoy the privacy of reading and writing letters; the advantage of greater ease in physical mobility through their ability to read signs and directions; less vulnerability in commercial transactions through their ability to read shopping lists, bills and other documents; and a new ease and facility in conversation with others. Their use of the mass media was changed only slightly, except for reading photo-novellas for relaxation, occasional newspapers, and religious materials.

> The newly literate adults' print reading is limited in range and amount. The reading that is done is used in terms of particular needs, and especially the respondents' position as migrants in a very different new environment. . . . There is little evidence of literacy increasing broadcast media use. [p. 3]

Other consequences of literacy for the individual are explored as revealed in case accounts by the women themselves.

Furthermore, de Sagasti proceeds to examine the possible implications of new adult literacy for the society. She notes that new adult literacy has a "multiplying effect" as skills of reading and writing are shared with illiterates and as new literates attempt to influence illiterates to learn to read. Literacy appears to have a clear, if modest, impact on occupational role performance and on new occupational goals. It has a greater impact on the new literate's educational and occupational aspirations for her children. And it has implications for the development of personal characteristics that may allow the migrant to better adapt to and function within her new urban environment. New literacy is associated with a desire to remain in the city rather than to return to the rural homeland, thereby potentially affecting patterns of residential mobility and stability in the society. And new literacy leads to the desire and determination to have one's children more fully participate in the opportunities of the new urban society. Thus, this study touches upon both the individual and social consequences of acquiring a new mode of communication, one customarily associated with exposure to the mass media. It illustrates the feasibility and benefits of future functional research conducted on such strategic populations undergoing changes in major modes of communication.

Institutional Analysis

A third application of the functional approach suggested in 1960 was in the institutional analysis of mass media and communication organizations, "examining the function of some repeated and patterned operation within that organization" (Wright, 1960: 608). Case studies, comparative analyses of differently organized media, and experiments were suggested as promising research strategies. During the past 15 years there has been a rise in the attention given to sociological analyses of mass communication organizations and institutions. Examples can be found in Halmos (1969), Tunstall (1970), and Wright (forthcoming). Several of these studies adopt a functional perspective. Space constrains us to one illustration here, and we chose one that addresses the topic at a broad level—television as a social institution.

An implicitly functional approach to the analysis of certain features of television as a social institution is provided by Katz (1973) in his article, "Television as a Horseless Carriage." Katz sets as his task an analysis of the problems faced in the introduction of television (especially in small and developing nations) and sees them, in part at least, as consequences of the uncritical transplantation of certain professional norms or conventions from radio broadcasting. Specifically, he considers three such professional norms (1973: 382): "(1) the goal of non-stop broadcasting; (2) the orientation toward an everybody audience; and (3) the striving for up-to-the-minute news." The norm of non-stop broadcasting is seen as having the dysfunction of making television trivial, through the exhaustion of talent and through resorting to repetitive formula dramatic series, with the further effect of leading viewers to use television more as a background for other activities than as a significant cultural experience deserving the viewer's full attention. The norm of striving for large heterogeneous audiences—of all ages and social classes—has the dysfunction of failing to meet the needs of minority audiences. And the norm for up-to-the-minute news prevents the development of in-depth "newsmagazine" treatments by television. Katz then proceeds to speculate on the consequences of these norms, inherited from radio, for television broadcasting in new nations. His central thesis is, to summarize, that (1973: 391)

> certain professional views—certain conventions—about the nature of television seem to me dysfunctional from the point of view of the inherent nature of the medium, and its essential, or at least potential, difference from radio. They are certainly dysfunctional from the point of view of the potential role of television in nation-building and in the stimulation of indigenous cultural expression and creativity.

Admittedly theoretical rather than empirical, Katz's presentation nonetheless illustrates the kinds of questions raised by a functional analysis of institutionalized practices in the mass media.

Examples of the consequences of other institutionalized practices in mass communication can be found in the work of Cantor (1971) on Hollywood television producers, Elliot (1972) on a television series production, Faulkner (1971) on hiring practices among Hollywood musicians, and Tuchman (1972, 1973a, 1973b) on conventions of objectivity in news making and reporting through newspapers and television.

Functional Analysis of Basic Communication Activities

The fourth level of functional analysis advocated in the earlier essay is rather abstract but crucial for the development of a functional theory of mass communication. The central arguments in its formulation are, in briefest summary, as follows: Mass communication, as institutionalized in modern societies, constitutes a social phenomenon qualitatively and quantitatively different from personalized communication. The several kinds of communication activities in which people engage (and four were identified at that time—surveillance of the environment or news activity, interpretation of the events surveyed and prescriptions for reactions to them, the transmission of social values and other elements of culture to new members of the society, young or old, and human amusement or entertainment) could be, and are, carried out both by means of mass communications and by other more personalized forms. The critical questions for research center on what are the consequences (manifest and latent) of carrying out these communications activities by means of mass communication; consequences for individuals, groups of individuals, societies, and culture.

An important distinction, sometimes blurred in subsequent reviews, is between functions and communication activities. Our working quartet of communications—surveillance, correlation, cultural transmission, and entertainment—was intended to refer to common kinds of activities which might or might not be carried out as mass communications or as private, personal communications. These activities were not synonyms for functions, which, as noted, refer to the consequences of routinely carrying out such communication activities through the institutionalized processes of mass communications.

As a preliminary step toward a functional analysis of these consequences, we presented a functional inventory of mass-communicated activities, a subject upon which we reflect in the following section.

BEYOND THE FUNCTIONAL INVENTORY

In functional analysis a distinction is made between functions and effects. Not all possible effects of mass communication are germane to the functional framework, but only those effects that are of serious consequence or significance for the system under examination, for example, the society.

Sensitivity to the distinction between mere effects and significant functions or dysfunctions is nicely illustrated in a much neglected early study of the impact of television on adolescents in Sydney, Australia (Campbell, 1962). The study employed a research design combining independent before-and-after surveys with a panel design. Two groups of 12-year-old and 15-year-old adolescents were studied in 1956, three months before the introduction of television into Sydney; in 1959 a new group of 12-year-olds was studied (three years after the introduction of television) and reinterviews were made with the original 12-year-olds (then aged 15). Data were gathered on the effects of television on leisure activities, family relations, neighborhood relations, and ego-ideals. Our example comes from the treatment of leisure activities. The researchers report on the impact of television in reducing time spent on a variety of leisure-time activities, such as viewing films, listening to the radio, and reading. They observe that the most striking change occurred in a sharp reduction in social interaction, and they go on to speculate upon the consequences of these effects for adolescent development (Campbell, 1962: 112):

> Some of these changes are unlikely to affect adolescent development, but the losses in *general neighborhood contacts* (excursions, miscellaneous activities and religion) and *social interactions* are more serious. The former is likely to make the adolescents' task of orienting to their own worlds more difficult, and, since most human development is dependent upon close social interactions with others, the latter is likely to retard maturity in almost all areas of development.

The functional inventory, presented in a three-page schema in the original essay, was intended as an aid in classifying various claims and findings about communication effects and as a device for reminding us to consider both the potentially dysfunctional and functional aspects of mass-communicated activities.

Admittedly a formal scheme (criticized by some as mechanical in its application; see Brown, 1970), the functional inventory has served its purposes well and it remains a useful heuristic device. But it has never succeeded as a paradigm for directing research about the functions of mass communication activities.

Much of the continuing debate about the macrosociological functions of mass communication takes the form of a polemic that pits opposite "functional" and "dysfunctional" outcomes. Proponents of the mass media see beneficial effects; critics dwell on the harm. An excellent summary statement of the opposing views is presented by Larsen (1960), who relates claims about the mass media to the continuing sociological concern with the problem of social order, "how society or elements therein can achieve stability midst constant demands for adjustment and change." Larsen (1960: 24) notes that many descriptive claims about media functions deal

> not so much with *whether* the media contribute to order as to the *kind of order* that emerges in a mass media oriented society, *i.e.,* does mass communication enhance social and political involvement and cultural creativity or does it induce apathy, indifference, and standardization and thus constitute a mechanism for the manipulation of the masses and the concentration of power?

Larsen concludes that this question "has been pursued mainly in terms of the activity versus the passivity potential of the media." His review of the literature examines statements about broad social effects of the mass media in terms of whether they tend to impute an *energizing* or *enervating* impact to mass communications.

Larsen's cogent summary serves precisely to illustrate the value of a functional orientation. The functional framework suggests that mass communication cannot be simply assigned one or the other broad social effect. But the theoretical framework can be extended beyond Larsen's summary question. A further theoretical orientation, and one which ought to direct future research, is *not* what kind of order mass communication facilitates, but rather to what *degree,* in what *manner,* and under what *conditions* does mass communication lead to greater (or lesser) social and political involvement?

Generalizing from this example suggests a family of related questions that serve to transform the functional inventory from a classificatory device into a source of more theoretically pertinent sociological questions. The first stage of such a programmatic approach remains, as the original inventory implied, a consideration of the possible functions and dysfunctions of some regularized mass communication activity. As an example, the institutionalized practice of transmitting news about an impending danger (e.g., flood) by means of mass media, publicly to all who are capable of receiving the message, might, on the one hand, aid in the society's survival through permitting its members, individually or in an organized manner, to escape catastrophe. On the other hand, such a broadcasting of "bad news" could be dysfunctional for the society if it led to panic, anti-social attempts at personal survival at the expense of others, and other undesirable effects. The generation of such lists of hypothetical consequences might be the product of speculation or it could be supported by research evidence that such effects occurred.

Contemporary theory and research add to the mounting inventory of alleged and/or demonstrated consequences of mass communication. To mention but a few examples, McCombs and Shaw (1972) have investigated the agenda-setting function of mass media, that is, their impact in determining for the public what seem to be the major political issues in an election campaign. Mendelsohn (1966) presents an analysis of the psychological and sociological functions of entertainment that is derived from the mass media of communication. Tichenor, Donohue and Olien (1970) have developed the hypothesis that one dysfunction of mass communicated information is an increase in the knowledge gap between various social strata in the society who are differentially likely to pay attention to these materials and to build upon prior knowledge. The list could be extended. A good review is provided by Kline (1972) and Robinson (1972).

But to settle for this type of accounting is insufficient. More critical for a sociological understanding of the functions of mass communication is consideration of the factors mentioned above. To what *degree* does mass communicated news of this sort lead to survival or to panic? In what *manner,* or by what social mechanisms are these varying consequences brought about? And under what *conditions* does mass communication lead to greater or lesser chances of organized survival or panic? Such a set of questions, hardly easily answered, point to new directions for research about the various functions and dysfunctions of mass-communicated surveillance, correlation, cultural transmission, and entertainment—as partially itemized in the functional inventory.

FORMULATING HYPOTHESES ABOUT COMMUNICATION SYSTEMS

A final use of functional theory suggested in the original article aimed at the functional analysis of mass communications themselves as systems. The focus here is to select some regularized feature of communications and to attempt to understand its existence and persistence in terms of the functions (significant consequences) that it has for the communication system of which it is a part. This section of the original paper was couched in terms of directions for the formulation and phrasing of hypotheses and propositions in functional terms, and supplied as an example a hypothetical analysis of the functions of mass communicated surveillance (news) for the "normal" operation of individuals in today's complex world. This hypothetical analysis was followed by some suggested strategies for research upon the problem. It seems significant now, in hindsight, that the article sought the "easy way out" by supplying an example of functional analysis on the level of the *individual.* It remained for De Fleur (1970) to arrive independently at a clear and insightful example of the application of this functional approach to the analysis of mass communication as a *social* system.

De Fleur applies functional analysis to explain the persistence of "low-taste" content in the mass media despite its opposition by prestigious critics. He arrives at the conclusion that

> the function of what we have called low-taste content is to maintain the financial equilibrium of *a deeply institutionalized social system which is tightly integrated with the whole of the American economic institution.* The probability that our system of mass communication in this respect can be drastically altered by the occasional outbursts of critics seems small indeed [p. 171].

Other examples of a functional analysis of the mass media as social systems are hard to find. Inkeles' (1950, 1968) descriptive analysis of the Soviet system of mass communication is an outstanding exception. De Fleur's example itself is more theoretical than empirical. He notes (p. 162):

> the analysis of social systems is extremely difficult. In fact, this strategy for the study of social phenomena is at the forefront of general sociological theory. . . . A functional analysis of the contribution of some item to the stability of a system, then, is a procedure that is somewhat less than completely rigorous.

He concludes, nevertheless, as we do, that this strategy offers a great deal of promise for understanding mass communication systems. And he too sees this form of functional analysis as a "strategy for inducing or locating hypotheses that can be tested empirically by comparative studies or other appropriate research methods."

USES AS FUNCTIONS VS. FUNCTIONS OF USES

Years have blurred (or else the initial formulations were inadequately sharp) the distinctions between several concepts central to a functional approach to the study of mass communications. Functions, as intended in the theoretical paradigm presented many years ago, referred to the *consequences* of certain routine, regular and standardized components of communications. As such, they were distinct from the intended effects, or purposes, of the communicator and from the intended use or motivations of the receiver. Thus, a network might intend that a television situation comedy attract a large number of viewers in order to provide an audience for the sale of its sponsor's products; but the program might have the consequence (among others) of making bigotry a socially acceptable topic for public observation, discussion, and laughter. Or a viewer might turn to televised entertainment of that type for the purpose of relaxation, but continued exposure to such a program might have the consequence of reducing his prejudice against minorities.

Although we do not regard needs as functions, it is possible to conceive of the satisfaction of felt needs as functional. That is, one consequence of a communication activity might be the satisfaction of certain users' needs. Such needs may be satisfied through the use of mass media or through other modes of communication. This multi-source range of functional alternatives for the satisfaction of human needs has been recognized most dramatically in the recent study by Katz, Gurevitch and Haas (1973).

Starting with a list of 35 social and psychological needs expected to be satisfied by exposure to the mass media, the researchers asked a cross-section of Israeli adults to specify how much each of five mass media (books, cinema, newspapers, radio, and television) helped to satisfy each need. In addition, each respondent was asked to say what else was more helpful to him than the media in satisfying each need. The results from this open-ended question were quite surprising. In all instances a majority of the respondents could nominate some non-media source that better served the particular need. The greatest dependence on the mass media appeared in satisfaction of the need to know what the world thinks about us (i.e., Israelis) and the need to strengthen knowledge, information, and understanding of sociopolitical matters. But even among these, as the authors note, "other sources of gratification taken together equal the mass media in importance." Among the several non-media sources of gratification specified, interpersonal communications (with friends, family, lectures) emerged most important. Katz, Gurevitch and Haas (1973: 180) observe that

> media-related needs are not, by and large, generated by the media. Most predate the emergence of the media and, properly, ought to be viewed within the wider range of human needs. As such, they have always been, and remain, satisfied in a variety of ways, most quite unrelated to the mass media. The surprising thing is to realize the extent and range of the media's encroachment on the "older" ways of satisfying social and psychological needs.

This study is of singular significance in sharpening our perspective on the relative importance of each of several mass media, mass communications in total, and interpersonal modes of communication as functional alternatives for meeting an individual's communications needs. Nevertheless, it brings us only to the edge of a tantalizing next order of theoretical question, namely, what are the functions of satisfying such needs regularly by the use of the mass media (or alternatives)? To put it another way, the "uses and gratifications" tradition in research tells us much about the extent to which certain personal needs are being fulfilled by one or another of the communications media. The next step is to ask, what are the social consequences of having these needs of individuals fulfilled in this manner rather than in some other way?

Such questions are not easily answered, even in one's imagination, let alone through rigorous research. The sociological value of strategic research on the uses of various media of communication and the gratifications and other consequences of such uses was forecast by Katz (1959) and Blumler (1964). It is entirely possible that other papers in the current volume contain examples precisely on this point. But if they do not, it seems singularly appropriate that this volume at long last brings together the challenge of the two orientations toward communication explicitly formulated by Katz and Blumler, on the one hand, and by myself on the other, some 15 years ago. I feel confident that these two editors of the current volume share with me the hope that at least some of our readers will be stimulated to join us in the exciting task of combining the two perspectives in future research on the role of mass communications and interpersonal communications in society.

NOTES

1. A functional perspective also reminds us of the need for research on the consequences which other social institutions have for mass communication. What, for example, are the functional requirements for the existence and operation of mass communication in a society? We need to consider not only the material resources and technology necessary for mass communication but also the social, economic, political, and other organizational arrangements required. And we need studies of the effects of changes in social, governmental, economic, and other institutional areas upon the nature and operations of the communication system. These problems, however, cannot be explored in the current essay.

2. For a recent study of television and politics that combines a concern about the political consequences of mass communication with a consideration for the gratifications of the audience see Blumler and McQuail (1969).

3. Clues to the functions normally performed by mass communication also may come through research during moments of social crisis in which the media are fully operative but the public is sensitized to their importance because of the crisis. Examples of such social crises are political assassinations, urban riots, commodity shortages, and episodes of a suspected "killer at large" in a community.

REFERENCES

BLUMLER, J. G. (1964) "British television—the outlines of a research strategy." British Journal of Sociology 15: 223-233.

——— and D. McQUAIL (1969) Television in Politics. Chicago: University of Chicago Press.

BROWN, R. (1970) "Approaches to the historical development of mass media studies," in J. Tunstall (ed.) Media Sociology. Urbana: University of Illinois Press.

CAMPBELL, W. J. (1962) Television and the Australian Adolescent. Sydney: Angus & Robertson, Ltd.

CANTOR, M. G. (1971) The Hollywood TV Producer. New York: Basic Books.

DE FLEUR, M. (1970) Theories of Mass Communication. New York: McKay.

DE SAGASTI, H. (1972) Social Implications of Adult Literacy: A Study Among Migrant Women in Peru. Ph.D. dissertation, University of Pennsylvania. (unpublished)

EDELSTEIN, A. (1966) Perspectives in Mass Communication. Copenhagen: Einar Harcks Forlag.

ELLIOT, P. (1972) The Making of a Television Series. London: Constable.

FAULKNER, R. (1971) Hollywood Studio Musicians. Chicago: Aldine-Atherton.

FREY, F. (1973) "Communication and development," in I. Pool et al. (eds.) Handbook of Communication. Chicago: Rand-McNally.

GERBNER, G. (1972) "Communication and social environment." Scientific American 227: 153-160.

——— (1967) "An institutional approach to mass communications research," in L. Thayer (ed.) Communication Theory and Research. Springfield, Ill.: Charles C Thomas.

GROSS, L. (1974) "The 'real' world of television." Today's Education (January): 86-92.

HALLORAN, J. (1964) The Effects of Mass Communication. Leicester: Leicester University Press.

HALMOS, P. [ed.] (1969) The Sociology of Mass-Media Communicators. Sociological Review Monograph 13.

HIMMELWEIT, H., A. M. OPPENHEIM, and P. VINCE (1958) Television and the Child. London: Oxford University Press.

HYMAN, H. H., G. LEVINE, and C. R. WRIGHT (1967) Inducing Social Change in Developing Communities. Paris: United Nations.

INKELES, A. (1950) Public Opinion in Soviet Russia. Cambridge: Harvard University Press.

——— (1968) Social Change in Soviet Russia. Cambridge: Harvard University Press.

KATZ, E. (1973) "Television as a horseless carriage," in G. Gerbner et al. (eds.) Communications Technology and Social Policy. New York: John Wiley.

——— (1959) "Mass communications research and the study of popular culture: an editorial note on a possible future for this journal." Studies in Public Communication 2: 1-6.

——— M. GUREVITCH, and H. HAAS (1973) "On the uses of the mass media for important things." American Sociological Review 38: 164-181.

KIMBALL, P. (1963) "New York readers in a newspaper shutdown." Columbia Journalism Review (Fall): 47-56.

KLAPPER, J, (1963) "Mass communication research: an old road surveyed." Public Opinion Quarterly 27: 515-527.

——— (1960) The Effects of Mass Communication. New York: Free Press.

KLINE, F. G. (1972) "Theory in mass communication research," in F. Kline and P. Tichenor (eds.) Current Perspectives in Mass Communication Research. Beverly Hills: Sage.

LANG, K. and G. E. LANG (1969) Television and Politics. Chicago: Quadrangle Books.

LARSEN, O. (1964) "Social effects of mass communication," in R. Faris (ed.) Handbook of Modern Sociology. Chicago: Rand-McNally.

——— (1960) "The social effects of mass communication as a research problem." Sociologiste Meddelesser 5.

LERNER, D. (1963) "Toward a communication theory of modernization," in L. Pye (ed.) Communications and Political Development. Princeton: Princeton University Press.

——— (1958) The Passing of Traditional Society. Glencoe: Free Press.

——— and W. SCHRAMM [eds.] (1967) Communication and Change in the Developing Countries. Honolulu: East-West Center Press.

LYLE, J. (1962) "Audience impact of a double newpaper merger." Journalism Quarterly (Spring): 145-157.

McCOMBS, M. and D. SHAW (1972) "The agenda setting function of the mass media." Public Opinion Quarterly 36: 176-187.

McQUAIL, D. (1969) Towards a Sociology of Mass Communications. London: Collier-Macmillan.

MENDELSOHN, H. (1966) Mass Entertainment. New Haven: College & University Press.

MERTON, R. K. (1957) Social Theory and Social Structure. Glencoe: Free Press.

MEYERSOHN, R. (1969) "Mass communications: dilemmas for sociology." Diogenes 68: 138-155.

PYE, L. [ed.] (1963) Communications and Political Development. Princeton: Princeton University Press.

ROBINSON, J. (1972) "Mass communication and information diffusion," in F. Kline and P. Tichenor (eds.) Current Perspectives in Mass Communication Research. Beverly Hills: Sage.

ROGERS, E. and L. SVENNING (1969) Modernization Among Peasants. New York: Holt, Rinehart & Winston.

SCHRAMM, W. (1964) Mass Media and National Development. Stanford: Stanford University Press.

——— J. LYLE, and E. PARKER (1961) Television in the Lives of our Children. Stanford: Stanford University Press.

STEINER, G. (1963) The People Look at Television. New York: Knopf.

TICHENOR, P., G. DONOHUE, and C. OLIEN (1970) "Mass media flow and differential growth in knowledge." Public Opinion Quarterly 34: 159-170.

TUCHMAN, G. (1973a) "Making news by doing work." American Journal of Sociology 79: 110-131.

——— (1973b) "The technology of objectivity: doing objective TV news films." Urban Life and Culture 2 (April): 3-26.

——— (1972) "Objectivity as strategic ritual: an examination of newsmen's notions of objectivity." American Journal of Sociology 77: 660-679.

TUNSTALL, J. [ed.] (1970) Media Sociology. Urbana: University of Illinois Press.

WRIGHT, C. R. (forthcoming) Mass Communication: A Sociological Perspective. Rev. and enl. ed. New York: Random House.

——— (1960) "Functional analysis and mass communications." Public Opinion Quarterly 24: 605-620.

——— (1959) Mass Communication: A Sociological Perspective. New York: Random House.

Chapter 10

TELEVISION AS A FUNCTIONAL ALTERNATIVE TO TRADITIONAL SOURCES OF NEED SATISFACTION

Jean Cazeneuve

UNDOUBTEDLY THE SOCIOLOGY OF MASS COMMUNICATIONS received its second wind when it departed from research into effects and began the study of functions. But, whatever the advantages of functionalism (especially when compared with the inadequate "stimulus-response" model), we should be alert to its dangers, at least when the notion of function implies a certain deliberate intentionality.

To say that television has a function or functions could simply mean that in order to understand the relationship effected between the transmission source, the programs, and the ultimate destination, the viewers, we must first ask ourselves what audience members seek in these programs and why they are motivated to watch them. That is, we have to find out ⎨what needs these programs fill and what satisfactions they bring to their public. This is all well and good, but, should we understand this approach in teleological terms, we would imply that televiewers always watch programs because they expect some satisfaction from them. This would often be incorrect, however, since, in many cases, people watch a certain program on TV either because it follows another one, or because their wives want to watch it, or just because they have nothing better to do at the moment. To say that any message from the mass media has a precise function is somewhat like taking up the famous theory of Bernardin de Saint-Pierre (much better known for his novel *Paul et Virginie* than for his more rigorously teleological, philosophical writings), stating that everything in the world must have a purpose. For him, the reason why a melon has lines on it is to let it be cut into slices and eaten at the family table. The reason why fleas are black is to make them visible on the skin and so caught more easily. Functionalists think they can escape these typical fallacies of philosophies of preestablished harmony by declaring that "functions," in the broadest sense of the term, also includes dysfunctions. But this is not an entirely satisfactory answer, since such dysfunctions should be regarded instead as negative effects. For instance, some sociologists, namely Lazarsfeld and Merton (1948), consider that the mass news media play the part of a "social drug." However, this thesis has the double disadvantage of (1) bringing us back to the study of effects and (2) passing a value judgment (for example, that this is a dysfunction, thus something bad), which in fact presupposes in turn a teleological point of view that would allow judgments to be made about what are the good and bad effects of mass communications.

By substituting a "functional analysis" aimed at the latent functions, as well as at the manifest ones, for the more rigid functionalism of Malinowski (1926), R. K. Merton (1957) avoided many stumbling blocks, kept his distance from teleological models, and ultimately gave up the idea of the functional unity of society, thus fixing for the study of functions objectives that were scientific precisely because they were limited. Still, the mass media sociologist must be constantly aware of the danger of confusing functions with final purposes or with value judgments that might seem to refer to the notion of an ideally functioning and well-integrated society.

In any case, an awareness of the dangers of a doctrinaire and teleological version of functionalism should engender caution whenever we are tempted to explain the role of TV in terms of the global purposes of modern society or of the shortcomings and frustrations associated with that society as a whole. For instance, it is certainly perceptive to suggest (McQuail, 1969) that, because of the social structure of modern society, most individuals are deprived of important material satisfactions and do not attain rewards commensurate with their economic efforts. In this situation, therefore, a system of compensating satisfactions is set up via identification with stars and through escapism, facilitated especially by television fiction. This implies that the function of television is to compensate for the insufficiencies of industrial society, which would otherwise fail to achieve the integration of its economically weaker members. Such an interpretation is reasonable and useful. But we must be careful not to be induced by it solely to associate the role of television with the integrative requirements of a particular social structure, which would mean, in fact, that television could be useful only in a society with high productivity and a highly unequal distribution of income. In other words, are we trying to prove that television has a place only in a society where prosperity is linked to inequality and to the frustrations resulting therefrom? It is true that television can exist only in industrialized societies, but that is because of the technical equipment needed. And who is to say that if a primitive society had an instrument like television, it would not have stimulated great interest? Moreover, by explaining TV use in terms of socially created frustrations, we imply that the underprivileged classes, more than other social groups, need this type of satisfaction via compensation. Is this really so? Do not the rich require compensation and escape from the tensions of social competition and the need to maintain their sociocultural standing? This truth is obscured from our notice simply because they have other means of finding escape than television. In short, we get the impression that by focusing functional analysis on the structure and integration needs of modern society, we merely state the facts and then note that these clearly correspond to the particular needs of this type of society.

Television did not make its appearance because it was needed. It appeared because it was invented, and it was technically possible to produce it. It then developed because it appeared to answer needs that were not typical only of the society where it was invented. Maybe television aroused new needs, or kindled needs long forgotten or that had been satisfied by something different from TV. For instance, it is certainly true that, to a large extent, television programs can satisfy the desire for escape sometimes felt by parts of the public. But it must be recognized that this desire, this escapism, is caused partly by constraints, tensions, and frustrations typical of the modern social system, and partly too by more profound and general inclinations. The same is true of the search for identification. Since its ancient origins, the history of literature, written or oral, and the mythology of archaic peoples prove that man has never contented himself with reality, and that he has even tried to escape from it by inventing a supernatural world, inhabited by extraordinary people, human enough to permit identification, but different enough to enable him to feel transported into an environment free from his everyday routines and miseries.

In short, in studying the role of television, one may distinguish among specific functions: firstly, those typical of industrial society (where it was devised); secondly, those that are provoked by TV itself; and thirdly, those that correspond to more general needs which, under different conditions, could and do find satisfaction by means other than television. It is this third type of function that will be considered here, first stressing their obvious importance but also the difficulty of studying them and the inevitable risk of generalizing about them. As a matter of fact, these functions can be studied only in comparison with societies very different from our own, thus drawing mainly from ethnography and less from prehistory and ancient or modern history. Of course we have to rely on analogy before detailed research can be started. So we will provide here only some landmarks and relatively open perspectives, while recommending the initiation of more thorough analyses.

THREE RESPONSES TO THE HUMAN CONDITION

When proceeding to list and classify functions, we have to look for a guiding principle. In other words, we have to find the raison d'etre or primary function of the functions. And it soon becomes clear that all functions are explained, one way or another, by the need to view man in relation to his own condition, or, more exactly, by his search for means of accepting his condition. But to accept the human condition, be it in primitive or modern society, always means, either directly or by symbolic detours, equivalences or substitutions, the achievement of a more or less satisfactory equilibrium, or, to put it even better, the achievement of a synthesis between the need to remain in this condition, defined by various boundaries and limits, and the need to escape from it. Possibly the mass media, especially television, by transposing reality into a spectacle, achieve what myths and rites had formerly effected by imbuing it with the sacred (Cazeneuve, 1972).

In order to understand better how the main function of the television show is rooted in the requirements of the human condition that first produced myths and rites, we must point, first, to the extreme irrationality displayed on television and at the extremely distorted picture it presents of our daily life. These features could be interpreted as manifestations of a fundamental metaphysical need: the urge to confront the human condition.

The feeling, or illusion, of liberty that is exclusive to man, is the cause of anguish, since every action appears to him as if resulting from a choice, thus implying responsibility. In order to escape from this feeling, man tends to bind himself to rules that offer him security. But, by the same token, he tends to regard anything trespassing these rules as a sign of power. There is, therefore, a contradiction between the tendency to confine one's horizons to a set of accepted rules, and the tendency to commune with that which is beyond the rules. But there is also a third path which avoids this contradiction by aiming at the transcendental, thereby placing both the guiding principle of the rules and their violation beyond the human condition in the realm of the Divine.

When studying the function of rites in primitive societies, the author realized (Cazeneuve, 1958, 1971) that, by referring to these three means for man of responding to the human condition, we could not only obtain guidelines for classifying these behaviors, but also find a means of solving certain difficulties encountered by most of the anthropological theories in this field. In particular, these theories could not define the relationship between religion and magic, because, whereas in certain aspects magical rites are opposed to religion, sometimes even aiming to fight it and scoff at it, they also present many similarities to religious ritual. A discredited religion can be considered a magical belief, priests can be the heirs of magicians, and between incantation and prayer there is antinomy together with continuity. On the other hand, how can we explain the fact that the magician often draws his power from the violation of taboos, and that religion, in some of its rites, like sacrifice, tries to contact a power free from taboo, while nevertheless respecting the taboos?

The only way to solve these contradictions is to explain rites by the three tendencies attached to the efforts of primitive man to confront his human condition; namely, the two contradictory tendencies, (1) security within a set of rules or constraints and (2) manipulating unrestricted power, plus (3) that tendency which represents a search for a synthesis between these two contradictory aims. We can attach to the first tendency all the rites that, by means of taboos, keep away, reject, or negate all symbols of the unrestricted, define them as unclean, against the rules, or endangering of security, for instance, whatever is peculiar, unusual, abnormal, anything extraordinary or that seems to break the rules of nature or of the tribe.[1] Contrary to this, the second tendency leads to magic, mobilizing the power of the unrestricted and the impure. The magician, through his initiation into the secrets of magic, and with the help of most of his rites, strives to escape from the normal human condition and to accept the anguish linked to the human condition, so as to be able to manipulate the supernatural immanent force. He puts himself forth as an unusual, exceptional person. Religion, then, belongs to the third tendency. It tries to reconcile the acceptance of rules and the relation with the supernatural power, taken as transcendental, thus permitting it to escape from impurity and to be truly sacred.

We can here only summarize very briefly this analysis of primitive rites and its underlying principles. We wish to suggest as a result that the attitude of modern man toward television could very well, at least partly, correspond to the three tendencies that help to explain archaic rites. This does not mean of course that TV must displace taboo, religion, and magic, nor that the use of this means of communication, entertainment, and information possesses magical or religious attributes. Nevertheless, a few sociologists, for example, Thayer (1972) and Gerbner (1967), have pointed out that the mass media could, in certain cases, fulfill symbolic functions that were formerly served by rites and myths. They have drawn attention to the fact that the scripts of broadcast series, soap operas, and dramatic serials have the same basic features and are really constructed like never changing rituals. On the other hand, when observing the traditional ceremonies of primitive tribes, for example, be they the *Intlchtuma* of the Australians, the *Corroboree* of the Canaques, the African initiation, or the *Shalako* of the Zunis Indians, we must admit that they contain a succession of scenes representing mythical episodes that could be compared to those repeatedly depicted in the familiar series on TV.

We should really look for the similarity of functions inherent in these analogies and not suppose, by basing oneself on a simplistic form of evolutionism, that what is happening today follows from archaic facts.

But it is useful to ask why it is that, in modern society, attitudes to the mass media, and especially television, best exemplify the functions that we have seen at work in primitive society (more exactly in the taboos, magic, and religion of these societies) rather than, say, orientations to any other products of modern technology (without excluding them completely).

Audiovisual communication, as opposed to conceptual communication, reaches the individual directly, without the need to decode written signs. It thus affects the individual's sensitivity without engaging his intellect, which is what gives television its suggestive power and fascination. By the same token, it is the best means (except, perhaps, for the cinema) of expressing symbolic thinking. And it is primarily through the development of symbols that the three-fold function of rites is fulfilled in primitive societies. Finally, television enters into the rhythm of everyday life more than does cinema, and exactly as did the magic and rituals of primitive tribes.

As we have previously mentioned, the first way to accept the human condition, at the ritual level, was to deny the anxieties derived from freedom of choice or its illusion. This involved a rejection of contact with anything that symbolized the undetermined and a sort of self-imprisonment in a network of constraints. Anything deviating from the norm or rule was taboo.

Today, as we can see, the mass media frequently present to the public events or social groups that are exceptional, abnormal or unusual. This applies especially to news items (accidents, catastrophies, crimes, offenses) which are the very kinds of happenings that are considered by primitive men as impure and awesome, and that would call for rituals of separation and exclusion (individual and collective purification, quarantine, expulsion, taboo). In particular, in many tribes, a person dead by accident was considered so unclean that he was thrown far away without being buried. So the view of the world, the *weltanschauung*, that we get through television is largely made up of those events that the primitive world rejected through taboo and purification, namely whatever was dangerous for its peace of mind. It is not sufficient to explain the return of the impure and this taste for the abnormal or accidental merely in terms of a process of "desacralization." There is at least one other source. The unclean, the object, person, or event considered taboo, is what cannot be incorporated in the framework of the known existing rules, thus being new in the context of what is usually seen and what one is used to. In effect, the primitive mentality abhors change and rejects the "becoming" (Cazeneuve, 1961). Thus Eliade (1949) rightly refers to the characteristic "terror of history" of archaic civilization. The rites of passage are symbolic systems which are designed to ignore the process of change by placing it in a framework of rules and regularities. The immobilism and conservatism of archaic societies result therefrom. Now, it was by overcoming the fear of the unusual or, if we prefer, by repelling or inverting the significance of the taboo, that humanity could get started on the path of progress. So the interest shown by the mass media in such news items as accidents, catastrophes, crimes, and in anything that was once taboo, is one facet of the entrance of humanity into history and of its acceptance of innovation.

It is quite remarkable, though, that not only is the "becoming" no longer impure, but that it is also the subject of the news transformed into a sensation. Humanity has made the unusual, the abnormal, and the different a symbol of its acceptance of history (by no longer considering unclean whatever is out of the ordinary, by triumphing over taboo). Here is a truly ambiguous, equivocal attitude. In effect, while still feeling the shiver of archaic anxiety in the presence of the unusual and the marginal, modern humanity lives under the illusion of mastering its historicity. The spectacle of assassinations, hold-ups, fires, floods, massacres, deadly explosions, car and airplane crashes, projected in its most striking pictures by television and the other mass media, is a cheap way of demonstrating emancipation. In fact, these are the bits and pieces of history, and it is the leftovers, or the parody, of human history that are delivered to us by sensational information. The inversion of the taboo is a means, for Promethean societies, of accepting the anxieties of the human condition by transforming the awesome[2] into a spectacle.

It is therefore natural that, on the same level, we may also observe the manifestations of a function that is the opposite of the one that corresponds to the taboo as we have seen in the ethnological and ritual domain. Let us repeat that the practice of magic is opposed in its very essence to the ritual of protection against the unclean, since on the contrary, it implies abandoning the normal condition in order to manage the awesome power. The rupture of the prevailing set of rules is then supposed to provide mastery over the world through contact with the superhuman.

Many sociologists who have observed the attitudes of little children to television have compared it to a magical instrument. For instance, by classifying very young children as "television embraced," Glick and Levy (1962) have referred to the fact that the "television embracing" viewers in general, and children in particular, regard the television set as being at their disposal and as obeying their will. The real world is then replaced by a world of substitute-reality that extends the human will and provides the same illusions as magic. The televiewer, like the magician, abandons the normal human condition, the one that is surrounded by laws and limitations, and becomes part of an unconfined world, where everything is possible and unpredictable, where the norms of space and distance are abolished, and where time itself is disrupted by the evocation of past, present, or future. The mixture of fiction and reality, the fact that information and imagination programs follow one another, supports this immersion in another world. The televiewer's attitude has shown that the psychological process of projection is important. It is this psychological process which makes it possible to achieve by symbol or substitution what cannot be done in real life, because it is impossible or forbidden, and because the tendencies that would push one to commit these acts have to be repressed. Like Prometheus, the hero of the legend who is nearer to magic than to the sacred religions (as shown by Callios, 1938), television is some kind of mediator which, by providing contact with a world where the limits of the possible are pushed away, turns will into power. So, by turning away from taboo and accepting the illusion of "becoming," and by endowing its public with a quasi-magical power, television abolishes one of the functions of rite but revives the other, that of magic, which goes together with the exaltation of the accidental by the sensational.

But at the same time the third path is opened up, although modestly and with less chance of solving the antinomies than is possible in primitive religious rites through "sacralization" and the search for transcendence. By transposing reality and fiction into the spectacular, we seem to obtain the comfort both of a circumscribed world governed by rules, and of a sharing with an undetermined realm. Many attitudes of televiewers can thus be explained, for example, by the facility of having an electronic instrument that can give them both the illusion of staying integrated in a secure society and of being linked to the world of the marvelous. In this way we can understand the blossoming of a certain kind of mythology, elaborated by the cinema and by television, and overflowing into the illustrated magazines. The stars, the actors, the presenters, the singers, all people who represent the transcendence of the show, are the personalities and nearly the gods of this new Olympus, and they therefore occupy a privileged place in the social stratification of prestige as well as of money.

Of course, there is no direct affinity between the modern spectator in front of his set and the primitive man who, guided by taboo, burns the hut of a man who has died by accident, or between him and the magician who claims to have acquired a frightening and unusual power or the believer who prays to the divinity and offers it sacrifices. But if television is so well integrated into everyday life, and has so quickly acquired a huge public, and if it seems to fill a gap in the life of the average modern man, it is because this medium has helped him to accept himself, to confront his own condition, between that which is determined and that which is unconfined. He does this, of course, in a way that is unrelated to primitive mentality, but which corresponds to the needs and possibilities of today's world, thrown into accelerated history. The effects of projection and identification, linked to the impact of the sensational, let the television viewer find his place in a changing world by responding to news items, give him a seeming power over reality by letting him switch from the real world to fiction, and, with the help of the medium's stars, allow a nearly mythical world to participate in his everyday world.

One can, with the help of the empirical evidence of the sociology of the mass media, then, try to distinguish between the needs and tensions typical of modern society and the ones that can be better explained by deeper, more stable, and more universal needs. This proposition is based on the three functions that stem from difficulties inherent in the human condition by which man is destined to search for security and to exercise an anxiety-laden freedom.

SOME IMPLICATIONS OF THE ANALYSIS

At this stage of the analysis one can also study how the more general functions may diversify, take on different aspects, and how one means of satisfaction may be replaced by another.

For instance, various analogies and permutations obtain between the ritual expression and the ludic expression as several authors have shown (Huizinga, 1939; Gallois, 1967). They have also shown that the spirit of play has much less opportunity for expression in modern society than in primitive society. It could therefore be the case that the introduction of television into the family circle could help to satisfy the ludic spirit, replacing what was once offered by primitive rituals. It can be seen that festivals belong more and more to folklore and have been slowly going out of fashion, as if they had become unnecessary since the advent of television. In fact, an interesting study could be made of the relationship between festivals and television. This would be a complex topic, since the relationship involved may be substitutive or complementary, or television might even take over the functions of festivals altogether. For example, by organizing and broadcasting group games, television enables its viewers to take part in a form of festivity.[3] Note also how successful quizzes have become, and even the verbal confrontations of political opponents.

We could also use this scheme of substitution and compensation between different ways of satisfying a general need and fulfilling a function, in order to correct some frequently accepted interpretations about the possible effects of television on violence (see, especially, Larsen, 1968). Does violence on TV stimulate aggression or does it offer a harmless outlet for it and avoid an acting out of aggression when there are no wars? Evidently Freudians would give an answer in favor of TV, considering that detective shows, for example, could have the positive effect of providing a symbolic satisfaction for drives that would be dangerous to repress. But this is an old thesis, since Aristotle (1969) had long ago presented it in a similar form with respect to the theater. By involving us in dramatic actions and presenting expressions of exacerbated feelings, Greek tragedy, said the great philosopher, acted as catharsis, a clearing of passions. In the same way, television may provoke youngsters to violence by showing violent scenes, but it may also serve the same cathartic function as the theater of antiquity and as those rituals and myths that glorified transgression, orgy, and the outburst of aggressive forces. The problem of violence on TV is thus highly complex and can only be considered if we take into account these diverse functions and dysfunctions, which afford us a readier comparison with more ancient and even primitive means of assuring a better control of aggression, either to provide a harmless form of "discharge" or, in some cases, to maintain warlike qualities through a reinforcement of aggression.

Looking at it from another standpoint, we could relate the success of television to a function that may also be served by such quite different experiences as drugs, alcohol, and yet other ways of transforming one's relationship to the world and to one's conscience. Of course, television is an inoffensive device and does not act directly on the nerve centers. In connection with viewing we may use the word intoxication only by way of analogy, but it is a fact that man has always tried to find ways of breaking away from everyday life and of placing himself in a different environment, nearer to a dream state. For instance, among the American Indians, the use of peyote is highly popular because of the change that the consumption of this hallucinogenic mushroom can bring about in their relations with the internal and external world. Television, in a very different way, can provide the same kind of satisfaction, when it becomes a habit or even a necessity.

We should also consider the role that this instrument can play for a large part of the population, which finds that television offers a means of relaxation, or simply entertainment, after a hard day's work. In order to fully understand to what very general function television is then directed, we should refer to Pascal's famous theory of divertissement, as illustrated by these few extracts from his *Pensees* (1900):

> . . . man is so unfortunate, that he would be bored even without cause for boredom, by the very nature of his character; and so frivolous, that having within him a thousand essential causes of ennui, the least trifle, such as a billiard table and a ball to drive, suffices to distract him.

. . . if man, however full of sadness he be, can be prevailed upon to enter on some diversion, he will be happy for the time being; and if man, however happy he be, is not diverted and occupied by some passion or amusement, which prevents ennui from asserting itself, he will soon be discontented and unhappy.

The only thing which consoles us in our troubles is diversion, and yet it is the greatest trouble of all. For it is chiefly that which prevents us from thinking of ourselves.

So, for Pascal, the function of entertainment is to save us from boredom, by stopping us from thinking about ourselves, by shifting our attention from ourselves, and thereby preventing us from becoming aware of our distressing condition. To achieve this aim, to be truly entertaining, an activity has to catch our attention and captivate us in a certain way. Pascal often chooses hunting and games as examples. These are diversions because man can forget himself by getting enthusiastic over these seemingly idle pursuits. He must catch this hare or win money at playing cards. But if he receives a hare without hunting it or money without winning it in a game, it is no longer entertainment.

Television is often a diversion in Pascal's sense but vicariously, that is, by identification or projection. This is the reason why all surveys, in every country, point to the fact that the best-liked programs are those telling a story (films, serials, dramas, comedies, and soap operas). We place ourselves unconsciously in the situation of one of the heros; we live together with him through dangers, joys and sorrows; we are excited over the unfolding of the story, just like the hunter chasing his prey or the card player over his game. In this way we forget, not only our daily worries, but also ourselves, our being. There is a metaphysical aspect in entertainment that Pascal described well and that we should take into consideration when speaking about the escapist function of television.

It is difficult to provide a profound analysis on the basis of these empirical data. Any survey undertaken in the framework of mass media sociology cannot help us directly to understand the deeper meaning of the satisfactions that audience members may derive from watching television. But it would be a mistake to ignore such functions, stemming from human nature, as such, when studying the uses and gratifications of TV. In other words, since the empirical surveys on these matters are necessarily conducted in modern societies, one is naturally tempted to explain everything they show on the basis of the specific characteristics of the same societies—for example, the tensions that are caused by industrial organization, competitive stratification, and the problems of urban life. Truly these factors are important when considering the origins of audience gratifications. But we should remember that other functions, not unique to our societies, may also play a part. These functions have provoked man in different types of societies, for instance in primitive society or in antiquity, or even in preindustrial society, to search for equivalent (if not identical) gratifications. Only the comparative method can help to discover more general functions and thereby widen the scope of research and thought in order to arrive at what may be most fundamental in the relationship between man and television.

NOTES

1. For instance, unusual or monstrous animals, hunchbacked people, albinos, twins, kings, leaders (above the common order), incestuous persons, criminals, people who have broken the social laws, and new objects are considered unclean and taboo.

2. What is here translated as "awesome" appears in the author's original French version as "numinous," a term that represents a central concept in the classic work of Rudolph Otto, *Das Heilige* (1959).

3. Programs like *Interville* (competition between two localities) or *Jeux sans Frontieres* are made in a locality where they are the occasion for a lively gathering and festivity.

REFERENCES

ARISTOTLE (1969) Rhetorica. Cambridge, Mass.: Harvard University Press.

CALLOIS, R. (1938) Le mythe et l'homme. Paris: Gallimard.

CAZENEUVE, J. (1972) La société de l'ubiquité. Paris: Dencel.

——— (1971) Sociologie du rite. Paris: P.U.F.

——— (1961) La mentalité archaique. Paris: A. Colin.

——— (1958) Les rites et la condition humaine. Paris: P.U.F.

ELIADE, M. (1949) La mythe de l'éternal retour. Paris: Gallimard.

GALLOIS, R. (1967) Les jeux et les hommes. Paris: Gallimard.

GERBNER, G. (1967) "Mass media and human communication theory," in F.E.X. Dance (ed.) Human Communication Theory. New York: Holt, Rinehart & Winston.

GLICK, I. O. and S. J. LEVY (1962) Living with Television. Chicago: Aldine.

HUIZINGA, J. (1939) Homo ludens. Paris: Gallimard.

LARSEN, O. N. (1968) Violence and the Mass Media. London: Harpers.

LAZARSFELD, P. F. and R. K. MERTON (1948) "Mass communication, popular taste and organised social action," in L. Bryson (ed.) The Communication of Ideas. New York: Harper.

McQUAIL, D. (1969) Towards a Sociology of Mass Communications. London: Collier-Macmillan.

MALINOWSKI, B. (1926) "Anthropology," in Encyclopoedia Brittanica, First Supplementary Volume. London and New York.

MERTON, R. K. (1957) Social Theory and Social Structure. Glencoe: Free Press.

OTTO, R. (1959) Das Heilige. Harmondsworth: Penguin.

PASCAL, B. (1900) Pensees. London: The Walter Scott Publishing Co., Ltd.

de SAINT-PIERRE, B. (1784) Etudes sur la Nature.

THAYER, L. (1972) "Communication and the human condition." International Symposium, Barcelona.

Chapter 11

POPULAR CULTURE AND USES AND GRATIFICATIONS:
NOTES TOWARD AN ACCOMMODATION

James W. Carey and Albert L. Kreiling

IN THE DECADE FOLLOWING WORLD WAR II, when Western thought rediscovered and wandered down so many strange corridors of thought, a major debate broke out concerning the nature of popular culture. The subject of the debate was never well defined, and the antagonists tended to talk past one another. Presumably, popular referred to certain objects and practices consumed or used by all strata of the population. Culture referred to expressive artifacts—words, images, and objects that bore meanings. In fact, the debate centered on popular entertainment—songs, films, stories. The growth of a popular culture, its history, meaning, and significance, was debated by an unlikely collection of disillustioned radicals who had turned from politics in the inhospitable fifties, outraged conservatives who saw popular culture as the penultimate threat to tradition, and smug liberal intellectuals who at last, following World War II, had achieved positions of power and influence. The leaders of the debate, if leadership was achieved by ability to outrage, were Dwight MacDonald (1962), Edward Shils (1959) and C. Wright Mills (1959). MacDonald, in contrast to his political Trotskyism, led the conservative anti-populist and anti-bourgeois assault on popular culture in the name of the folk and the elite. Mills attacked the popular arts from the left, in the name of authentic democratic community and against the manipulation of political, economic, and academic elites who controlled the system of industrial production in culture. Shils in the name of liberal progress defended the center: taste was being neither debased nor exploited; artists were freer and better compensated and audiences better entertained; artistic creativity and intellectual productivity were as high as they had been in human history.

Gradually the debate evaporated and the protagonists went on to other more tractable but less elevating subjects. There was, as with most intellectual debate, no resolution of the issues. When the whole matter was stated in the undressed form the protagonists finally adopted, it was clear they were all correct: surely tradition was being evaporated, surely things in many ways were better than ever before and certainly no worse for the mass of men, and surely ordinary people were under a constant barrage of shallow and manipulative culture controlled by a "power elite." But if that was the prudent conclusion, it illustrates that in intellectual matters prudence is not always the most desirable course; for rather than resolving a debate, they lost a subject matter. Since then, with rare·and notable exception, the study of popular culture has drifted into triviality and bemusement disconnected from any passionate concern or pressing intellectual puzzle.

What is important about this disappearance is that the original debate raised and then promptly obscured a still puzzling intellectual question: what is the significance of conceiving the world on the terms laid down by popular art, and what is the relationship between this form of consciousness and other forms—scientific, ethnic, religious, mythological—which popular art variously displaces, penetrates, or merely co-exists with?

The late film critic Robert Warshow (1964) intuitively grasped the reason for the expiration of the popular culture debate. In proposing a study of the cinema, Warshow observed that two kinds of students went to the movies: critics and social scientists. Unfortunately, neither of them saw the movies. Critics went looking for art and only responded when what they saw on the flickering screen could be transformed into a formal aesthetic. Social scientists watched the audience and responded only when what they saw could be transfigured into an "effect," a behavioral response of the audience. What Warshow sensed was that the entire issue of the movies, an issue that depended on having what we have learned to call a semiotic of cultural form, was being lost, and, therefore, neither the question of the relationship between art and society which so vexed the critic, nor the problem of audience effects which so stimulated the social scientist, could be effectively treated. As a result critics and social scientists went their separate and undistinguished ways.

However, one social scientist, Elihu Katz (1959), attempted to produce a marriage between the critical work on popular culture and the study of audience effects. He adopted for this new attitude and subject matter the awkward label "uses and gratifications research" and pinned to it the question that he took popular culture critics to be implicitly asking, namely, what is it that people do with, what uses and gratifications do they find in, mass produced news and entertainment? While popular culture critics asked such questions in a strictly conjectural, speculative, and ideologically biased manner, Katz now proposed to treat these concerns as empirical hypotheses based on a functional theory of mass communication.

The marriage that Katz proposed in heaven, however, has not been consummated in the drawing rooms of actual research. And part of the reason remains that advanced by Warshow: uses and gratifications researchers still are not "seeing the movies," still have not incorporated any theory of cultural forms into their analyses. Therefore, the marriage between studies in popular culture and research into the uses and gratifications of mass communication will only be achieved with a considerably higher dowry than has heretofore been offered. Something of the theoretical goals and operating assumptions of popular culture theorists will have to be actively incorporated into uses and gratifications research. In this essay we would like to prepare the ground for such influence through a critical analysis of the assumptions of uses and gratifications research and by tentatively charting the assumptions of a cultural theory of communication that could enrich and partially transform current studies.

FROM CAMPAIGN EFFECTS TO USES AND GRATIFICATIONS

Uses and gratifications research emerged because of the discovered inadequacy of the older tradition of campaign or effects studies. Setting out to show the effects of mass communication, the campaign studies instead mainly demonstrated the limited incidence of direct effects and adduced a range of intervening factors, such as selective exposure and selective perception, that mediated direct effects. The chief value of the campaign studies was that they demonstrated, as Blumler (1964) points out, the relative lack of short-term effects and persuasive power of the mass media. The newer approach treats uses and gratifications sought or experienced by the audience as intervening variables standing between mass-communicated messages and their impact upon the audience. Exploring these uses and gratifications, Blumler suggests, may offer a more adequate route than the older strategy toward the eventual discovery of media effects, since any effects would depend upon the influence of the intervening variables.

The uses and gratifications approach recognizes that two kinds of influence shape the intervening variables. First, it assumes that uses of the media depend upon the sociological milieu of the audience: the structure of groups and contexts in which the audience is situated. Second, uses and gratifications research rests upon the psychological principle that human perception is not a passive registering process but an active organizing and structuring process. Thus, gratifications sought by the audience are assumed to result from active psychological processes of constructing lines of action. Various authors pointed communications research away from the campaign studies tradition by arguing that audiences' uses of mass media had little relation to the uses expected or intended by producers (for example, Bauer, 1958, 1964; Davison, 1959). In sum, uses and gratifications researchers shifted the impact of mass media from the effects of producers' intentions to the effects of audiences' intentions, which are understood to depend upon sociological context and active psychological processes.

When this by now standard interpretation of the emergence of uses and gratifications research is presented, it is rarely acknowledged, however, that such research rests upon assumptions imported from other areas of the behavioral sciences. This silence concerning underlying assumptions in turn disguises the fundamental grounds of the position. These assumptions are considerably more controversial than the standard history allows. The assumption that the intentions of the audience are partly shaped by the surrounding sociological context is a legacy of functional and system theories in sociology. These theories made themselves felt in the uses and gratifications studies of the 1950s which attempted to relate uses to sociological categories and to psychological dispositions now explicitly conceptualized as resulting from social-structural factors. The assumption that audiences formulate their intentions in an actively structuring perceptual process came chiefly from the various streams of functional and Gestalt psychology. Not surprisingly, the uses and gratifications approach received wide acclaim among communications researchers about the same time as cognitive dissonance theory and various other psychological equilibrium models surfaced in modern psychology.

Very early, functional psychologists made the concept of system central to their explanatory schemes, Whitaker (1965) points out, and the systemic formulation has remained characteristic of the derivative equilibrium models applied in communications studies. The system concept, of course, also stands at the center of sociological functionalism. Chiefly growing out of these two bodies of thought, uses and gratifications studies are ineluctably wedded to the logic of the system model.

The assumption by uses and gratifications researchers that mass media consumption is governed by the recipient's actively structuring perceptual habits represents a decided gain over the psychological assumptions underpinning the older research tradition. However, to the degree that uses and gratifications research is tied to functional models, to the notion that the phenomena of communications are systemic and to the related model of perceptual processes as utilitarian acts of juding stimuli in terms of self-generated needs, it will prove difficult to integrate this research with the study of popular culture.

FROM PROPHETIC TO PRIESTLY COMMUNICATION ANALYSIS

Blumler (1964) and Katz (1959) have argued that uses and gratifications research offers a way of conceptually clarifying and empirically testing hypotheses concerning the consumption of mass communication proposed by popular culture critics. However, uses and gratifications research does much more than simply clarify and operationalize these ideas. Instead, it casts the subject up in an entirely different language and in doing so alters the entire nature of the problems studied.

This criticism should not be construed as a defense of the popular culture theorists' position, for we agree with Blumler, Katz and others that the debate between critics and defenders of mass culture has led to a stalemate. The uses and gratifications approach, however, should not be presented as a new and superior way of unlocking answers to old questions. The uses and gratifications approach and the theories of the popular culture critics are totally different languages for describing and therefore conceptualizing the subject. In the words of Burke (1957), they are alternative "terministic screens" which apprehend different realities. Like all terminologies they cast up selective and therefore somewhat simplified and distorted images of the reality for which they are taken as models.

As Katz, Blumler and Gurevitch (1974) point out, the debate about popular culture has been couched in "technological, aesthetic, ideological, or other more or less 'elitist' terms." To abandon these terms is probably a step in the right direction, but it should be recognized that aesthetic, ideological, and "elitist" problems are also being abandoned and about that loss we can be less sanguine. Unhappily, some advocates of uses and gratifications studies seem to want it both ways: having renounced as unanswerable and unproductive questions that are historical, aesthetic, ideological, and bound up with the interests of class and status groups, they nevertheless assert that their data are somehow germane to the debate on these questions. Thus, having renounced the elitist terms, Katz, Blumler and Gurevitch go on to say they "suspect that a full understanding of what lies behind audience behavior would neutralize at least some part of the criticism that is typically directed against it from elite quarters." Similarly, in the midst of his excessive defense of mass culture, Mendelsohn (1966) concedes that "admittedly, the language of mass entertainment is mostly contrived, stereotyped, and shallow."

From the standpoint of a popular culture theorist there is some double-talk here, but it is not altogether unusual. For example, in *Television in the Lives of Our Children,* Schramm, Lyle and Parker (1961) declared that they were not asserting that television supplied the "best" means of satisfying certain functions as judged from the perspectives of historians or philosophers or as it might appear from the vantage point of later generations, but only that television offered the "best" means of satisfying certain functions from the standpoint of the children who consumed it. This sort of declaration is ritualistically advanced by uses and gratifications researchers, but all too often ignored in suggesting implications of their findings. For in the decision to adopt the perspective of children rather than that of philosophers, historians, or future generations is buried a series of assumptions of serious ideological import—indeed, just the import popular culture theorists were concerned about.

As the critical conclusions of popular culture theorists are shaped by their ideological and aesthetic terminologies, the generally positive and supportive conclusions of uses and gratifications researchers are shaped by their terminology, which is, as Katz, Blumler and Gurevitch (1974) point out, an "audience-related" terminology. It is not surprising that this terminology yields a series of apparently positive and valuable functions of mass communication. Moreover, there is no reason to attribute to these self-reports of audience members any more finality than can be attributed to the critics' negative conclusions. Communities of drinkers find positive reasons for drinking and television viewers similarly justify viewing. In any universe of discourse persons construct legitimations that make their own normative patterns of behavior appear right and reasonable, and social scientists often conspire with such communities to heighten the plausibility of their activities. Uses and gratifications researchers collect lists of audiences' descriptions of their own media use. However methodologically clever the elicitation, researchers face the danger that they may make such a description appear to be a "real" or objective description of the behavior and then a legitimate and positive pattern of behavior by translating the audience's description into the statistical rhetoric of social research.

It is not enough in dealing with this issue merely to suggest, as Katz, Blumler and Gurevitch (1974) do, that value "judgments about the cultural significance of mass communication should be suspended while audience orientations are explored on their own terms." Such a statement is made in reaction to the explicit ideological biases of many popular culture theorists. However, in most studies such value judgments are introduced through the very nature of functionalism, through the very language used to explore audience orientations "on their own terms" and to name audience needs.

These issues raise that long-standing charge about which functionalists are most touchy—that their methodology is conservative and defensive of the status quo. The charge should come as no surprise. After all, radical and conservative critics of popular culture often directed their attacks at the liberal center of modern society, a center represented, at least in the United States, by behaviorists who executed the campaign studies and now by functionalists who sponsor the uses and gratifications studies. Therefore, no consideration of uses and gratifications research can avoid the question that most popular culture theorists would automatically put to it—Does not the whole methodology of uses and gratifications research—adducing imputed needs and functions satisfied by mass media—smack of a mere defense of the media operators' oldest argument: "We only give the people what they want"?

Uses and gratifications researchers often sidestep the worst excesses of this sort, and cautious functional theorists have devoted considerable attention to the potential pitfalls of the functionalist methodology. A cultural practice may not be functional for the society as a whole, Merton (1957) points out, but only for some subgroup sufficiently powerful to perpetuate it—which is, of course, precisely the suspicion about mass culture harbored by many critics. After concluding his analysis of the latent functions fulfilled by the political machine, Merton carefully adds that the analysis is not a defense of the political machine but might instead be taken as the basis for attempts to replace it by other social mechanisms regarded as more desirable and capable of satisfying the same latent functions. Hempel (1959) has pointed out that a functional analysis does not explain the existence of a cultural practice but only of that practice or any one of its possible functional alternates, most of them, of course, unknown. In showing that mass media consumption has functions, uses and gratifications research does not show that it is the only way or the optimum way of satisfying these functions. Moreover, such research can easily slide into an unwarranted defense on matters of taste and quality.

Defenders of functionalism have argued that the methodology is not inherently conservative but may become so in the hands of practitioners. Pertinent here is a noticeable difference, on the whole, between uses and gratifications studies conducted in the forties and those conducted in the fifties. Studies of the forties were more likely to describe adduced functions and gratifications in negative terms, such as Herzog's (1944) evident dismay about the use of soap operas for advice, while studies of the fifties were more likely to focus on functions that could be cast in a positive light, such as "social utility." This suggests that the methodology is sufficiently ambiguous to permit the injection of various ideological and evaluative points of view.

Indeed, Hempel (1959) has argued that the core terms of functional analysis, which have fairly clear meanings in reference to biological systems, are sufficiently ambiguous when transferred to the analysis of social systems as to create considerable danger of the injection of an investigator's values by virtue of the construction he explicitly or implicitly attaches to the functional terms. The problem is magnified in uses and gratifications research insofar as researchers have mostly been content to adduce lists of uses and functions without explicitly connecting their findings with the underlying functional assumptions. Unarticulated core concepts and assumptions remain even more susceptible to value-laden biases.

Blumler (1964) was certainly correct in maintaining that the condemnation of mass culture is mainly a reflection of the anxieties of the intellectuals who attack it. But it is equally important to be aware of the sociological roots of the posture that dominates uses and gratifications research. Gouldner (1970) has argued that a system of social theory may be accepted as plausible by its adherents because it reflects what Williams (1961) called the "structure of feeling" in their own milieu. The shift in tone and focus in uses and gratifications studies between the forties and the fifties mirrored a changing structure of feeling among the investigators, and that shift paralleled a general shift in the structure of feeling among communications researchers.

In short, the sociological analysis and discussion of mass communication has undergone a transformation parallel to what Friedrichs (1970) described as the shift from the "prophetic" mode to the "priestly" mode in sociology. The pessimism of early discussions of mass communication—captured in such terms as "alienation" and "mass society"—was the legacy of nineteenth century and early twentieth century social theorists who were, as Blum (1961) has pointed out, marginal men who felt considerable personal alienation from the burgeoning industrial society. But communications research, like the larger sociological milieu from which it draws much of its inspiration, has undergone what Burke (1957) called a "bureaucratization of the imaginative," and positive and optimistic terminologies and styles of thought now dominate the center of the field.

A peculiar liability of the functionalist language for dealing with popular culture is its inadequate aesthetic theory. Implicit throughout much of the communications literature is a contrast made explicit by Schramm, Lyle and

Parker (1961) in their discussion of "reality content" and "fantasy content." They note that there have been two classical types of aesthetic theory. One type regards art as a contributor to insight and cognitive development, while the other treats it as a vehicle to irrational pleasures.

Popular culture theorists often assume this contrast, placing high art in the first category and popular culture in the second. Typically, uses and gratifications researchers have not questioned or abandoned the contrast, but have simply attempted to move much of popular culture consumption from the second category to the first. This feat is accomplished through various rhetorical strategies, including the argument that much of what appears to be escape is not really, or at least is not entirely, because it has social utility functions or contributes to "incidental learning" or socialization. Mendelsohn (1966) makes explicit the assumption that mass culture consumption is escapist or dysfunctional only when it totally severs the individual from his everyday world. Many popular culture theorists believe this is frequently true, while uses and gratifications researchers seem intent on showing that it is typically true only of "isolated," "abnormal," and "maladjusted" people. Turned around, Mendelsohn's proposition implies that the consumption of cultural products is functional, non-escapist, and therefore approved when it has a payoff or utility external to the experience of consumption itself, that is, in the "real world" instead of in the "symbolic world" of cultural forms themselves.

Uses and gratifications research fails to link the functions of mass media consumption with the symbolic content of the mass-communicated materials or with the actual experience of consuming them. Yet Dewey (1934) argued that the characteristic property of aesthetic experience was its immediately pleasurable quality, which he called the "consummatory moment." Stephenson (1967) picked up the insight in his "play theory" of mass communication, which recognizes that the motivations for mass media consumption include a peculiar kind of aesthetic satisfaction, self-contained within the consuming experience itself—a satisfaction which differs in kind from the functionalists' utilitarian needs. Uses and gratifications researchers translate the aesthetic or cultural dimension of mass media consumption into an ill-fitting mechanical language of sociological functions, such as "incidental learning," and psychological functions, such as "tension reduction," instead of applying a model more appropriate to cultural experience. Gouldner (1970) regards this as a consequence of a general disposition among persons in a utilitarian culture to dismiss the reality of things in themselves and to treat them instead in terms of their consequences.

It is difficult to specify "functions" of the symbolic experience itself apart from its psychological and sociological consequences because the language of functionalism is ill-equipped to express the significant qualities of that experience. Katz and Foulkes (1962) point out that the largest escapist pastime, dreaming, is regarded as unreal and irrelevant in our society. That same mental set is characteristic throughout the social sciences, and uses and gratifications research shares with many other approaches an inability to conceptualize the significance of symbolic experience and thus a tendency to translate it into more "real" phenomena in "normal" cases and to relegate it to a special realm of pathology in "abnormal" cases.

Uses and gratifications researchers condemn popular culture theorists for inferring appeals and effects from content, but the functionalists have done an unproductive about-face by dropping any attention to symbolic content. Or, to the extent that content is treated as in any sense symbolic, it is so regarded only in the myopic sense that it may trigger psychological reactions or represent such sociological elements as values and role-expectations to which persons are thereby socialized. Like much of the social sciences, uses and gratifications research regards psychological and sociological variables as real and primary, and culture as a derivative agent and manifestation of them. That attitude will have to be replaced by a cultural point of view if research on popular culture and uses and gratifications is to go forward.

THE FUNCTIONALIST AND UTILITARIAN UNDERPINNINGS

We have identified two shifts in communications studies: first, from the study of campaign effects to uses and gratifications, from a causal model to a functional model, or, to use cybernetic language, from the study of persons conceived as relatively trivial machines to complex systems. The second change, orthogonal to the first, is from a prophetic to a priestly mode of study, from the general pessimism of popular culture theorists to the optimism of contemporary studies, from the dysfunctions to the functions of mass communications. The central problem in comprehending this shift and relating it to the study of popular culture is comprehending something of the nature of functionalism as an intellectual program.

Implicitly or explicitly, research on uses and gratifications relies on functionalism for whatever intellectual underpinnings it possesses. This reliance on functionalism is not merely a product of the narrow history of mass communication research but reflects, more importantly, the general history of the social sciences, particularly when the social sciences attempt to deal with artifacts and expressions that are explicitly symbolic. There is a sense, of course, in which all human activity is in both origins and endings symbolic. But there is still a useful analytic distinction (to steal from Burke, 1957) between building a house and drawing up a blueprint for building a house, between making love and writing a poem about making love. However much the symbolic and the artifactual are fused in everyday life, it is nonetheless useful to separate them for analytic purposes. Unfortunately, whenever the symbolic component is inescapably present, a certain theoretical clumsiness overtakes the social sciences. Faced with making some explicit statements about cultural forms, social scientists retreat to obscurantism and reduce their subject matter to social structures or psychological needs. They seem incapable of handling culture in itself—as an ordered system of symbols—and treat merely the social and psychological origins of the symbols.

The several subfields of the social sciences in which symbols and meanings are of critical importance exhibit a similar history. In the study of ideology, religion, and mythology as well as popular culture, the same attempt is made to reduce symbolic forms to antecedent and causal variables. When this strategy fails, as it inevitably does, a switch in strategy is announced which reduces cultural phenomena to system-maintaining phenomena—that is, to a functional explanation. Behind the switch in research strategy there is a concurrent switch in imagery: from a power model of phenomena to an anxiety model, from an interest theory of action to a strain theory, and from a passive and arational notion of behavior to an active and utilitarian conception.

Mass communication research begins as an attempt to explain communication effects by deriving them from some causally antecedent aspect of the communication process. Inspired by both behavioristic psychology and information theory, this explanatory apparatus gave rise to a power model of communication wherein the emphasis was placed upon the action of the environment, however conceived, upon a relatively passive receiver. This model was made both possible and necessary by a scientific program that insisted on reducing cultural phenomena to antecedent causes. While some of these causes were explicitly conceptualized as psychological variables—source credibility, appeal of the message—others were rooted in the structural situation of the receiver—class, status, religion, income (Hovland, Janis and Kelley, 1953; Lazarsfeld, Berelson and Gaudet, 1948).

An advantage of this model of antecedent causality was that it rooted cultural phenomena in the solid ground of social structure or the conditioning history of individuals. However, it had the disadvantage of yielding ambiguous predictions of behavior. At best, modest correlations of antecedent and resultant variables were achieved, and even modest success was often purchased by carefully screening test populations (Katz and Lazarsfeld, 1955) to heighten the likelihood of significant results.

The history of mass communication research parallels that of other areas of the social sciences which deal with cultural forms. Whether it be delinquency (Matza, 1964), ideology (Geertz, 1973), or religion (Berger, 1967), the attempt is first made to predict the presence of a creed, ideology, deviant pattern, or behavior change on the basis of antecedent exposure and stimulation or on the basis of a social-structural variable—race, class, income, etc. The results are usually meager and the final conclusion comes down to "some do, some don't." On the basis of conditioning or class or any other of these families of antecedent variables, one concludes that some hold to the creed, some do not; some vote one way, some another; some join Fascist movements, some remain apathetic. Unfortunately, one is unable to predict the doers from the underlying model, for only a minuscule amount of variation in the generated data—significant correlations, but usually less than .5—can be explained by even complex sets of variables. Finally, the entire imagery of culture as a power—the opiate of the people, the hypodermic needle, the product of the environment—denies the functioning of autonomous minds and reduces subjects to trivial machines. The rich history of cultural symbolism, the complex, meaningful transactions of, for example, religion end up no more than shadowy derivatives of stimuli and structures.

The functional model arises in response to the empirical difficulties encountered in models of antecedent causality. Moreover, it engenders a shift in imagery and in attention: from a view of communication as a power to one of communication as a form of anxiety release and from an interest in the source to an interest in the audience. But most importantly, it involves a shift in the explanatory apparatus. For in functional analysis the primary emphasis is not upon determining the antecedents or origins of behavior but upon determining the import or consequences of behavior for the maintenance of systems of thought, activity, or social groups. One explains social phenomena not merely etiologically but teleologically: the way they act as mechanisms to maintain or restore equilibrium within a system.

Functional analysis turns, then, from causes to consequences, which are viewed as a contribution to maintaining (or disrupting) the individual personality or more complex systems of social life. Whether the subject is ideology, religion, or mythology, the effect is the same. Religion, no longer characterized as a product of historical conditioning, is now shown to maintain social solidarity: the "we're all in this together" theory. Ideology, now no longer merely caused by class interest, is shown to provide catharsis by fixating and dispelling anxiety on scapegoats: the "even paranoids have enemies" theory. Mass communication, rather than causing certain attitudes or behaviors, provides, by diverting audiences from their troubles, feedback into the maintenance of normalized social roles: the "everything we do is useful" theory.

Functionalism starts, then, from the potential malintegration of systems —social, personality, cognitive. It explains phenomena by attaching them not to causal antecedents but to future states which they erode or more often maintain. At the level of society functional mechanisms deal with strain—surveying hostile environments; at the level of personality with anxiety or, in the psychological equivalent to sociological functionalism, with dissonance.

Functional analysis appears, of course, in some of the earliest literature of mass communication, but does not receive any explicit and programmatic formulation until the name "uses and gratifications" is associated with it and until Wright (1960) gives functionalism explicit formulation in the context of mass communication. Unfortunately, Wright states the case for functionalism on very general grounds and then defends it on very narrow terrain. In the first part of his essay he uses the notion of function in the loosest imaginable way, confusing terms like function, consequence, and activity, and in the latter portion of the essay he defends the program by reliance on the writing of Hempel (1959). Unfortunately, Hempel uses the term function in a very narrow sense and lays down a series of conditions for functional analysis—quoted by Wright—that Wright's program is in no way capable of meeting; perhaps, in principle, is incapable of meeting.

Wright follows upon the sociological school of communications researchers

—Riley and Riley (1959), for example—who attempted in the 1950s to articulate communications studies with a general sociological system model so that mass media effects or functions could be interpreted in a sociological context. These efforts pretty much came to naught, and uses and gratifications studies remain predominantly individualistic—on the surface at least. At least no one has been able to convincingly show functions of mass communications for anything other than individuals, or mechanical aggregates thereof, beyond the trivial and obvious—such as calling the activity of writing news stories the functional mechanism for "surveying the environment."

In the absence of a linkage with a general social system theory, the mere collection of lists of uses and gratifications suffers from the lack of any demonstration that functional logic has a bearing upon the subject being studied. The idea that a cultural practice has functions presumes that it has functions for some system. Gouldner (1959) argues that the two defining properties of a system are equilibrium and interdependence but the degree of these two properties and thus of "systemness" must be treated as variable. To argue that mass communications have functions, the researcher must specify the system for which they have functions and show that it can be characterized as possessing some degree of "systemness." Failure to specify the relevant system, Rudner (1956) argues, denies any explanatory value to functional conclusions, which must instead be regarded as sheer descriptions.

Moreover, as Bredemeier (1955) points out, functional analysis requires showing not only that a cultural practice satisfies some need but also the origin of the need. Further, as Hempel (1959) argues, the conclusion that cultural practices are functional or dysfunctional for the operation of some system requires a specification of the "normal" state of the system. Clearly, these requisites are not explicitly satisfied in uses and gratifications studies, but implicit assumptions lurk in the background. Reducing culture to social and psychological variables, the uses and gratifications approach regards the relevant systems as the "personality system," which is conceived as the bearer of a string of crudely conceptualized individualistic utilitarian needs, and the "social system."

Part of the problem with functionalism arises from the plurality of meanings of the term "function" in sociological literature. Martindale (1960) notes four prevalent meanings of the term, of which three are relevant in the present context: (1) useful activity, (2) appropriate or normal activity, and (3) the contribution to a system. In empirical studies, the explanatory logic of the third meaning is often claimed for imputed functions conceptualized from the standpoint of other meanings.

As the label "uses and gratifications" suggests, the functions adduced in these studies are, in the main, those that can be characterized as "useful" or "utilitarian" consequences. Gouldner (1970) suggests that functionalism is not much more than a resurrection of utilitarianism as an agency for bourgeois defense of the existing social order on nontraditional grounds. Whatever the relevance of this sweeping charge, it is certainly pertinent to question whether utilitarian models, however applicable to certain behaviors, are adequate as models of the consumption of cultural products. We believe that the utilitarian model is a fairly poor one for consumption choices that hinge upon considerations of taste, style, or aesthetics.

In the work of Katz, conducted with a variety of colleagues, there is an attempt to treat the functions of mass communication for the individual and to treat them in a way which connects directly with the literature of popular culture. Katz's first attempt at achieving this integration was an essay written with Foulkes (1962) on the concept of escape. Escape was an indictment of popular culture theorists, particularly Marxists, regularly laid at the door of popular entertainment. According to the critics, alienation drives persons to seek escape in the mass media, but what they get there has mainly "negative feedback" to their everyday roles. However, Katz and Foulkes argue that even if it is alienation or deprivation which drives people to the mass media, what they get upon arriving there often functions as positive feedback to other roles. They present a wide range of impressive evidence to support the view that what is called escapist content can restore and maintain normal activity, serve unintended functions such as heightening social solidarity, serve as a "cover" for a variety of desirable activities, and generally provide a sanctioned mode of escape from ordinary responsibilities.

This brief example reveals a number of characteristic things about the functional study of uses and gratifications. First, if function turns out to mean useful consequences, the question arises, useful for what? Researchers sometimes assume that mass media consumption is useful for satisfying purely individual-istic needs. But the imputed functions often are useful consequences for needs induced by social roles.

Second, the term "dysfunction" seldom appears in empirical studies. Yet the idea of a division of media uses into functions and dysfunctions runs implicitly throughout communications studies. Uses characterized approvingly, as func-tions, are those connected with "real" social roles, while uses characterized negatively, as dysfunctions, are those that involve a flight from "real" roles. Much of communications research questionably characterizes as bizarre and abnormal, but fortunately confined to a minority of isolated and maladjusted people, all uses of mass communication that appear to be purely symbolic in the sense that they do not contribute to everyday roles. In short, positive functions are connected with social roles, which derive from the social system. Hence the present workings of the social system constitute its "normal" state, the needs that it generates are approved, and the means of satisfying them are positive functions.

Only the evaluation, not the logic, of this line of reasoning differs from a frequent charge of popular culture theorists, especially Marxists. According to the critics, the social structure (now evaluated negatively) generates various needs (now also evaluated negatively) which popular culture satisfies. Thus popular culture contributes to the present state of the personality and the social structure, both of them evaluated negatively by popular culture theorists and positively by uses and gratifications researchers. We submit that the underlying logic, regardless of which way it is evaluated, is inadequate for the study of popular culture.

Third, the presumption of the chronic malintegration of social life, while truthful, probably inevitable and universal, gets the entire analysis not only into ideologically murky waters but into some questionable scientific presumptions as well. We are left with a case in which some people derive positive functions from mass communication while others derive dysfunctions. But there is no way on scientific grounds of choosing between the possibilities. And this studied vagueness haunts functional analysis throughout the social sciences. Mass communication may upset or confirm social consensus, survey the environment or deceive an audience, promote solidarity or enhance animosity, relieve or exacerbate social tensions, correlate a response to crisis or fragment a community. Anecdotal evidence can be introduced to support all of these contentions, but there is no way of specifying when and under what circumstances mass communication does any or all of these things.

While a uses and gratifications analysis on occasion comes close to motives that lie behind the consumption of mass communications, in attempting to discriminate the consequences of the behavior the analysis becomes ambiguous. A pattern of behavior shaped by a certain set of motivations turns out by a plausible coincidence to serve remotely related ends. A person sits down to watch a television program because he wants to be entertained and by some mysterious process ends up dispelling his tensions, restoring his morale, or establishing solidarity with a larger community. These consequences are related to the motivations for the action in an extremely vague, unspecific, and unconvincing way. This problem, again, haunts all functional analysis. As Geertz (1973) has summarized the dilemma,

> a group of primitives sets out, in all honesty, to pray for rain and ends up by strengthening its social solidarity; a ward politician sets out to get by or remain near the trough and ends by mediating between unassimilated immigrant groups and an impersonal governmental bureaucracy; an ideologist sets out to air his grievances and finds himself contributing, through the diversionary powers of his illusions, to the continued viability of the very system that grieves him.

The idea of a latent function is usually rushed in to disguise this anomalous conclusion, but its effect is merely diversionary.

Latent functions are the device by which irrational motives are transformed into rational ones and thus made available for analysis. This trick was inherited from Malinowski (1962) and his arguments concerning the nature of the primitive mind. In Malinowski's scheme, human action that on its face was patently irrational, superstitious, and magical was linked by what we would now call a latent function to meanings inherently rational and commonsensical: the primitive mentality disclosed a utilitarian mind. This form of thought left us with but two alternatives in treating behavior; it was either intrinsically primitive and hence irrational and superstitious or it was susceptible to transformation into utilitarian forms of thought by indication of its intrinsic sensibleness: it contributed functionally to the stability of the personality or the ordering of society.

Either strategy has the effect of dissolving the content of the experience—the particular ritual, prayer, or entertainment—into something pre- or proto-logical without ever inspecting the experience itself as some ordered system of meaningful symbols. The difficulty is, of course, the virtual absence in functional analysis of anything more than a most rudimentary conception of symbolic processes. There is much talk about escape, finding symbolic outlets or solidarity being created, but how these miracles are accomplished is never made clear. In functional analysis one never finds serious attention being paid to the content of experience. For example, functional studies of religion claim that religion is not completely "irrational" because it eases tension and promotes solidarity—claims that seem ridiculous to anyone who has witnessed his community divided into saints and sinners by religious commandment. What one rarely finds is any analysis of the voice in which the religion speaks. There is an emphasis on everything except what the religion is concretely all about.

The link between the causes of mass communication behavior and its effects seems adventitious because the connecting element is a latent function and no attention is paid to the autonomous process of symbolic formation. Functional analysis, like causal analysis, goes directly from the source to the effect without ever seriously examining mass communication as a system of interacting symbols and interlocked meanings that somehow must be linked to the motivations and emotions for which they provide a symbolic outlet. Content analyses are done, but they are referred for elucidation not to other themes nor to any sort of a semantic theory but either backward to the needs they mirror or forward to the social system they maintain.

In summary, functional analysis, or that part of it which is of interest to us, focuses upon the individual, though often upon the individual conceptualized as the occupant of a role which carries with it socially induced strains and tensions. It takes the needs of the individual, the receiver, to be the determinant of the effects realized in the communication process. While it may tell you something about the uses and gratifications of the receiver, it tells you little about the consequences of this use or even, except implicitly, about the motivations that lie behind it. To explain behavior, functional theory must assume a homeostatic system—one that tends toward an equilibrium. Thus, such an analysis assumes that persons have needs, for example, to escape, to establish social relations; for normal people, these vary within understandable limits. When the needs are not satisfied, behavior ensues to reestablish the equilibrium values, and for the needs in question, this behavior involves utilization of the mass media. Presumably then, the media are a functional equivalent to other kinds of devices that could perform the same functions. Thus functionalism in mass communication is a theory of personality that disguises as a theory of communication. To illustrate these weaknesses, let us look at the phenomenon of pornography.

PORNOGRAPHY: AN OBJECT LESSON IN IGNORING CULTURE

Two general kinds of inquiry have been made into pornography, paralleling the history of mass communications research generally. First, there has been an attempt to establish direct effects of erotic material by linking certain untoward attitudes and behavior to antecedent, causal variables in the material consumed, the setting of the consumption, or the background of the receiver or interactions among them.

All this research pretty much came to naught and led to the by now standard conclusions of the President's Commission on Obscenity and Pornography (1970). While it is possible to identify forms of sexual behavior and aggression that are untoward, it is impossible to predict this behavior from antecedent variables. While weak correlations exist between certain patterns of exposure, certain life histories, and certain behaviors, they are not strong and regular enough to support restrictive social policy or to claim scientific reliability. Pornography cannot be conceptualized as a power because it cannot, in conjunction with personality, structural and situational variables, independently or together, predict either attitudes—as incipient acts—or behavior.

When this conclusion is reached, a switch is made to a functional mode of interpretation. The functional explanation buttresses the conclusion reached by the earlier mode of analysis by demonstrating whatever effects of pornography exist are positive contributions to social stability. According to Polsky's (1967) representative argument, human sexuality is both polymorphous and perverse. Sexual energy can attach itself to any object and can be expressed within any form of social relation. However, society hooks this natural energy into social ends, thereby constraining it and channeling it into normatively approved forms. There is, therefore, an inherent strain at the social level between the biological nature of humans and the apparent requisites of social order. What is experienced at one level as strain is experienced in the personality of social actors as tension and anxiety.

Society places sexuality under a double bind. First, it defines a range of suitable sexual objects and acts that are far narrower than what is biologically permissible. Second, it places temporal constraints on behavior by defining some activity as appropriate only during sanctioned periods, for example, adolescence or post-marriage.

Looking at the conflict between society and nature from the male side only, masturbation, visiting prostitutes, consuming pornography are three functional equivalents to the same end: the displacement of tension generated by conflict between biological drive and social constraint. Which activity is chosen will vary by class—lower classes more often visiting prostitutes, upper classes more often consuming pornography; by situation—what is available in prisons, colleges, street corner societies; and by personality types—varying capacities to be stimulated by vicarious experience.

However, whichever alternative is chosen, two functions are seen to follow: first, a cathartic release of dammed-up sexual energy; and, second, at the social level, a strengthening of the family. The discharge of sexual energy is pictured as feeding back into the performance of normalized social roles in the family, or, to reverse the image, disruptions in family life occur when mechanisms for dealing with personality needs and disorders generated within society are not provided. Also, to get to the ideological side of the argument, the same analysis can be used to remove restrictions on pornography and prostitution.

This sketch of the typical analysis of pornography, while slightly burlesqued, reveals the typical weaknesses of uses and gratifications analysis. First, while there is greater specification of content—at least it is more precise than speaking of news or television—nonetheless the analysis apparently requires no explicit attention to the symbolic form itself. No semantic theory is deemed necessary to assess its meaning, and no effort is made to determine the subjective meaning of the material for the audience. Second, the extraordinary diversity of the material itself—diversity over time and across cultures—is reduced to the idea of a functional alternative. This reduction assumes that human needs exist independent of the symbolic material through which they are satisfied; exist as some kind of biological and psychological substratum that emanates in, is expressed by or is satisfied through symbolic materials, the materials being affectively and cognitively neutral. Consequently, symbolic objects themselves as patterns of meaning which shape and give reality to whatever needs exist can be ignored.

Third, the material can only be treated when its usefulness can be demonstrated to the person and society. A person sits down to read a "dirty" book and not only dissipates the very urges he is trying to titillate but ends up strengthening the nuclear family. The relationship between the motive and the function—even if labeled latent—is far from necessary and seems merely adventitious. Moreover, what is one to do with all the energy that goes into consuming pornography but cannot be shown to lead to derangement or positive functions? The only options seem to be to label its consumption as abnormal—no matter how widely practiced—dismiss it as insignificant or laboriously attempt to twist it unconvincingly to utilitarian practices.

Finally, a functional approach to pornography drains the subject of historical and cultural significance. While examples of erotic art can be found in many ancient societies, pornography as we know it is a creation of the sixteenth century, emerging as a distinctive and cumulative genre with the birth of printing. The explanation of this is not merely technical but social, for as a form pornography is a product, in both production and consumption, of the middle class, and its expansion parallels the expansion of this class and its achievement of cultural power. It is a form created by and almost solely directed at men. Moreover, pornography is stylistically related to the novel, and its conventions evolve along the same path. It works through, in altered forms, the same social relations found in the novel. Pornography also characteristically centers on the same social relations found in popular art except in inverted form. If women dominate men in the comic strips, these same men dominate the same women in the pornographic equivalent of the funny papers. Pornography, then, is not solely or perhaps even largely about sexuality. It is an exploration of the grammar of human relations. It is a fantasy, a fiction, something made, but it is a making of collective images of men, women, classes, races, and ethnic groups. It is above all an exploration of mysterious groups—maids and aristocrats, college girls and professors, blacks and Orientals—and the sexual imagination that is taken to possess them.

Far from mechanically serving functions, pornography maps a world of sexual relations, effectively or no, and the social relations that obtain within it. It is not enough to call this fantasy or escape, for it is precisely the inability of uses and gratifications researchers to effectively treat this mapped world of relations that prevents any effective marriage between popular culture and this form of analysis.

TOWARD AN ACCOMMODATION

The tone of this critique has been negative, for, as we said at the outset, any merger between uses and gratifications research and the study of popular culture will be consummated only at a considerably higher price than uses and gratifications researchers have imagined. We agree with Katz, Blumler and others that the traditional, direct effects model of communication has exhausted whatever limited utility it once had, and we are indebted to them for aiding in releasing communication researchers from it. We welcome the emergence of an audience-centered communication model and the liberating assumption of an active, goal-oriented receiver as opposed to the older, passive, dependency conception. But these positive contributions hardly go far enough if the study of popular culture is to be freed from ideological stalemates and polemical standoffs. Uses and gratifications research will have to cast off its functional model of explanation, its systems model of social order, its naive and undeveloped aesthetic theory, and its implicit utilitarianism if it is to effectively treat popular culture. We can point to three crucial assumptions that will have to be adopted for a more viable modus vivendi.

First, an effective theory of popular culture will require a conception of man, not as psychological man or sociological man, but as cultural man. Such a model would assume that culture is best understood, not by tracing it to psychological and sociological conditions, but as a manifestation of a basic cultural disposition to cast up experience in symbolic forms that are at once immediately pleasing and conceptually plausible, thus supplying the basis for felt identities and meaningfully apprehended realities. In the 45 years since Edward Sapir (1929) called for a theory of culture and communication grounded in symbolic action, halting, episodic but persistent success has been realized in this enterprise. Major contributions have come from semiotics, cultural anthropology, literary criticism, intellectual history, phenomenology, hermeneutics, and that branch of modern philosophy deriving from Wittgenstein. It is now of some importance that news of these advances reach communications researchers.

If human activity is not passive or fully dependent on external stimulation, then a corollary is that activity is not merely an emanation of some substratum of biological needs or socially induced dispositions. Instead, human activity, by the very nature of the human nervous system (Geertz, 1973), is cultural, involving the construction of a symbolic container that shapes and expresses whatever human nature, needs, or dispositions exist. As with much else in this essay, Max Weber (1946) has expressed it best, in the context of the sociology of religion:

> Many . . . varieties of belief have, of course, existed. Behind them always lies a stand towards something in the actual world which is experienced as specifically "senseless." Thus, the demand has been implied: that the world order in its totality is, could, and should somehow be a meaningful "cosmos." . . . The avenues, the results and the efficacy of this meta-physical need for a meaningful cosmos have varied widely.

When the idea of culture enters communications research, it emerges as the environment of an organism or a system to be maintained. But culture must first of all be seen as a set of practices, a mode of human activity, a process whereby reality is created, maintained, and transformed (Carey, forthcoming), however much it may subsequently become reified into a force independent of human action (Berger and Luckmann, 1966). This activity allows the human nervous system to function by producing and maintaining a meaningful cosmos at once both aesthetically gratifying and intellectually plausible. It is precisely such a theory of culture—or, if you prefer, a theory of meaning, semantics or semiotic—that is necessary if culture is to be removed from the status of a power or an environment.

Such a theory is usually avoided by setting human needs and motives outside of history and culture—the eighteenth century rationalist view that human nature is everywhere the same if its cultural, that is symbolic, trappings can be stripped away (Geertz, 1973). Yet uses and gratifications analysis only attains any precision or persuasiveness when it is placed within history and culture; within, that is, the historical experience of particular peoples, as Katz (1973) does when he applies the general mode of analysis to Israel.

The second assumption that needs to be shared we can call, following Schutz (1970), the assumption of multiple realities. Functional analyses of fantasy, for example, assume that there exists some hard existential reality beyond culture and symbols to which human imaginative productions can be referred for final validation. It is comic to see this argument in analyses of, for example, popular music in which commercial love songs are defined as fantasy and Negro blues or war protest songs as reality (Hayakawa, 1957; Carey, 1972). The difference between these forms is not that one is real and the other fantastic, but rather that they reflect the tastes of audiences for different modes of casting up experience.

Rather than grading experience into zones of epistemological correctness, we can more usefully presume that the nature of man, culture, and their interactions leads persons to live in qualitatively distinct zones of experience which cultural forms organize in different ways. Few people are satisfied apprehending things exclusively through the flattened perceptual glasses of common sense. Most insist on constantly transforming perception into different modes—religious, aesthetic, scientific—in order to see the particular marvels and mysteries these frames of reference contain. The scientific conceit is the presumption that living in scientific frames of reference is unequivocally superior to aesthetic, commonsensical or religious ones. The debilitating effect of this conceit is the failure to understand the meaningful realms of discourse in terms of which people conduct their lives.

The debate on popular culture raised and then promptly obscured the question of the significance of apprehending reality in the terms laid down by popular art. This significance has little to do with effects or functions. Popular art is, first of all, an experience, in Warshow's terms an "immediate experience," that must be apprehended in something like its own terms. However long or intensively one lives in the world of popular art, it is only one of several cultural worlds, by no means consistent or congruent, in which people live. In general, there is little or no relation among these worlds except when people, in answering social science questionnaires, must produce a merger between their entertainment and other regions of life. At most what one finds within popular art is the creation of particular moods—sadness, joy, depression—feelings which descend and lift like fogs, and particular motives—erotic, aggressive, which have vectorial qualities (Geertz, 1973). But whether these moods or motives ever reach beyond the domain in which they exist—theaters and concert halls—into laboratories, street corners, and churches where other dramas are being enacted and other melodies played is radically problematic. Usually, they do not. But any merger of uses and gratifications research and popular culture will have to examine the several cultural worlds in which people simultaneously exist, the tension, often radical tension, between them, the patterns of mood and motivation distinctive to each and the interpenetration among them. Simultaneously, it will have to release the assumption that needs and motives encountered in scientific worlds are anything more than one cultural version among many and not some final court against which to judge the veridicalness of other modes of experience.

As a third necessary assumption, uses and gratifications researchers will have to adopt a new view of human needs and motives. Uses and gratifications researchers assume that mass media consumption is purposive or goal directed. Put more technically, they assume that mass media use fits a "means-end" model of behavior, according to which an actor perceives a line of behavior as the means to some desired end or the means to satisfying some felt need. The actor's rational perception of the means-end relationship is then regarded as the motive for his mass media use.

Seemingly, the chief reason for assuming that mass media use fits the means-end model is that subjects offer motives of this kind, or at least offer descriptions that can be classified into types that fit the means-end model. Mills (1940) argued that motives are merely words accepted as reasonable and plausible descriptions and explanations for behavior in some universe of discourse. These verbal explanations may be adduced either before or after the behavior, and they are susceptible to all the vagaries of any form of linguistic expression. The point is not that subjects lie or investigators fudge, but simply that the final list of imputed motives depends upon unstated assumptions concerning reasonable and plausible types of motivation held by either the subjects or the investigators or, more likely, both.

The motives adduced for media consumption probably fit the means-end model chiefly because both subjects and investigators assume that behavior is governed by motives of this type. Schutz (1970) and Sorokin (1947) contrasted this type of motivation, which Schutz called "in-order-to" motives and Sorokin called action "for the sake of," with another type of motivation, which Schutz called "because" motives and Sorokin called action "because of." Whereas "in-order-to" or "for-the-sake-of" motives are imagined future states or consequences, "because" motives have their origin in past experience that motivates present action in a nonpurposive way. Schutz and Sorokin were trying to show that all action does not fit the model of rational or purposive or goal-directed action. As Schutz wrote, "What I wish to emphasize is only that the ideal of rationality is not and cannot be a peculiar feature of everyday thought, nor can it, therefore, be a methodological principle of the interpretation of human acts in daily life."

The assumption of purposive action rests on an ideal-typical model of one type of action, which is probably seldom if ever matched completely by real action and certainly is not an adequate model for all action. To suggest alternative models of action that would require alternative conceptions of motivation, we might turn to the four ideal types of action described by Weber (1947)—traditional, affectual, *Zweckrational* (purpose rational), and *Wert-rational* (value rational). Purposiveness is characteristic of only one of the four types, *Zweckrational*, whereas in at least two of the others, Weber wrote, "the meaning of the action does not lie in the achievement of a result ulterior to it but in carrying out the specific type of action for its own sake."

We again confront the suggestion that some actions are not purposive, but instead are engaged in for their own sake, or for what was earlier called, following Dewey, their consummatory value. Uses and gratifications studies, Weiss (1969) observes, have occasionally noted, but not given sufficient attention to, consummatory gratifications. This is not an accidental oversight, but a result of the language and assumptions about motivation of the methodology. A more illuminating approach to popular culture would be one founded on a model of action and motivation more appropriate to aesthetic types of experience than the purposive model.

Following the functionalist logic, the needs that mass media consumption presumably satisfies could as well be satisfied in many other ways. Yet obviously they are not satisfied randomly in any one of a large number of functionally alternative ways. One must, therefore, attempt to link cultural behavior, not with psychologically and sociologically generated needs for classes of functional alternates, but instead with culturally constructed "tastes" for specific cultural styles and forms. For uses and gratifications research to deal with popular culture, matters of style and taste, which slip into unexplained and unexamined interstices in the functionalists' language of needs and uses, should be elevated to focal concern. Communications research, Ennis (1961) argued, might "more wisely wed itself to the expressive rather than the cognitive or instrumental symbol." More recently, Burns (1967) wrote approvingly of one study which "rescues the concept of 'style of life' from the status of a dependent variable, an extra and perhaps superfluous appendage of class or occupational status."

Ennis proposed treating a mass media audience as a "social group" created by the communicative process itself. Chaney (1972) has echoed the call, noting that leisure and communicative activities result in shared affinities for common "means for the expression and integration of social character and identity." In sum, popular culture should not be studied in relation to predefined sociological categories, but as a cultural process in which persons create shared expressive and conceptual models that supply common identities and apprehended realities. Thereby its use results, Chaney writes, in a "consensus about the world, or at least a discord that is minimally disturbing." Entertainment, Burns (1967) writes,

> can be construed as contemporary society's response to the enduring need to ritualize the unfamiliar and disconnected.
>
> Like ritual, it domesticates the unattainable and the threatening and reduces the increasing range and strangeness of the individual's world to the synthesized, rehearsed, and safely repeatable form of a story, a documentary, a performance, a show. The structures of leisure exist as repositories of meaning, value and reassurance for everyday life.

REFERENCES

BAUER, R. (1964) "The obstinate audience." American Psychologist 19: 319-328.
——— (1958) "The communicator and the audience." Journal of Conflict Resolution 2: 67-77.
BERGER, P. (1967) The Sacred Canopy. Garden City, N.Y.: Doubleday.
——— and T. LUCKMANN (1966) The Social Construction of Reality. Garden City, N.Y.: Doubleday.
BLUM, A. (1961) "Popular culture and the image of Gesellschaft." Studies in Public Communication 3: 145-158.
BLUMLER, J. G. (1964) "British television—the outlines of a research strategy." British Journal of Sociology 15: 223-233.
BREDEMEIER, H. (1955) "The methodology of functionalism." American Sociological Review 20: 173-180.
BURKE, K. (1957) The Philosophy of Literary Form. New York: Vintage Books.
BURNS, T. (1967) "A meaning in everyday life." New Society 9, 243 (May 25): 760-762.
CAREY, J. T. (1972) "Changing courtship patterns in the popular song," pp. 198-212 in R. S. Densioff and R. Peterson (eds.) The Sounds of Social Change. Chicago: Rand-McNally.
CAREY, J. W. (forthcoming) "A cultural approach to communications." Communication 1, 2.

CHANEY, D. (1972) Processes of Mass Communication. New York: Herder & Herder.

DAVISON, W. (1959) "On the effects of communication." Public Opinion Quarterly 23: 343-360.

DEWEY, J. (1934) Art as Experience. New York: Minton, Balch.

ENNIS, P. (1961) "The social structure of communication systems: a theoretical proposal." Studies in Public Communication 3: 120-144.

FRIEDRICHS, R. (1970) A Sociology of Sociology. New York: Free Press.

GEERTZ, C. (1973) The Interpretation of Cultures. New York: Basic Books.

GOULDNER, A. (1970) The Coming Crisis of Western Sociology. New York: Basic Books.

——— (1959) "Reciprocity and autonomy in functional theory," pp. 241-270 in L. Gross (ed.) Symposium on Sociological Theory. Evanston, Ill.: Row, Peterson.

HAYAKAWA, S. (1957) "Popular songs vs. the facts of life," pp. 393-403 in B. Rosenberg and D. White (eds.) Mass Culture. Glencoe, Ill.: Free Press.

HEMPEL, C. (1959) "The logic of functional analysis," pp. 271-307 in L. Gross (ed.) Symposium on Sociological Theory. Evanston, Ill.: Row, Peterson.

HERZOG, H. (1944) "What do we really know about daytime serial listeners?" in P. F. Lazarsfeld and F. N. Stanton (eds.) Radio Research 1942-1943. New York: Duell, Sloan & Pearce.

HOVLAND, C., I. JANIS, and H. KELLEY (1953) Communication and Persuasion. New Haven: Yale University Press.

KATZ, E. (1973) "Culture and communication in Israel: the transformation of tradition." Jewish Journal of Sociology 15: 5-21.

——— (1959) "Mass communication research and the study of popular culture: an editorial note on a possible future for this journal." Studies in Public Communication 2: 1-6.

——— J. G. BLUMLER, and M. GUREVITCH (1974) "Utilization of mass communication by the individual: an overview," in J. G. Blumler and E. Katz (eds.) The Uses of Mass Communications: Current Perspectives on Gratifications Research. Beverly Hills: Sage.

KATZ, E. and D. FOULKES (1962) "On the use of the mass media as 'escape': clarification of a concept." Public Opinion Quarterly 26: 377-388.

KATZ, E. and P. LAZARSFELD (1955) Personal Influence. Glencoe, Ill.: Free Press.

LAZARSFELD, P., B. BERELSON, and H. GAUDET (1948) The People's Choice. New York: Columbia University Press.

MacDONALD, D. (1962) Against the American Grain. New York: Random House.

MALINOWSKI, B. (1962) Sex, Culture and Myth. New York: Harcourt, Brace & World.

MARTINDALE, D. (1960) The Nature and Types of Sociological Theory. Boston: Houghton Mifflin.

MATZA, D. (1964) Delinquency and Drift. New York: John Wiley.

MENDELSOHN, H. (1966) Mass Entertainment. New Haven: College & University Press.

MERTON, R. (1957) Social Theory and Social Structure. Rev. ed. New York: Free Press.

MILLS, C. W. (1959) The Power Elite. New York: Oxford University Press.

——— (1940) "Situated actions and vocabularies of motives." American Sociological Review 5: 904-913.

POLSKY, N. (1967) Hustlers, Beats, and Others. Chicago: Aldine.

President's Commission on Obscenity and Pornography (1970) Report of the Commission on Obscenity and Pornography. New York: Bantam.

RILEY, J. W., Jr. and M. W. RILEY (1959) "Mass communication and the social system," pp. 537-578 in R. K. Merton et al. (eds.) Sociology Today. New York: Basic Books.

RUDNER, R. (1966) Philosophy of Social Science. Englewood Cliffs, N.J.: Prentice-Hall.

SAPIR, E. (1929) "The status of linguistics as a science." Language 5: 207-214.

SCHRAMM, W., J. LYLE, and E. PARKER (1961) Television in the Lives of Our Children. Stanford: Stanford University Press.

SCHUTZ, A. (1970) On Phenomenology and Social Relations. Chicago: University of Chicago Press.

SHILS, E. (1959) "Mass society and its culture," pp. 1-27 in N. Jacobs (ed.) Culture for the Millions? Princeton: D. Van Nostrand.

SOROKIN, P. (1947) Society, Culture and Personality. New York: Harper.

STEPHENSON, W. (1967) The Play Theory of Mass Communication. Chicago: University of Chicago Press.

WARSHOW, R. (1964) The Immediate Experience. Garden City, N.Y.: Anchor Books.

WEBER, M. (1947) The Theory of Social and Economic Organization. New York: Oxford University Press.

——— (1946) in H. Gerth and C. W. Mills (eds.) From Max Weber: Essays in Sociology. New York: Oxford University Press.

WEISS, W. (1969) "The effects of the mass media of communication," pp. 77-195 in G. Lindzey and E. Aronson (eds.) Handbook of Social Psychology. Volume 5. Rev. ed. Reading, Mass.: Addison-Wesley.

WHITAKER, I. (1965) "The nature and value of functionalism in the social sciences," pp. 127-143 in Monograph no. 5. Philadelphia: American Academy of Political and Social Science.

WILLIAMS, R. (1961) The Long Revolution. New York: Columbia University Press.

WRIGHT, C. (1960) "Functional analysis and mass communication." Public Opinion Quarterly 24: 605-620.

Chapter 12

USES AND GRATIFICATIONS RESEARCH:
A CRITIQUE AND A SOCIOLOGICAL ALTERNATIVE

Philip Elliott

AS A GENERAL RULE mass communication researchers seem to be dissatisfied with the history of their subject. The literature is full of attempts to repudiate old approaches, to start new ones and to direct attention to aspects of the subject hitherto untouched. This chapter fits into this negative tradition in that it aims to provide a comprehensive critique of the "uses and gratifications" approach to audience research. However, it is not so much the past as the present that is the target for this attack. In recent years there has been a simultaneous revival of interest in the approach in a variety of countries (Lundberg and Hultén, 1968; McQuail, Blumler and Brown, 1972; Rosengren and Windahl, 1972; Katz, Gurevitch, and Haas, 1973). Moreover, its proponents claim that this revival is part of the long march of media research away from simple, direct effect, stimulus-response models of the communication process toward more sophisticated and complex attempts to capture the communicator-audience relationship and to set this within a wider social context (Katz, Blumler, and Gurevitch).[1] So far as the uses and gratifications approach itself is concerned, this claim will be disputed in the following critique.

In general, this version of the subject's history seems to be little more than a slogan used in a restricted debate within mass communication research. There have been few attempts to use media research to address broader issues in

AUTHOR'S NOTE: A previous version of this chapter was given at the 1973 Conference on "The Future of Uses and Gratifications Studies" sponsored by the Audience Research Department of Sveriges Radio in Stockholm. I am indebted to the participants at the conference for helping me to clarify my position, and subsequently to my colleagues at the Centre for Mass Communication Research, in particular Paul Hartmann, Dennis Howitt, Robin McCron, and Graham Murdock, for commenting on an earlier draft.

sociology or to integrate its concerns with other ongoing debates about social structure and process. The mass media generally receive little more than a passing reference in such debates. One reason for this is that mass communication research has been too preoccupied with its own problems and methods, too attached to its empiricist past, to contribute much to a sociological understanding of the part that the mass media play in modern society. The alternative approach outlined in the final section of this chapter is intended not just as a replacement for uses and gratifications within media research but to show how such research could begin to address wider issues within sociology.

There are a number of reasons why the uses and gratifications approach should be currently in vogue. The concept of gratifications seems to add a new dimension to traditional audience research (Emmett, 1968). It suggests that one can measure not just how big the audience is but also what its members are getting out of the communication experience. This distinction between size and satisfaction has dogged broadcast audience research from its infancy. In addition, research using traditional socio-demographic background variables has proved singularly unrevealing when applied to the consumption of the mass media and especially television. Research using such variables as education and social class has established that while people may differ in what they say they do, they differ very little in actual patterns of consumption behavior (Abrams, 1959, 1968; McQuail, 1970; Marplan, 1965; Steiner, 1963; Wilensky, 1964). But the main focus of empirical methods in social research is on explaining differences between groups. This has led to the proposition that there is a set of intervening variables between media output and media consumption that may provide more effective predictors of media behavior differences than crude classifications of output or demographic indicators.

This proposition links the various approaches to be found under the uses and gratifications heading. The proposition is most commonly formulated in psychological terms emphasizing the needs and gratifications experienced by the individual in the mass communication process, but there are also variants that appear to be more sociological and employ the language of functionalism (Rosengren and Windahl, 1972, 1973). There is some uncertainty within the approach about whether these internal states are independent, dependent, or intervening variables. There is also considerable variation in terminology and in whether explicit reference is made to needs as well as gratifications. In general, it seems that whereas the early studies carried out in the United States in the 1940s were content to deal with gratifications, more recent work has made more explicit reference to needs. Even so there are exceptions (Fearing, 1947). The trend, however, seems to be toward identifying general patterns of gratification and need and using these as independent variables to explain media consumption (Katz, Blumler and Gurevitch, 1974).

The functional variant also relies on the concept of need (Rosengren and Windahl, 1972, 1973). Individuals experience basic human needs that may be met through media use or by other patterns of behavior. In this case there is less emphasis on the individual purposively using one channel in place of another to find his satisfaction. Rather the frustration of some "natural" way to satisfy a need will necessarily lead to the substitution of a "functional alternative" —media consumption.

The concept of need is the source of most of the difficulties to be found in uses and gratifications research in general. In the psychological formulation individuals are allowed to identify their own needs or at least the gratifications from which needs may be inferred. The difficulty of providing independent evidence for the existence and importance of the intervening mental states and processes becomes more acute as they proliferate. The more one aspect of the process has to be used as evidence for another the more the argument becomes circular and unnecessarily complex. In both variants—use leads to the gratification of need or need leads to satisfaction through functional behavior—need is the residual factor and yet it is also put forward as an explanation for the process. As explanatory variables, "needs" appear to exist outside time and space. In searching for "basic human needs" the aim is to find needs that are true of human beings qua human beings. The basic concept tends to set the approach off in a direction that is too general, too static, and too asocial for it to be effectively redirected at a later stage by the reintroduction of social or psychological variables. Such variables are unlikely to turn out to be powerful predictors of need distribution and satisfaction if the needs themselves have been selected to represent the general human condition.

Attempts have been made in other fields in social science to use mental constructs or unidentifiable internal states or drives to explain behavior. These have run into difficulties similar to those which are to be found in the uses and gratifications approach. Familiar examples are the problem of the relationship between attitude and behavior and the problem of identifying instincts. Another is to be found in the normative approach to the study of professional education (Merton, Reader and Kendall, 1957).[2]

According to this view, education provides aspiring professionals not only with knowledge and technical skills but also with norms and attitudes which they can use later to guide their conduct in the practice situation. Students and practicing professionals will subscribe to such norms when presented with them as verbal tests. But other evidence from the study of professional education and practice suggests that it would be rash to conclude that such norms actually exist as mental regulators in the way assumed. Firstly, studies attempting to measure the acquisition of norms through the education process have shown little consistent change. Given the premise, the inevitable conclusion seems to be that education has little effect—a conclusion that should be familiar to media researchers in another context. Secondly, within each profession it is possible to point to sets of qualifying and conflicting norms. This suggests that instead of acting as regulators, such norms may simply be available for use as public justifications or excuses. Thirdly, the behavior of practicing professionals varies according to the problems and demands of different practice situations. Such situational explanations are drawn from an alternative approach to the whole field which can be ranged against the normative (Becker, Hughes, Geer and

Strauss, 1961). The contrast between the two is especially relevant when considering alternatives to uses and gratifications in the media field.

The approaches differ in their assumptions, methods, and findings. In place of internal self-regulation, the situational approach sets the individual within specific changing social settings and identifies the goals, pressures, and demands experienced within them. Instead of administering tests and scales, the dominant method in the situational approach is participant observation. A prime focus in the study of professional education has been the student culture, the body of shared understandings on how to order and cope with the problems of the student role. This seems a particularly fruitful concept to take over into the field of media research. There the problem can be seen as one of interaction and interpenetration between two types of culture—that relayed through the media and founded on their structure, organization, personnel, and methods of work and contrasting situationally based cultures founded on the life experiences of different groups in society. I shall return to this in a final section outlining an alternative approach.

First, however, I shall consider the theory and assumptions, the methods and the policy implications of the uses and gratifications approach itself. The discussion above of the concept of need has already hinted at the general strategy to be followed in this critique. The uses and gratifications approach is basically *mentalistic*, relying as it does on intervening mental states and processes. But their introduction only adds to the confusion and circularity of the argument because their existence and importance can only be assessed indirectly. The approach is *individualistic* in the sense that it deals with intra-individual processes. These can then be generalized to aggregates of individuals, but they cannot be converted in any meaningful way into social structure and process. It is *empiricist.* The existence of the intervening states and processes appears to be proved by the methods used, but they may also be an artifact of these methods. Moreover, although there are exceptions in the literature, the methods are usually imposed upon the subjects rather than taken from them. Tests too often contain items that cannot be answered and that no self-respecting researcher would (or should) consider trying to answer himself.[3] As the approach is not informed by any initial social theory, findings have to be explained post hoc. Given an association between variables, the difficulty is to know what they mean.[4]

This lack of social theory contributes to another characteristic of the approach, its *static-abstraction.* The mass communication process is treated in isolation from any other social process. Social variables may be introduced at a late stage in the analysis, but these too are abstracted from the social context, posing once again the problem of meaning. The sampling and analysis techniques used ensure that respondents are wrenched from their social situation, from ongoing social process, from the groups and subcultures that provide a framework of meaning for their activities, especially in a symbolic field like media consumption.

Static-abstraction is largely responsible for another general problem with the approach–its *low explanatory power*. There seems to be an inverse relationship between the level of abstraction and generality of the studies and the interest of the results produced. Although uses and gratifications studies seem to have developed partly because demographic variables proved so ineffective in explaining different patterns of media consumption, uses and gratifications variables themselves have not so far been spectacularly revealing or effective. This may be because they are simply a more cumbersome way of tapping the original demographic variables.

Finally, the approach raises all the problems commonly associated with *functionalism*, and more besides, since it is based on a peculiarly individualistic variant of functionalism. Because of the inferences involved, the argument that use leads to the gratification of needs is at best circular and at worst imprisons research within a stable system of functional interdependencies from which there is no escape. Functionalism at the individual level is matched by a very generalized view of society. No attempt is made to differentiate between media or people on the basis of the interests they represent or the power they possess; no analysis is made in terms of the functions and dysfunctions for different power groups and their ideologies.[5] Dysfunctions, when they appear at all, tend to be negatively labelled phenomena which might prevent society (as a whole) from reaching its ideals, as for example the narcotizing dysfunction identified by Lazarsfeld and Merton (1957).

There is considerable overlap between the criticisms advanced under these different headings. Partly this is because they are all based on an alternative, sociological perspective which will be further elaborated in the final section, and partly because there is inevitably a unity of theory and method to be found in any approach. Given the asocial, individualistic, and mentalistic assumptions of the uses and gratifications approach, and given the desire to generalize about the relationship between the media and mankind, it is no accident that the dominant field method should be broad surveys of the general population and the dominant data-handling method, cluster or factor analysis. This means that to a large extent the various aspects of the approach must stand or fall together. The room for maneuver within it is necessarily limited.

CRITIQUE–THEORY AND ASSUMPTIONS

Underlying the broad characteristics of the approach outlined above, are a number of more specific assumptions about audience behavior and the mass communication process. One of these, the idea of an active audience consciously selecting its media fare in order to maximize its gratifications, brings out the ideological ambiguities involved in this supposedly value-free approach. The idea of an active audience has its attractions when fitted into a broader model of the communication process. Overarching the stimulus-response model was the fear that the new media had put people and society directly at the mercy of those who controlled them. The idea of an active audience is apparently more optimistic. People are credited with more control over their own activities. But if the audience can take care of itself, there is less reason to be concerned about the ownership and control of the media, or with the quality of the output or with any problem of long-term or short-term effect.

Claims to value freedom for the approach also founder on its empirical naiveté. The attempt to find out new facts about the world, uncontaminated by a priori, theoretical assumptions, inevitably means that the findings lack explanatory power and significance. Conclusions about the mass communication process abstracted from culture and social structure ignore all the problems associated with the differential distribution of power and opportunity in society, and in practice this empiricism is founded on functionalism. As we shall see in a later section, the uses and gratifications approach can only support one policy conclusion, the preservation of the status quo.

It may be questioned whether mass communication research has really provided the evidence for an active audience. Stimulus-response models seem to have been neglected more because the assumption they made of an atomized, individual audience was shown to be false, than because evidence accumulated showing the audience was especially active or purposive in its media behavior. Bauer (1964) supports his plea for introducing a transactional model of the communication process in place of the direct influence model with the following arguments: social survey studies have shown no effect, uses and gratifications studies have shown a variety of gratifications, various types of selective perception have been identified, and diffusion studies have shown that specific groups use specific media selectively under various conditions. But only the last can be taken as evidence of conscious, purposeful, selective use by audience members. In that case too the findings apply mainly to minority audiences using specialized media, not to the mass audience and mass media. So far as television is concerned, some evidence will be cited in the next section suggesting an opposite conclusion—that use depends on availability. On the other hand, the uses and gratifications approach, like the stimulus response model, still tends to treat the audience as individuals, abstracted from their social environment.

In itself, "active" is an ambiguous concept. The distinction has often been made between active and passive audience behavior by critics of popular culture. The distinction is largely evaluative, lining up the active consumption of traditional media or pursuits against the passive activities of listening to or viewing broadcast output. Except in so far as it makes a point about the availability of different media, it has no relevance to the idea of activity current in uses and gratifications research.

This idea brings us back to needs. Active in this case means purposive. The activity of media consumption is directed toward the achievement of certain goals—the gratification of certain needs. But, in the immortal phrase of Gilbert Ryle (1949), is there really a "ghost in the machine"? Do people really orient themselves by reference to internal mental states? There is no doubt that the language is available so that behavior and reported gratifications can be converted into needs, just as the language of norms and morals is available to describe professional education. Tests and scales using these ideas may well produce results, but there are a number of reasons for doubting their worth. Intelligent introspection, a method much despised by empiricists, suggests that it is an extremely complex task to explain one's media tastes. If one did, one would be unlikely to refer to needs. Katz et al. (1973) confidently assert that "methodologically the study rests on the assumption that people are aware of their needs and able to identify their sources of satisfaction." In the study, however, respondents were asked how important various feelings, activities, and states of mind were to them. The title of the paper refers to these, perhaps more accurately, as "things." In the paper needs are inferred, clustered, and labelled from these things, but there is no evidence to show that people are "aware of their needs" and the doubt remains whether they would themselves use the concept.

"Needs" are founded on the idea of deficit motivation, but, as Maslow (1964) has pointed out, this is only plausible when applied to basic or deficiency needs, cases where lack of satisfaction produces physiological consequences. Maslow contrasts these needs with the growth needs that motivate healthy people toward "self-actualization (defined as ongoing actualization of potential capacities and talents, as fulfilment of mission . . . as a fuller knowledge of, and acceptance of, the person's own intrinsic nature, as an unceasing trend toward unity . . . within the person)." If we must talk of needs in relation to media consumption, then, it seems clear that they are growth needs, not deficiency needs, that they are learned, not innate, that media consumption is founded on growth rather than deficiency motivation. But learned needs are a product of social experience. In that case media consumption should be explained as part of a positive process of self-development taking place in a series of social situations.

To reject the idea of an active, purposive audience out of hand would be to adopt a completely determinist view. But the problem lies in the equation of goals and needs. To reinstate man as a conscious actor, it is only necessary to suggest that he orients his behavior toward the external world rather than internal mental states. To translate this into a verstehen perspective, the task then becomes one of identifying the social meaning of different media and their outputs for groups differentially located in society. This also sidesteps another difficulty with the goal-needs equation. Need-goals appear to operate outside time and space. On occasion they are used as if they were once for all properties of individuals forming a basis from which the media consumption behavior of groups with different needs can be assessed. At bottom there is something fundamentally illogical in the claim that basic human needs are differentially distributed through society; that this distribution can be explained by reference to social and psychological factors; and that the needs themselves will explain differences in behavior. What is more, there seems every reason to declare the needs redundant and to go back to social and psychological factors as direct explanations of behavior.

A further advantage claimed for the uses and gratifications approach is that it suggests a new way of looking at the producer-audience relationship to give the latter more influence over the former. There seems little evidence to support such a view. If producers know little about the behavior of their audience, there seems every reason to suppose that they know less about its mental state. And yet the suggestion is that audience need-goals play some part in structuring the communicator's situation. As production studies accumulate, so too does the evidence for regarding the two sides of the communication process as largely separate, self-contained systems (Burns, 1969; Elliott, 1972b). But maybe the suggestion is simply that audience need-goals should or would play a part in the communication process if information about them were available to producers. In a later section it will be argued that such information would be no help in policy making unless the aim were simply to justify current practices.

CRITIQUE—METHOD AND FINDINGS

The attention given above to uses and gratifications theory should not obscure the fact that it is basically a very atheoretical approach. On occasion its protagonists are inclined to turn this into a virtue, taking the line that if it can be measured it exists, and if it can be associated it is significant.[6] This line can be taken even further to the claim that if it does not work, it has been measured wrongly, a claim that effectively lets even the most hard-nosed empiricist off the hook (Rosengren and Windahl, 1973). If we continue for the moment to put the argument in slogans, the answer to these claims is that you can measure anything if you ask the right questions, and giving old associations new labels does not advance the cause of knowledge. If it can be shown that the methods of data collection themselves construct reality, and that the new processes identified coincide with and obscure ones that were already known, then the foundations are cut away from the impressive edifices of statistical analysis that are the tour de force of contemporary uses and gratifications researchers.

This critique is directed specifically at this newer type of uses and gratifications research. The older studies carried out in the United States in the 1940s were methodologically less sophisticated but in many ways sociologically more significant. Researchers were content to enumerate the various functions that media output served directly for their audience without looking for underlying structures of need and gratification. Moreover, they mostly dealt with specific types of content and relatively specific audiences. They were sufficiently focused to throw up new information about media use and attitudes toward it among specific groups in the population, information which, in the case of Herzog's (1941) housewives, for example, could be used to say something about the way they were integrated into the social structure and the way in which power and authority were legitimated to them. By contrast the modern approach has been to search for wider and more general categories of need and gratification from the general population (Blumler et al., 1970; Katz et al., 1974).

The argument that the methods used themselves construct reality rests on the type of questions commonly asked. The aim is to assess the importance of various need-goals to the respondent and the importance he attaches to different media and other types of behavior as means of achieving them. Both the need-goals and the media are selected on the assumption that they are important (Lundberg and Hultén, 1968; Kjellmor, 1973; Katz et al., 1973). In most cases respondents can only be differentiated according to the degree of importance they attach to goals and means.

Given the level of generality at which the questions are aimed, it is not surprising to find that people will subscribe to them. One can hardly reject truisms out of hand. The difficulty is whether they are truisms about the people—whether, for example, some people really have a greater need than others to avoid boredom—or whether they are truisms about the situations in which people find themselves—boredom varies according to situation and also according to the social meaning of the concept. But as soon as this possibility is introduced, it becomes clear that measuring boredom avoidance or indeed any other need-goal is liable to be a way of measuring variance in the social situation, or available social meanings, variance that could be more directly expressed in terms of familiar demographic variables.

For all their methodological ingenuity Rosengren and Windahl (1972, 1973) seem to have run into the same difficulty in their studies of mass media consumption as a functional alternative to actual interaction. Their claim that people less involved in actual interaction will become more involved in media consumption is backed up by data collected around four indices: degree of involvement in mass media output, interaction potential, actual interaction, and amount of mass media consumption. The names given to these indices make the argument sound plausible, but it must be questioned whether the first three indices are such discrete measures of newly identified phenomena as is suggested.

Degree of involvement, for example, is based on whether respondents answer in personal terms when asked what type of media output they like. The authors themselves recognize that the tendency to think in personal terms may be a class phenomenon. More than that, however, when dealing with television output, there is more scope for giving a personal answer about entertainment programs, which commonly include well-known stars, than about news or information programs. The whole notion of personal involvement has some problems when applied to newspapers, but answers in terms of local people seem much more likely to come from geographically stable, lower-class people with a local orientation to their community.

The construction of the next two indices, interaction potential and actual interaction, seems to confirm these suspicions that what we are really dealing with is a class phenomenon. Among the six indicators of interaction potential are education, car ownership, and leisure time. Actual interaction is based on the number of contacts at work and with friends outside. It seems, therefore, that the association between lack of interaction and degree of involvement can be translated into the more familiar terms that lower-class people tend to say they like entertainment programs (and tend to be locally oriented) more than middle-class.

Such a conclusion is the stock in trade of many uses and gratifications studies (Weiss, 1971).[7] It is also a reason why such research invites the accusation that it lacks explanatory power. The contrast between information and entertainment usually turns up in some guise as a classification both of media output and of audience need-goals. It is then not surprising to find that these differences in tastes, reported consumption behavior, or need-goals can in turn be related to social class and similar variables. It may be questioned, however, whether this is a step forward, since it is already known that, at least so far as television is concerned, it is reported behavior, not actual behavior, which differs along this dimension (Steiner, 1963; Marplan, 1965; Wilensky, 1964). Uses and gratifications researchers often make a virtue out of the fact that they have to rely on their respondents' ability to recognize and verbalize their needs and gratifications. It may be a good thing to trust people, but it is naive to suppose that people can give answers as if they were in a social vacuum. The various media and the consumption behaviors associated with them are already socially stratified (Murdock and McCron, 1973). Their social meaning will be clear to people and so too will the social meaning of the associated need-goals.

This underlines another flaw in the empiricist approach. People are not simply objects available for study. They are located in the social structure. In giving answers to social researchers they will draw on the different systems of meaning available to them, according to their position in the social structure (Blumer, 1956). Frank Parkin (1972) has distinguished three broad meaning systems currently available in Western societies: the dominant, the subordinate, and the radical. He uses this distinction to point out another weakness of survey methods compared to situated, observational studies.

> Studies of working class attitudes which rely on questions posed in general and non-situational terms are likely to produce findings which emphasise class consensus on values; this is because the dominant value system will tend to provide the moral frame of reference. Conversely studies which specify particular social contexts of belief and action, or which rely on actual behavioural indices are likely to find more evidence for a class differentiated value system; this is because in situational contexts of choice and action the subordinate value system will tend to provide the moral frame of reference.

The evidence that there is more difference between reported and actual media consumption behavior and that television consumption is more a matter of availability than selection undercuts the idea of an active, purposive audience and the claim that needs and gratifications can be used effectively to explain differences in media consumption. Ever since *Steptoe and Son* revived a flagging *Panorama* program, planners have tried to use the phenomenon of the inherited audience to their advantage. Ehrenberg and Goodhart (1969) have suggested, however, that in a multichannel situation there is only a marked inheritance effect between programs that are directly adjacent. Overlap between the audiences for pairs of programs separated by more than one other program was no higher than that predicted by their general "duplication of viewing law."

This law states that "the percentage of the audience of a TV programme who watch another programme on another day of the same week is approximately equal to the rating of the latter programme times a constant." Stated in abstract form, the implications of this law are difficult to grasp, but Ehrenberg and Goodhart have applied it to viewing patterns for standard program categories to show that there is very little tendency for people watching one program in a category to watch more programs of the same type, beyond the level predicted by the law. In other words, there is no evidence to suggest that viewing behavior can be explained by a preference for program types. One of their conclusions is that "there is . . . no evidence of any 'informed elite' who watch a lot of news features." This ties in with other findings that low viewers do not constitute a specially selective audience for minority programs but simply join the majority audience in watching popular programs (Höijer and Berg, 1972).

Availability is not just a matter of what is provided through each medium but also a matter of access to the media depending mainly on individuals' personal and family circumstances. In a sense availability also depends on familiarity (Chaney, 1972). The audience has easier access to familiar genre partly because they understand the language and conventions and also because they already know the social meaning of this type of output with some certainty. Their self-concept will already include the idea that they are consumers of westerns, romances, avant-garde comedy, or whatever. This type of explanation can become particularly complex and effective when one moves away from such general mass media as television toward more specific media and audiences such as the adolescent audience for pop music (Murdock and Phelps, 1973; Murdock and McCron, 1973). But availability in any sense rarely finds a place in uses and gratifications research.

CRITIQUE—POLICY IMPLICATIONS

The uses and gratifications approach is commonly put forward as an advance on traditional "head-counting" techniques of broadcast audience research (Emmett, 1968). The substance of this claim was questioned in the previous section. But the claim also includes the idea that measuring audience gratifications and needs would provide more useful data to guide broadcasting policy. Audience figures have an accepted place in program planning. We may all agree that broadcasters should know more about their audience, but it seems unlikely that they will learn much from uses and gratifications data. The approach is effectively neutered by its assumptions.

The difficulty stems from the basic tautology that use leads to gratification. Different gratifications may be identified independently of use, but there is no way of distinguishing between them according to the level of satisfaction they supply. The difficulty is well illustrated by the few references to dysfunctions that are to be found in the uses and gratifications literature. In most cases dysfunctions are types of gratifications that the researchers suppose will have harmful consequences for society. At the individual level, to label some gratifications functional, others dysfunctional, would clearly be to reintroduce the critical judgments of popular culture theorists by the back door. But the social dysfunctions identified have no firmer basis, especially so long as they are applied to society as a whole or to the general quality of life within it. Thus the only basis for policy is to decide normatively which gratifications should be encouraged, which suppressed.[8]

This problem also underlies Brian Emmett's scheme to replace the maximization of audience size with the maximization of audience satisfaction. If audience satisfaction can be concluded from use, it is just as effective to count heads. If not, then some place will have to be found in the uses and gratifications approach for dissatisfaction. But even if it were, the fundamental difficulty would remain. Different types of gratification are not additive. It may also be questioned how far they are stable entities dependent directly on media content, as Emmett's model would suppose. Taking the view that media consumption is a specifically situated, social process, on the other hand, would suggest that gratification depends on a dynamic relationship between the individual and his whole social environment. Of course the problem could always be sidestepped by throwing the onus on the long-suffering respondents and asking them to provide a general satisfaction score. While the respondent tries to work out what he is being asked, the researcher will have time to pause and wonder what the answer will be worth when he gets it. Uses and gratifications research is effectively hoist with its own petard. Research has led to "a growing consensus that almost any type of content may serve practically any type of function" (Rosengren and Windahl, 1972), but research cannot produce any criteria for differentiating between them.

Having argued that the approach provides no basis for policy making, it may seem perverse, if not illogical, to go on to argue that if it were used, its effect would be positively harmful. But this follows given the tautological and functional assumptions behind the approach. In themselves, uses and gratifications data can only point in one direction, toward a justification of the present situation. One example is the finding cited above that any content may serve any function (yield a variety of gratifications). In other words, the audience may not be getting what was intended from media output, but at least they are getting something.

Another example may be taken from Katz, Blumler and Gurevitch's (1974) attempt to defuse the radical critique of mass communications as a dysfunctional "latter-day opiate of the masses" by suggesting that uses and gratifications research would be peculiarly suited to exploring the supposed "media-output audience-satisfaction nexus." The implication is that "dysfunction" as used here is simply a negative evaluation, as it would be in the uses and gratifications approach itself. It rests, however, on a social analysis in which it is seen to be in the interests of those controlling the media to distract others in society from a true recognition of their own interests. If the media-output audience-satisfaction nexus were explored in uses and gratifications terms, the only possible conclusion would be that the audience was getting something out of it. But that is not in dispute. The issue in dispute is whose interests are being served in the process, and that is an issue which the approach itself is powerless to elucidate.

Nordenstreng (1970) raised the same issue when he pointed out that needs develop within the existing social structure and so that any approach based on identifying such needs would inevitably provide support for the status quo. The conclusion to be drawn from this critique is not that individual opinions do not matter, as Katz, Blumler and Gurevitch interpret it, but that some prior analysis of social structure is necessary to know what such opinions are worth. The quest to identify functions for "society as a whole" or basic underlying human needs must inevitably rule out any consideration of the differential distribution of power and opportunity in society, of the conflict of interests between different groups, and of the development and use of different ideologies to protect them. If the media are in business to maintain false consciousness throughout society, then asking people about their satisfactions and dissatisfactions will simply record their experience of the present system and their acceptance of the consciousness it provides. To find out whether or not it is *false* consciousness requires an entirely different approach. Just to assume that it is not false, to talk in terms of the interests of society as a whole, is to assume that all men are equal and to ignore social structure. "Society as a whole" or "basic human needs" are devices for obscuring or ignoring the issue of who controls society and who defines the ways in which such needs are experienced and learned. The problem can even be formulated within the language of functionalism if we ask, functional or dysfunctional for whom?

CONCLUSION

This critique has been informed by a very different sociological perspective from that which underlies the uses and gratifications approach. There has been a long debate in sociology about the relative merits of the functional and conflict perspectives (Cohen, 1968). Fundamentally, it is these two that are at issue here. Even on its own terms uses and gratifications research has not been particularly revealing or effective, but there is no reason to take it on its own terms. The underlying theoretical assumptions create most of the difficulties to be seen in the research whether they revolve around the psychological concept of need or a variant of functionalism. This is at once individualistic and over-generalized, so that it is especially vulnerable to traditional critiques of functionalism. Rather than go over the general debate between the two perspectives once again or summarize the specific critique set out above, it is perhaps more useful to consider what an alternative approach to audience research based on the conflict perspective might look like.[9]

Such an approach would start by placing the different media and their audiences in the social structure. In the case of the media it is necessary to analyze ownership, control, and production processes to see which groups and interests are directly represented and which are used as a source in the production of the output (Halloran, Elliott and Murdock, 1970; Elliott, 1972b; Elliott and Golding, 1974; Murdock and Golding, 1973). Different media vary in prestige and in the social valuation placed on their output and consumption. Analytically it is possible to distinguish between their subjective and objective location in the social structure though usually the two overlap. There have been cases, however, particularly with the development of a new medium, when practitioners have found it hard to win the social evaluation to which they felt entitled. British television, for example, was long despised by sections of the educated middle class, even though the BBC itself had every claim to being an established institution.

On the other side different audience groups face different social situations posing various problems and defining different interests that are met by common solutions and understandings about the means to be used. Evidence from both sides of the communication process, showing how media production tends to take place within bounded organizational systems and how audience members are integrated into society through such mechanisms as roles and group membership, supports an initial focus on the way the two sides are separately involved in the social structure. This is an alternative to the view that explanations of media output or audience behavior are to be found in the direct links of the communication process itself.

Nonetheless, media-based and situationally based cultures meet, intermingle, and interact. In a broad sense the media provide an ideology for the groups they represent, legitimating their activities and interests. But this does not mean that they constitute a monolithic ideological system controlling the development of thought and behavior in society. Internal differences are to be found within any loosely defined ruling class, differences that are also likely to find their way into media output. More important, the ideology purveyed by the media does not directly determine audience response. It is only one factor contributing to it. The most powerful way in which this factor operates would seem to be in providing a general view of society, a mapping of social roles and activities, and a rhetoric through which these are labelled, evaluated, and explained. Oppositional systems may be found with more or less thoroughly worked out alternative views, but even so, given the ubiquity of modern mass media, it is difficult for such alternative views to avoid using the same labels or to ignore completely the terms of the debate as defined by the established media.

An example of this process can be taken from Frank Parkin's (1972) analysis of change in the radical value system available in Western societies. These systems, which provided the basis for a specifically class consciousness, were associated with the mass, left-wing parties that developed to represent the interests of the working class. In all societies there has been a long-term trend toward the de-radicalization of such parties and their associated value systems. Parkin rejects the view that this is due to a change in the views and interests of their supporters. Instead he points to changes in the organization, recruitment, and roles of the parties themselves.

It is no accident, however, that the first view has been widely used in the British mass media to support the argument that the electorate will not stand for left-wing policies. The thesis of embourgeoisement has held a continuing fascination for the mass media, first as an argument why the Labour Party should move right following its defeat in 1959, and more recently as an argument for a new party in the center, given that the Labour Party appeared to be moving left. In Europe generally this de-radicalization has coincided with a period in which the party press and other direct channels of communication between political parties and the public have disappeared. In their place mass media have developed, more closely integrated into the corporate economic structure of society, and standing between the mass audience and political activities and other sources of radical or class ideologies. In this intermediary position they have been able to comment on and interpret political developments and so to contribute to the process of de-radicalization. Thus, for example, there has been considerable support for what Parkin has called meritocratic socialism, on the grounds of both fairness and efficiency.[10] By contrast egalitarian socialism, looking forward to radical changes in the distribution of rewards and the structure of ownership and authority, has been ridiculed as impractical and dangerous.

Such a climate of opinion is not just created through the editorial columns but more generally through the way news events are selected and angled (Halloran et al., 1970; Elliott and Golding, 1973, 1974). Labour Party policy debates, for example, are commonly treated as divisive battles between a militant left-wing minority and a moderate majority. By translating events into a leadership battle or a personality conflict, the policy issues themselves can be left out. The study of the news coverage of the Anti-Vietnam War Demonstration of October 27, 1968, showed the same process at work. The image of a violent confrontation was built up in the press and used by both press and television to present and interpret the events of the day. Demonstrators appeared not as political activists but as violent subversives or as unwitting fellow travelers in violence planned by foreign agitators. This study also provided some clear examples of the way in which this image came to define reality. Both the demonstrators and various representatives of the authorities began to act within it, so providing further evidence for it in a self-fulfilling cycle. This image was not a result of deliberate bias on the part of the journalists but followed simply from the use of accepted professional assumptions, practices, and routines (see also Hartmann and Husband, 1972, 1974).

Another way in which media and audience interact is through the social meaning given to the consumption of different types of media output. The problem is to discover the discriminations that different audience groups make between different types of output. Such discriminations appear to be much more subtle than those commonly made by researchers between information and entertainment or between standard content types. They come to mark the boundaries between different social groups, so that involvement in a particular type of media output becomes an important part of an individual's self-concept, symbolizing his membership or aspiration to membership in particular groups. The study of different types of media output as symbols defining social boundaries, reflecting conflicts and contradictions at a variety of levels, seems likely to lead further into the social structure than the standard analysis with straightforward demographic variables (Murdock and Phelps, 1973; Murdock and McCron, 1973).

Phil Cohen (1972), for example, has provided an intricate analysis of social change in East London showing how structural changes in housing, employment, and population composition led to internal conflicts within the traditional culture of the respectable working class. These were played out in generational conflict as a series of youth groups appropriated a variety of symbols from the media and other leisure and fashion industries to form their own subcultures:

> The succession of subcultures . . . can . . . all be considered as so many variations on a central theme—the contradiction at an ideological level, between traditional working class puritanism and the new hedonism of consumption; at an economic level between a future as part of the socially mobile elite, or as part of the new lumpen. Mods, Parkers, skinheads, crombies, all represent, in their different ways, an attempt to retrieve some of the socially cohesive elements destroyed in their parent culture, and to combine these with elements selected from other class fractions, symbolising one or other of the options confronting it.

Those responsible for media output commonly emphasize the unpredictable nature of audience response. It is rarely possible to predict what will be taken up by the general audience or by particular groups within it. Again this is a reason for treating the two sides of the communication process as largely separate but interacting systems. Apart from using their intuition, producers have little access to the information about social process which might cue them in to what would be particularly useful or relevant symbols given current trends in social conflict and change. Most of the information they have comes through the media system itself, so that it has already been selected and processed through the same production system. One technique, however, is to incorporate into the mass media and mass culture performers and performances that have already achieved some success or prominence at a more local level.

Nevertheless, there are some striking examples to be found of particular types of media output that have set off wholly unexpected responses and become the focus and symbol for a loosely defined social position, marking out social boundaries and the lines of potential social conflict. This has even occurred through television, the most mass of the media in the sense that it seems to have the most generalized and undifferentiated appeal. Take, for example, the discovery of satire on BBC TV in the early 1960s. Given the subsequent careers of those involved, it seems unlikely that they saw themselves as providing the focus for a radical critique of the established social and political order. But this is what the programs came to symbolize, and they did so for a much larger audience than had initially been expected. For Sir Hugh Greene (1969), the Director-General of the BBC at the time, *That Was the Week That Was* was one example of the flowering of creative talent allowed by the introduction of new men and new methods inside the organization. He has ridiculed more purposive interpretations of the part he played in the development:

> It was in my capacity as a subversive anarchist that I yielded to enormous pressure from my fellow subversives and put "TW3" on the air; and it was as a pillar of the Establishment that I yielded to the fascist hyena-like howls to take it off again.

But the social meaning that the program acquired gave some validity to both these interpretations.

A final problem with the uses and gratifications approach is that it would deny the media this creative role in contributing to social change. The problem of long-term effect is one of the most difficult and challenging in media research, especially because, as Hartmann and Husband (1972) have pointed out, "if the media do influence events they seldom do so directly, but through the way people think." The aim, therefore, should be to study the media as one of the most important sources and channels for the different meaning systems available in contemporary society. To link media output to stable gratifications based on generalized needs, as in the uses and gratifications approach, is to lock media and audience into a stable equilibrium. As a description of social reality it seems inaccurate; as a normative prescription, undesirable and unexciting.

NOTES

1. The Katz, Blumler and Gurevitch paper on "Utilization of Mass Communication by the Individual," which appears elsewhere in this volume, was also presented at the Stockholm Conference (see Author's Note) and provided the initial focus for this critique. Unless otherwise stated, this paper is the source for claims made on behalf of the approach.

2. The argument in the next two paragraphs is condensed from Elliott (1972a, especially Chapter 3). Further references are cited there.

3. For example, "How important is it for you to understand the true quality of our leaders?" or "How important is it for you to feel satisfied with the way of life in Israel as compared with other countries?" (Katz et al., 1973).

4. For example, in describing the correlates of a tendency to seek "excitement" from quiz program viewing, McQuail et al. (1972) state that "The highest scoring group consisted of working-class viewers who were late-born children of large families. While the significance of the role of family background here is not clear. . . ." And, in presenting data from a functional study of children's media uses, Brown et al. (1973) write: "As with the earlier table we cannot attempt to explain many of the findings. Instead we will conclude by offering a few conjectures which might help to integrate and explain the somewhat disjointed data presented."

5. Thus "not all effects of mass communication are germane to functional analysis, only those which are relevant and important if the system under analysis is to continue to function normally" (Wright, 1960).

6. "Estimating the social grade of a child is fraught with difficulty. We based our classification on school and/or the child's home address. Perhaps the best justification for that technique is that it produced significant results, as can be seen in Table I" (Brown et al., 1973).

7. The same argument, that uses and gratifications concepts only work because class

relationships are already built into them, applies especially to Schramm, Lyle and Parker (1961).

8. Emmett (1968) recognizes this: ". . . one other matter has to be considered. That is the relative importance, or weight, to be given to the gratification of various needs. The decision about these weights is crucial, since they ultimately determine the solution. It is not too extreme to say that they must encapsulate the philosophy or value system of the organisation. . . ."

9. The following sketch draws on the approach set out by Chaney (1972).

10. The period before the General Election of 1964 provides some support for these speculations. The "conservative" press turned against the Conservative government for a variety of reasons, but among these was the feeling that it was out-dated in style and inefficient in practice. By contrast, claims to meritocratic efficiency played a large part in the Labour Party's election campaign. The changed climate of opinion in the media does seem to have had a direct effect on public opinion (Butler and Stokes, 1970).

REFERENCES

ABRAMS, M. (1968) Education, Social Class and Readership of Newspapers and Magazines. London: JICNARS.

——— (1959) "The mass media and social class in Great Britain." Paper presented at the Fourth World Congress of Sociology, Stresa, Italy.

BAUER, R. A. (1964) "The obstinate audience." American Psychologist 19: 319-328.

BECKER, H. S., E. C. HUGHES, B. GEER, and A. L. STRAUSS (1961) Boys in White. London: University of Chicago Press.

BLUMER, H. (1956) "Sociological analysis and the 'variable'." American Sociological Review 21: 683-690.

BLUMLER, J. G., J. R. BROWN, and D. McQUAIL (1970) "The social origins of the gratifications associated with television viewing." Leeds: University of Leeds. (mimeo)

BROWN, J. R., J. K. CRAMOND, and R. J. WILDE (1973) "Children's use of the mass media: a functional approach." Paper presented at the Annual Conference of the Social Psychology Section of the British Psychological Society, Bristol.

BURNS, T. (1969) "The public service and private world." The Sociological Review Monograph 13.

BUTLER, D. and D. STOKES (1970) "The national press and partisan change," in J. Tunstall (ed.) Media Sociology. London: Constable.

CHANEY, D. (1972) Processes of Mass Communication. London: Macmillan.

COHEN, P. S. (1968) Modern Social Theory. London: Heinemann.

COHEN, P. (1972) "Sub-cultural conflict and working class community." Cultural Studies 2.

EHRENBERG, A.S.C. and G. J. GOODHART (1969) "Practical application of the duplication of viewing law." Journal of the Market Research Society 11: 6-24.

ELLIOTT, P. (1972a) The Sociology of the Professions. London: Macmillan.

——— (1972b) The Making of a Television Series: A Case Study in the Sociology of Culture. London: Constable.

——— and P. GOLDING (1974) "The image of development and the development of images," in E. De Kadt and G. Williams (eds.) Sociology and Development. London: Tavistock.

——— (1973) "The news media and foreign affairs," in R. Boardman and A.J.R. Groom (eds.) The Management of Britain's External Relations. London: Macmillan.

EMMETT, B. P. (1968) "A new role for research in broadcasting." Public Opinion Quarterly 32: 654-665.

FEARING, F. (1947) "Influence of the movies on attitudes and behaviour." Annals 254: 70-80.

GREENE, H. (1969) The Third Floor Front. London: Bodley Head.

HALLORAN, J. D., P. ELLIOTT, and G. MURDOCK (1970) Demonstrations and Communication: A Case Study. Harmondsworth: Penguin.

HARTMANN, P. and C. HUSBAND (1974) Racism and the Mass Media. London: Davis Poynter.

——— (1972) "The mass media and racial conflict," in D. McQuail (ed.) Sociology of Mass Communications. Harmondsworth: Penguin.

HERZOG, H. (1941) "On borrowed experience." Studies in Philosophy and Social Science 9: 65-95.

HOIJER, B. and U. BERG (1972) Audience Mechanisms and Programme Selection. Stockholm: SR/PUB.

KATZ, E., J. G. BLUMLER, and M. GUREVITCH (1974) "Utilization of mass communication by the individual: an overview," in J. G. Blumler and E. Katz (eds.) The Uses of Mass Communications: Current Perspectives on Gratifications Research. Beverly Hills: Sage.

KATZ, E., M. GUREVITCH, and H. HAAS (1973) "On the use of the mass media for important things." American Sociological Review 38 (April): 164-181.

KJELLMOR, S. (1973) "Basic subjective broadcasting media functions." Paper presented to the Stockholm Conference on Uses and Gratifications Studies.

LAZARSFELD, P. F. and R. K. MERTON (1957) "Mass communication, popular taste and organized social action," in B. Rosenberg and D. M. White (eds.) Mass Culture—The Popular Arts in America. New York: Free Press.

LUNDBERG, D. and O. HULTEN (1968) Individen och Mass Media. Stockholm: Norstedts.

McQUAIL, D. (1970) "The audience for television plays," in J. Tunstall (ed.) Media Sociology. London: Constable.

——— (1969) Towards A Sociology of Mass Communications. London: Collier-Macmillan.

——— J. G. BLUMLER, and J. R. BROWN (1972) "The television audience: a revised perspective," in D. McQuail (ed.) Sociology of Mass Communications. Harmondsworth: Penguin.

Marplan Ltd. (1965) Report on a Study of Television and the Managerial and Professional Classes. London: ITA.

MASLOW, A. B. (1964) "Deficiency motivation and growth motivation," in R. C. Teevan and R. C. Birney (eds.) Theories of Motivation in Personality and Social Psychology. London: Van Norstrand.

MERTON, R. K., G. G. READER, and P. L. KENDALL [eds.] (1957) The Student Physician. Cambridge, Mass.: Harvard University Press.

MURDOCK, G. and P. GOLDING (1973) "For a political economy of mass communications," in R. Miliband and J. Saville (eds.) The Socialist Register. New York: Humanities Press. (Also published by London: Merlin, 1974.)

MURDOCK, G. and R. McCRON (1973) "Scoobies, skins and contemporary pop." New Society (March 29).

MURDOCK, G. and G. PHELPS (1973) The Mass Media and the Secondary School. London: Macmillan.

NORDENSTRENG, K. (1970) "Comments on 'gratifications research' in broadcasting." Public Opinion Quarterly 34: 130-132.

PARKIN, F. (1972) Class Inequality and Political Order. London: Paladin.

ROSENGREN, K. E. and S. WINDAHL (1973) "Mass media use: causes and effects." Lund. (mimeo)

——— (1972) "Mass media consumption as a functional alternative," in D. McQuail (ed.) Sociology of Mass Communications. Harmondsworth: Penguin.

RYLE, G. (1949) The Concept of Mind. London: Hutchinson.

SCHRAMM, W., J. LYLE, and E. B. PARKER (1961) Television in the Lives of Our Children. Stanford: Stanford University Press.

STEINER, G. A. (1963) The People Look at Television. New York: Knopf.

WEISS, W. (1971) "Mass communication." Annual Review of Psychology 22.

WILENSKY, H. (1964) "Mass society and mass culture: interdependence or independence." American Sociological Review 29, 2: 173-197.

WRIGHT, C. R. (1960) "Functional analysis and mass communication." Public Opinion Quarterly 24: 605-620.

Chapter 13

USES AND GRATIFICATIONS:
A PARADIGM OUTLINED

Karl Erik Rosengren

WHEN THE HISTORY OF MASS COMMUNICATION RESEARCH is written, the early 1970s are likely to be treated as a time when the tradition of uses and gratifications studies was revived and a number of attempts were made to realize its early promise. Questions first raised in classic papers dating from the heroic days of communication research in the late 1940s were asked again, reformulated, and pursued with sometimes sophisticated attempts at quantification. By piecing together some of the questions asked and answers given by participants in this new wave of study, it should now be possible to outline a paradigm for uses and gratifications research. It would seem to be a timely enterprise to aim in this way to distill the essential elements of the several independent efforts to re-establish an important tradition in the mass communication field.

A simple paraphrase of something like the famous Lasswellian formula, however, will not suffice: "Who uses which media, under what circumstances, for what reasons and with what effects?" What is needed instead is a somewhat more elaborate paradigm, with brief comments on each of its several components, providing examples of research relevant to them, criticisms of such research, and also, perhaps—where the paradigm directs our attention to lacunae within the work carried out to date—suggestions for new research.

A first outline of such a paradigm is presented in Figure 1. In Figure 2 the paradigm is graphically visualized. (For a similar graphic model, cf. von Feilitzen and Linne, 1972.) Each item in the paradigm will now be discussed, using, as points of reference, material from a number of recent papers in the uses and gratifications tradition. The construction of any paradigm of course entails simplifications. Some of these will be touched upon and, hopefully, clarified in the following pages. The elucidation of others must await further research and critical discussion.

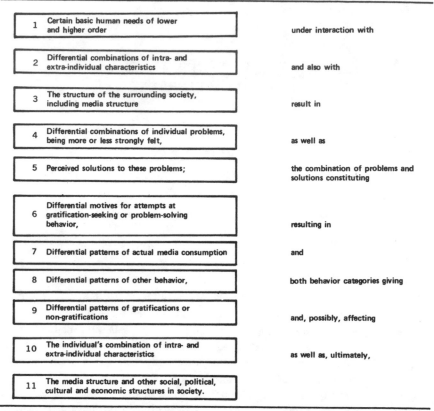

1	Certain basic human needs of lower and higher order	under interaction with
2	Differential combinations of intra- and extra-individual characteristics	and also with
3	The structure of the surrounding society, including media structure	result in
4	Differential combinations of individual problems, being more or less strongly felt,	as well as
5	Perceived solutions to these problems;	the combination of problems and solutions constituting
6	Differential motives for attempts at gratification-seeking or problem-solving behavior,	resulting in
7	Differential patterns of actual media consumption	and
8	Differential patterns of other behavior,	both behavior categories giving
9	Differential patterns of gratifications or non-gratifications	and, possibly, affecting
10	The individual's combination of intra- and extra-individual characteristics	as well as, ultimately,
11	The media structure and other social, political, cultural and economic structures in society.	

Figure 1: OUTLINE FOR A PARADIGM OF USES AND GRATIFICATIONS RESEARCH

The first item of the paradigm epitomizes the biological and psychological infra-structure that forms the basis of all human social behavior. We all carry with us a bundle of biological and psychological needs that make us act and react. It can hardly be the task of uses and gratifications research to clarify the human need structure at this underlying level. But neither should relevant findings of biology, psychology, and social psychology in this respect be neglected. Rather, they should be incorporated into the theoretical argument and related to variables of a more social character.

Maslow (1954) has outlined a need hierarchy which may be drawn upon to give some structure to the argument. He distinguishes five sets of basic needs: (1) physiological needs; (2) safety needs; (3) belongingness and love needs; (4) esteem needs; and (5) a need for self-actualization (cf. also Huizinga, 1970; Erickson, 1973; as well as Etzioni, 1968, and Alderfer, 1969). In terms of this hierarchy, the needs that deserve the attention of the uses and gratifications researcher are especially sets (3), (4), and (5), the last sometimes being characterized as growth needs (as contrasted with physiological or deficiency needs).

The point to be made is that these needs do not develop in a vacuum but in

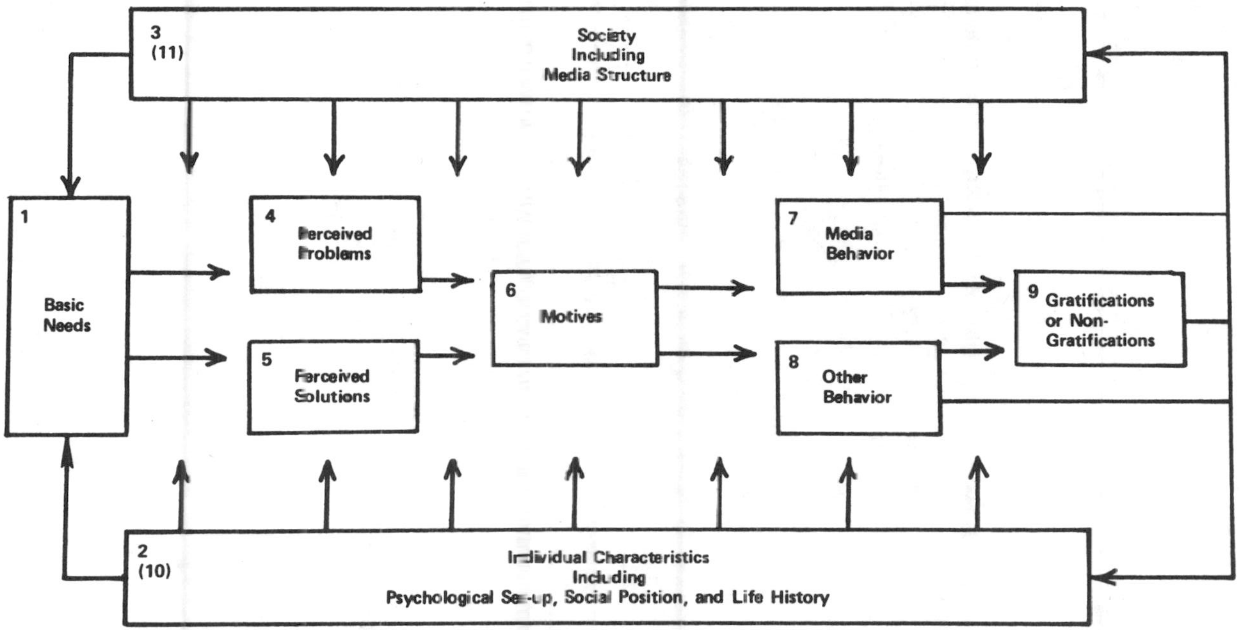
3
(11)
Society
Including
Media Structure
1
Basic
Needs
4
Perceived
Problems
5
Perceived
Solutions
6
Motives
7
Media
Behavior
8
Other
Behavior
9
Gratifications
or Non-
Gratifications
2
(10)
Individual Characteristics
Including
Psychological Set-up, Social Position, and Life History

Figure 2: VISUALIZED PARADIGM FOR USES AND GRATIFICATIONS RESEARCH

interaction with a host of other variables, subsumed under items 2 and 3 of the paradigm: characteristics of the individual *and* his society. Students of audience gratifications never perceived man as oriented only toward his inner world or even as more inward looking than outward regarding. But they did object to attempts to treat him as if determined by outside forces only.

The fact, then, that basic needs are incorporated into the theoretical structure should not be construed to mean that these needs are regarded as the sole and only determinants of behavior, that they are necessarily innate deficiency needs, or that they are considered to be immune from any societal influence. They are innate and yet affected by society. Thus there is nothing at all "fundamentally illogical in the claim that basic human needs are differentially distributed" in and between societies as Elliott maintains in a brilliantly biased paper elsewhere in this volume. There is a society characterized by a unique combination of structures and institutions, and within this society individuals behave, react, act, and interact, subject to the potentialities and restrictions presented to them by interacting bundles of biological, psychological, and social variables. This complicated pattern of interaction is symbolized in the paradigm by items 1, 2, and 3.

Although the term "need" is often encountered in writings about uses and gratifications, item 1 has not been subject to direct investigation within this tradition—and for a very good reason. This must be the task of biologists and psychologists. When the term "need" is introduced, then, what is typically meant is what has here been called problems or even motives (items 4 and 6 of the paradigm). On those occasions when the concept has been used to represent item 1 in the paradigm, the need has often been taken for granted and regarded as more or less constant. Rosengren and Windahl (1972, 1973) offer examples of this, basing their theoretical argument on the individual's need for interaction with others. If, in doing so, they reify aspects of human nature—as the Marxist criticism would and does run—at least they are not the only sinners against nature. "There is good reason to consider this *basic drive for contact* the most important factor in keeping all communication in operation" (Nordenstreng, 1969; cf. also Nordenstreng, 1970, italics added).

Leaving basic needs for a moment, let us turn to items 2 and 3, individual and societal characteristics. The interest of researchers has been heavily concentrated on item 2, individual characteristics, and within this, it has been equally heavily concentrated on extra-individual characteristics (social position, etc.), while intra-individual characteristics (personality variables, etc.) have been all but neglected. (On the other hand, the whole tradition, of course, is very much concerned with intra-individual processes; witness items 1, 4, 5, 6, and 9 of the paradigm.) Naturally, the border line between intra- and extra-individual variables is rather diffuse. Moreover, this distinction must not be confused with the difference between individual and societal characteristics.

Within a given society, different individuals may occupy different positions and enact different roles, each being ascribed, and achieving, a special combination of values on a number of extra-individual variables. In another society, of a different structure, the same individuals would have been assigned, perhaps, not only different values but also values on different variables. This is the essential difference between items 2 and 3, between individual and societal characteristics.

Since in connection with items 2 and 3 the interest of researchers has been focused more often on extra-individual characteristics than on intra-individual or societal ones, let us consider some illustrations of the neglected factors, starting with the intra-individual variables of item 2.

The point of departure of Rosengren and Windahl (1972, 1973) is a cross-tabulation of intra- and extra-individual possibilities to satisfy a given need in a given way. To them, extra-individual characteristics encompass such variables as status, partner availability, and leisure time, combined into an index of interaction potential. To represent intra-individual characteristics, they adopted Eysenck's well-known introversion/extraversion and neuroticism scales (Eysenck and Eysenck, 1969), and in four different surveys they have examined the relationships between these intra- and extra-individual characteristics, regarded as some of the many factors affecting media use and media gratifications. Since the samples are small and some of the indicators imperfect, the details of their results must in some respects be regarded as suggestive only. Further research may be able to establish what is tenable and what is not in this particular approach. And developments within psychology and social psychology may ultimately provide us with personality variables, and corresponding scales, tapping more dynamic and creative aspects of personality than introversion/ extraversion. That personality variables of some kind must be incorporated into such research seems almost self-evident. Only thus could we hope to understand the dynamic relationship between the individual and his social environment.

If intra-individual variables—regarded as moderator variables in the uses and gratifications process—are somewhat neglected in this research tradition, so too are societal variables in the proper sense of the word. It is true that several papers have been devoted to the "social origins of audience gratifications" (Blumler, Brown and McQuail, 1970; McQuail, Blumler and Brown, 1972). But social origins in this sense of the term are nothing but the extra-individual characteristics of item 2 in the paradigm. To include societal variables proper, it would be necessary to resort to a comparative design, studying the uses and gratifications process in different societies. Otherwise, there would be no variation on the societal, as distinct from the individual, level.

Comparative designs have so far been adopted only rarely in the uses and gratifications tradition. Greenberg (see Chapter 4 in this volume) has investigated British children's motivations for TV viewing, having previously studied the equivalent orientations of American adolescents, but no explicit cross-cultural comparison is attempted. It is true that the author expects the same kinds of motivation categories to be relevant to the viewing behavior of American children, but that remains an untested hypothesis as yet. Some of the inter-media comparisons on which the substantial Israeli investigation of audience gratifications was based (Katz, Gurevitch and Haas, 1973) are currently being replicated and further developed by Blumler and Gurevitch and their associates at the Centre for Television Research in Leeds, but the new project has not yet reached the stage of report. Rosengren and Windahl (1972, 1973) have carried out four parallel surveys in Swedish communities and cities ranging in size from a few hundred inhabitants to a quarter of a million. They hoped to find meaningful differences among relationships between public and media in the four communities, on the assumption that community size would consistently affect them, but the findings did not support this hypothesis.

One of the most interesting comparative investigations with a uses and gratifications emphasis was conducted by Edelstein (1973). Surveys were carried out in three cities—Belgrade, Ljubljana, and Seattle. The author examined how various media are used by the individual to help him understand, and make up his mind about, various local and world problems perceived by him as important. Much of the study focused on descriptions of media use in each of the three cities individually rather than on comparisons between them. Nevertheless, influences from the differential societal and cultural conditions in the research sites did make themselves felt. For instance, the relationship between sex and media use was affected by the differential social and cultural conditions in the three cities. However, it was repeatedly found that differences between men and women in one of the cities (Belgrade, supposedly the city with the most traditional value system of the three) were more pronounced than those within each sex and between the two cultures (North American and Southeast European).

The value of these and other findings can only be tested against the background of yet more comparative research. (Such comparative investigations could be undertaken, of course, with respect to each of the items of the paradigm.) It would be especially interesting to make similar comparisons between yet other capitalist and socialist countries than the United States and Yugoslavia. However, the full implementation of such a research program would prove difficult. This difficulty may be regarded as mitigating the occasionally voiced criticism to the effect that the importance of power relations on a macro level is too often neglected.

Now, to request a combined study of the influence of intra-individual and societal variables on the uses and gratifications process is to ask for very much indeed. Only concerted action by a number of leading researchers in different countries could achieve this. A first step in this direction would be to try to develop transculturally valid measures of some of the key components in the process. Measures of personality and society would have to be provided by psychology and macro-sociology respectively. (And it is a rather safe guess that the psychologists would have the most to offer.) Measures of other variables would be procured within the uses and gratifications tradition itself. Items 4 and 5 (perceived problems and problem solutions) of the paradigm are examples of concepts that are in the process of being thus operationalized.

The term "problem" should not invariably be supposed to imply a high degree of intellectual awareness of the "problems" created by the interaction of needs, individual characteristics, and surrounding social conditions. In some cases the term "requirement" might be more appropriate.[1] However, "requirement" might be mistaken for "needs," something which must be avoided. The terminology is far from agreed upon in this area, nor is the conceptual apparatus behind the terms crystal clear. As a result of this confusion, the term "problem" as used in the paradigm covers roughly what Katz et al. (1973) call "needs," at the same time that their expression "needs" also seems to refer to parts of my item 1: basic human needs of higher and lower order.

Lundberg and Hultén (1968) report the results of some interesting attempts to quantify items 4 and 5 (problems and solutions). However, their conceptualization was slightly different from that proposed in the paradigm. Instead of problems, the authors were concerned with goals. In spite of this terminological difference, the substantive parallelism is evident. Respondents were asked to rate the perceived importance to them of certain goals, and also the perceived instrumentality of the media in helping the respondent to achieve such goals. The two measures were then combined into an index and used to predict reported media use. The relationships obtained as a rule were highly significant.

The most ambitious recent attempt to arrive at a better understanding of these phenomena is undoubtedly represented by the theoretical and empirical typologies of Katz et al. (1973). Thirty-five media-related "need statements" were collected from the literature. (For instance: "How important is it for you to spend time with your family?") The 35 statements were classified according to whether they concerned (a) the strengthening or weakening of (b) certain resources (information, contact, emotional experiences, etc.) with respect to (c) self, family, friends, etc. This a priori classification was then compared with an empirical clustering of respondent endorsements of the items. In the main the empirical data supported the validity of the fourteen groups of needs that had been differentiated in advance on theoretical grounds.

Two precautions seem important, if not essential, when developing this approach. First, the distinction between needs and problems as outlined in the paradigm should probably be heeded (or some similar distinction be made). Second, one should investigate not only media-related problems as has been the case up to now, but also—as Katz et al. (1973) themselves underline—"the larger context of human needs of which these form but a small segment." A suitable point of departure for such an approach might be found in the needs hierarchy constructed by Maslow (1954). The end product would presumably be a new typology and a new measuring instrument, in design, however, similar to that of Katz and his associates.

Given the availability of such an instrument, one would have the means of measuring in a more meaningful way the strength with which the individual experiences his various problems, as well as the aggregate level at which they make themselves felt in different societies. Data such as these might then be related to intra-individual, extra-individual, and societal variables of various kinds, and comparisons between the "problem structures" within and between societies might be undertaken. This would make an interesting comparative investigation in itself; within the uses and gratifications tradition the results could be placed within the frames of our paradigm, to be related to, for instance, item 5 (perceived solutions).

In fact, item 5 has already been touched upon in the preceding paragraphs. It corresponds to the second type of question posed by, for instance, Lundberg and Hulten (1968) and Katz et al. (1973). (First type of question: How important for you is it to . . . ? Second type: How effective is, e.g., TV, in gratifying this need or achieving this goal?) It should be remembered, of course, that media consumption is not the only way of solving problems, just as there are other problems than media-related ones. Furthermore, the solutions perceived as available and appropriate must be highly dependent on the individual's inner and outer characteristics, as well as on features of the surrounding society. Consequently, there must be different "solution structures," and these could be compared within and between different societies. So could the relationship between the problem structure and the solution structure. On the individual level, however, perceived problems and perceived solutions might combine to form a motive (item 6).

Motives may be difficult to distinguish empirically from needs and problems, but analytically they are different, and consequently they should be kept apart. (The academic terminology varies considerably in this area. What has here been called a need is often called a motive, while our term "motive" is often labelled motivation—cf., for example, Atkinson, 1958.) According to our paradigm, however, biological and psychological needs in conjunction with characteristics of an individual and his environment give rise to problems. Problems in combination with perceived means for solving them may then give rise to a motive for action. According to this point of view, Rosengren and Windahl (1972) probably go too far when they regard their four types of motives for seeking a functional alternative (change, compensation, escape, and vicarious satisfaction) as if they were *defined* by the combination of intra- and extra-individual possibilities to satisfy the given need in a given way.

Rather, one should establish an independent typology of motives and then look into the empirical relationships that may obtain between distributions over these types of motives, distributions over the various types of problems and solutions, and also over the various patterns of actual media consumption. The typology of motives should be more comprehensive than that of Rosengren and Windahl (1972), which comprises only motives for seeking a functional alternative (to mass media consumption). Of course mass media may be consumed for their own sake—not merely as an alternative activity. As a matter of fact, this might be one of the more important distinctions to include in the proposed typology of motives: the difference between motives for mass media consumption as a valued activity in its own right, and as a functional alternative, more or less "second-best" in character.

Within the area of motives for mass media consumption, as here conceived, very little systematic research has actually been published. Very often, motives have been loosely equated with either needs, problems, goals, or gratifications, although, strictly speaking, they are neither. Consequently, the way to a typology of motives proper is probably rather long. Presumably, it should start with a literature review, which would probably yield at least some pure "motive-items" (as distinct from "gratifications items" or "problem items"). It would then have to continue over tape-recorded discussions and possibly depth interviews, and only later arrive at the stage of more structured interviews. Although this is a protracted process, it is one that should be opened up for the benefit of the tradition of uses and gratifications study. (A model for such work may be derived from the careful qualitative work preceding the typology of "media-person interactions" established by the Leeds group; cf. Blumler et al., 1970; McQuail et al., 1972.)

Item 7, differential patterns of actual media consumption, has received more attention from researchers than have the motives as here conceived. It may be taken broadly to correspond to the "uses" side of the "uses and gratifications" label so often attached to work in this tradition. Three main areas are discernible: (a) media consumption in terms of amounts of time spent on the various media; (b) types of media content consumed; (c) various relations between the individual consumer and either the media content he is consuming or the media more generally.

Media consumption is a fairly simple and well-researched area, although unwarranted conclusions have sometimes been drawn from sheer amount of media exposure to motives, needs, gratifications, effects, and what not. The whole uses and gratifications tradition tends to be skeptical about the insights to be gained from evidence of mere quantity of media consumption on its own. Spokesmen for this approach are more concerned to investigate the types of content consumed and especially the uses made thereof.

However, we still lack a typology of mass media content sufficiently widely accepted to make research comparisons possible. In principle, two ways seem to be open: to look for an "objective" or for a "subjective" taxonomy, the latter being based on the public's own more or less implicit conceptualization. The standard content typologies of the various media corporations offer examples of "objective" taxonomics. A thorough and methodologically meticulous attempt at creating a "subjective" classification instrument has been made by Nilsson (1971, 1972).

Using the repertory grid interview technique, Nilsson generated 46 bipolar semantic scales that were assumed to represent a wide range of perceptions of TV programs. The aim was to ascertain whether there existed any general factor structures for the experience of television programs, and whether, on the basis of such factors, television programs could be clustered into homogeneous groups. Five generally valid factors emerged, called Information, Evaluation, Dynamics, Difficulty, and Controversialism, respectively. It also seemed that these factors could be used to cluster programs into homogeneous groups. That is, the instrument could be regarded as at least a step toward the development of a subjective taxonomy of media content. (For another attempt in this direction, cf. Emmett, 1968-1969.)

Nilsson has also suggested that his factors of Evaluation, Dynamics, and Difficulty are comparable with Osgood's well-known factors of Evaluation, Activity, and Potency. This opens up important possibilities of tying in the uses and gratifications tradition with theoretically and methodologically more sophisticated branches of behavioral science. In the light of such a possible confluence of two traditions, it may well be that the above-mentioned distinction between "objective" and "subjective" taxonomies of media content could also be expressed as a distinction between denotative and connotative meaning. (A typical Osgood scale, it will be remembered, aims preferably to measure connotative meaning, while, in several papers and reports Fishbein, 1967, reports the results of his attempt to develop scales to measure denotative meaning; cf. also Guerrero and Hughes, 1972.)

In any case, the distinction between objective and subjective taxonomies of media content must not be neglected. It is quite possible or even probable that actual media consumption takes place more in terms of subjectively structured media content than in terms of "objective" taxonomies like the standard program categories of, say, the Swedish Broadcasting Corporation or the BBC. This may be one explanation of the startling findings of Ehrenberg and Goodhardt (1969) to the effect that "all special viewing tendencies or clusters (of duplicately viewed programmes) were unrelated to programme content as such." A replication based on a subjective taxonomy might reveal that such clusters were related to distinctions between program contents other than those of the more standard categories. The strange idea—so contrary to all subjective experience—that actual viewing behavior cannot be explained by a preference for program types disregards precisely this vital distinction between subjective and objective taxonomies.

The consumption of different amounts of different kinds of media content—however these variables may be measured—occurs in the context of different types of relations between consumer and content consumed. Two types of such relations should be kept apart: relations during the very act of consumption; and relations to media and their content outside the act of consumption. Let us call them "consumption relations" and "outside relations," respectively. Both types of relationship may show individual patterns, stable over time, and differentially distributed in society.

Consumption relations may be exemplified by the little boy looking at a Western on TV, imagining himself right in the saddle of the hero, shooting down one rustler after another. The relations obtaining between this boy and the media content during the act of consumption could be described as identification (with the hero) and interaction (with the rustlers).

By cross-tabulating the two variables of identification and interaction, Rosengren and Windahl (1972) arrive at four types of relationships, termed detachment (neither identification nor interaction), parasocial interaction, solitary identification, and capture (both identification and interaction). Although not explicitly stated as such in their paper, this is a typology of "consumption relations," not to be mistaken for a typology of "outside relations." As a matter of fact, a typology of the latter is still lacking, despite the fact that uses and gratifications researchers have been at least as interested in the carry-over of media uses into audience members' social roles as in relationships established with content at the time of exposure as such.

The notion of "outside relations" may be illustrated by the possibility that the little boy considered above may think of himself as a TV cowboy even when he is no longer viewing or following the Western that gave rise to this tendency. He may even do so for rather long periods of time—several weeks or months, perhaps—albeit intermittently. Whereas this is an example of "identification" extended beyond the moment of consumption, other relationships might be carried over into outside life as well. For example, the parasocial relationship of fictitious friendship between the popular entertainer and the lonely housewife may live on in the latter's mind quite vividly during the intervals between his daily or weekly appearances on the screen: an instance, then, of "outside" parasocial interaction.

Of course the two kinds of relations (consumption and outside relations) may readily be confused with each other, since there is probably a high empirical correlation between their occurrence. Indeed, certain consumption relations may typically provide the mechanism through which certain outside relations are established, but in the latter case terms like identification and interaction assume quite different meanings from those that apply to the former.

The development of fruitful typologies of both kinds of relationship should be given a high priority in gratifications research, for an understanding of consumption relationships, as well as of outside relationships, is essential for a full understanding of media behavior as a whole. There is every reason to expect associations between, for instance, type of relationship, type of media content consumed, motives for consumption, and individual constellations of perceived problems and their solutions. Also, some of these media relationships may be related to other activities than media consumption, and also to some of the gratifications derived from such activities.

Of course the entertainment industry has been well aware of the two types of relationship for a long time and has deliberately exploited its understanding of human needs for interaction and companionship and how people try to satisfy such needs in modern society. To have such phenomena as these illuminated from the perspective of uses and gratifications research as well is long overdue.

Item 8, differential patterns of behavior other than mass media consumption, may seem to lie somewhat beyond the range of a uses and gratifications researcher's interests. However, a full appreciation of the meaning of media uses and gratifications demands their assessment in the context of other activities and the gratifications obtained therefrom. This could be attempted in two ways. One would aim to estimate the relative importance of mass media consumption vis-a-vis other activities by comparing them in terms of certain indicators, such as the time spent on them and the perceived utility of different activities for serving various purposes. Another approach could follow causal or functional lines: a certain pattern of media consumption (including time spent on the different media, type of content consumed, and consumption and outside relations) might be regarded as having causal or functional relations to other activities.

Katz et al. (1973) found that even for the gratification of media-related needs, certain other activities (family, friends, sleep, drugs, etc.) were equally important as or more important than the mass media. Lundberg and Hultén (1968) arrived at similar conclusions. Many examples of functional or causal relations between mass media consumption and other activities could also be cited from the uses and gratifications tradition. And of course the whole effects tradition in mass communication research is concerned with this problem: the causal relations between mass media consumption and other behaviors or characteristics of the consumer (deviant behavior, prejudice, aggression, etc.).

But now we have crossed the borderline to item 10, individual characteristics, as affected by mass media consumption among other influences. Because of the complex net of functional and causal relations that are bound to exist between patterns of media consumption and patterns of other behavior, it is difficult, perhaps impossible, to distinguish empirically between "other behavior" as affected by, as affecting, and as having the same origin as mass media consumption. Precisely because this is so, the item "Differential patterns of other behavior" represents a potentially fruitful area of contact between two main traditions in mass communications research.

Item 9, differential patterns of gratifications or non-gratifications, is generally considered to be one of the central foci of uses and gratifications research concern. However, gratifications are not always explicitly included in the design of investigations within this tradition. This is because, quite in accordance with its name, the tradition encompasses at least two groups of studies: studies of mass media use; and studies of the gratifications derived from that use. Uses as well as gratifications may be conceptualized and operationalized in various ways, and causes as well as effects of differential uses and gratifications may also feature prominently in research designs. Some of the papers already referred to illustrate quite well this rather wide spectrum of attention.

Nilsson (1971, 1972) investigated the way that television programs are perceived or experienced (item 7). Rosengren and Windahl's (1972, 1973) main dependent variable was degree of involvement (relationship between media and public, item 7), which they saw as dependent on the respondent's "interaction potential" (item 2). Edelstein (1973) investigated the mass media as more or less used and useful sources of information (item 7), about world and local problems, important to the respondent (item 4). Katz et al. (1973) ranked and compared the media with respect to their perceived helpfulness (item 5) in satisfying (item 9) clusters of media-related "needs" (item 4). The Leeds project (Blumler et al., 1970; McQuail et al., 1972) was and is centered on the social origins (item 2) of the gratifications associated with television viewing (items 5, 9). Greenberg investigated the gratifications that young people seek (item 6) or obtain (item 9) from TV. According to this somewhat schematic overview, then, Nilsson, Rosengren and Windahl, and Edelstein would be seen as dealing mainly with uses, while Katz and his associates, as well as the Leeds group and Greenberg, would be dealing mainly with gratifications.

However, uses and gratifications are probably functionally related in the sense that uses can lead to gratifications, and gratifications may derive from uses. Consequently any individual researcher may in practice concentrate upon one of the two components and yet be aiming, more or less explicitly, at both of them.

In the work of Rosengren and Windahl (1972, 1973), for example, the main dependent variable is "degree of involvement," which is an aspect of "use." But only partly explicit in their argument there is the assumption that from a high degree of media involvement may be derived a gratification of a kind more or less similar to the type of gratification to be enjoyed in real interaction. Use is measured, gratifications assumed. Katz et al. (1973), on the other hand, purport to measure gratifications while presumably taking for granted the assumption that they have counterparts in actual uses or media behaviors.

Indeed, the two concepts of uses and gratifications, although analytically distinct, are empirically so intimately intertwined that even when the researcher is explicitly setting out to measure one of them, elements of the other may slip in. For example, the Leeds group (Blumler et al., 1970; McQuail et al., 1972) established a typology of gratifications, while Nilsson (1971, 1972) found some factors showing audience perceptions or experience of TV programs. However, some of the gratification types and perception factors that feature in the two investigations turn out to be quite similar to each other (e.g., the gratifications category of surveillance, and the perception factor of information). In fact, this similarity sometimes approaches identity when the individual items and scales representing the various factors and types are considered.

Gratifications, of course, as defined in the paradigm are extremely difficult to measure. One difficulty is that over the years a folklore of conventions and norms about the various media, what they are good for and at, has developed. Simply asking people—as Katz et al. (1973) did—how much, for example, radio helps in gratifying this or that need—may be to invite them to reproduce popular stereotypes about gratifications rather than their own experience of gratifications as such. The notions of media in general, and needs or problems in general, may be too abstract to elicit valid answers about gratifications truly obtained. In the two projects by Blumler and his associates and Edelstein and his associates, different attempts were made to overcome these difficulties.

Edelstein (1973) tried to anchor the respondent's opinions about media usefulness in concrete situations, using a funnel-type series of questions ending up with questions about how the respondent learned about this or that local or world problem, personally important to him, which of these sources of information was most (least) useful, and why. Blumler and his colleagues (Blumler et al., 1970; McQuail et al., 1972) turned the other way round, as it were, trying to anchor statements of gratifications in concrete experiences of programs actually viewed, using a technique of questioning especially devised for this purpose. It would seem that in both cases serious and at least partly successful attempts have been made to anchor the respondent's answers in concrete situations rather than in general and relatively vague stereotypes. Continued work along these lines should prove rewarding.

The following two items of the paradigm (10 and 11) are more difficult to incorporate into a single uses and gratifications study. They represent the effects of media uses and gratifications on the audience member and his society. It is common practice to contrast effects studies and uses and gratifications studies. But Klapper (1960) in his authoritative review of investigations of the effects of mass communication had already included a chapter on uses and gratifications. Not surprisingly, he noted some differences between the two traditions. According to Klapper, uses and gratifications studies had always concentrated on the functions that media material serves for its consumers, "rather than on the occurrence or nonoccurrence of specific effects of which the media material was presumed to be the primary cause," a principal difference between the two traditions, of course. Effects studies take media content and its consumption as their starting-point; uses and gratifications studies start with the individual and his problems. The effects tradition has to a considerable extent been concerned with short-term individual effects intended by the *communicator* (for instance, commercial and political communications effects), while uses and gratifications researchers have been examining short-term individual effects more or less consciously intended by the *consumer* (functions such as mood manipulation and vicarious companionship). In addition, the effects tradition has also been concerned with certain more long-term effects that are intended by nobody (for instance, the gratuitous learning effects of exposure to violence and sex in the media). This aspect has been more or less neglected by empirical uses and gratifications research, although it has been much discussed. Whereas audience functions have been actively studied, the long-term effects of the existence of such functions have so far only been an object of speculation.

Sometimes the debate has touched on controversial issues that are quite central to the evaluation of mass communication in modern society. An example may be noted in Klapper's discussion of the contrast between two classic studies of radio serial listeners by Herzog (1944) and Warner and Henry (1948). The two studies agreed about the functions the serials served for their fans. Herzog, however, blamed them for making their listeners less socially aware and less capable of controlling their environment, while Warner and Henry commended them "for helping their devotees adjust to the facts of their lives and their inability to control the environment" (Klapper, 1960).

The debate has recurred intermittently since the 1940s, but very few empirical results supportive of one or the other position have actually been produced. Recently, however, Rosengren and Windahl (1973) reported that for certain subgroups—introverts with a high social potential for interaction—a high degree of involvement in the media content consumed could result in increased neuroticism. Since the findings are based on two very small subsamples, they must be regarded as suggestive only. But they do at least represent an attempt to move from items 7 (uses) and 9 (gratifications) on to item 10 (individual characteristics as affected by differential uses and gratifications).

If the individual effects of differential uses and gratifications have so far been only sporadically calculated by research, their societal effects have not been investigated at all. A scientific, empirical study of these effects would be extremely difficult to carry out and could not be designed in the near future. It would demand macro research on a comparative level over a long period of time, so long, perhaps, that even secondary analyses of survey data originally collected for other purposes would be precluded. One way out of this dilemma might be offered by the conduct of content analyses of media output distributed over time, perhaps along lines pioneered by Lowenthal's (1944) classic study of heroes in the mass media. The results of such content analyses might then be correlated with other time series of social and economic data (cf. Funkhouser, 1973).

But so long as we know next to nothing about the correlations between "objective" and "subjective" classifications of content, and little more about the uses made of, and the gratifications derived from, the consumption of media content, we will not know much about the mechanisms through which media content affects social structure. Uses and gratifications studies, in combination with effects studies on the individual level, seem to be a prerequisite for a deeper understanding of the interplay between society and media.

Before concluding this paper on some key elements in the uses and gratifications process, it may not be altogether out of place briefly to consider some recent developments within two mother disciplines of communications research, sociology and psychology.

The most important development in sociology during the last decade or so has been the theoretical vitalization resulting from the confrontation between Marxism and traditional academic sociology. One enduring result of this confrontation will undoubtedly be an increased attention to class perspectives and power relations on a macro level.

In psychology, a dispute of a quite different nature may be more relevant to the mass communication researcher, namely, the old quarrel between "trait theorists" and "situationists." According to two recent impressive overviews (Mischel, 1973; Bowers, 1973), a synthesis may well be under way between these two seemingly diametrically opposed schools of thought. The interaction between the two sets of factors—traits and situation—will probably come to the fore, and when personality characteristics are referred to, it would seem that personality will be regarded much more in dynamic terms of capacities and activity than in static terms of traits and types. If carried to its utmost, such a development will ultimately tend to transcend the very distinction between personality and situation, the active subject being regarded as in a sense creating the situation to which he later on reacts.

Now, what lessons may the communication researcher draw from tendencies such as these in sociology and psychology? Sooner or later they will probably affect all communication research, but here we are concerned primarily with a subset of the field, the tradition usually called uses and gratifications research. Let us start with some theoretical and methodological perspectives, taking the sociological development first.

An example of Marxist sociology having reached communication research may be found in the contribution by Philip Elliott referred to earlier in this paper. Elliott is highly critical of the uses and gratifications tradition. For example, he condemns its alleged tendency to wrench respondents "from their social situation." I have described above some attempts that have been made to anchor statements about uses and gratifications in concrete problems and concrete experiences of media content. Against the background of these and other attempts, this critique does not seem entirely warranted.

Following Nordenstreng (1970), Elliott also considers that the uses and gratifications tradition must "inevitably provide support for the status quo." But knowledge of gratifications derived from mass media consumption may equally well be used as a stepping-stone for attempts at change. *Without* such knowledge, these attempts may be doomed beforehand; *with* it, they may stand a better chance of success. But suppose it could be demonstrated in an intellectually satisfying manner that an understanding of uses and gratifications as here described would inevitably provide support for the status quo. Would that automatically entail a ban on such research? What kind of knowledge —indeed, what kind of a world—would we end up with, if only one type of truth was allowed? To this question Elliott has no answer, for he forgets to ask it.

Elliott also maintains that to study, for instance, the social origins of the gratifications derived from media consumption is only to study class relations in disguise. The same observation could also be positively formulated: central aspects of uses and gratifications research are highly relevant to a sociology oriented toward a class perspective. That this is so may be regarded as a positive attribute indeed. But one should take care not to make the main object of uses and gratifications research one of demonstrating the validity of a class perspective. Any grand perspective of sociology will always have to draw upon results obtained from a large number of subspecialties, and it would perhaps be presumptuous to demand that all these special sociologies should necessarily couch their results and conceptual apparatus directly in terms of the preoccupations of this or that overarching perspective. Perhaps it would be wiser to let the various subdisciplines develop according to their own conditions. It may be that the variation resulting from such a generous and pluralistic policy will be more fruitful in the long run than the uniformity that would arise should one single perspective be allowed to dominate. On the other hand, it goes without saying that the specialist researchers must not make such a policy an excuse for ignoring important developments in other specialties and in general sociology. No doubt papers like Elliott's serve an important function in preventing the specialists from isolating themselves too much.

The recent developments within psychology and social psychology seem to fit in excellently with the paradigm of uses and gratifications research outlined in this paper. The interplay between what has here been called intra- and extra-individual variables (item 2) corresponds closely to the interaction between traits and situation recommended for closer study by both Mischel (1973) and Bowers (1973). Also, the individual's capacities as an acting and purposeful subject may well be taken into consideration in terms of the paradigm's items 4,

5, and 6 (problems, solutions, and motives). A recent attempt to incorporate an "actor-oriented perspective" into the uses and gratifications tradition (Dembo and McCron, forthcoming) clearly demonstrates that much may be gained from pursuing this development in psychology and social psychology.

Finally, what methodological demands should be satisfied if uses and gratifications research is to learn from some of the trends discernible in sociology and psychology? Macro variables and power relationships could be included by means of comparative research organized at an international level. Probably the experiences gained by the "three cities project" (Edelstein, 1973) and by the cooperation established between the Leeds and the Jerusalem groups could be used as stepping-stones toward such comparative research. To cover more fully the complex interaction between intra- and extra-individual variables, it is probably necessary to supplement the instruments and techniques used up to now. By and large, uses and gratifications researchers have been working either with rather small, exploratory studies of a qualitative nature, or with traditional surveys of a cross-sectional type. These two types should probably be complemented and—if possible—combined with an experimental approach and/or panel studies. Brown (1973) has outlined a project that seems to promise much in this respect. And it may well be that other examples of similar designs are being conceived or implemented right now—to be reviewed, perhaps, in some future overview of uses and gratifications research.

NOTE

1. Suggested in a personal communication by J. R. Brown.

REFERENCES

ALDERFER, C. P. (1969) "A new theory of human needs." Organizational Behavior 4: 142-175.

ATKINSON, J. W. [ed.] (1958) Motives in Fantasy, Action and Society. Princeton: D. Van Nostrand.

BLUMLER, J. G., J. R. BROWN, and D. McQUAIL (1970) "The social origins of the gratifications associated with television viewing." Leeds: The University of Leeds. (mimeo)

BOWERS, K. S. (1973) "Situationism in psychology: an analysis and a critique." Psychological Review 80: 307-336.

BROWN, J. R. (1973) "Children and television: interpersonal and intrapersonal features of the effects process." Leeds: The University of Leeds. (mimeo)

DEMBO, R. and R. McCRON (forthcoming) "Social mapping and media use," in J. R. Brown (ed.) Children and Television. London: Cassell & Collier-Macmillan.

EDELSTEIN, A. S. (1973) "Communication and decision-making in Yugoslavia and the United States." Final Report, Seattle. (mimeo)

EHRENBERG, A.S.C. and G. J. GOODHARDT (1969) "Practical applications of the duplication of viewing law." Journal of the Market Research Society 11: 6-24.

EMMETT, B. P. (1968-1969) "A new role for research in broadcasting." Public Opinion Quarterly 32: 654-665.

ERICKSON, G. M. (1973) "Maslow's basic needs theory and decision theory." Behavioral Science 18: 210-211.

ETZIONI, A. (1968) "Basic human needs, alienation and inauthenticity." American Sociological Review 33: 870-883.

EYSENCK, H. J. and S.B.G. EYSENCK (1969) Personality Structure and Measurement. London: Routledge & Kegan Paul.

FEILITZEN, C. v. and O. LINNE (1972) "Masskommunikationsteorier," in Radio och tv möter publiken. Stockholm: Sveriges Radio.

FISHBEIN, M. [ed.] (1967) Readings in Attitude Theory and Measurement. New York: Wiley.

FUNKHOUSER, G. R. (1973) "The issues of the sixties: an exploratory study in the dynamics of public opinion." Public Opinion Quarterly 37: 62-75.

GUERRERO, J. L. and G. D. HUGHES (1972) "An empirical test of the Fishbein model." Journalism Quarterly 49: 684-691.

✓ HERZOG, H. (1944) "What do we really know about daytime serial listeners?" in P. F. Lazarsfeld and F. N. Stanton (eds.) Radio Research 1942-43. New York: Duell, Sloan & Pearce.

✓HUIZINGA, G. H. (1970) Maslow's Need Hierarchy in the Work Situation. Groningen: Wolters-Noordhoff.

KATZ, E., M. GUREVITCH, and H. HAAS (1973) "On the use of the mass media for important things." American Sociological Review 38: 164-181.

✓KLAPPER, J. T. (1960) The Effects of Mass Communications. Glencoe: Free Press.

LOWENTHAL, L. (1944) "Biographies in popular magazines," in P. F. Lazarsfeld and F. N. Stanton (eds.) Radio Research 1942-43. New York: Duell, Sloan & Pearce.

LUNDBERG, D. and O. HULTEN (1968) Individen och massmedia. Stockholm: Norstedts.

McQUAIL, D., J. G. BLUMLER, and J. R. BROWN (1972) "The television audience: a revised perspective," in D. McQuail (ed.) Sociology of Mass Communications. Harmondsworth: Penguin.

MASLOW, A. H. (1954) Motivation and Personality. New York: Harper.

MISCHEL, W. (1973) "Toward a social learning reconceptualization of personality." Psychological Review 80: 252-283.

NILSSON, S. (1972) "Om programupplevelse," in Radio och tv möter publiken. Stockholm: Sveriges Radio.

——— (1971) "Publikens upplevelse av TV-program." Stockholm. (mimeo)

NORDENSTRENG, K. (1970) "Comments on 'gratifications research' in broadcasting." Public Opinion Quarterly 34: 130-132.

——— (1969) "Consumption of mass media in Finland." Gazette 15: 249-259.

ROSENGREN, K. E. and S. WINDAHL (1973) "Mass media use: causes and effects." Lund. (mimeo)

——— (1972) "Mass media consumption as a functional alternative," in D. McQuail (ed.) Sociology of Mass Communications. Harmondsworth: Penguin.

WARNER, W. L. and W. E. HENRY (1948) "The radio day time serial: a symbolic analysis." Genetic Psychology Monographs 38: 3-71.

Chapter 14

EXPLAINING AUDIENCE BEHAVIOR:
THREE APPROACHES CONSIDERED

Denis McQuail and Michael Gurevitch

THIS CHAPTER IS CONCERNED with the frameworks and theories which can be deployed in trying to account for the phenomenon of the highly patterned and predictable form of behavior that supports mass communication. For the most part, this question has been approached by adopting the perspective of the audience member and by asking what uses and satisfactions he derives from media content and what appeal media content has for him. The uses and gratifications approach has appeared as a mainly empirical and pragmatic mode of inquiry, treating evidence about audience gratifications as of intrinsic interest, or seeking objective relationships between such evidence and, on the one hand, content and, on the other, the psychological or sociological characteristics of the audience member. The context of debate in which the approach matured was one that opposed an audience perspective against a message or communicator perspective (Bauer, 1964). The limit of theoretical development was reached in this debate by stating a transactionist alternative to an earlier stimulus-response model of the communication process. Insofar as investigators have been more theoretically inclined, either explicitly or implicitly, one brand of theory has tended to dominate the field, namely, functionalism. One can see why this should have been so. Functional analysis has seemed both relevant and attractive because of its capacity to handle relations of causality or interdependence between behavioral phenomena and because of the appropriateness of functional terminology to questions of motivation and need satisfaction.

Although a case can be made out for continuing studies in the more empirical, atheoretical, and possibly less pretentious, vein of earlier work, this chapter is written in the belief, first, that future research on audience behavior will benefit from a greater clarification and explication of theory. Secondly, we wish to argue that there are theoretical perspectives other than functionalism which may be drawn upon by audience gratification studies and which these studies can in their turn help to illuminate. Our intention is both to summarize the main features of the functionalist position on audience gratification studies and to offer a comparative outline of two different theoretical approaches which either have been implicit in past work or might be developed in future. In discussing these alternative approaches we are deliberately widening the scope of discussion to include studies that are not normally classified as examples of uses and gratifications research. By so doing, we hope also to show that this line of study is not just a narrow specialism within the field of mass communication research but one contribution, among several, to the wider task of accounting for the links between society and its cultural products.

The alternatives that we propose derive from different models of human behavior and consequently have different implications for the choice of appropriate methods of research and for the ways in which findings should be interpreted by policy-makers. We have labelled the non-functionalist alternatives as "action/motivation" and "structural/cultural" approaches, respectively, and they may be summarized as follows. The former is concerned with the individual actor, his choice of media behavior, and the meanings and expectations that attach to his choices. The "structural/cultural" perspective concentrates instead on patternings of contents and exposure behaviors and on those determinants of the audience situation—in the form of rules, customs, and conventions—that are seen as socially regulated. By contrast to these two, the "functional" perspective, with which we begin, focuses on relations of cause and effect between all components of the situation and especially on those aspects of media use that can be expressed as "need-gratifications."

THE FUNCTIONAL PERSPECTIVE

Functional sociological analysis, from which this perspective derives, is based on the assumption that the actions and phenomena of the social world are functionally interdependent, i.e., systematically related in causal chains and circles. Accordingly, behavior is explained in terms of meeting certain needs, the origins of which might be varied. Media consumption by the individual is seen as behavior that meets (or fails to meet) needs generated through an interaction of the individual's psychological dispositions and experience of his social situation. Clearly, however, mass media use is not necessarily seen as related to all, or even most, human needs, but rather to certain well-defined, albeit varied, areas of need for which mass communication might be especially suited. It either meets a need (e.g., for information) for which it is the "natural" solution, or it stands in as a substitute, or "functional alternative," for some missing "natural" solution to a need (e.g., for personal contact as in Rosengren and Windahl, 1972). Thus, media consumption is seen as a factor contributing to system equilibrium and to the capacity of the individual to function in his regular manner. The "explanation" of behavior is to be found in a person's own response to his perceived needs, either to maintain his established behavioral patterns, or to adapt to environmental changes, so that system maintenance can be assured.

Because of its emphasis on causal explanation, the functional approach is readily amenable to a paradigmatic formulation, in which needs (and their "origins"), motivation, action, and subsequent gratifications are linked in an essentially sequential manner (see Rosengren elsewhere in this volume). However, in spite of its apparent linearity, the functional paradigm allows room for varied explanatory foci, based on different views of the origins of action and behavior. Thus, hypotheses might focus on different stages of the paradigm, depending on the nature of the explanation sought. Two such foci have characterized some of the studies recently conducted within this general approach: the first has been concerned with explaining media gratifications in terms of the intensity and extensity of "felt needs" (e.g., for information, diversion, social integration) and the social and social-psychological origins of these needs (McQuail et al., 1972; Katz et al., 1973). The second attempts to explain media gratifications in terms of individual capacities and inclinations for satisfying these needs in a variety of different ways, including attendance to mass communication (Rosengren and Windahl, 1972). While the first focus assumes direct causal relationships between media gratifications and their social and psychological determinants, the second underlines the importance of differential social and psychological resources available to different people, the various options for action open to them, and the choices they then exercise among these options, for explaining the ways in which they go about satisfying their needs, either through media exposure or via other "functional alternatives." Clearly, however, even when this second focus is adopted, individual differences are also explained in causal terms.

In line with the behaviorally deterministic character of this perspective, the hypotheses generated within it tend to be *predictive,* deriving media gratifications from social and psychological determinants. These include at least three major categories of variables relating to the life circumstances of individual members of the audience: (1) personality characteristics; (2) social roles and social experience (both past and present); and (3) variations in environmental and situational circumstances. Hypotheses might be based either on discrete variables (e.g., age, sex, level of education, degree of anxiety, loneliness) or on "typical" combinations of interrelated variables (e.g., educational level, occupation and income) constituting *types* of individuals with common social background.

Data about media gratifications may, in the functional perspective, come in diverse forms. Earlier studies in this tradition have favored an *unobtrusive, inferential* approach, in which inferences about media gratifications were derived from the needs that people in various social circumstances were assumed to have (Riley and Riley, 1951; Maccoby, 1954; Bailyn, 1959). More recently, a greater emphasis has been placed on eliciting from respondents *retrospective and subjective* versions of why they attend to the media in general or to specific media contents in particular, and what they have derived from such behavior by way of need gratification. Yet another approach to data collection may be termed *clinical,* in which the investigator attempts to probe, either with or without the respondent's help, for inferences about underlying needs and motives which might be implicit in the respondent's own account of media use (Mendelsohn, 1964, offers one example). Data gathered by "subjective" and "clinical" techniques can then be examined in relation to other evidence about the individual and his social situation, and explanations of these relationships sought in functional terms.

The functional perspective seems to facilitate the formulation of a large number of relatively plausible hypotheses, some of which are illustrated below. The examples given here are based not on an indiscriminate number of discrete social and psychological variables that might activate communication needs, but rather on *types* of social and psychological circumstances that might give rise to certain orientations toward the media. If, for example, we seek to formulate hypotheses concerning use of the media for "escape," we might, following McQuail et al. (1972), first differentiate among "escape from the constraints of routine," "escape from the burdens of problems," and "emotional release," respectively. Accordingly, it is possible to hypothesize that (1) *escape from the constraints of routine* will be sought by those whose job or family circumstances provide restricted or repetitive environments, e.g., assemblyline or shift workers and non-working mothers of small children. Those who seek escape from routine through media exposure are also more likely to be less gregarious, e.g., they will prefer to look for means of diversion in the context of the home environment. Alternatively, they might be those who, because of life circumstances (e.g., geographical mobility, lack of financial or other resources) have limited access to social or commercial means of diversion. (2) *Escape from the burdens of problems* might be sought by individuals employed in work situations that are taxing or productive of tension (e.g., those engaged in work involving high responsibility and/or strain; incumbents of dangerous occupations; or those exposed to precarious or insecure job situations); by persons in difficult family circumstances (e.g., those with low incomes and large families) or troubled by personal and life-cycle worries (e.g., ill health, old age). It might also be sought by those who are ill equipped to cope with their problems (e.g., those with little education, in low status position, or the downwardly mobile). (3) *Emotional release* might be sought by those with limited outlets in personal relationships for emotional expression (e.g., the lonely) or by those whose cultural norms and psychological dispositions restrict emotional expression (e.g., middle-class women, introverts).

In a similar fashion, hypotheses might be formulated for other gratification categories suggested in the typology of "media-person interactions" formulated by McQuail et al. For example, hypotheses concerning use of the media for *substitute companionship* might focus on those with limited opportunities for social contacts; those who because of certain circumstances (e.g., geographical mobility) have lost touch with former social contacts; or those in the above circumstances who particularly value, and have a more salient need for, intensive social contacts. On the other hand, *social utility* gratifications, i.e., use of the media to facilitate or "lubricate" social contacts, might be more characteristic of those with diverse opportunities for such contacts; those in need of accessible materials to facilitate conversion; or those occupying opinion-leadership roles. Such hypothesized relationships between media gratifications and diverse social positions are, of course, by no means exhaustive and merely illustrate the kinds of relationships that can be sought in the functional approach.

THE STRUCTURAL/CULTURAL PERSPECTIVE

By using this term and distinguishing it as a separate approach, we are acknowledging and invoking one of the dominant concerns that has brought some investigators to the study of the media audience. This concern has to do with the character of human experience in urban industrial society, with the overall characterization of such a society and with the potential for future change in its quality of life. Thus, in the study of media audiences, we may perhaps separate a functional interest in the dynamics of a behavioral pattern from a structural/cultural interest in the dynamics of a societal and social situation. The latter assumes a determining connection between the social structure on the one hand and, on the other, both the dominant culture and the attitudes and orientations of individual members of society. No such assumption is called for if we are solely concerned with audience behavior as a more or less self-contained system. Thus the dominant theme of the structural/cultural perspective, as the term is used here, is the idea that audience expectations and satisfactions derived from the media should be explained primarily in terms of (1) the patterns of media materials that are made available and (2) the customs, norms, and conventions—defining what counts as appropriate ways of using and reacting to media provision—that prevail in particular societal settings. Both of these are molded, in turn, by social-structural and cultural factors. Thus, audience behavior is seen as being *prescribed* by structural and cultural factors which, on the one hand, shape media contents and the intimations they hold for the gratifications that might be gained from them and, on the other hand, help to institutionalize the approved ways of using the mass media and responding to cultural goods of various kinds. Differentiation in audience behavior may stem either from subcultural variations within a given society (such as social class distinctions) or from variations across societies. Since this approach regards audience gratifications as derivative from structural and cultural forces that are external to the individual, explanations in terms of personal choices or internal need-states are avoided. Rather, the nexus of interaction between media output and audience response is treated as if shaped by an independent social fact which, like many cultural phenomena, is in a sense arbitrary (that is, not itself open to a further causal explanation). Of course each individual has some opportunity to make choices within the range of available outputs and socially supported behaviors. But the emphasis is on how the dominant cultural definitions constrain that range, the possibilities of escaping from which are then highly limited. Within such an overall framework one might approach the question of why audience members attend as they do to mass communication and what they derive from it.

Evidence drawn from individual audience members concerning the appeals for them of mass media materials remains of central importance in this perspective, but in contrast to the functional approach, the consumer's account of what is going on cannot be regarded as the sole source of knowledge. Instead, the focus is on more collective features of mass communication phenomena—for example, interrelating aggregate findings about media contents, audience orientations, and social and cultural contexts. And the interpretation of such evidence is influenced by the observer's overall view of the social-structural and cultural situation, offering a holistic style of explanation that would take account of as many concurrent features of the situation as possible.

The hypotheses about the determinants of audience tastes and preferences that can be deployed from this standpoint also tend to derive from rather general views about the nature of social and cultural phenomena. For instance, they might start from a social-critical view of the typical mass media "article" as a standardized product that is shaped by the dominant forces of industrial society and is consumed by people whose lives are conditioned by the same forces. Thus, Irving Howe (1957) has written in the following vein about mass culture:

> Whatever its manifest content, mass culture must . . . not subvert the basic patterns of industrial life. Leisure time must be so organized as to bear a factitious relationship to working time: apparently different, actually the same. It must provide relief from work monotony without making the return to work too unbearable.

If one applies such a line of reasoning to the case of television in many Western democracies, it might be proposed that the medium is defined by its producers, and by and for its audience, as a leisure pastime. Its predominant meanings are linked to diversion and relaxation; the scheduling of programs confirms this definition. Features of the home and family context of use add more, still consistent, elements to this view of what television is for and how it should normally be regarded. Whereas production is on an industrialized basis, industry "releases" viewers to watch and recuperate. Such a general view is spelled out by critical writers like Mills (1956) and Marcuse (1964). A similar line of reasoning might be applied to more detailed problems of audience behavior—for example, to explain patterns relating to age or social-class differences. Particular groups in the total public may be faced with limited alternative media sources and encouraged by their social and cultural environment to make a particular kind of choice, which is reinforced in turn by their media experiences.

Leaving aside the work of social critics and mass society theorists, we may identify two main lines of research that have reflected such a perspective. First, there are studies that have taken the form of a general survey of the audience for a particular mass medium or a particular section of the audience. Perhaps the clearest examples are Steiner's (1963) examination of the American television public and its follow-up study a decade later by Bower (1973), which offer some explanations of subgroup differences defined by such conventional classificatory variables as age and educational background. Such an analysis might be criticized, however, for isolating respondents from the structural forces that actually bear on their situations, an omission which the work of Wilensky (1964) largely makes good, though he is no more than suggestive about the precise uses and gratifications involved in mass media consumption. Janowitz (1952) on the Chicago local press also provides some of the elements of an explanatory model along structural/cultural lines in his portrayal of a form of mass communication that arose out of commercial requirements and exists with its readership in a particular urban context which in turn patterns both its contents and its functions—for example, in promoting the integration of the neighborhood and the city social system. Studies of the child audience (Maccoby, 1954; Schramm, Lyle and Parker, 1961) are especially suited to this approach, with its emphasis on constraining context and on content as given. Children are typically placed in situations defined rather arbitrarily for them by others and are much influenced in their expectations and behaviors by their immediate social environment.

Another line of research that fits under this general heading consists of work on the context of media use and on the rules and meanings that apply in given cases. In this connection the work of Freidson (1953), Bailyn (1959), and Geiger and Sokol (1959) might be cited, even if they cannot all be regarded as fully fledged uses and gratifications studies. By focusing attention on the actual situation of cinema-going, watching television at home, or reading the newspaper on the journey to and from work, such research has increased our awareness of the force of custom and habit and of the fact that definitions of appropriate behavior are built into such patterned social activities.

It should be evident from this brief discussion and from the examples cited that this perspective is especially valuable in providing a theoretical framework in which to place findings about patterns of audience behavior; and in directing research along lines that are likely to be fruitful for purposes of macro-sociological analysis. While the interpretation of audience use data could take a functional form, the framework does not require this. For instance, it would be possible to account for established patterns of media use as in some sense functional for maintaining a particular form of social structure and culture. Thus, Marcuse (1964) speaks of "modes of relaxation which soothe and prolong" a "stupefaction" which effectively suffocates needs that demand liberation and of the "irresistible output of the entertainment and information industry" that binds the "consumers more or less pleasantly to the producers and through the latter, to the whole." The whole line of his argument is that the mass media are inimical to change and "functional" for a repressive form of society. We should note, however, that the proponents of this line of argument would typically reject the "functionalist" label for their theory, since it is basically a conflict theory, viewing mass media, their content, and the devices that attach mass audiences to the media as instruments of class domination, rather than neutral mechanisms of tension-reduction. To take a different example, De Fleur (1970) writes that the "function of what we have called low taste content is to maintain the financial equilibrium of a deeply institution-alized social system which is tightly integrated with the whole of the American economic institution." Both this view and that of Marcuse are examples of a macro-level functionalism that is distinct from the individual psychological functionalism of many uses and gratifications formulations. On the other hand, the same overall perspective and the same kinds of data allow one to deploy alternative types of explanation. For instance, one could propose a "cultural reflection" thesis according to which media content and audience taste are accounted for in terms of their consistency with, though not necessarily functionality for, dominant societal and cultural forms. Examples would have to be drawn mainly from content studies, though ones that make inferences about audience gratifications. Thus Johns-Heine and Gerth (1957) show a reflection in magazine themes of social changes in America following the Depression. Similarly, Lowenthal (1961) traces a historical shift in popular biography subjects from "idols of production" to "idols of consumption" during the first four decades of this century. What we hope to have shown by these examples is the potential relevance of uses and gratifications evidence to non-functionalist social theory. As it happens, the writers cited do not produce any evidence about actual audience uses. But they do employ assumptions about audience motivation and gratification and could well have followed the procedures of uses and gratifications research to support their respective analyses.

THE ACTION/MOTIVATION PERSPECTIVE

Of the three, this approach has been least adopted in any deliberate way, yet it represents a position that many researchers in this field would recognize as at least partly their own, and it may also hold out most promise for future work. The action/motivation perspective can best be explained in terms of phenome-nological sociology, especially as developed by Alfred Schutz (1972). His distinction between "conscious behavior" and "unconscious behavior" is echoed by those working in the uses and gratifications field who stress the idea of media use as a rational, goal-directed activity. According to Schutz, "An action is conscious in the sense that, before we carry it out, we have a picture in our mind of what we are going to do. This is the 'projected act'." While not all media use fits this conception of behavior, the researcher working within this perspective would be concerned with situations in which media use appears to be purposeful and in which the actor is able to explain his choices.

Certain assumptions implicit in the action/motivation perspective can be distinguished. First, human action implies freedom of choice, not merely freedom to choose between different courses of action but also freedom to attach different personal meanings to what may seem to be similar actions and experiences. Second, although unconscious motivation may exist, only those actions whose meanings and purposes can be described by the actor are suitable objects of study. Third, the future, particularly the future as perceived by the actor, is emphasized. The future is seen as distinct from the past and present, and neither present nor future is merely a function of the past. The essence of a motivated action, then, is its meaningfulness for and orientation to some future state.

In applying these assumptions to audience behavior, media use is regarded as an act of free choice by an actor who seeks to gain some immediate or delayed future benefits, to be or do what he wishes. The observer or investigator makes no presuppositions about the causes of behavior, on either a personal or a situational level. Although this approach may appear unrealistic, given the extent of social constraints on media use, its adoption may lead to observations, explanations, and insights that would not be produced by more deterministic perspectives. This is not merely a matter of adopting a general scientific openmindedness in advance of specific evidence, but rather one of rejecting explanatory frames of reference that are not those of the actor and that therefore might be alien to him. The primary source of evidence is the actor's own view of what he is doing.

When these assumptions of the action/motivation perspective are translated into methodological rules for studying the experience of the mass media audience, the following guidelines emerge:

(1) To find out why viewers, listeners, or readers attend to media, *ask them*. They are likely to have some awareness of their motivation, and in any case their answers are the only relevant explanation of the actions in question.

(2) Do not assume that any experience has a *unitary meaning*. Different people will give different accounts of the same media experience and will attribute personal meanings to that experience. Let the respondents provide the components of any explanatory framework.

(3) In asking questions, focus on the *anticipated outcomes* of a communication experience. Direct inquiry to the future, not to the past.

(4) Concentrate so far as possible on the *communication experience*. The personality, life circumstances, and past experiences of the person, as well as the content of the message, are secondary to the *relationship* between the message and the recipient.

Moreover, the adoption of this approach would tend to confine the investigator to certain types of research problems and to favor techniques that encourage respondents to give subjective accounts of their media experiences. The assumption of conscious choice and action requires finding an audience situation in which this level of awareness is likely to exist. This suggests a concentration on "fans"—either of a particular and established type of content or of an item typical of a genre, or possibly fans of a given medium in general. Established genres are most likely to give rise to clear expectations in prospective audience members, and fans are more likely to have, and to be aware of, motives for exposure than are casual members of the audience who simply "drop in." While we are here more concerned with representing the principles of a research approach, we can find several examples of uses and gratifications studies that have exemplified this strategy (e.g., Herzog, 1944; Blumler et al., 1970). Of course in a "pure" action/motivation approach fans can only represent themselves. However, some investigators have regarded fans as spokesmen for the less committed or articulate consumers of the same media content, who are then perceived as paler and less distinct versions of the former.

Since this perspective requires that data be collected from the vantage point of the media receiver, descriptive, qualitative, and exploratory procedures are more appropriate than carefully controlled experiments and representative sample surveys. Interviewing in depth and participant observation are techniques well suited to the approach. Studies are likely to be small in scale but detailed and intensive. A significant problem arises in devising techniques to obtain information about an individual's motivation for *future* behavior, since, ideally, motivation for future behavior and past experience should be separated, at least on a conceptual level. The investigator should, at least, aim to avoid obtaining rationalizations of past behavior, unprobed stereotypes, and current popular ideas about the appeal of the content.

The main prescription for data collection from this perspective is that it should explore the source of *meanings* present in media use situations and indicate the frequency of given types of interpretations. In this way, it might be possible to enhance our understanding of certain processes of media reception and to develop something approaching an ideal type for particular media use situations. Although the connection of media behavior with other features of a person's social situation should not be ignored, this connection should be established through the person's own perception rather than by a pattern of correlations. And although generalizations about a wider population and prediction of patterns of behavior for individuals or groups would not be the primary goal, research of this kind might yield statements of expectation about the occurrence of audience use phenomena structured in particular ways.

Given the basic assumptions and modes of research outlined, it would be inappropriate to state formal hypotheses for testing. This is not to suppose, however, that there would be no pattern in the findings. While assuming choices to be freely made, the investigator would also assume them to be rationally and meaningfully related to other acts and experiences in the individual's situation. Thus, patterns might show themselves because individuals sharing a set of situational circumstances are likely to choose, and give meaning to their choices, in similar ways—not because common circumstances *cause* common behavior but because the meanings given to acts of choice *take account of,* and are consistent with, what is involved in those circumstances. In addition, a given kind of content that has attracted a patterned set of associations and expectations may generate characteristic interpretations among its audience members, even though these may also vary according to other features of the individual's experience.

Underlying this argument there is a more general hypothesis that audience members' recurrent objectives and aspirations are likely to be linked to some extent with regularities and standardization in content themes. Otherwise, however, this approach requires the least specific hypotheses to guide research designs, and there is no pressure to force its lines of reasoning into a hypothetico-deductive mould.

As we noted at the outset, this perspective has not been consciously adopted as a model for audience studies, and yet much of what has been said will be recognizable to anyone familiar with uses and gratifications research as describing procedures and commonsense assumptions of fieldwork. The theoretical distinctiveness comes from the rejection of interpolated "explanations" based on correlational evidence, the avoidance of any concept of unconscious or latent motivation, the stress on motivation as having a necessary future reference instead of being open to inference by introspection. If data were to be collected and these prescriptions adhered to, one would have a theoretically consistent study of the audience deserving a uses and gratifications label and yet in no way functionalist in concept.

THE THREE APPROACHES COMPARED

In conclusion, it may be helpful to offer an overall comparison of the three perspectives in terms both of their characteristics as models of behavior and of implications for policy which they contain, were they to guide applied research. One way of highlighting differences is to think in terms of three different models of the communication process. Thus the action/motivation perspective allots a dominant role to the receiver. The act of receiving communication is regarded in principle as a free and meaningful act, which essentially defines the event. The structural/cultural approach views communication as dominated by the source and limited in definition and meaning by the context and rules that govern the communicative situation. The functional view, on the other hand, focuses on communication as systematic interaction, a process of homeostatic adjustment within a larger social system. Communication is two-way and, ultimately, balanced.

Another set of comparisons emerges when we turn to the formulation of the uses and gratifications approach by Blumler, Katz and Gurevitch (Chapter 1 in this volume) as concerned with (1) the social and psychological *origins* of (2) the *needs* which generate (3) *expectations* of (4) the *mass media* or *other sources,* which lead to (5) differential patterns of *media exposure* or engagement in other activities, resulting in (6) *need-gratification* and (7) other consequences. Figure 1 attempts to relate certain aspects of each of the three approaches to the main terms in this paradigmatic sentence. Some difficulty arises because the terminology of this formulation is suited mainly to the functional approach, but, despite this, we can see how it applies differentially to the three models that have been outlined.

	Origins	Needs	Expectations of Mass Media	Media Exposure	Gratification of Needs	Consequences for Media Use	Consequences for Individual and/or Social System
Action/ Motivation	Reason; chance; individual and varied	Personally chosen projects	Actively formulated; open-ended	Selective; varied; unpredictable	Individual judgment of satisfaction	Further choice-making	Self-enhancement and development
Structural/ Cultural	Generally patterned by culture and social structure; conditioned by past experience of content	Externally imposed and defined, with limited choice	Culturally given; shaped by contextual and group norms; result of socialization	Predictable and regular; unselective	Fulfillment of a given expectation	Reinforcement of pattern of media use	Consistency and continuity of individual-collective link
Functional	Personality; past and present social situation and opportunities	Responses to stimuli in environment	Individual need satisfaction	Systematically related to needs and expectations through selective exposure and perception	Homeostasis; Need-reduction	Varies according to variation in needs-salience	Contribution to more effective performance of personality and social systems

Figure 1: A PARADIGMATIC COMPARISON OF THE THREE APPROACHES

Thirdly, since the uses and gratifications approach in general has attracted the attention of some of those who either plan or produce media content, it is of some relevance to trace out some of the policy implications of our challenge to the idea of a single theoretical orientation. The attraction of gratifications research to some communicators is partly accounted for by its capacity to make audience research data qualitatively more meaningful. However, it has also been heralded as offering an objective basis for planning a service to meet audience needs (Emmett, 1968-1969), a proposal which has been criticized, partly on the grounds (Nordenstreng, 1970; Elliott in this volume) that the uses and gratifications approach would inject a static principle into policy making by justifying existing provision and enshrining prevailing patterns of culture in society. The point of this reference is to note that this particular charge is directed especially at research that is formulated in functional terms. The alternatives we have outlined would seem, in principle, immune from this objection.

The other approaches which we have described appear, in any case, to have a different kind of relevance for policy making. Neither framework would help very much to give direct answers to media planners with specific problems. The action/motivation perspective would seem, however, with its stress on the objectives and purposes of self-conscious consumers, best suited to helping to plan for the more well-defined needs of subgroups and minority audiences rather than for the *mass* audience as such. (This would be consistent with the philosophy outlined, for example, in the Report on Broadcasting of the Pilkington Committee, 1962.) To attempt to understand audience behavior in this way could also help to reinforce a non-manipulative, service attitude toward the individual audience member which might, in the final analysis, be regarded by many, especially in Western democratic societies, as the raison d'etre of the entire mass communication process. The policy implications of the structural/cultural perspective, because of its socially deterministic emphasis, are more problematic, and evidence obtained within this framework has fewer policy prescriptions than either of the other approaches. At one level this position might imply that the responsibility for audience behavior rests squarely with media professionals, who are entrusted with the shaping of media contents, and with members of other culturally dominant groups, who perform the function of articulating the dominant cultural meanings and definitions extant in a given society. Adoption of this perspective might also suggest, however, that even these groups are to some extent constrained by the very social-structural and cultural factors that determine the norms of media provision and the customs that regulate the patterns and expectations of cultural consumption. It follows, then, that changes in audience behavior would hinge upon a restructuring of the media and of the structural and cultural forces that provide their underpinnings.

Finally, the question arises whether the three approaches are to some degree compatible with each other or whether they are totally antithetical and, if so, how the choice between them should be made. First, on the issue of compatibility, it is clear that, at least at one level, these approaches reflect basic disagreements over the task of social science and the nature of social reality, and as such they would appear to be irreconcilable. At another level, however, they can be regarded as alternatives which complement each other and which cumulatively may provide a more comprehensive explanatory picture of audience behavior. To the extent that the three approaches focus on different aspects of the relationship between the individual, the mass media and the social system, and that no single approach can describe this web of relationships in its totality, then it might be argued that the three approaches are complementary *by definition.* Any concern to secure a balanced account of audience responses to mass communication would ultimately demand that more than one approach be deployed.

As to the issue of choice, constraints on researchers arising from limits to their material resources (as well as to their reserves of time and energy) would normally require that one or another approach be adopted for implementation. In any case, as we have argued above, intellectual clarity and analytical rigor will be better served by a readiness on the part of individual investigators to work within the perspectives afforded by a single approach. Such choices are likely to be influenced as much by personal taste and intellectual fashion as by judgments upon the inherent strengths and weaknesses of each orientation. Indeed, in the present state of the social sciences, it would seem rash to commend any one alternative as intrinsically superior to the others. Rather we would argue that since at present the uses and gratifications approach is indeed just that—a provisional orientation to data collection in one problem area in the study of mass communication—research as a whole should proceed in as eclectic a spirit as possible. At the same time it should be borne in mind that, precisely because of the multiplicity of available perspectives, this field is perhaps rather too liberally endowed with alternative conceptualizations and competing value positions. These underlie some of the criticisms that have been leveled against uses and gratifications research, especially by those who would prefer a more unitary approach. But perhaps the time for the latter is not yet ripe. What is true and useful in this research tradition might, for the time being, be best protected by a clarification of theoretical alternatives combined with a respect for the potential contributions of different approaches that are at one and the same time divergent yet complementary.

REFERENCES

BAILYN, L. (1959) "Mass media and children: a study of exposure habits and cognitive effects." Psychological Monographs 71, 1: 1-48.
BAUER, R. A. (1964) "The obstinate audience." American Psychologist 19: 319-328.
BLUMLER, J. G., D. McQUAIL, and J. R. BROWN (1970) "The social origins of the gratifications associated with television viewing." Leeds: University of Leeds. (mimeo)
BOWER, R. T. (1973) Television and the Public. New York: Holt, Rinehart & Winston.
De FLEUR, M. L. (1970) Theories of Mass Communication. New York: McKay.
EMMETT, B. (1968-1969) "A new role for research in broadcasting." Public Opinion Quarterly 32, 4: 654-665.

FREIDSON, E. (1953) "Communication research and the concept of the mass." American Sociological Review 18, 3: 313-317.

GEIGER, K. and R. SOKOL (1959) "Social norms in television watching." American Journal of Sociology 65, 3: 174-181.

HERZOG, H. (1944) "What do we really know about daytime serial listeners?" in P. F. Lazarsfeld and F. N. Stanton (eds.) Radio Research. New York: Duell, Sloan & Pearce.

HOWE, I. (1957) "Notes on mass culture," in B. Rosenberg and D. M. White (eds.) Mass Culture. Glencoe: Free Press.

JANOWITZ, M. (1952) The Community Press in an Urban Setting. Chicago: University of Chicago Press.

JOHNS-HEINE, M. and H. GERTH (1957) "Values in mass periodical fiction, 1921-40," in B. Rosenberg and D. M. White (eds.) Mass Culture. Glencoe: Free Press.

KATZ, E., M. GUREVITCH, and H. HAAS (1973) "On the use of the mass media for important things." American Sociological Review 38, 2 (April): 164-181.

LOWENTHAL, L. (1961) Literature, Popular Culture and Society. Englewood Cliffs, N.J.: Prentice-Hall.

MACCOBY, E. E. (1954) "Why do children watch television?" Public Opinion Quarterly 18, 3: 239-244.

McQUAIL, D., J. G. BLUMLER, and J. R. BROWN (1972) "The television audience: a revised perspective," in D. McQuail (ed.) Sociology of Mass Communications. Harmondsworth: Penguin.

MARCUSE, H. (1964) One Dimensional Man. London: Routledge.

MENDELSOHN, H. (1964) "Listening to radio," in L. A. Dexter and D. M. White (eds.) People, Society, and Mass Communications. Glencoe: Free Press.

MILLS, C. W. (1956) The Power Elite. New York: Oxford University Press.

NORDENSTRENG, K. (1970) "Comments on 'gratifications research' in broadcasting." Public Opinion Quarterly 34: 130-132.

Report of the Committee on Broadcasting, 1960 (1962) CMND 1753 (The Pilkington Report). London: HMSO Publications.

RILEY, M. W. and J. W. RILEY (1951) "A sociological approach to communications research." Public Opinion Quarterly 15, 3: 444-460.

ROSENGREN, K. E. and S. WINDAHL (1972) "Mass media consumption as a functional alternative," in D. McQuail (ed.) Sociology of Mass Communications. Harmondsworth: Penguin.

SCHRAMM, W., J. LYLE, and E. PARKER (1961) Television in the Lives of Our Children. Stanford: Stanford University Press.

SCHUTZ, A. (1972) The Phenomenology of the Social World. London: Heinemann.

STEINER, G. (1963) The People Look at Television. New York: Alfred A. Knopf.

WILENSKY, H. (1964) "Mass society and mass culture: interdependence or independence?" American Sociological Review 29, 2: 173-197.

Chapter 15

SOME POLICY IMPLICATIONS OF THE
USES AND GRATIFICATIONS PARADIGM

Harold Mendelsohn

CONCEPTUALLY IT IS A SIMPLE MATTER to link media uses and gratifications to human needs. In this mode how the public uses the media, and the satisfactions they derive therefrom, help to explain the mass communications process at least from the perspective of audiences. Newspapers are read in order to sustain societal linkages; broadcast "marathons" are attended to in order to assess the endurance capacities of revered personalities; and televised football matches are watched assiduously in order safely to ventilate pent-up feelings of hostility. Just as the behaviorist is able to come up with a response manifestation for every conceivable stimulus, so too the functionalist can conceptualize a predisposing "need" of one sort or another that precedes any and every particular instance of media usage.

DIFFICULTIES OF DERIVING MEDIA POLICY
FROM AUDIENCE "NEEDS"

From a scientific point of view the conceptualization of prior needs as motivating forces for media usage and gratification is not only legitimate; it is extremely useful in helping to explain a variety of mass communications behaviors as well. However, when it comes to formulating media policy on the basis of public needs, the matter becomes troublesome, giving rise to at least two major difficulties. First off, critics of the mass media, and particularly of their content, generally operate from a posture of specifying a priori the kinds of material that audiences *should* have or *need* to have. More on this later on. Second, more often than not "needs" can be used as post hoc rationalizations for submitting content of questionable quality and merit to audiences. Thus "gossip" columns can flourish under the pretense of meeting the public's "need to know." Explicit sex films can be purveyed as affording "everything you wanted to know about sex—but were afraid to ask." And blatant one-sided propaganda of all sorts can be presented as satisfying the "information" needs of various publics. I am not arguing for the elimination or censorship of gossip columns, so-called pornographic films, or advertising and publicity. I merely wish to point up how the needs-uses-gratifications model can easily be distorted on the level of media policy-making—distorted to convey an aura of legitimacy where such is not at all intrinsic.

A serious shortcoming of the "needs" concept, particularly in its a priori form, is its anchorage in the value systems of those making the determination. Thus, the teacher sees only the need for education; the physician, for therapy; the preacher, for morality; the communicator, for information and entertainment. Yet, the physician often offers education; the teacher tries to inculcate principles of ethics and propriety; the preacher presents varieties of information many times in a dramatic or entertaining milieu; and television's Dr. Marcus Welby offers medical therapy on a continuing basis. Moreover, research into audience gratifications has indicated that a serious discrepancy often exists between the intent of the source and what actually happens as outputs of various interactive processes. It is precisely because numerous publics with varieties of social and psychological attributes, and with differing interests, motivations, expectations, and tastes, come away from the media with varying experiences, that formulating media policies on any given predetermined catalogue of audience needs will be self-servingly unrealistic. In this respect, the attacks on popular culture by elitist humanists stand out as rather presumptuous hollow assertions regarding human needs (mostly alleged aesthetic needs) as well as human behavior. To the elitist critic of popular culture, the mass media serve but one fundamental need (and, one might add, an evil need), the need for passive escape. The media well serve this one overriding need, albeit dysfunctionally, the argument goes, with disastrous psychological, social, political, and aesthetic consequences.

Policy recommendations flowing from subjectively determined audience needs generally are one-sided, undemocratic, and insensitive to the actualities of media audiences' expectations and behaviors. Two cases in point are illustrative.

Returning to the elitist critics momentarily, the one policy recommendation recurring in the writings of such essayists as MacDonald (1957), Arendt (1971), Van den Haag (1957, 1971), and Howe (1957) is Platonic in essence. Just as Plato would banish the diversionary poets from his ideal state, so would the elite critics simply do away with the media and thereby uplift the intellectuality of the masses, curb juvenile delinquency, and avoid the threat of a totalitarian political takeover. Based on the assumption that bad art drives out the good, only "good" art would be offered for appreciation via what media were allowed to remain—with "good" to be determined not by the audiences, but by the critics. That is to say, the needs, uses, and gratifications of the critics, rather than those of the audiences, would serve as the bases for the neo-Platonic media policies of the elite humanistic critics of popular culture.

The second illustration stems from the development of educational television —now labeled "public" television—in the United States. Accompanying the widespread acceptance of American commercial television in the 1950s was a shrill protest cry among educators and reformers for an "alternative" night-time broadcast mode that would be primarily "educational" or serious in nature. Again, the "need" was pre-determined mostly on a subjective non-empirical basis—certainly so far as audiences were concerned. The night-time offerings of educational television in its inception phase were simply disastrous. Mostly structured "lessons" in such matters as calligraphy, flower-arranging, flamenco guitar-playing, and the like, night-time educational television quickly earned an enduring reputation for being dull, esoteric, and of interest only to minuscule highly self-selected audiences. Here, policy had been developed with regard to satisfying the highly circumscribed needs of tiny, educationally elite, audiences, rather than those of elite critics as in the first example. In its developmental phase American educational television offered no "alternative" whatever to commercial television. At best it served a convenience function mainly by bringing certain kinds of "educational" materials into the homes of highly selected, well-educated, well-to-do families, who may have been spared the annoyance of acquiring that information elsewhere. "Educational" television ultimately changed into "public" television, abetted by public financing. As the structure of non-commercial TV changed, so did its programming. No longer was PTV confined to didactics; now an attractively broad array of entertainment and information fare was made available. Nevertheless, large audiences still avoid PTV in the belief that its offerings are elitist and therefore esoteric, dull, and irrelevant. Current PTV viewers continue to be dominated by the better-educated and the well-to-do, even though all sectors of the public contribute to the financial support of public television through their taxes. In effect the large majority of taxpayers who ostensibly are not greatly interested in viewing PTV are now subsidizing a vehicle that is still addressed primarily to the needs of a culturally elite minority. Where in the past it has been customary for the affluent to underwrite the costs of bringing "culture" to the masses, the current non-commercial television situation in the United States has reversed that policy dramatically. From a policy perspective, PTV poses a serious problem indeed: namely, the cultural needs of taste minorities cannot be overlooked in a democracy. Yet, how fair is it to ask *everyone* to pay for the satisfaction of the needs primarily of the relatively few who are affluent and already well-educated?

There is another problem—that of control. Implicit in the policy formulations of both the humanistic critics and the educator-reformers is the need for more and more government control over the content of programming. The argument here is that the interests of private owners of the television enterprise are fundamentally selfish and are oriented primarily to the fiscal needs of stockholders rather than to the real needs of the public at large. Government is seen as an impartial altruistic source of control, interested only in the public's welfare. The announced public telecommunication policies of the Nixon Administration may have altered that particular image. Rather than formulating policies derived from the needs of the public, the telecommunications policies of the White House had been addressed principally to the needs of the Nixon Administration itself. Charging PTV with a liberal "anti-Nixon bias," the White House actually proposed the elimination of all "controversial" public affairs programming on PTV, a measure that ultimately floundered in the wake of Watergate. Another thrust by the Nixon Administration succeeded, however, with the firing of several alleged liberal PTV commentators who had earlier come under pressure from the President's associates.

Clearly the needs component of the uses and gratifications model is the most difficult to handle. One problem stems from the observation that many individual and societal needs are not at all media related, and indeed are not directly relevant to the study of media uses and gratifications. What precisely is meant by "needs" when the mass media are being discussed, then, is not always self-evident. Another problem grows out of the fact that as society becomes more complex, needs increase and also become more complex. It would be far simpler to catalogue both macro and micro needs, say, for 1674 than it is for 1974. A third problem pertains to the fact that while many individual and societal needs are indeed universal in nature, it appears that it is precisely media related needs that seem to be culturally anchored and uniquely responsive to specific societal expectations and norms and that vary therefore from group to group. What serves the entertainment functions for American audiences, for example, may not necessarily satisfy the needs for amusement and diversion among audiences in Spain, Indonesia, or Ghana in precisely the same way. Further, because needs have an attribute of universality, the needs concept alone is frequently too general and gross to be useful in explaining specific instances of uses and gratifications. To illustrate, for entertainment some people read detective stories; others prefer listening to a chorale; and still others choose to tune in to an episode of *Gunsmoke*. The gross needs for entertainment cannot and does not explain the differentiations in either usage patterns here or the presumed differences in derived gratifications therefrom. On the level of policy-making it is difficult to see how decisions about the provision of detective stories, choral music, or Western adventure dramas can be made on the basis of an observed gross need for entertainment. Finally, because needs are both manifest and latent, researchers must depend on both their scientifically rooted observations and the reports of individual subjects in determining their incidence. Observation often entails inferential deduction—always a risky business. Individual reportage, particularly of latent or quasi-conscious motives, very much depends on the skills of the analyst as well as on the capability for in-depth introspection on the part of the subject. It is one thing to discover that individuals A and B both wear wrist watches in order "to know what time it is." But it is far more difficult to ascertain that individual A sports a $1,500 solid gold timepiece in order to achieve social status, while individual B displays a modest stainless steel Timex in a reverse-snobbism effort to avoid an image of ostentation.

FINDING A POINT OF DEPARTURE

Perhaps we can do away with some of the problems attending the needs component by lowering our sights somewhat. Suppose we turn our attention momentarily to a middle-range construct such as audience wants and expectations. "Wants" in this context would refer to feelings that particular phenomena or conditions can fulfill particular self-experienced lacks or desires (i.e., longings-for). "Expectations" would refer to affective anticipations regarding the prospects of particular events occurring in conjunction with certain associated consequences. I am not here proposing an abandonment of the needs construct. I am merely suggesting laying it aside temporarily to be returned to, possibly in a modified form, at a later stage in the discussion.

By turning our attention to audience wants and expectations, we begin a more realistic approach to the problem of formulating media policy from the perspective of what might be preferred and sought after by audiences rather than from what is absolutely necessary for them. In any case, media institutions operating in a relatively free marketplace are geared more frequently to offerings of "what the public wants" rather than to what the public may need. It is precisely because critics of the media see a discrepancy between the two that they are so bitter in their attacks on the popular media.

The answer to what the public wants is not much easier to ascertain than is the reply to the question of what the public needs. On the one hand, elitist critics, believing that whatever the public wants is meretricious by definition, see no policy relevance in either asking the question or seeking an answer to it. On the other hand, researchers attempting to find out what the public really wants, have been frustrated to the point where many believe that the question is not at all amenable to systematic investigation. Yet, decisions based on perceptions of what the public wants permeate the pragmatic operations of vast numbers of media entrepreneurs every day—be they publishers of magazines of books, newspaper editors, disc jockeys, film producers, museum curators, art gallery managers, or philharmonic conductors. Whether the question of what the public wants should be asked or can be answered satisfactorily appears to be peculiarly insignificant to media practitioners. The ability of these practitioners to assess public wants—whether by intuition, experience, or systematic empiricism—has generally been neglected by researchers. Theoretically, systematic study of entrepreneurial assessments of public wants could serve as benchmarks against which more scientifically grounded investigations of these same wants could be compared. Much more attention should be given by researchers to this entire matter.

How realistic is it for contemporary researchers to try to ascertain public wants and expectations as they relate to the mass media of communication? Without a number of provisos it probably is not too realistic at the moment. This is not to say that the task is impossible. Far from it.

Before we can begin the quest realistically, however, the matter of what people expect from the various media must first be opened up for sustained national discussion, debate, and dialogue over a considerable period of time. In other words, the public must first of all become aware that their wants will be subjected to systematic investigation and, as a consequence, that they are under an obligation to give serious thought to the issues involved and to their personal interests and concerns prior to the time of investigation.

Secondly, in order for the public to free itself from habit and customary usage, the discussions, dialogues, and debates generated in the sensitizing awareness stage of the process should present realistic alternative possibilities for consideration. All too often public wants and expectations focus on what has been rather than on what might be.

Finally, the public should be allowed actually to experience several alternative possibilities before it expresses its wants. For example, do people prefer to view motion pictures via home video cassettes or in movie theaters? Will individuals begin to rely on newspapers projected into the home via cable television in contrast to reading the newsprint version? How would the public react to a ban on paid political advertising? What would the free distribution of paperbacks by public libraries do to the reading habits of different publics?

Obviously this road map is rather an ambitious one requiring much time and enormous inputs of effort yet to be made. What are some of the policy implications that flow from our current, albeit seriously limited, knowledge of audience wants and expectations? Let us examine several of the more prominent contemporary examples.

Individuals in modern technological societies seek news, information, and entertainment from the media primarily because they want to be forewarned about imminent danger; because they want instrumental guidance in order to give coherence to their every-day activities, and because they seek respite. At the very least modern society requires a *system* of mass communications which in toto addresses itself to these basic expectations. That is to say, no one component of the system is required to address itself to all the fundamental expectations of audiences simultaneously. Because each of the media is capable of performing specific communications functions extremely well and others not so well, one fundamental policy implication calls for each of the media to concentrate on what it is best capable of accomplishing. However, because the mass media always have the capacity of reaching (not necessarily affecting) enormous aggregates of individuals, the temptation is always present to push each of them separately into multi-functional modes. This seems to be particularly the case with regard to the broadcast media, where efforts to turn them simultaneously into newspapers, classrooms, museums, pulpits, lecture halls, sports arenas, salons, live and cinema theaters, and concert halls persist. Surely, if the media-related wants, uses, and gratifications of audiences are multi-faceted, should there not be a greater division of labor and specialization within the mass media spectrum?

With regard to broadcasters in the United States, their response to the demands of various interests, including government, simultaneously to satisfy diverse and often incompatible public expectations has resulted in a policy of

offering "balanced programming." More often than not "balanced programming" is reflected in presenting little more than a bits-and-pieces potpourri
of news, information, religion (almost exclusively on Sundays), entertainment,
and public service (almost exclusively after most audiences have retired to bed).
The desperate attempt of American radio and television outlets to comply with
the Federal Communication Commission's regulations regarding the satisfaction
of what it—the Commission—has pre-determined to be public "needs," has
generally resulted more in a numerical "balance" than in a high quality
substantive one. By literally being required to be all things to all individuals,
American broadcasters have not been able to concentrate on developing
materials that may be uniquely amenable to radio and television alone and
specifically to the broadcast-related wants and expectations of audiences.

Frequently the mass media neglect the actual media-related wants and
expectations of significant sub-populations as a result of trying to cater to
unspecified "mass audiences" as well as a consequence of their own subjective
determinations of mass audience "needs." In the United States the interests of
numerous cultural and demographic minorities, as well as ethnic, racial, and
religious subgroups, are generally ignored by most national mass media.
Thus, one is hard put to find realistic portrayals in the mass media as a
whole of women, farmers, Spanish-surnamed people, Blacks, blue-collar workers,
intellectuals, the elderly, the poor, to cite but a few instances. Additionally, with
rare exceptions it is difficult to uncover materials in the mass media that are
uniquely oriented to the particular wants, expectations, or cultural tastes of such
substantial subpopulations. At best one must search through "specialized"
publications such as *Ms.*; tune in to local farmer-oriented radio stations in the
Midwest corn and wheat belts; get insights (distorted as they may be) into the
life-styles of blue-collar workers from TV's unique *All in the Family*; or learn
about the life experiences of Southern poor Black sharecroppers or those of
Caucasian "hard hats" from an occasional motion picture such as *Sounder* or
Joe.

This phenomenon of the mass media neglecting the wants and expectations of
substantial subpopulations, while attempting to cater to everyone, affords us an
opportunity to examine how general research on the predispositions of
audiences and their media-related uses and gratifications can first delineate a
problem and, second, point to policy alternatives that may help ultimately to
resolve it.

Currently some 60 million Americans, composing more than three-fourths of
the total labor force, work in manual or clerical jobs for an hourly wage, jobs
requiring neither a college education nor substantial utilization of cognitive
output. These working persons make up the overwhelming majority of the adult
population in the United States, and in addition to sharing attributes such as
limited education and income attainment, they hold in common many similar
norms, values, attitudes, aspirations, life-styles, and media habits.

Among the cultural themes that permeate the life experiences of working
status persons in the United States are (1) feelings of inadequacy with regard to

intellectuality and especially vis-a-vis persons with economic, political, and social power; (2) feelings of intense insecurity, particularly in the economic sphere; (3) an orientation of suspiciousness toward out-groups and the individuals who compose them; (4) a disdain for abstractions and matters intellectual; (5) a high regard for traditional norms and life-ways, particularly as they pertain to family, morality, and male-female relationships; (6) distrust of and resistance to innovation and change; (7) a chronic sense of economic and political powerlessness.

Gleaned from the social stratification research conducted by large numbers of sociologists, cultural anthropologists, social psychologists, economists, and manpower experts, this thematic array, purposefully oversimplified for the sake of discussion, suggests a number of fundamental needs around which media policies of all sorts might be envisioned. In this sense of the term, "needs" would refer to those wants or lacks which, if fulfilled, would tend to facilitate purposeful activity and behavior. It is thus to be distinguished from the various conceptions of needs considered in the first part of this essay, such as that of a subjectively postulated set of requirements or that of a supposedly universal set of primary necessities. For example, one sees clearly a need, arising from the circumstances of their life-situations, for enhanced self-esteem among many working persons, as well as a need for security; a need to understand how cognitive processes can solve concrete problems; and a need to realize how political, social, and economic power is achieved and sustained in American society through associations and organizations. Customarily, such needs—which by no means are in the exclusive domain of working people—are seen as being met by that peculiarly American institutional cure-all, education. But here we are faced with a social cohort that actively eschews education as a viable pathway leading to need satisfaction. Can one formulate media policies that might help to meet some of these needs? Possibly such an attempt could be made, but only in an indirect and limited fashion.

We must first examine the media-related wants and expectations of working people. Research conducted by Bogart (1965), Gans (1966), Mendelsohn (1966, 1969, 1973), and Rainwater, Coleman and Handel (1959) indicates that working people are oriented much more so than are other individuals to television as a prime source of information and entertainment. Working people are generally less critical of TV than are others. In fiction and drama working men tend to prefer explicit melodramatic plots that feature the triumph of good over evil as a consequence of considerable explicit "action." Male protagonists who are strong, silent, know how "to handle women," and who can take care of themselves in the preservation of their homes, their working-class values, and their wives', mothers', and sisters' virtue, are preferred to heroes who are middle or upper class, intellectual in bent, indecisive, sensitive to nuances, and need institutional support in the resolution of problems. Working women tend to prefer "romantic" fictional and dramatic fare that supports working-class values, upholding the "woman's place" as a home-tender and as an indispensable aide in the service of husbands and offspring. Heroines who are unglamorous, good women, and who endure and overcome temptations to abandon principles of sexual morality as they pertain to virginity, early marriage, faithfulness in marriage, and child bearing, are preferred over those heroines who may be glamorous, career-oriented, unmarried, and morally fancy-free and footloose, unburdened by obligations to and responsibilities for home, mate, or children.

Both working men and women show considerable interest in performers as "personalities" and in straight-forward plots in orthodox story form with clearly delineated beginnings, mid-points, and "happy" resolutions of conflicts, issues, and problems. Both males and females in the working-class cohort derive considerable instrumental information and guidance from narrative materials in the mass media in contrast to strictly informational sources. Thus, disc jockeys, comic strips, cinematic films, soap operas, and show business "personalities" are more apt to be used for school-of-life purposes than are news commentators, learned publications, or acknowledged experts and authorities.

A number of policy suggestions offer themselves from the preceding observations.

First, simply by making more explicit efforts to address themselves to the needs and media-related expectations of working persons, the media—and specifically television—can serve to enhance the self-esteem of this subpopulation, thus blunting the sharp edge of insecurity and perceived victimization that cuts through the fabric of working-class life. It has often been noted that the media have a capacity to confer status by merely focusing attention upon individuals, groups, events, and phenomena (Lazarsfeld and Merton, 1948). By simply allotting more space and time on the part of acceptable "personalities" to matters of interest to working persons, the media can be expected to afford them a sense of enhanced worth and importance.

Second, we can begin to overcome the reluctance of working persons to become involved with the arts by not insisting that, in order to enjoy them, individuals must approach them with special intellectual skills, reverence, and a mystical sense of awe. It is a fact of life that, when offered a TV hour of *Mannix* versus an hour of the Boston Symphony, nine out of ten working persons will consistently choose the former. If more and more working persons are to be attracted to the arts, considerably much more must be done than simply putting artistic presentations on TV at precisely the times when they must compete with more interesting, exciting, and less confounding fare—at least from the taste perspectives of working persons. When we realize how drab, routine, and hum-drum the every-day lives of most working persons are, it is easy to empathize with their desire for "excitement" in their leisure activities. When the arts are presented in imaginative and exciting ways, the response of working persons is enthusiastic. Thus, New York's Shakespeare-in-the-Park productions; Pennsylvania's Symphony-on-the-Barge program, which features tours of the river towns of that state literally via river barge; and the Metropolitan Museum's "art train," which whistle stops through remote areas of the Western half of the United States, all have enjoyed outstanding success in attracting large first-time audiences to the arts. The mass media must follow suit, break with tradition, and imaginatively develop fresh means of presenting the arts if they are to interest working persons to any significant degree.

A third policy suggestion concerns the presentation of news by the media and again, television in particular—with an eye to the needs and wants of working people. Given the desire of working persons for comforting anchorages in tradition, and their general suspicion of change as disrupting and altering tradition, it is small wonder that many become confused and feel threatened by the diversity and swiftness of the technological, social, political, economic, and institutional changes that contemporaneously seem to confront Americans at every turn. Yet, a common theme in the news these days focuses precisely on occurrences of profound changes—be they related to new patterns of sexual mores or to the uses of fossil-fuel energy, to rising rates of inflation and unemployment, to the trustworthiness of government, or to explorations of outer space. By merely reporting events reflecting change, then, the media undoubtedly can be dysfunctional so far as working people are concerned. Here, straight reportage—without concomitant explanation and interpretation—can serve only to raise already-present levels of anxiety. What is called for is a policy of linking reports of change with explanations and interpretations of the factors causing these changes; the processes by which changes occur; the likely effects of changes on the overall society generally, and on working persons in particular; and explicit guidelines for coping with change rationally and without fear.

THE ROLE OF RESEARCH

What we have attempted to demonstrate is the possibility of formulating *operational* mass media policies for one specific cohort from two kinds of social-science research efforts—general observations of life patterns and the needs they reflect plus general investigations of mass-media-related wants, expectations, and uses-gratifications as they pertain to a particular subpopulation. The post hoc "conclusions" drawn from the integration of such social science data cannot stand as such on purely scientific grounds. Scientifically, they are at best hypotheses yet to be proved, rather than reflections of iron-clad principles or laws. Nevertheless, "soft" as they may be, "conclusions" of this sort can offer a considerably more rational grounding for intelligent policy formulation than can either sheer viscerally subjective a priori speculation or self-serving hypocritical post hoc rationalization.

In addition to providing a scientifically empirical basis for policy-making, the integration of generalized social science intelligence regarding specific audiences, together with media-related information about them, allows for the development of policies for filling important gaps in the media enterprise. Thus social science research can provide a basis for *changing* media policy in line with the media-related needs, expectations, uses, and gratifications of particular audiences rather than serving as endorsements of the status quo as some critics of the uses and gratifications paradigm have vainly argued.

If it has accomplished anything at all, uses and gratifications research has applied a corrective to the notion of mass audiences as enormous monolithic aggregates of heterogeneous publics who simultaneously converge on the mass media. Although there may be some reason at times to consider audiences for particular media—such as the audiences for cinematic films or radio or television—as masses, uses and gratifications research has shown a significant degree of differentiation among audiences for particular types of media and especially for particular media formats and content. Rather than being uniformly monolithic, mass media audiences are viewed by functionalists as being segmentalized, the various component elements being considerably more homogeneous than had previously been observed—at least in terms of sharing many common social and psychological characteristics, tastes, needs, perceptions of the media, and media-related expectations, uses, and gratifications.

The segmentalization factor bears significantly on the problems of formulating media policies out of research into audience gratifications. Briefly, segmentalization affords researchers an opportunity to focus their inquiries on delineated, identifiable, relatively homogeneous subaudiences, rather than on a total population that is heterogeneously amorphous. It would appear to be a relatively easier task to develop media policy ideas based on the needs and media-related wants of pre-school children between the ages of three and six, for example, than it would be for just "children" generally. Or the task of developing media policies for urbanized Mexican-American audiences earning no more than $5,000 annually would become considerably more manageable than attempting to generate media policy for "poor people" as a whole.

By concentrating on explicitly designated target audiences, it is possible to focus on the needs, wants, uses, and gratification syndromes of one specific audience at a time in a coherent and systematic fashion. Once a determination of a specific target audience is made, research strategies can be developed in terms of specific media goals. By working together with communications practitioners the researcher can use the explicitly stated intentions, objectives, and assumptions of the practitioner as guidelines for the development, testing, and ultimate evaluation of viable hypotheses. Data from the tests then become sound empirical bases for policy formation in the middle range.

Two examples serve to illustrate this possibility. In developing both the *Sesame Street* and *Electric Company* televised educational services, the Children's Television Workshop created a modus operandi wherein elaborately detailed research on both needs (i.e., the needs for reading and arithmetical skills) and media-related expectations (i.e., the expectation to be entertained) of specifically identified child audiences served as direct inputs for the creation of highly specialized programming formats and content. Evaluations reported by the Children's Television Workshop suggested that such research-guided inputs into the creative process had helped the production team to develop some highly effective communication modes. Far from sustaining the status quo, the experience of the Children's Television Workshop stands out as a prime example of the fresh, innovative, and imaginative communications pay-off that may be reaped from careful, customized uses and gratifications research in all three stages of the mass communications process—formative, implemental, and evaluative.

The author enjoyed a similar experience in his development of an ameliorative series of programs addressed specifically to low-income Mexican-American audiences (Mendelsohn, 1969, 1971). Working in concert directly with Mexican-American writers, directors, and authors, the research team for this project conducted no fewer than twelve separate studies that were designed (1) to delineate a distinctive target audience (urbanized Mexican-Americans earning less than $5,000 yearly and manifesting above-average levels of anomie); (2) to assess important audience needs (e.g., the need for supportive messages designed to alleviate feelings of personal powerlessness); and (3) to determine patterns of media-related wants, uses, and gratifications which might help to attract audiences who were unaccustomed to strictly informational mass media vehicles. This research effort resulted in a particularly unique "educational" innovation —the creation of televised "soap operas" of an informative nature that superficially emulated the "novellas" from which target audiences appeared to derive considerable pleasure as well as information. In addition, the research provided for (4) a number of on-going assessments of audience reactions as individual programs were being aired, so that these reactions might guide the efforts of programming still to be written and produced; as well as (5) evaluations of the overall effects of the series in toto on the lives of viewers as compared to non-viewers. (In fact the series proved extremely effective in many respects, particularly in the provision of ameliorative sentiments.)

Once more, the *Cancion de la Raza* experience demonstrates the viability of uses and gratifications research in offering guidelines for the development of sound, innovative, rational media policy that can actually serve particular public needs and expectations without reinforcing the status quo.

The discussion regarding the policy implications of uses and gratifications research is a multi-faceted and multi-leveled affair. If we consider *all* possible uses and gratifications as they pertain to *all* people and to *all* the media, we shall, as researchers, be embarking upon a hopeless task. It is a task better suited to the talents of poets and philosophers who relish subjective speculation rather than hard data upon which to base their policy recommendations. We must also avoid endorsing media policies that come to us in the guise of pre-packaged, pre-digested stereotyped "responses" to trumped-up artificial "needs." Of course it is premature to think seriously of the grand theory and design approach to policy formulation with regard to the media. The best we can presently hope for is a recognition that the mass media operate within a pluralistic context in which diverse media perform diverse functions for diverse publics at diverse times. This has resulted in considerable specialization among and between the media in addressing the various specialized needs, wants, and expectations of segments of so-called mass audiences. Technological developments in video cassettes, interactive cable television, rapid facsimile reproduction and transmission promise even a greater segmentalization in the capacity of more specialized media to cater for highly specialized audience needs and wants. Before these innovations can be harnessed in the service of actual audience requisites, we must find out considerably more than we now know about what those requisites actually are. To accomplish this we have three options—we can rely on the humanists to structure policy; we can rely on the operational assessments of practitioner entrepreneurs; or we can begin the arduous task of systematically delineating the media-related needs, wants, and uses-and-gratifications problems of explicitly identified segments of that elusive entity, the mass media audience.

SUMMARY AND CONCLUSIONS

Whether grounded in a scientifically conceived empiricism or in subjective speculation, contemporary policies regarding the functions of the mass media are derived mainly from observations of audience uses and gratifications. To argue that mass communication policy ought not to be derived from such data simply ignores the realities of mass communication decision-making as it actually occurs. Nor does the rather antiquated proposition that functionalism serves to reinforce the status quo take into account Robert K. Merton's (1957) contemporary process corrective of Radcliffe Brown's (1935) and Malinowski's (1926) rather static functional paradigm. It is peculiarly unwarranted to suggest that, while all other aspects of human behavior are complex, dynamic, and undergo change, the uses to which individuals put the media, and the gratifications derived therefrom, are simplistic, static, and immutable.

The assertion that uses-and-gratifications guidelines for media policy simply undergird the status quo does not stand up before even the most casual observation of media offerings. Motion picture films of 1974, for example, bear little or no resemblance whatever to the films of 1944 or, for that matter, 1964. The current nostalgia vogue in the United States regarding films produced thirty or forty years ago is due precisely to this generation's curiosity about the changes that have occurred over the years, not only in society but in that particular medium's reflections of such changes. Observations that neither the media nor media audiences are cemented in place for all time abound when we examine the newspapers, radio and TV programs and popular novels and magazines of today as compared with just a decade ago. Bear in mind that changes in media content generally reflect changing patterns of audience needs, wants, expectations, uses and gratifications, as well as changes in mass media technology. What, then, can possibly be meant by critics of the uses-and-gratifications model when they refer to the "status quo?" Status quo as of when—1974, 1954, or 1924?

Critics of the uses and gratifications approach to mass communications policy join with the humanistic critics of the mass media in denying the ability of audiences to determine for themselves what will serve them best. Further, they see no relevance whatever of data about audience gratifications for media policy. This elitist stance argues that only self-appointed arbiters of public taste are best suited to make mass communications policy for everyone else in the realization of some ambiguously outlined aesthetic utopia in which the media are presumed to be totally functional. In this mode, rather than formulating policy that is rooted in the needs, wants, uses, and gratifications of audiences, media policy must be reflective solely of the needs, wants, uses, and gratifications of minuscule minorities of dictatorial taste-makers. Thus, what is viewed as functional policy for the elitist critic becomes dysfunctional for a democratic society. For the issue here revolves around the critical matter of censorship.

As agents of socialization and social control, the media are simultaneously functional and dysfunctional; they are both integrative and disintegrative. No man-made institution is either completely functional or dysfunctional or totally integrative or disintegrative. Utopias exist entirely in the minds of poets and philosophers. Sociologically, we have yet to uncover one. From the perspective of policy-making vis-a-vis the media, the problem is to control so far as possible their dysfunctional and disintegrative potentialities. These cannot be eliminated entirely. Initiating such controls without data relative to actual audience uses and gratifications reflects a dictator-like arrogance on the part of such initiators, which is at one and the same time wholly subjective and repugnant to the principles of democracy.

Nor is it possible to develop sound functional policies for the media on the basis of simple head-counts of audiences alone. At best such measures afford rather gross estimates of exposure to specific media and content as a function of what types of media and content are available to which types of individuals and groups at what points in time. In no way can we determine the media-related wants, uses, and gratifications of audience members from exposure measurements alone.

In order for uses and gratifications data to serve as keystones for media policy decisions, far more research effort is required. Thus, the full range of social and psychological conceptualization and methodology must be put into play. Crucial for developing useful media policies for varying audiences is the need for considerably more data than are now available on two major variables. On the micro level, what is called for is a better understanding of precisely what roles the media play in the socialization process. On the macro level, we need far more insight than we now have into the integrative-disintegrative functions of the media in relation to groups and communities.

Just as the process of socialization touches different strata of society differentially, so too may we expect that media needs, wants, expectations, uses, and gratifications will differ accordingly. For the isolated, culturally deprived ghetto child, television may serve a nearly exhaustive variety of socializing functions otherwise more aptly fulfilled by non-media institutions such as the family, museums, concert halls, libraries, and the live theater. In the isolated ghetto TV becomes an absolutely essential life element, and the media gratifications sought throughout his maturation by a ghetto child will be significantly different from those that are experienced by a child reared in a typical upper middle-class suburban milieu. For the latter, television is likely to be perceived as a relatively prosaic and mundane source of information and diversion—just one expendable source amidst a plethora of far more exciting communications opportunities available to him for his pleasure and enlightenment. Just as one medium by itself cannot possibly address all the socialization requisites of the ghetto child effectively, so too will it fail by itself in the effective socialization of the suburban youngster. What is needed, then, is a system of mass communications with enough variety and flexibility in it to cover the media-related needs and wants of diverse population subsets, a system that is intimately linked to non-media institutions more adequately suited in many instances to disseminating knowledge, culture, and diversion. The uses and gratifications orientation affords us two significant opportunities in this respect. First, by uncovering pertinent needs, wants, and expectations, determinations can be made relative to the kinds of needs, wants, and expectations of diverse subgroups that can be best met by the media as a whole. Second, uses and gratifications research affords a means for evaluating whether and the extent to which varying media-related needs and expectations are actually being effectively met by the media, either singly or in concert.

Far from reinforcing the status quo, properly used, audience gratifications research becomes a powerful instrument for changing those media policies that do not facilitate the satisfaction of actual media-related needs, wants, and expectations. Further, uses and gratifications research can spur the generation of fresh and imaginative modes for fulfilling needs, wants, and expectations that for whatever reason the mass media have either overlooked or neglected in the past.

REFERENCES

ARENDT, H. (1971) "Society and culture," in B. Rosenberg and D. M. White (eds.) Mass Culture Revisited. New York: Van Nostrand Reinhold.

BOGART, L. (1965) "The mass media and the blue-collar worker," in A. B. Shostak and W. Gomberg (eds.) Blue-Collar World: Studies in the American Worker. Englewood Cliffs, N.J.: Prentice-Hall.

GANS, H. (1966) "Popular culture in American social problems in a mass society or social asset in a pluralistic society," in H. S. Becker (ed.) Social Problems: A Modern Approach. New York: Wiley.

HOWE, I. (1957) "Notes on mass culture," in B. Rosenberg and D. M. White (eds.) Mass Culture: The Popular Arts in America, Glencoe: Free Press.

LAZARSFELD, P. F. and R. K. MERTON (1948) "Mass communication, popular taste and organised social action," in L. Bryson (ed.) The Communication of Ideas. New York: Harpers.

MACDONALD, D. (1957) "A theory of mass culture," in B. Rosenberg and D. M. White (eds.) Mass Culture: The Popular Arts in America. Glencoe: Free Press.

MALINOWSKI, B. (1926) "Anthropology," in Encyclopaedia Britannica, First Supplementary Volume, London and New York.

MENDELSOHN, H. (1973) "The neglected majority: mass communications and the working person," in I. de Sola Pool (ed.) Talking Back: Citizen Feedback and Cable Technology. Cambridge, Mass.: MIT Press.

——— (1971) "*Cancion de la Raza* evaluated: audiences' reactions to televised social-amelioration programming." Educational Broadcasting Review: 45-53.

——— (1969) "What to say to whom in social amelioration programming." Educational Broadcasting Review: 19-26.

——— (1966) Mass Entertainment. New Haven: College and University Press.

MERTON, R. K. (1957) Social Theory and Social Structure. Glencoe: Free Press.

RADCLIFFE-BROWN, A. R. (1935) "On the concept of function in social science." American Anthropologist 37: 395-396.

RAINWATER, L., R. COLEMAN, and G. HANDEL (1959) Workingman's Wife. New York: Oceana Publications.

VAN DEN HAAG, E. (1971) "A dissent from the consensual society," in B. Rosenberg and D. M. White (eds.) Mass Culture Revisited. New York: Van Nostrand Reinhold.

——— (1957) "Of happiness and despair we have no measure," in B. Rosenberg and D. M. White (eds.) Mass Culture: The Popular Arts in America. Glencoe: Free Press.